Published by
BLACK MASK STUDIOS
BRETT GUREWITZ | MATTEO PIZZOLO | STEVE NILES

First Edition | Printed In Canada
10 9 8 7 6 5 4 3 2 1

EXIT

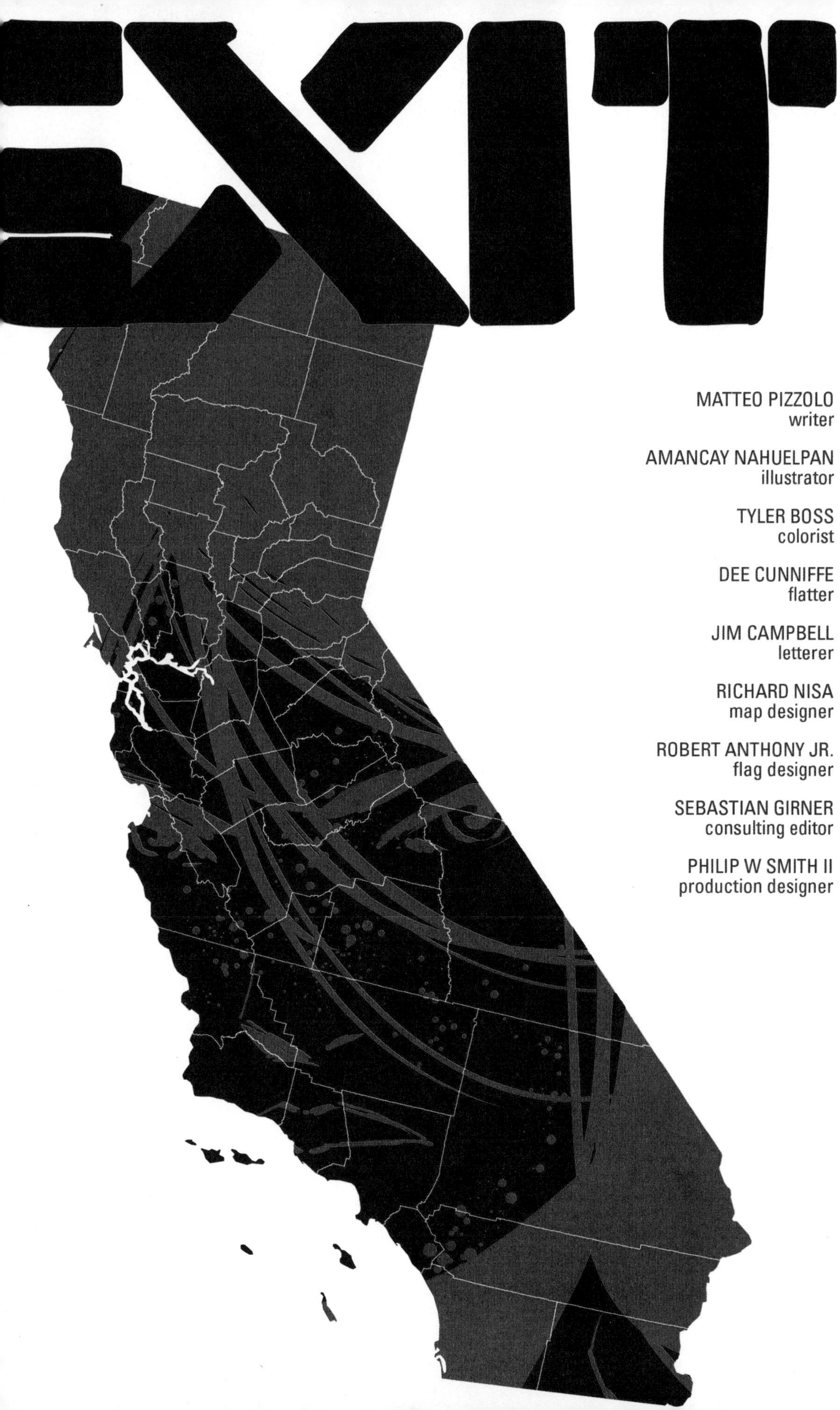

MATTEO PIZZOLO
writer

AMANCAY NAHUELPAN
illustrator

TYLER BOSS
colorist

DEE CUNNIFFE
flatter

JIM CAMPBELL
letterer

RICHARD NISA
map designer

ROBERT ANTHONY JR.
flag designer

SEBASTIAN GIRNER
consulting editor

PHILIP W SMITH II
production designer

CHAPTER ONE

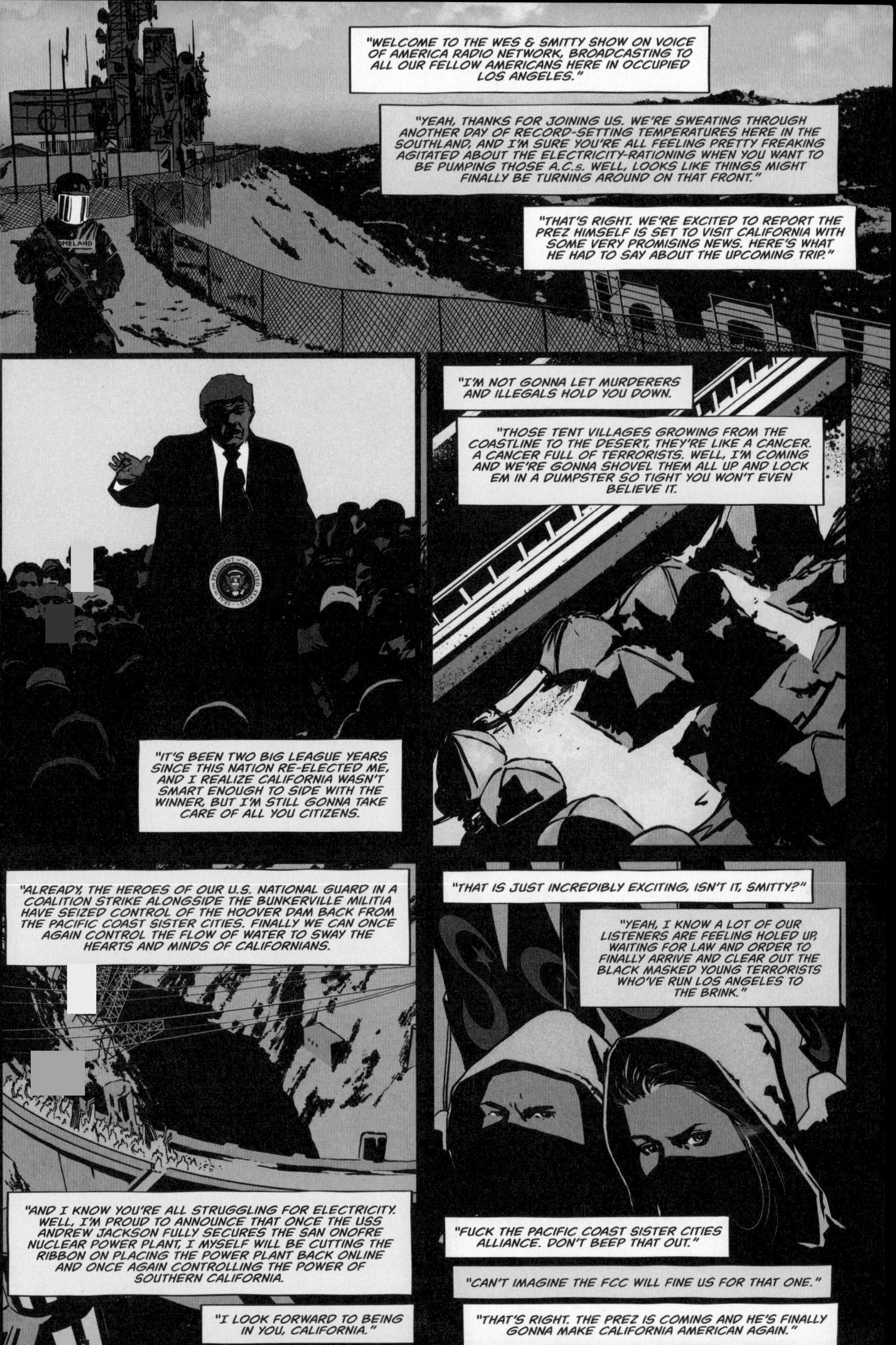
"WELCOME TO THE WES & SMITTY SHOW ON VOICE OF AMERICA RADIO NETWORK, BROADCASTING TO ALL OUR FELLOW AMERICANS HERE IN OCCUPIED LOS ANGELES."
"YEAH, THANKS FOR JOINING US. WE'RE SWEATING THROUGH ANOTHER DAY OF RECORD-SETTING TEMPERATURES HERE IN THE SOUTHLAND, AND I'M SURE YOU'RE ALL FEELING PRETTY FREAKING AGITATED ABOUT THE ELECTRICITY-RATIONING WHEN YOU WANT TO BE PUMPING THOSE A.C.s. WELL, LOOKS LIKE THINGS MIGHT FINALLY BE TURNING AROUND ON THAT FRONT."
"THAT'S RIGHT. WE'RE EXCITED TO REPORT THE PREZ HIMSELF IS SET TO VISIT CALIFORNIA WITH SOME VERY PROMISING NEWS. HERE'S WHAT HE HAD TO SAY ABOUT THE UPCOMING TRIP."
"IT'S BEEN TWO BIG LEAGUE YEARS SINCE THIS NATION RE-ELECTED ME, AND I REALIZE CALIFORNIA WASN'T SMART ENOUGH TO SIDE WITH THE WINNER, BUT I'M STILL GONNA TAKE CARE OF ALL YOU CITIZENS.
"I'M NOT GONNA LET MURDERERS AND ILLEGALS HOLD YOU DOWN.
"THOSE TENT VILLAGES GROWING FROM THE COASTLINE TO THE DESERT, THEY'RE LIKE A CANCER. A CANCER FULL OF TERRORISTS. WELL, I'M COMING AND WE'RE GONNA SHOVEL THEM ALL UP AND LOCK EM IN A DUMPSTER SO TIGHT YOU WON'T EVEN BELIEVE IT.
"ALREADY, THE HEROES OF OUR U.S. NATIONAL GUARD IN A COALITION STRIKE ALONGSIDE THE BUNKERVILLE MILITIA HAVE SEIZED CONTROL OF THE HOOVER DAM BACK FROM THE PACIFIC COAST SISTER CITIES. FINALLY WE CAN ONCE AGAIN CONTROL THE FLOW OF WATER TO SWAY THE HEARTS AND MINDS OF CALIFORNIANS.
"AND I KNOW YOU'RE ALL STRUGGLING FOR ELECTRICITY. WELL, I'M PROUD TO ANNOUNCE THAT ONCE THE USS ANDREW JACKSON FULLY SECURES THE SAN ONOFRE NUCLEAR POWER PLANT, I MYSELF WILL BE CUTTING THE RIBBON ON PLACING THE POWER PLANT BACK ONLINE AND ONCE AGAIN CONTROLLING THE POWER OF SOUTHERN CALIFORNIA.
"I LOOK FORWARD TO BEING IN YOU, CALIFORNIA."
"THAT IS JUST INCREDIBLY EXCITING, ISN'T IT, SMITTY?"
"YEAH, I KNOW A LOT OF OUR LISTENERS ARE FEELING HOLED UP, WAITING FOR LAW AND ORDER TO FINALLY ARRIVE AND CLEAR OUT THE BLACK MASKED YOUNG TERRORISTS WHO'VE RUN LOS ANGELES TO THE BRINK."
"FUCK THE PACIFIC COAST SISTER CITIES ALLIANCE. DON'T BEEP THAT OUT."
"CAN'T IMAGINE THE FCC WILL FINE US FOR THAT ONE."
"THAT'S RIGHT. THE PREZ IS COMING AND HE'S FINALLY GONNA MAKE CALIFORNIA AMERICAN AGAIN."

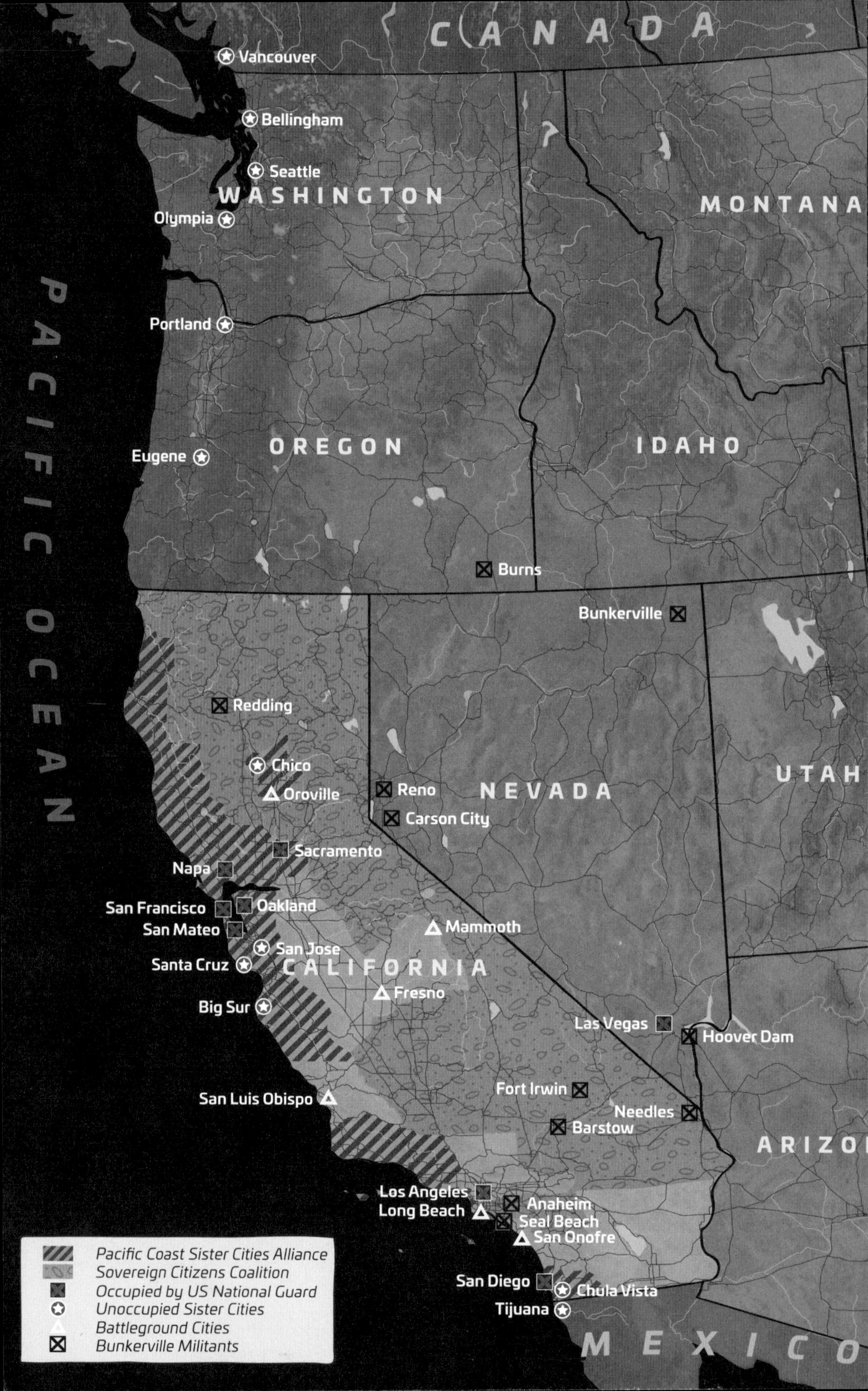
CANADA
Vancouver
Bellingham
Seattle
WASHINGTON
MONTANA
Olympia
PACIFIC OCEAN
Portland
OREGON
IDAHO
Eugene
Burns
Bunkerville
Redding
Chico
Oroville
Reno
NEVADA
UTAH
Carson City
Sacramento
Napa
San Francisco
Oakland
San Mateo
Mammoth
San Jose
Santa Cruz
CALIFORNIA
Fresno
Big Sur
Las Vegas
Hoover Dam
Fort Irwin
San Luis Obispo
Needles
Barstow
ARIZO
Los Angeles
Anaheim
Long Beach
Seal Beach
San Onofre
San Diego
Chula Vista
Tijuana
MEXICO
Pacific Coast Sister Cities Alliance
Sovereign Citizens Coalition
Occupied by US National Guard
Unoccupied Sister Cities
Battleground Cities
Bunkerville Militants

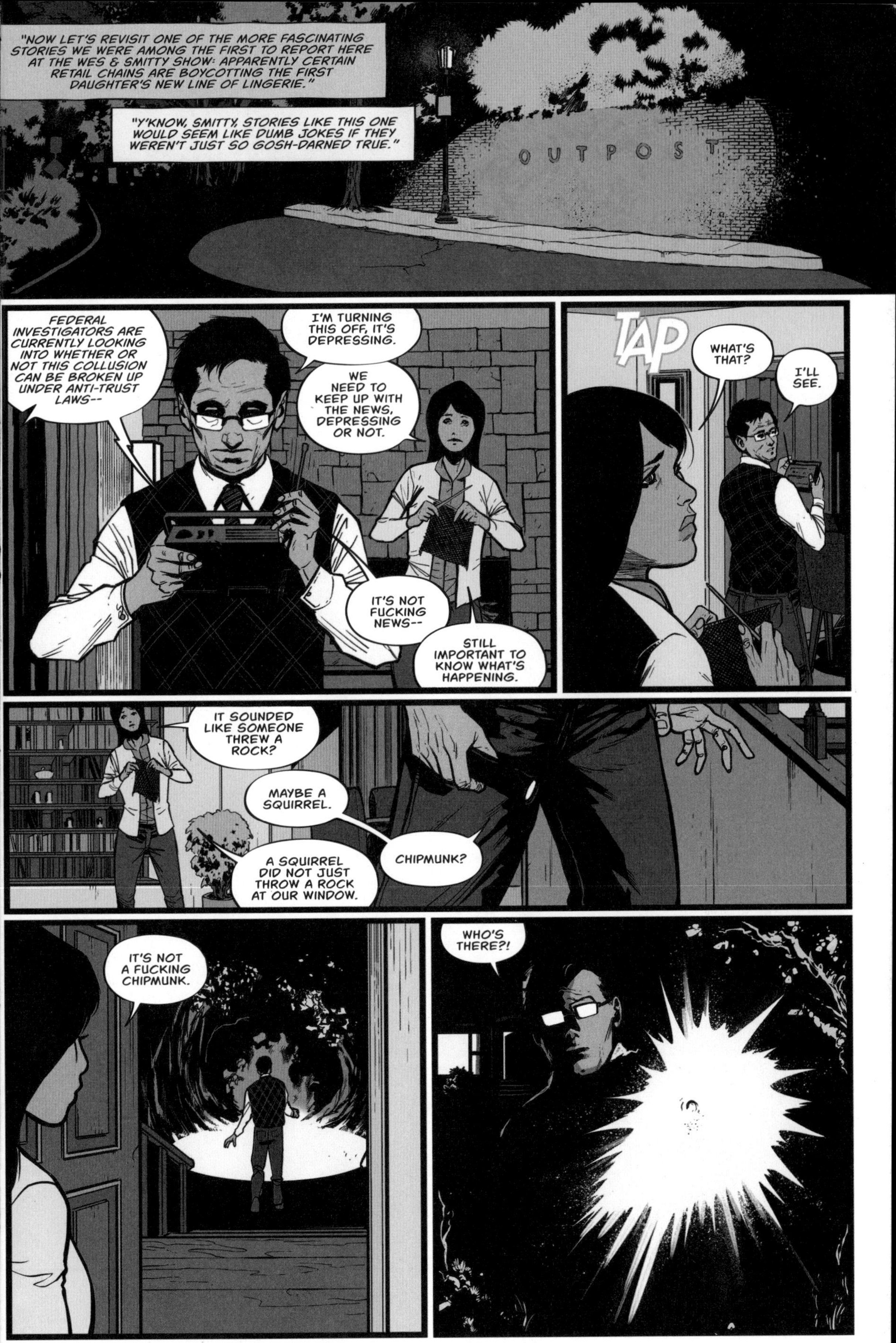
"NOW LET'S REVISIT ONE OF THE MORE FASCINATING STORIES WE WERE AMONG THE FIRST TO REPORT HERE AT THE WES & SMITTY SHOW: APPARENTLY CERTAIN RETAIL CHAINS ARE BOYCOTTING THE FIRST DAUGHTER'S NEW LINE OF LINGERIE."
"Y'KNOW, SMITTY, STORIES LIKE THIS ONE WOULD SEEM LIKE DUMB JOKES IF THEY WEREN'T JUST SO GOSH-DARNED TRUE."
OUTPOST
FEDERAL INVESTIGATORS ARE CURRENTLY LOOKING INTO WHETHER OR NOT THIS COLLUSION CAN BE BROKEN UP UNDER ANTI-TRUST LAWS--
I'M TURNING THIS OFF, IT'S DEPRESSING.
WE NEED TO KEEP UP WITH THE NEWS, DEPRESSING OR NOT.
IT'S NOT FUCKING NEWS--
STILL IMPORTANT TO KNOW WHAT'S HAPPENING.
TAP
WHAT'S THAT?
I'LL SEE.
IT SOUNDED LIKE SOMEONE THREW A ROCK?
MAYBE A SQUIRREL.
A SQUIRREL DID NOT JUST THROW A ROCK AT OUR WINDOW.
CHIPMUNK?
IT'S NOT A FUCKING CHIPMUNK.
WHO'S THERE?!

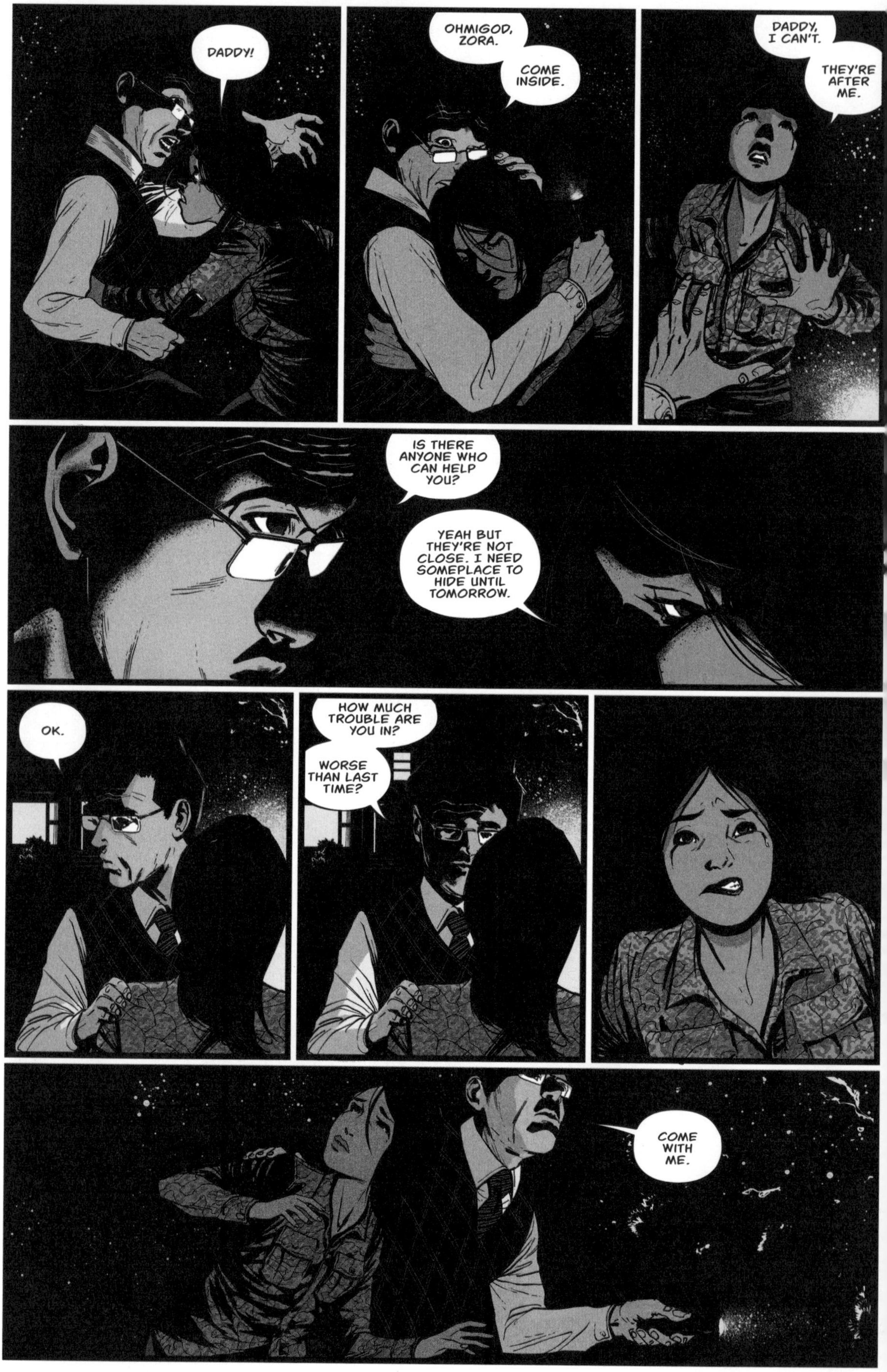
DADDY!
OHMIGOD, ZORA.
COME INSIDE.
DADDY, I CAN'T.
THEY'RE AFTER ME.
IS THERE ANYONE WHO CAN HELP YOU?
YEAH BUT THEY'RE NOT CLOSE. I NEED SOMEPLACE TO HIDE UNTIL TOMORROW.
OK.
HOW MUCH TROUBLE ARE YOU IN?
WORSE THAN LAST TIME?
COME WITH ME.

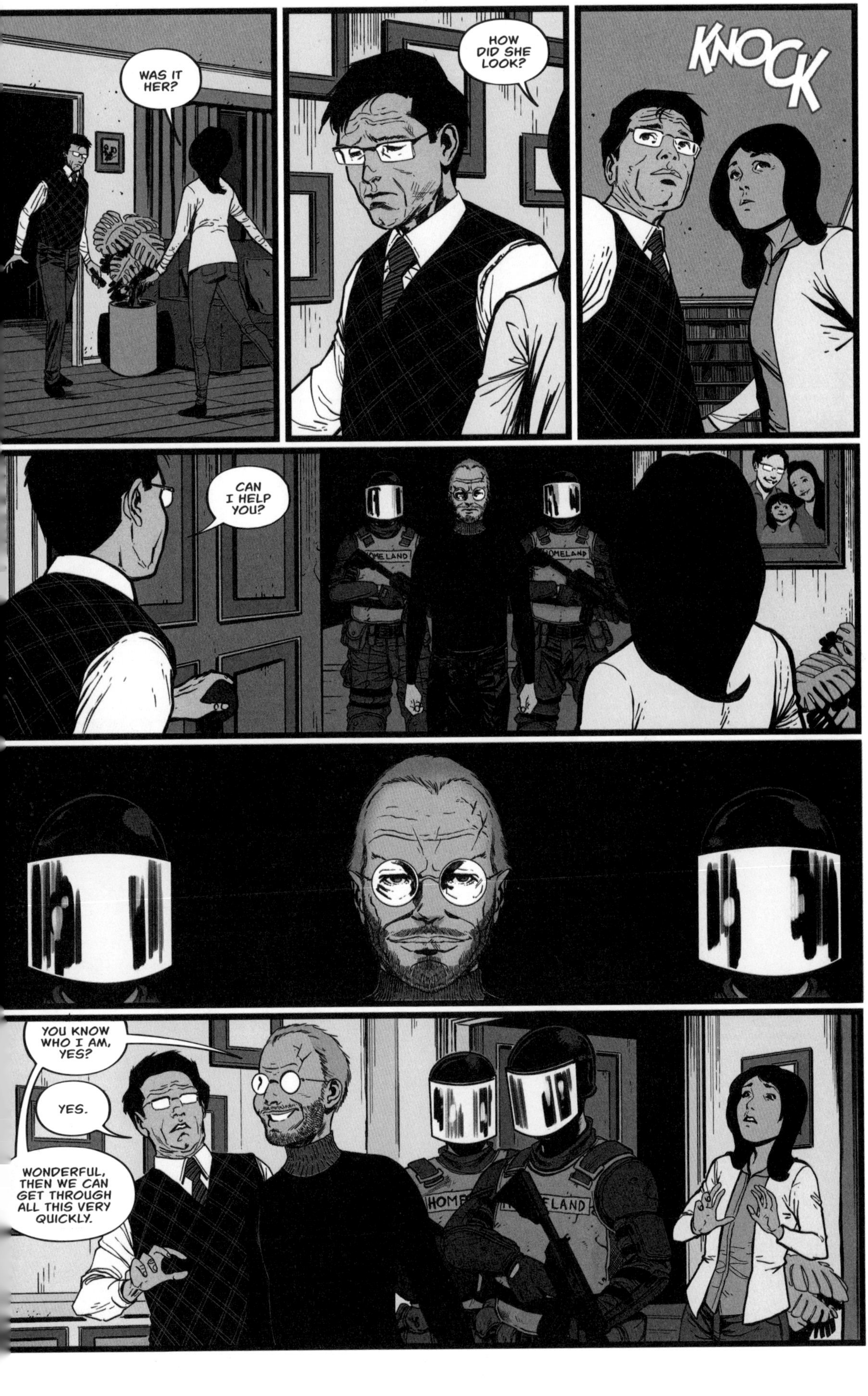
WAS IT HER?
HOW DID SHE LOOK?
KNOCK
CAN I HELP YOU?
HOMELAND
YOU KNOW WHO I AM, YES?
YES.
WONDERFUL, THEN WE CAN GET THROUGH ALL THIS VERY QUICKLY.

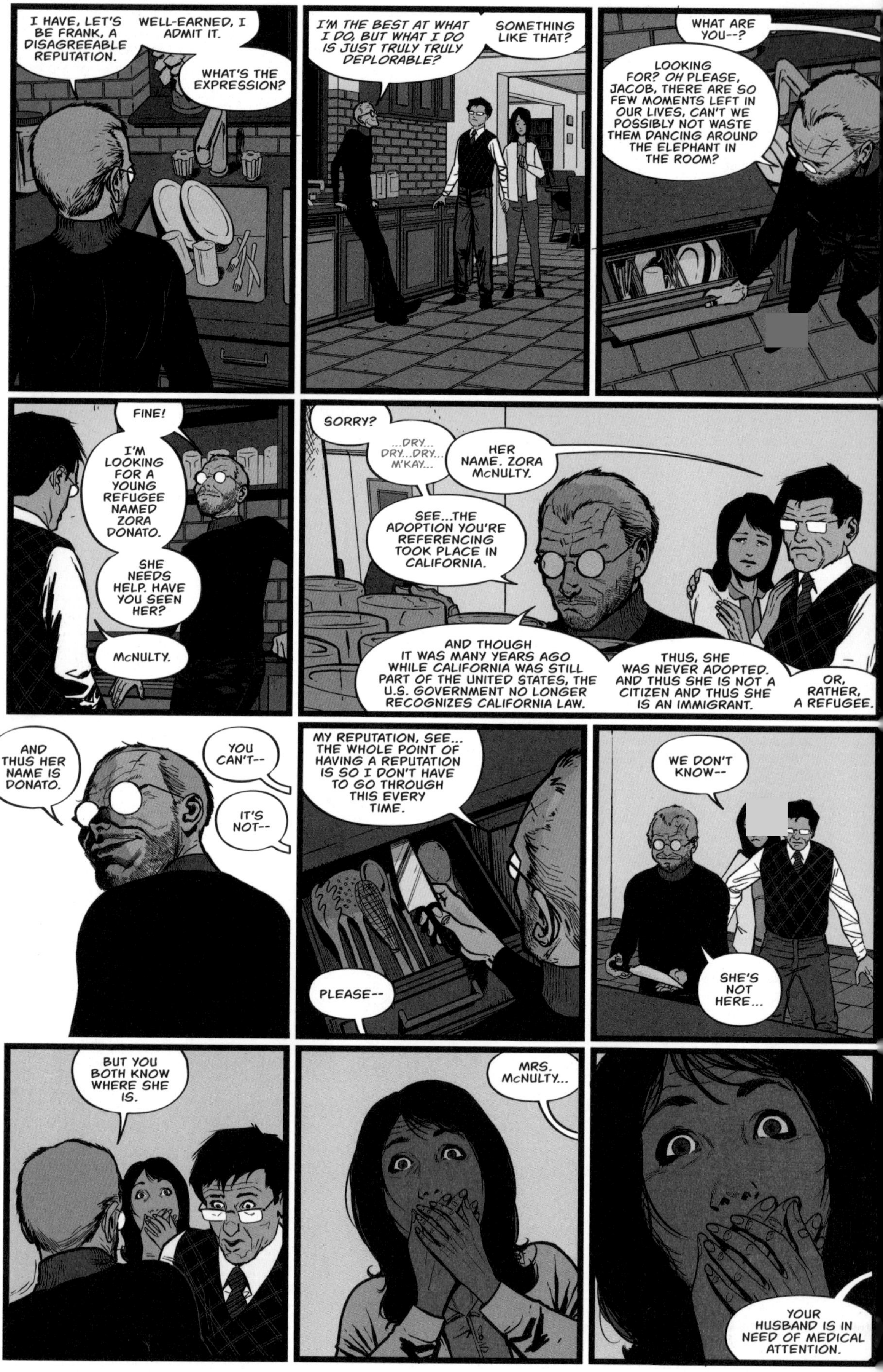
I HAVE, LET'S BE FRANK, A DISAGREEABLE REPUTATION.
WELL-EARNED, I ADMIT IT.
WHAT'S THE EXPRESSION?
I'M THE BEST AT WHAT I DO, BUT WHAT I DO IS JUST TRULY TRULY DEPLORABLE?
SOMETHING LIKE THAT?
WHAT ARE YOU--?
LOOKING FOR? OH PLEASE, JACOB, THERE ARE SO FEW MOMENTS LEFT IN OUR LIVES, CAN'T WE POSSIBLY NOT WASTE THEM DANCING AROUND THE ELEPHANT IN THE ROOM?
FINE!
I'M LOOKING FOR A YOUNG REFUGEE NAMED ZORA DONATO.
SHE NEEDS HELP. HAVE YOU SEEN HER?
McNULTY.
SORRY?
...DRY... DRY...DRY... M'KAY...
HER NAME. ZORA McNULTY.
SEE...THE ADOPTION YOU'RE REFERENCING TOOK PLACE IN CALIFORNIA.
AND THOUGH IT WAS MANY YEARS AGO WHILE CALIFORNIA WAS STILL PART OF THE UNITED STATES, THE U.S. GOVERNMENT NO LONGER RECOGNIZES CALIFORNIA LAW.
THUS, SHE WAS NEVER ADOPTED. AND THUS SHE IS NOT A CITIZEN AND THUS SHE IS AN IMMIGRANT.
OR, RATHER, A REFUGEE.
AND THUS HER NAME IS DONATO.
YOU CAN'T--
IT'S NOT--
MY REPUTATION, SEE... THE WHOLE POINT OF HAVING A REPUTATION IS SO I DON'T HAVE TO GO THROUGH THIS EVERY TIME.
PLEASE--
WE DON'T KNOW--
SHE'S NOT HERE...
BUT YOU BOTH KNOW WHERE SHE IS.
MRS. McNULTY...
YOUR HUSBAND IS IN NEED OF MEDICAL ATTENTION.

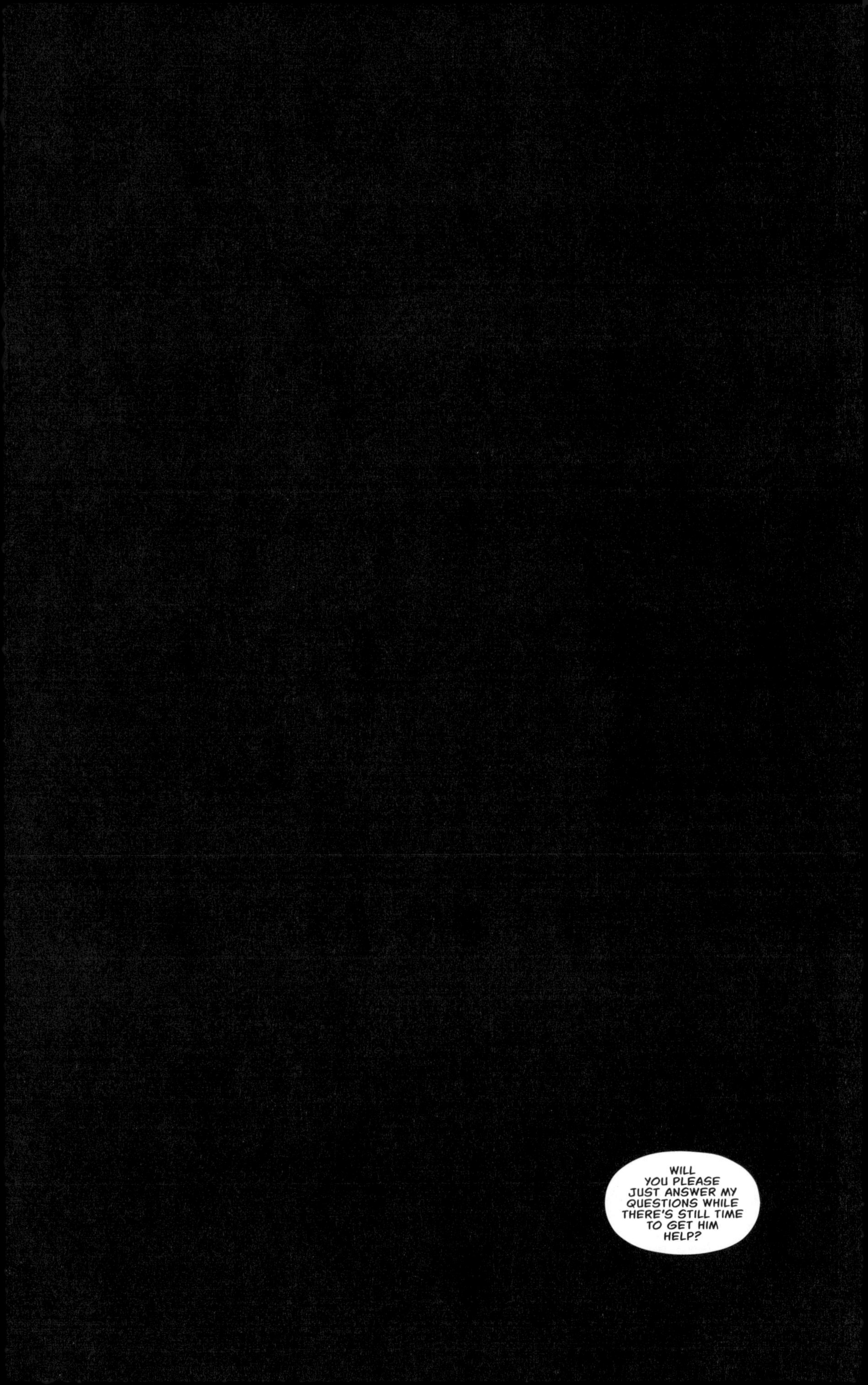
WILL YOU PLEASE JUST ANSWER MY QUESTIONS WHILE THERE'S STILL TIME TO GET HIM HELP?

BLACK MASK STUDIOS PRESENTS

CALEXIT

CHAPTER 1: IF YOU WANNA SCREAM, SCREAM WITH ME

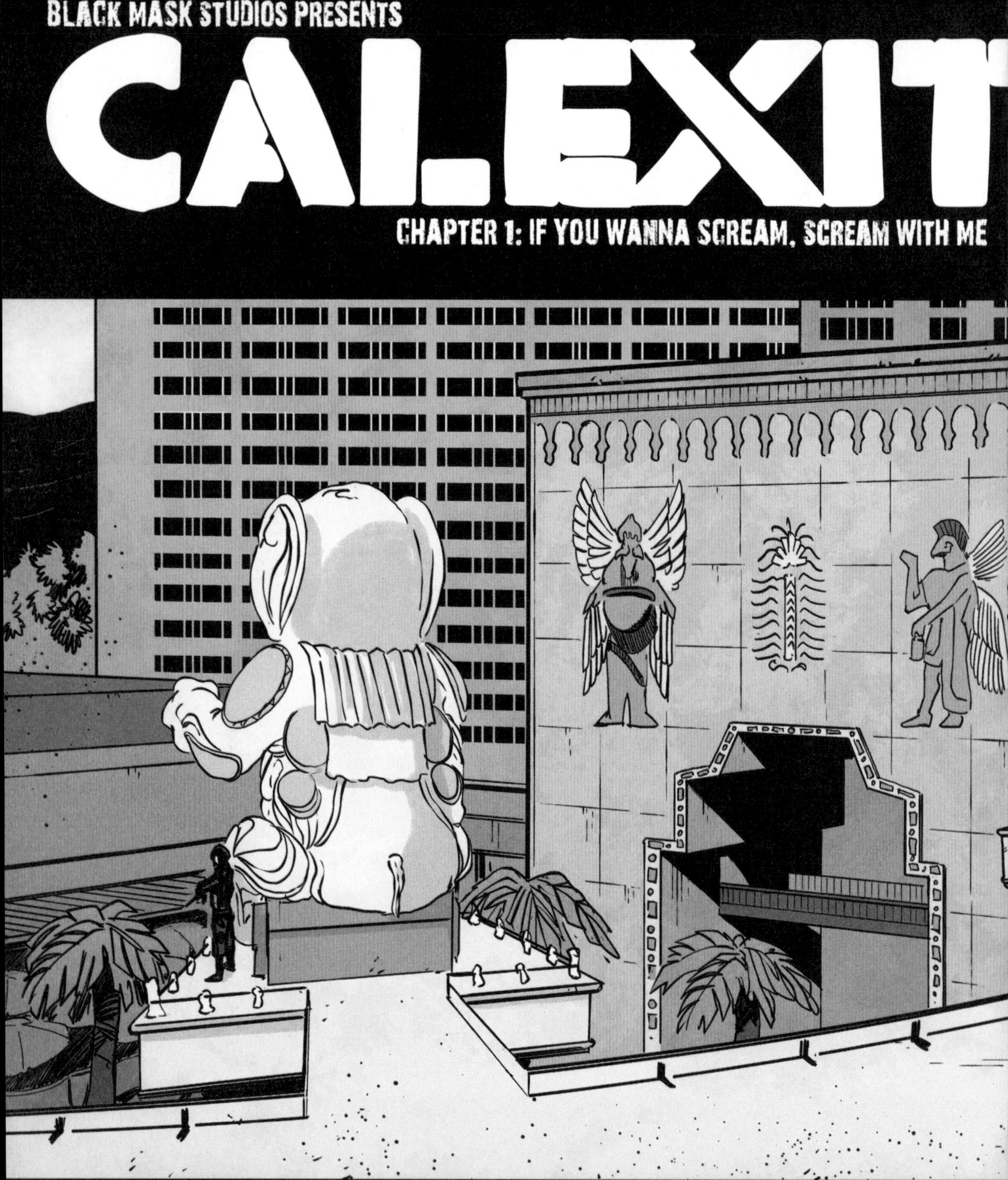

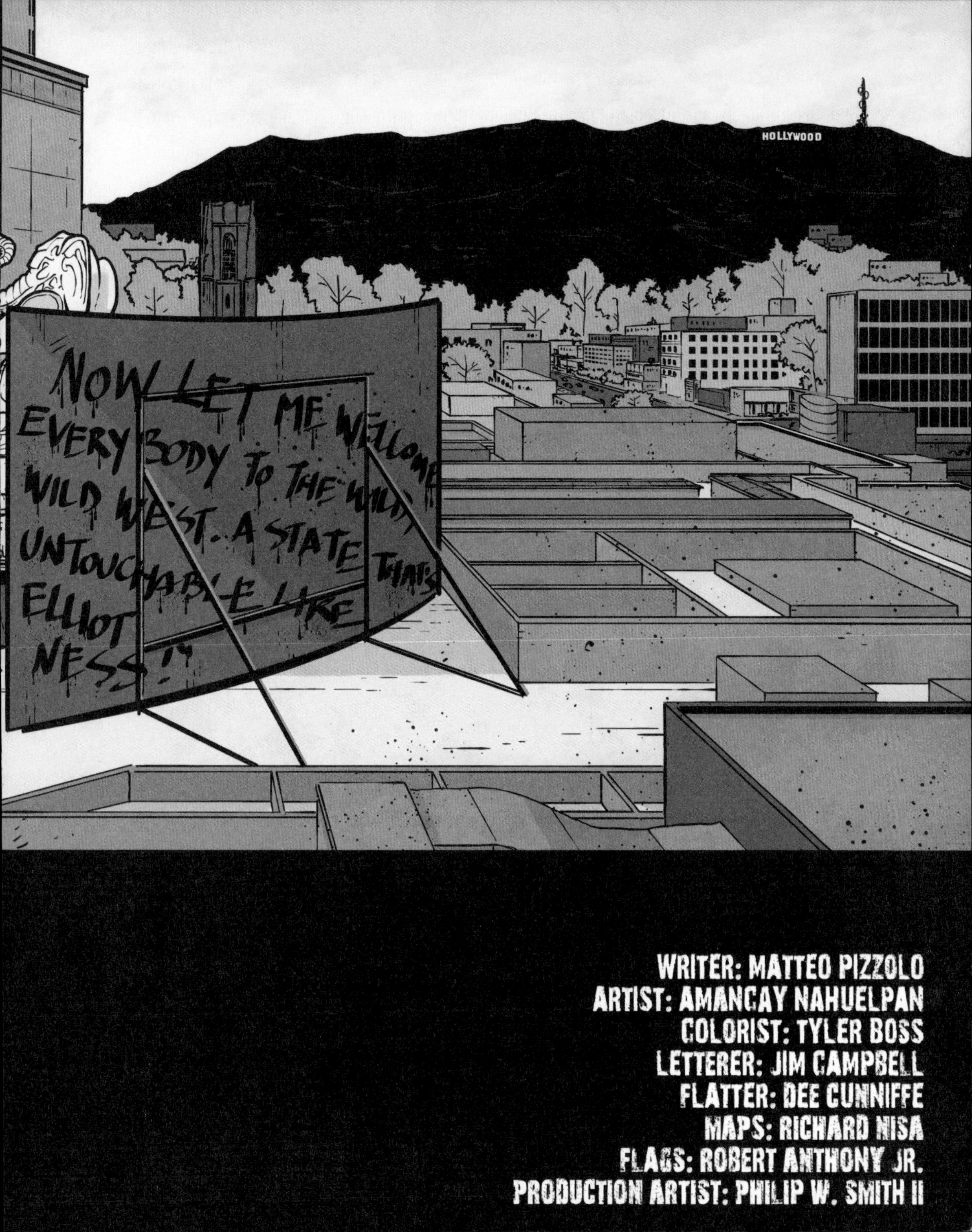
HOLLYWOOD
NOW LET ME WELCOME EVERYBODY TO THE WILD WILD WEST. A STATE THAT'S UNTOUCHABLE LIKE ELLIOT NESS!

WRITER: MATTEO PIZZOLO
ARTIST: AMANCAY NAHUELPAN
COLORIST: TYLER BOSS
LETTERER: JIM CAMPBELL
FLATTER: DEE CUNNIFFE
MAPS: RICHARD NISA
FLAGS: ROBERT ANTHONY JR.
PRODUCTION ARTIST: PHILIP W. SMITH II

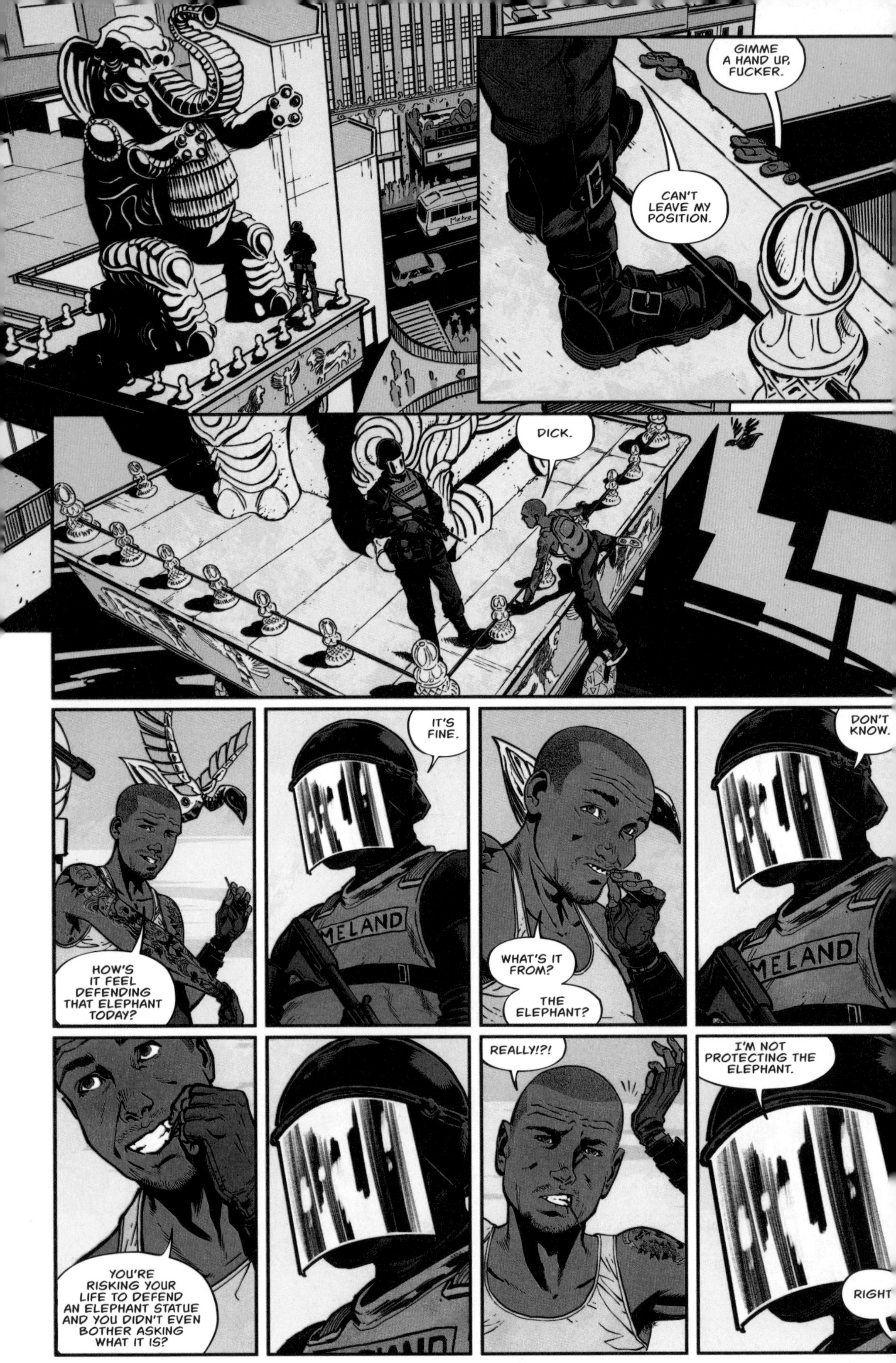
GIMME A HAND UP, FUCKER.
CAN'T LEAVE MY POSITION.
DICK.
MELAND
HOW'S IT FEEL DEFENDING THAT ELEPHANT TODAY?
IT'S FINE.
WHAT'S IT FROM?
THE ELEPHANT?
DON'T KNOW.
MELAND
YOU'RE RISKING YOUR LIFE TO DEFEND AN ELEPHANT STATUE AND YOU DIDN'T EVEN BOTHER ASKING WHAT IT IS?
REALLY!?!
I'M NOT PROTECTING THE ELEPHANT.
RIGHT

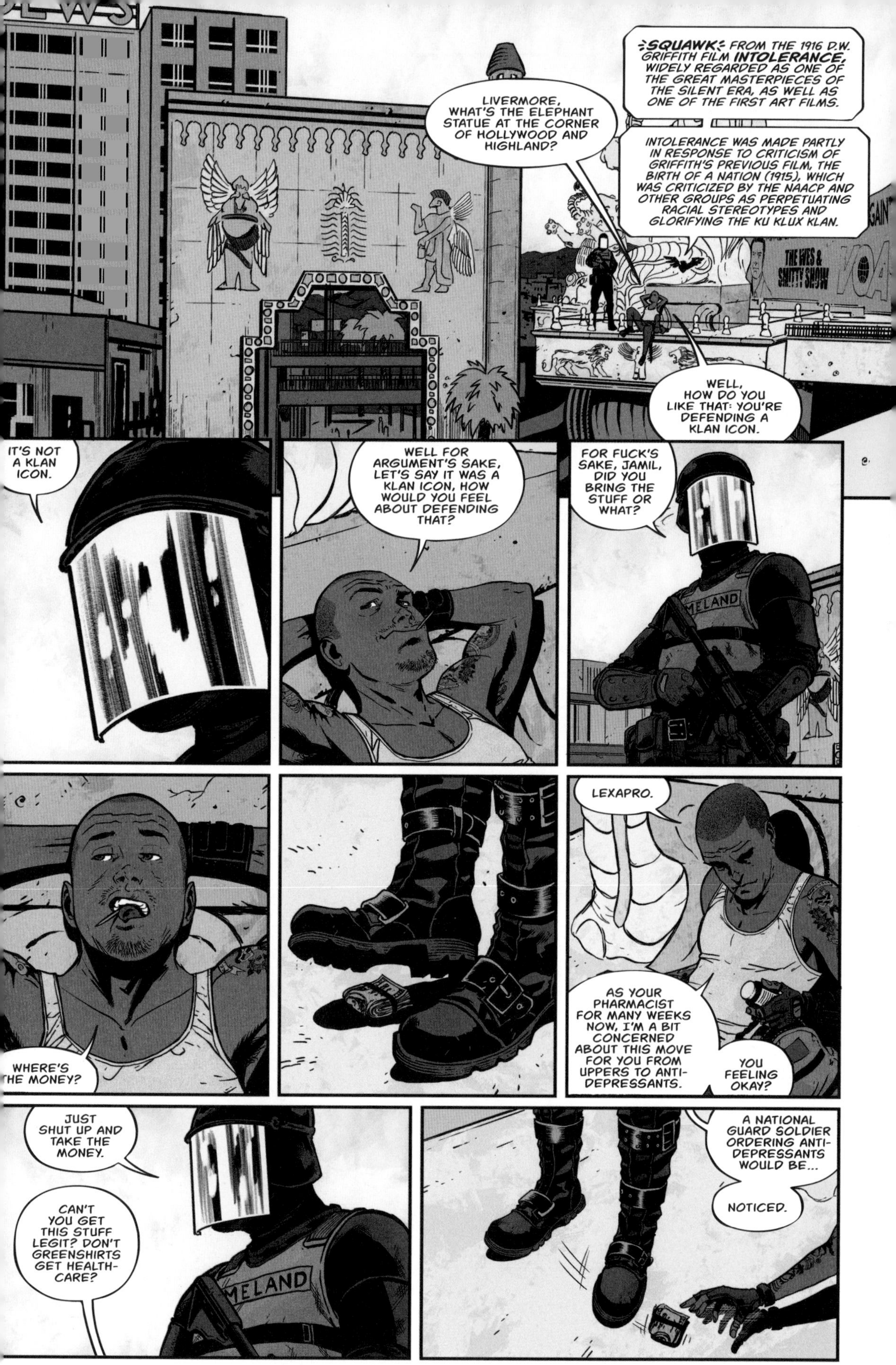
LIVERMORE, WHAT'S THE ELEPHANT STATUE AT THE CORNER OF HOLLYWOOD AND HIGHLAND?
SQUAWK: FROM THE 1916 D.W. GRIFFITH FILM INTOLERANCE, WIDELY REGARDED AS ONE OF THE GREAT MASTERPIECES OF THE SILENT ERA, AS WELL AS ONE OF THE FIRST ART FILMS.
INTOLERANCE WAS MADE PARTLY IN RESPONSE TO CRITICISM OF GRIFFITH'S PREVIOUS FILM, THE BIRTH OF A NATION (1915), WHICH WAS CRITICIZED BY THE NAACP AND OTHER GROUPS AS PERPETUATING RACIAL STEREOTYPES AND GLORIFYING THE KU KLUX KLAN.
THE WES & SHITTY SHOW
WELL, HOW DO YOU LIKE THAT: YOU'RE DEFENDING A KLAN ICON.
IT'S NOT A KLAN ICON.
WELL FOR ARGUMENT'S SAKE, LET'S SAY IT WAS A KLAN ICON, HOW WOULD YOU FEEL ABOUT DEFENDING THAT?
FOR FUCK'S SAKE, JAMIL, DID YOU BRING THE STUFF OR WHAT?
MELAND
WHERE'S THE MONEY?
LEXAPRO.
AS YOUR PHARMACIST FOR MANY WEEKS NOW, I'M A BIT CONCERNED ABOUT THIS MOVE FOR YOU FROM UPPERS TO ANTI-DEPRESSANTS.
YOU FEELING OKAY?
JUST SHUT UP AND TAKE THE MONEY.
CAN'T YOU GET THIS STUFF LEGIT? DON'T GREENSHIRTS GET HEALTH-CARE?
MELAND
A NATIONAL GUARD SOLDIER ORDERING ANTI-DEPRESSANTS WOULD BE...
NOTICED.

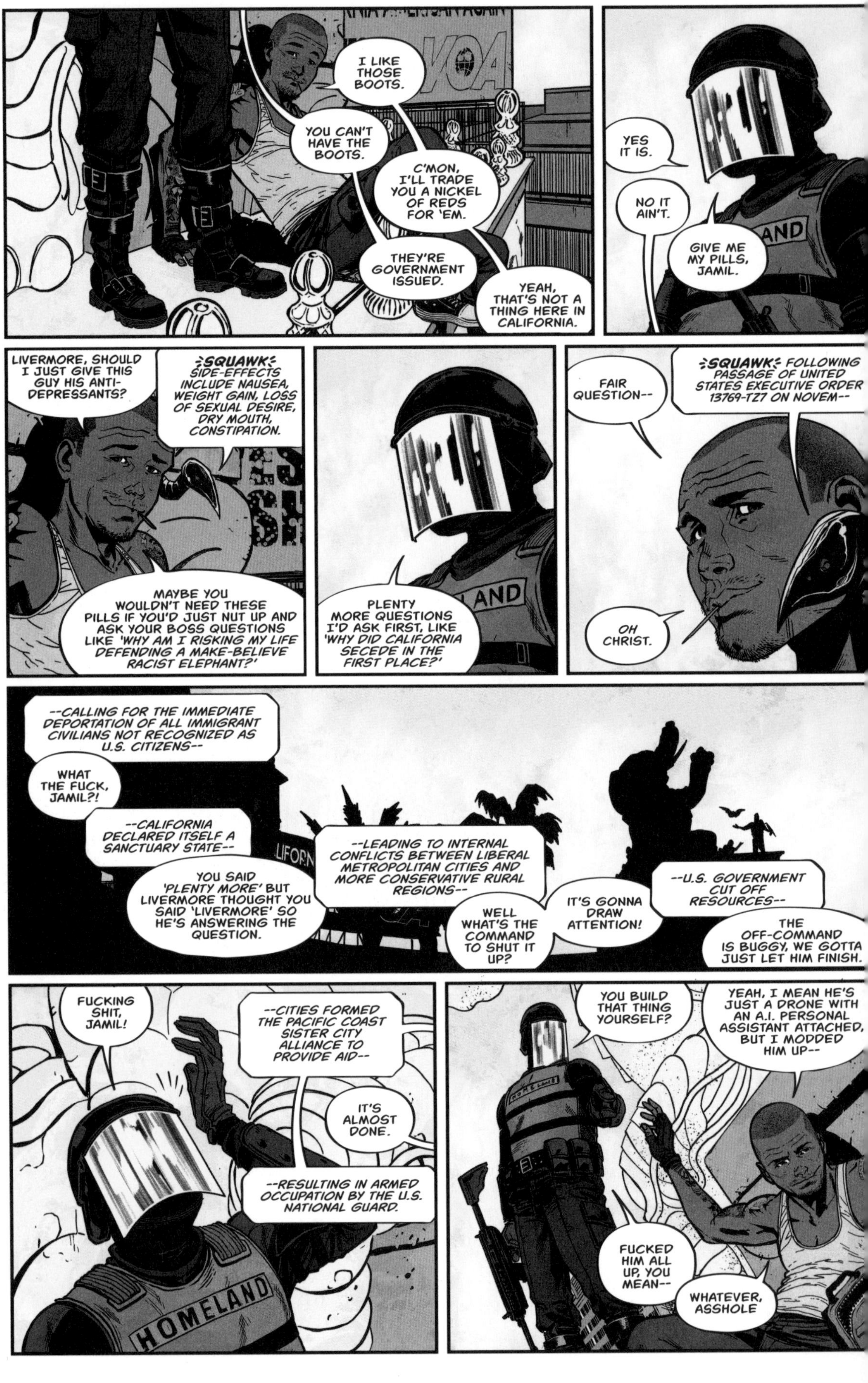
I LIKE THOSE BOOTS.
YOU CAN'T HAVE THE BOOTS.
C'MON, I'LL TRADE YOU A NICKEL OF REDS FOR 'EM.
THEY'RE GOVERNMENT ISSUED.
YEAH, THAT'S NOT A THING HERE IN CALIFORNIA.
YES IT IS.
NO IT AIN'T.
GIVE ME MY PILLS, JAMIL.
LIVERMORE, SHOULD I JUST GIVE THIS GUY HIS ANTI-DEPRESSANTS?
SQUAWK SIDE-EFFECTS INCLUDE NAUSEA, WEIGHT GAIN, LOSS OF SEXUAL DESIRE, DRY MOUTH, CONSTIPATION.
MAYBE YOU WOULDN'T NEED THESE PILLS IF YOU'D JUST NUT UP AND ASK YOUR BOSS QUESTIONS LIKE 'WHY AM I RISKING MY LIFE DEFENDING A MAKE-BELIEVE RACIST ELEPHANT?'
PLENTY MORE QUESTIONS I'D ASK FIRST, LIKE 'WHY DID CALIFORNIA SECEDE IN THE FIRST PLACE?'
FAIR QUESTION--
SQUAWK FOLLOWING PASSAGE OF UNITED STATES EXECUTIVE ORDER 13769-TZ7 ON NOVEM--
OH CHRIST.
--CALLING FOR THE IMMEDIATE DEPORTATION OF ALL IMMIGRANT CIVILIANS NOT RECOGNIZED AS U.S. CITIZENS--
WHAT THE FUCK, JAMIL?!
--CALIFORNIA DECLARED ITSELF A SANCTUARY STATE--
YOU SAID 'PLENTY MORE' BUT LIVERMORE THOUGHT YOU SAID 'LIVERMORE' SO HE'S ANSWERING THE QUESTION.
--LEADING TO INTERNAL CONFLICTS BETWEEN LIBERAL METROPOLITAN CITIES AND MORE CONSERVATIVE RURAL REGIONS--
WELL WHAT'S THE COMMAND TO SHUT IT UP?
IT'S GONNA DRAW ATTENTION!
--U.S. GOVERNMENT CUT OFF RESOURCES--
THE OFF-COMMAND IS BUGGY, WE GOTTA JUST LET HIM FINISH.
FUCKING SHIT, JAMIL!
--CITIES FORMED THE PACIFIC COAST SISTER CITY ALLIANCE TO PROVIDE AID--
IT'S ALMOST DONE.
--RESULTING IN ARMED OCCUPATION BY THE U.S. NATIONAL GUARD.
HOMELAND
YOU BUILD THAT THING YOURSELF?
YEAH, I MEAN HE'S JUST A DRONE WITH AN A.I. PERSONAL ASSISTANT ATTACHED, BUT I MODDED HIM UP--
FUCKED HIM ALL UP, YOU MEAN--
WHATEVER, ASSHOLE

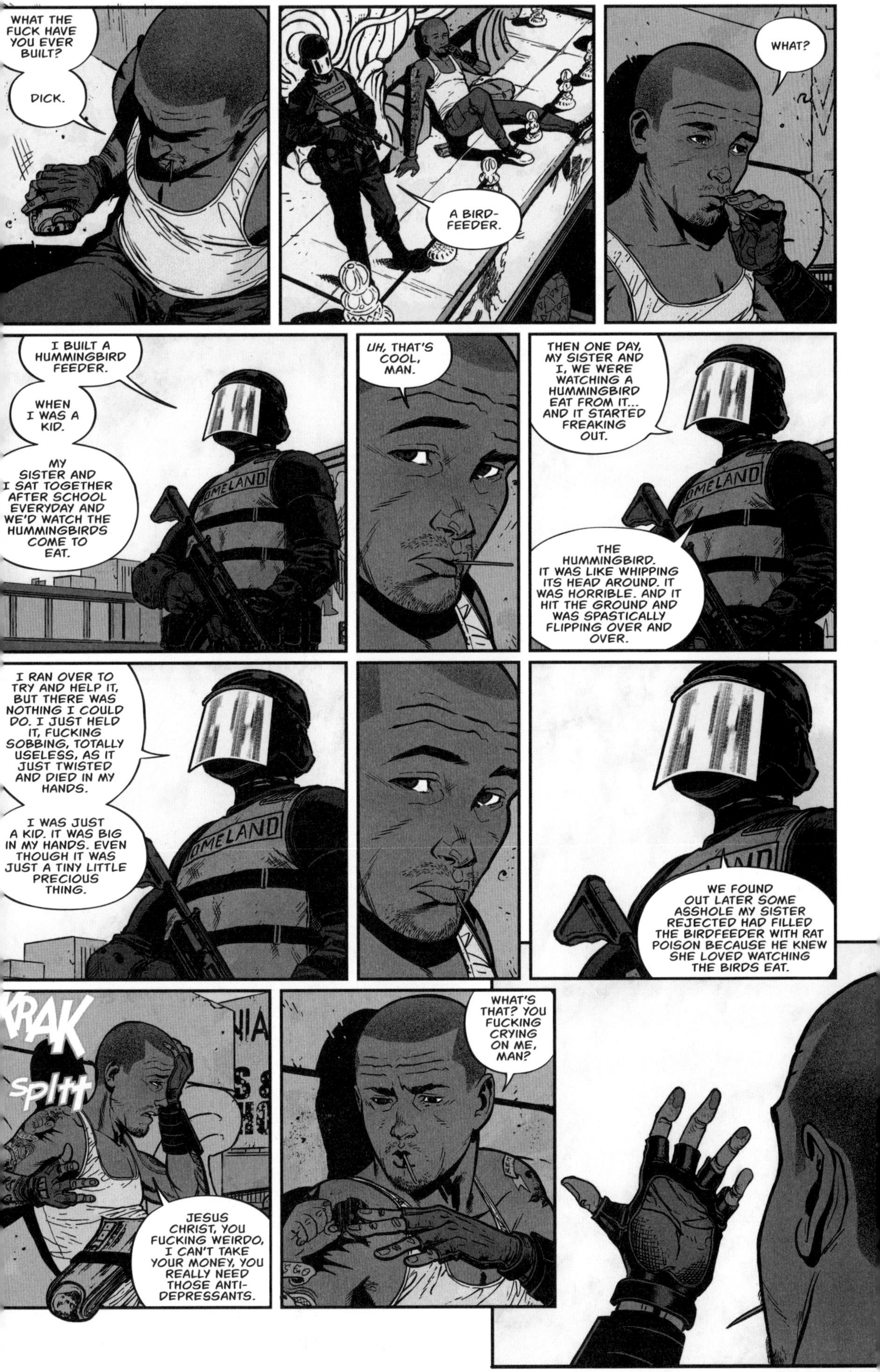
WHAT THE FUCK HAVE YOU EVER BUILT?
DICK.
A BIRD-FEEDER.
WHAT?
I BUILT A HUMMINGBIRD FEEDER.
WHEN I WAS A KID.
MY SISTER AND I SAT TOGETHER AFTER SCHOOL EVERYDAY AND WE'D WATCH THE HUMMINGBIRDS COME TO EAT.
OMELAND
UH, THAT'S COOL, MAN.
THEN ONE DAY, MY SISTER AND I, WE WERE WATCHING A HUMMINGBIRD EAT FROM IT... AND IT STARTED FREAKING OUT.
OMELAND
THE HUMMINGBIRD. IT WAS LIKE WHIPPING ITS HEAD AROUND. IT WAS HORRIBLE. AND IT HIT THE GROUND AND WAS SPASTICALLY FLIPPING OVER AND OVER.
I RAN OVER TO TRY AND HELP IT, BUT THERE WAS NOTHING I COULD DO. I JUST HELD IT, FUCKING SOBBING, TOTALLY USELESS, AS IT JUST TWISTED AND DIED IN MY HANDS.
I WAS JUST A KID. IT WAS BIG IN MY HANDS. EVEN THOUGH IT WAS JUST A TINY LITTLE PRECIOUS THING.
OMELAND
WE FOUND OUT LATER SOME ASSHOLE MY SISTER REJECTED HAD FILLED THE BIRDFEEDER WITH RAT POISON BECAUSE HE KNEW SHE LOVED WATCHING THE BIRDS EAT.
KRAK
SPLTT
JESUS CHRIST, YOU FUCKING WEIRDO, I CAN'T TAKE YOUR MONEY, YOU REALLY NEED THOSE ANTI-DEPRESSANTS.
WHAT'S THAT? YOU FUCKING CRYING ON ME, MAN?

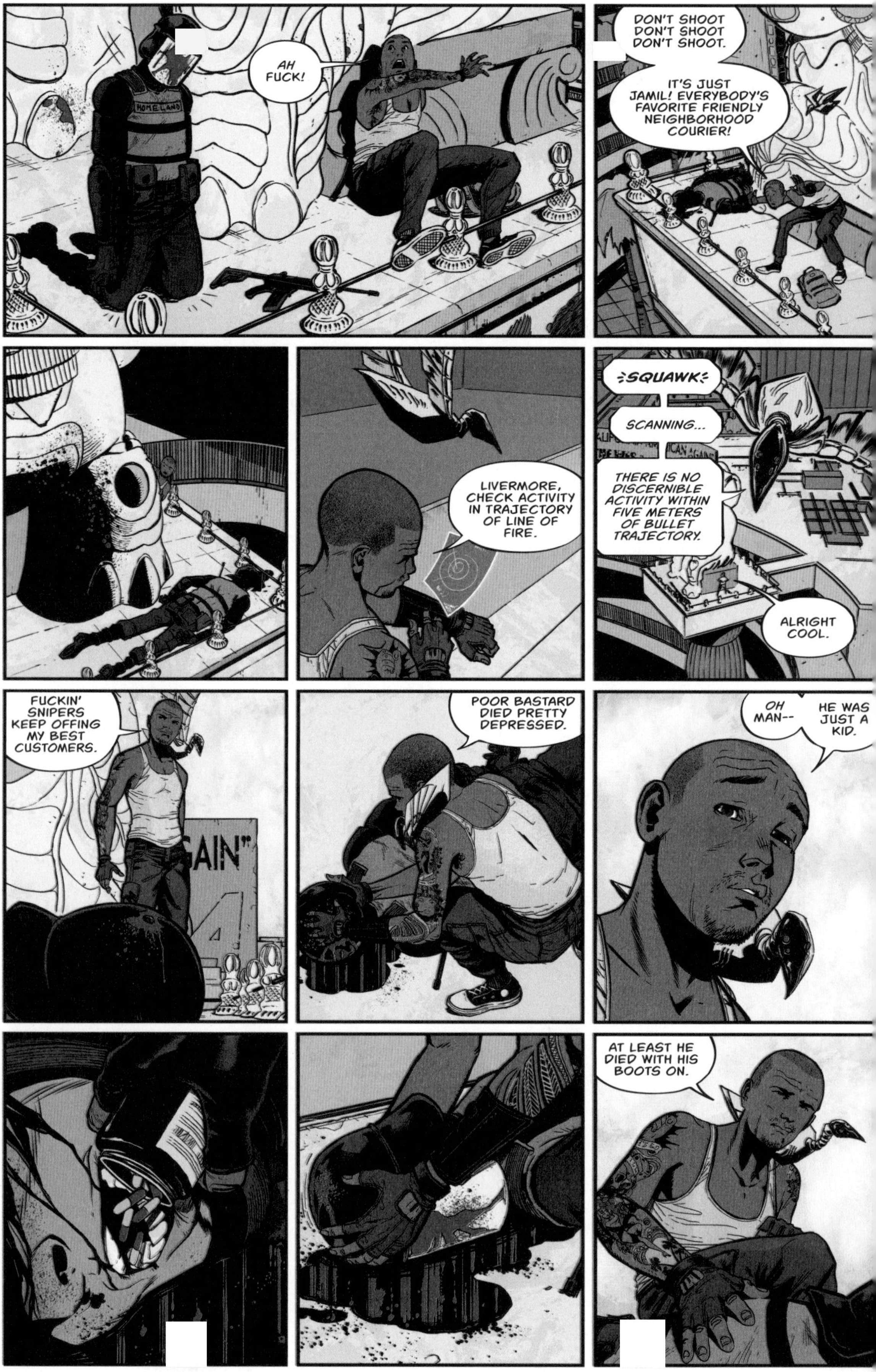
AH FUCK!
DON'T SHOOT DON'T SHOOT DON'T SHOOT.
IT'S JUST JAMIL! EVERYBODY'S FAVORITE FRIENDLY NEIGHBORHOOD COURIER!
LIVERMORE, CHECK ACTIVITY IN TRAJECTORY OF LINE OF FIRE.
SQUAWK
SCANNING...
THERE IS NO DISCERNIBLE ACTIVITY WITHIN FIVE METERS OF BULLET TRAJECTORY.
ALRIGHT COOL.
FUCKIN' SNIPERS KEEP OFFING MY BEST CUSTOMERS.
POOR BASTARD DIED PRETTY DEPRESSED.
OH MAN--
HE WAS JUST A KID.
AT LEAST HE DIED WITH HIS BOOTS ON.

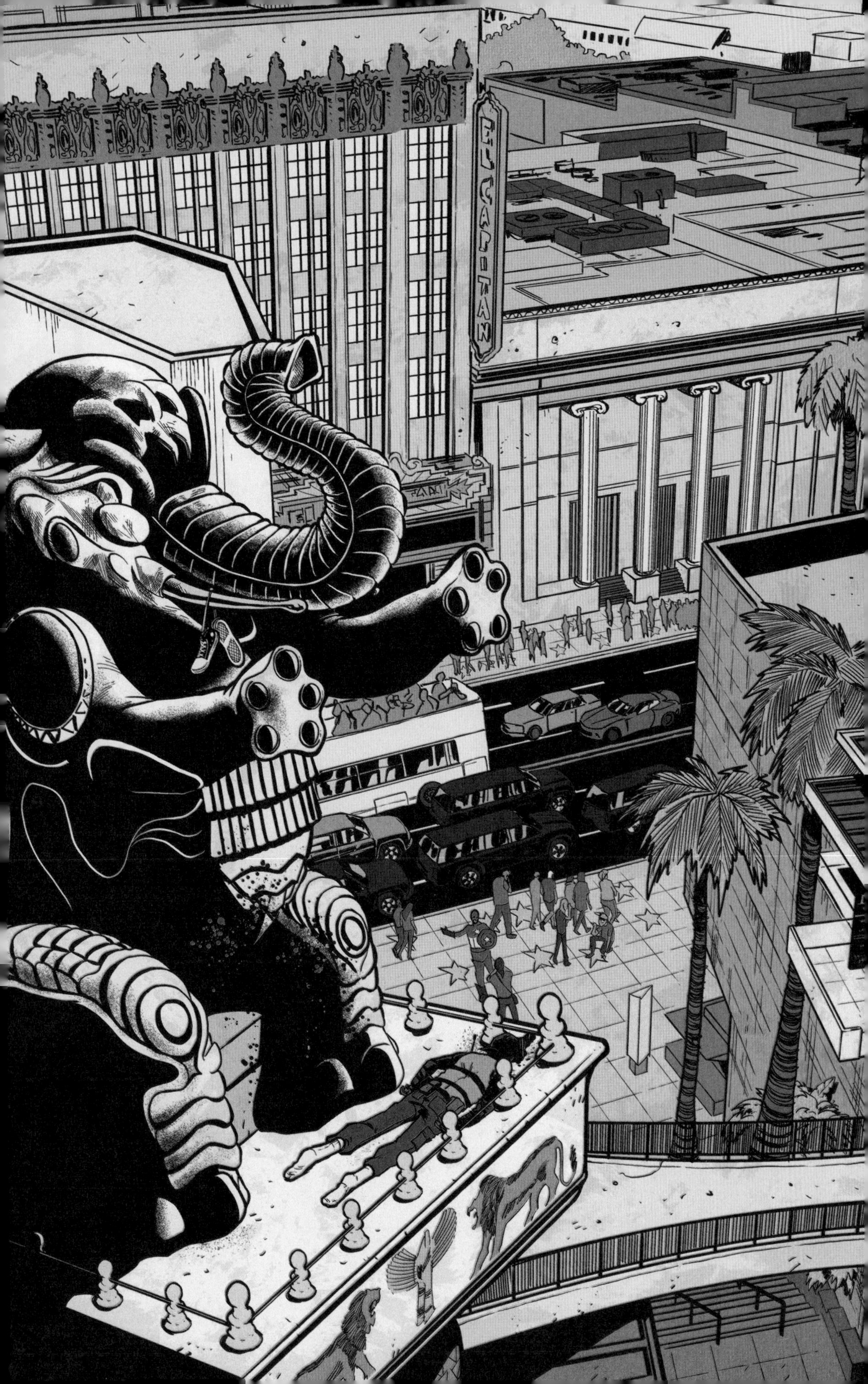
EL CAPITAN

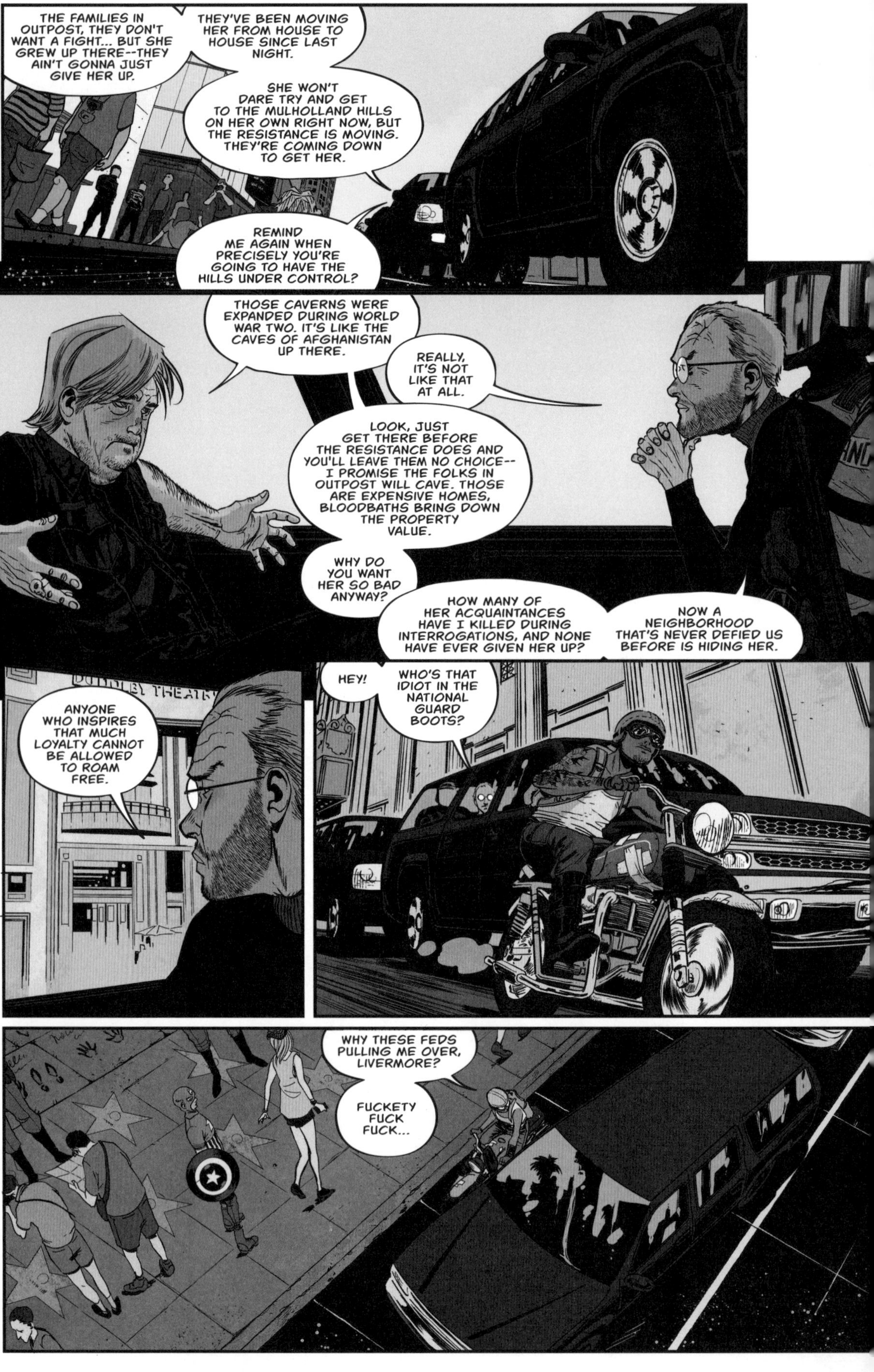
THE FAMILIES IN OUTPOST, THEY DON'T WANT A FIGHT... BUT SHE GREW UP THERE--THEY AIN'T GONNA JUST GIVE HER UP.
THEY'VE BEEN MOVING HER FROM HOUSE TO HOUSE SINCE LAST NIGHT.
SHE WON'T DARE TRY AND GET TO THE MULHOLLAND HILLS ON HER OWN RIGHT NOW, BUT THE RESISTANCE IS MOVING. THEY'RE COMING DOWN TO GET HER.
REMIND ME AGAIN WHEN PRECISELY YOU'RE GOING TO HAVE THE HILLS UNDER CONTROL?
THOSE CAVERNS WERE EXPANDED DURING WORLD WAR TWO. IT'S LIKE THE CAVES OF AFGHANISTAN UP THERE.
REALLY, IT'S NOT LIKE THAT AT ALL.
LOOK, JUST GET THERE BEFORE THE RESISTANCE DOES AND YOU'LL LEAVE THEM NO CHOICE-- I PROMISE THE FOLKS IN OUTPOST WILL CAVE. THOSE ARE EXPENSIVE HOMES, BLOODBATHS BRING DOWN THE PROPERTY VALUE.
WHY DO YOU WANT HER SO BAD ANYWAY?
HOW MANY OF HER ACQUAINTANCES HAVE I KILLED DURING INTERROGATIONS, AND NONE HAVE EVER GIVEN HER UP?
NOW A NEIGHBORHOOD THAT'S NEVER DEFIED US BEFORE IS HIDING HER.
ANYONE WHO INSPIRES THAT MUCH LOYALTY CANNOT BE ALLOWED TO ROAM FREE.
HEY!
WHO'S THAT IDIOT IN THE NATIONAL GUARD BOOTS?
WHY THESE FEDS PULLING ME OVER, LIVERMORE?
FUCKETY FUCK FUCK...

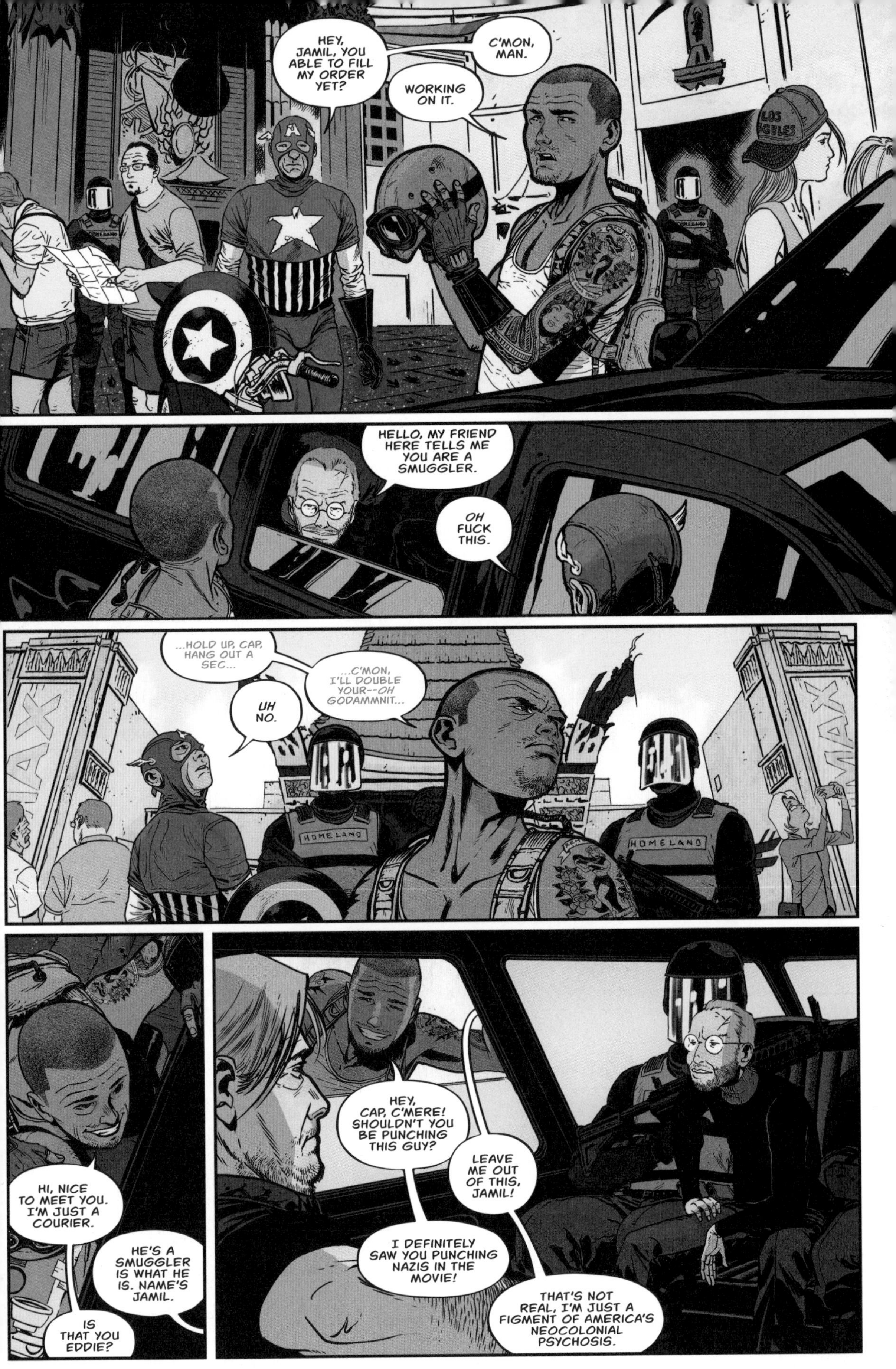
HEY, JAMIL, YOU ABLE TO FILL MY ORDER YET?
C'MON, MAN.
WORKING ON IT.
HELLO, MY FRIEND HERE TELLS ME YOU ARE A SMUGGLER.
OH FUCK THIS.
...HOLD UP, CAP, HANG OUT A SEC...
UH NO.
...C'MON, I'LL DOUBLE YOUR--OH GODAMMNIT...
HOMELAND
HOMELAND
HI, NICE TO MEET YOU. I'M JUST A COURIER.
HE'S A SMUGGLER IS WHAT HE IS. NAME'S JAMIL.
IS THAT YOU EDDIE?
HEY, CAP, C'MERE! SHOULDN'T YOU BE PUNCHING THIS GUY?
LEAVE ME OUT OF THIS, JAMIL!
I DEFINITELY SAW YOU PUNCHING NAZIS IN THE MOVIE!
THAT'S NOT REAL, I'M JUST A FIGMENT OF AMERICA'S NEOCOLONIAL PSYCHOSIS.

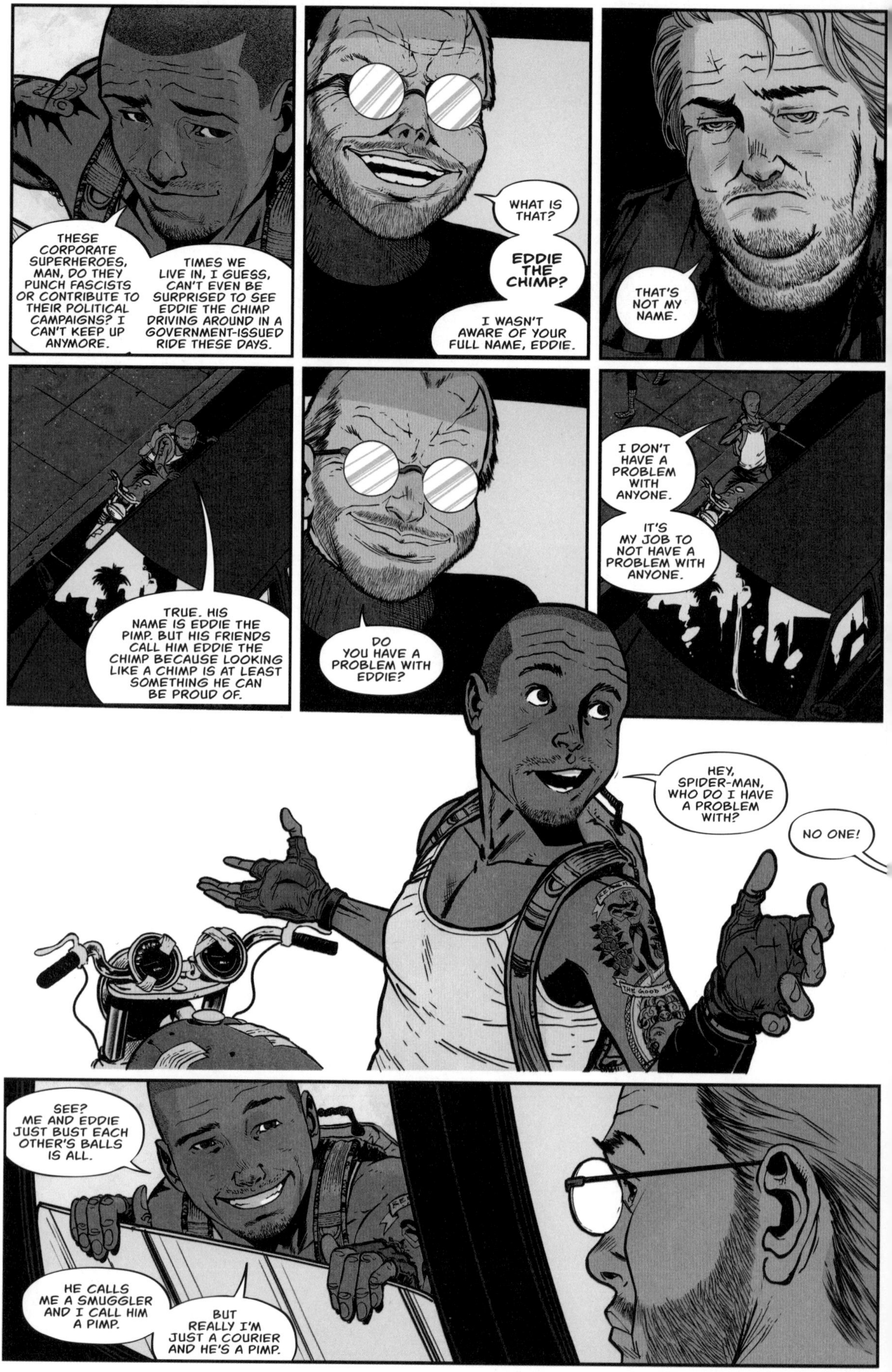
THESE CORPORATE SUPERHEROES, MAN, DO THEY PUNCH FASCISTS OR CONTRIBUTE TO THEIR POLITICAL CAMPAIGNS? I CAN'T KEEP UP ANYMORE.
TIMES WE LIVE IN, I GUESS, CAN'T EVEN BE SURPRISED TO SEE EDDIE THE CHIMP DRIVING AROUND IN A GOVERNMENT-ISSUED RIDE THESE DAYS.
WHAT IS THAT?
EDDIE THE CHIMP?
I WASN'T AWARE OF YOUR FULL NAME, EDDIE.
THAT'S NOT MY NAME.
TRUE. HIS NAME IS EDDIE THE PIMP. BUT HIS FRIENDS CALL HIM EDDIE THE CHIMP BECAUSE LOOKING LIKE A CHIMP IS AT LEAST SOMETHING HE CAN BE PROUD OF.
DO YOU HAVE A PROBLEM WITH EDDIE?
I DON'T HAVE A PROBLEM WITH ANYONE.
IT'S MY JOB TO NOT HAVE A PROBLEM WITH ANYONE.
HEY, SPIDER-MAN, WHO DO I HAVE A PROBLEM WITH?
NO ONE!
SEE? ME AND EDDIE JUST BUST EACH OTHER'S BALLS IS ALL.
HE CALLS ME A SMUGGLER AND I CALL HIM A PIMP.
BUT REALLY I'M JUST A COURIER AND HE'S A PIMP.

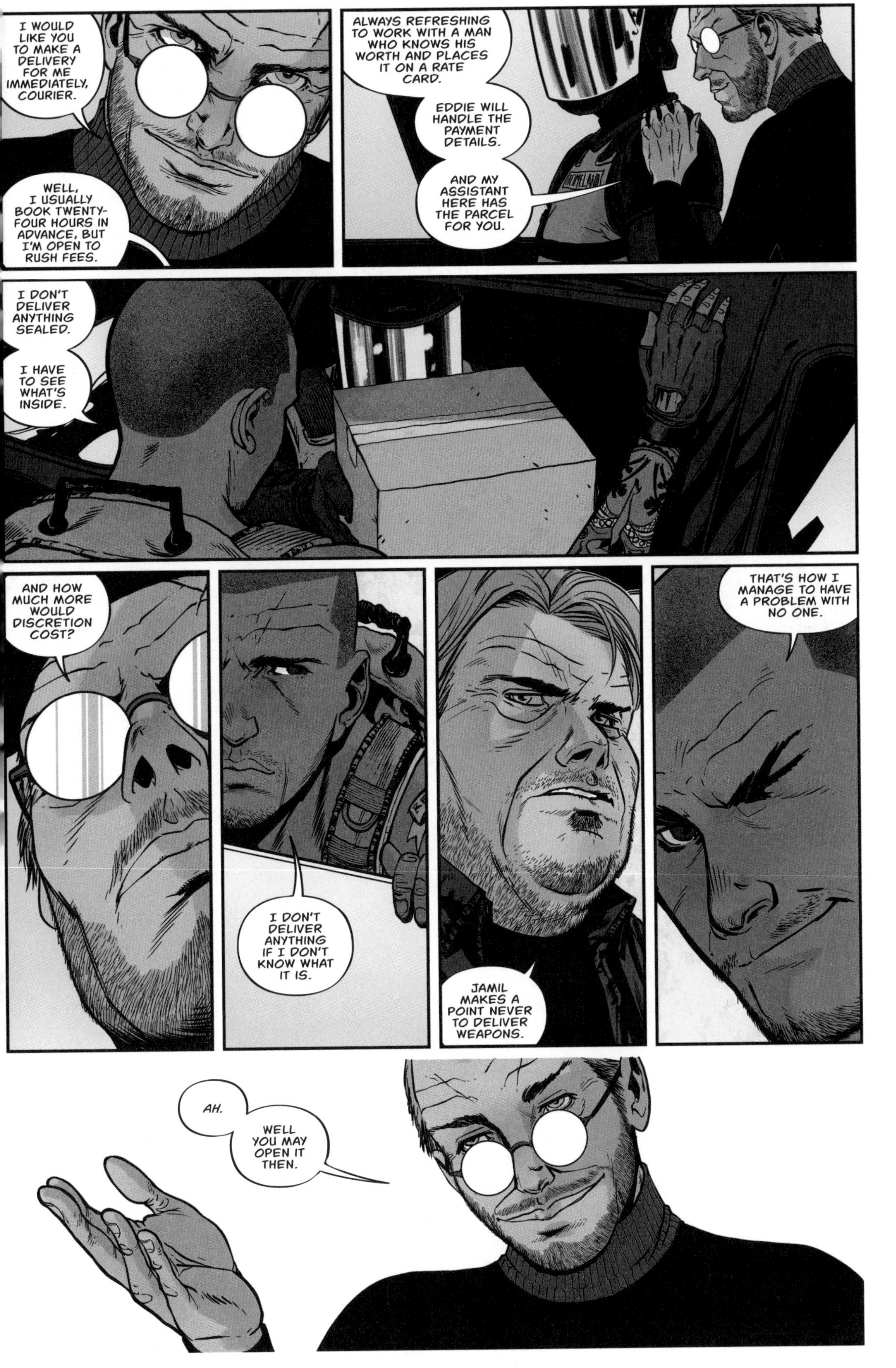
I WOULD LIKE YOU TO MAKE A DELIVERY FOR ME IMMEDIATELY, COURIER.
WELL, I USUALLY BOOK TWENTY-FOUR HOURS IN ADVANCE, BUT I'M OPEN TO RUSH FEES.
ALWAYS REFRESHING TO WORK WITH A MAN WHO KNOWS HIS WORTH AND PLACES IT ON A RATE CARD.
EDDIE WILL HANDLE THE PAYMENT DETAILS.
AND MY ASSISTANT HERE HAS THE PARCEL FOR YOU.
I DON'T DELIVER ANYTHING SEALED.
I HAVE TO SEE WHAT'S INSIDE.
AND HOW MUCH MORE WOULD DISCRETION COST?
I DON'T DELIVER ANYTHING IF I DON'T KNOW WHAT IT IS.
JAMIL MAKES A POINT NEVER TO DELIVER WEAPONS.
THAT'S HOW I MANAGE TO HAVE A PROBLEM WITH NO ONE.
AH.
WELL YOU MAY OPEN IT THEN.

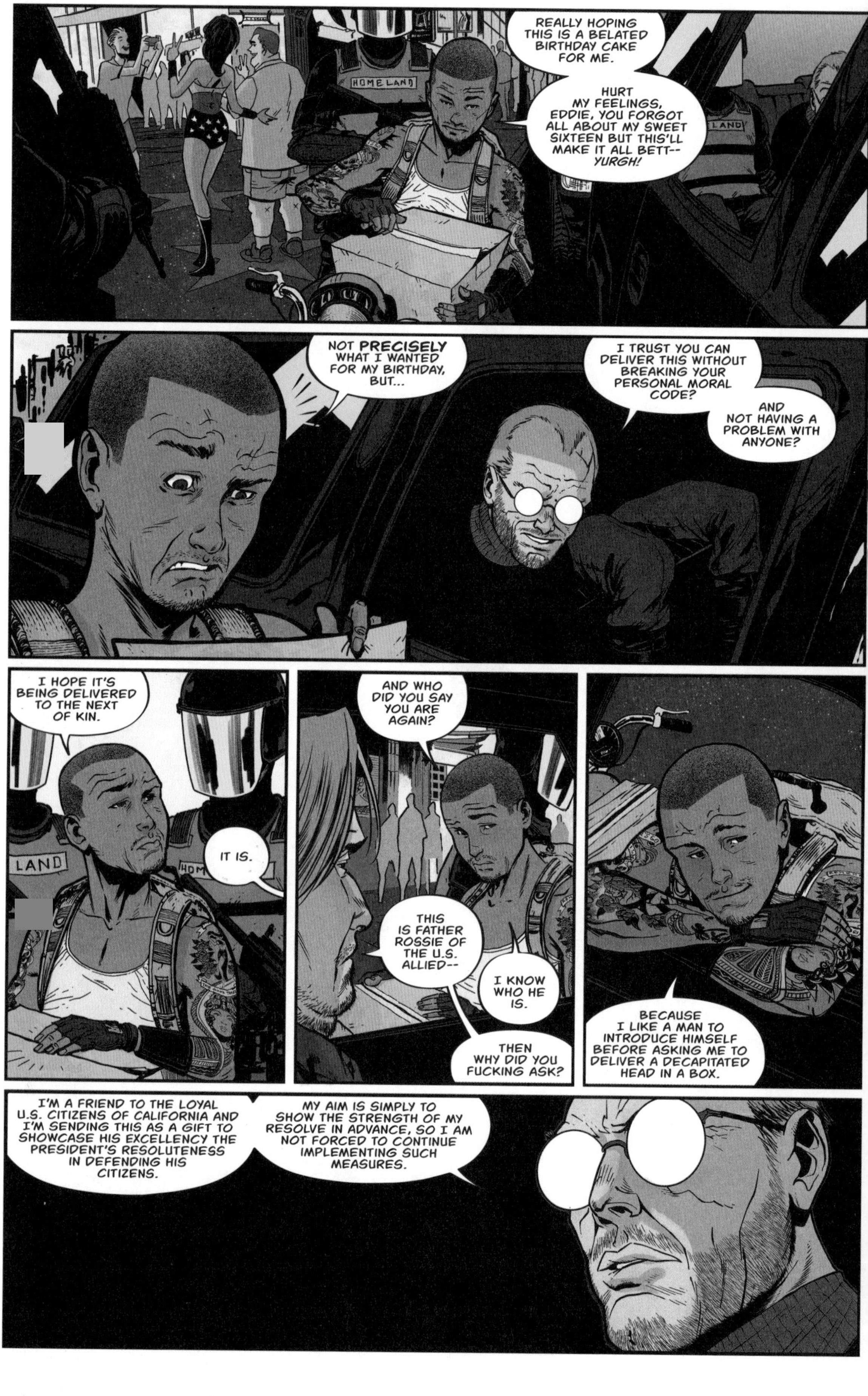
REALLY HOPING THIS IS A BELATED BIRTHDAY CAKE FOR ME.
HURT MY FEELINGS, EDDIE, YOU FORGOT ALL ABOUT MY SWEET SIXTEEN BUT THIS'LL MAKE IT ALL BETT-- YURGH!
HOMELAND
NOT PRECISELY WHAT I WANTED FOR MY BIRTHDAY, BUT...
I TRUST YOU CAN DELIVER THIS WITHOUT BREAKING YOUR PERSONAL MORAL CODE?
AND NOT HAVING A PROBLEM WITH ANYONE?
I HOPE IT'S BEING DELIVERED TO THE NEXT OF KIN.
IT IS.
AND WHO DID YOU SAY YOU ARE AGAIN?
THIS IS FATHER ROSSIE OF THE U.S. ALLIED--
I KNOW WHO HE IS.
THEN WHY DID YOU FUCKING ASK?
BECAUSE I LIKE A MAN TO INTRODUCE HIMSELF BEFORE ASKING ME TO DELIVER A DECAPITATED HEAD IN A BOX.
I'M A FRIEND TO THE LOYAL U.S. CITIZENS OF CALIFORNIA AND I'M SENDING THIS AS A GIFT TO SHOWCASE HIS EXCELLENCY THE PRESIDENT'S RESOLUTENESS IN DEFENDING HIS CITIZENS.
MY AIM IS SIMPLY TO SHOW THE STRENGTH OF MY RESOLVE IN ADVANCE, SO I AM NOT FORCED TO CONTINUE IMPLEMENTING SUCH MEASURES.

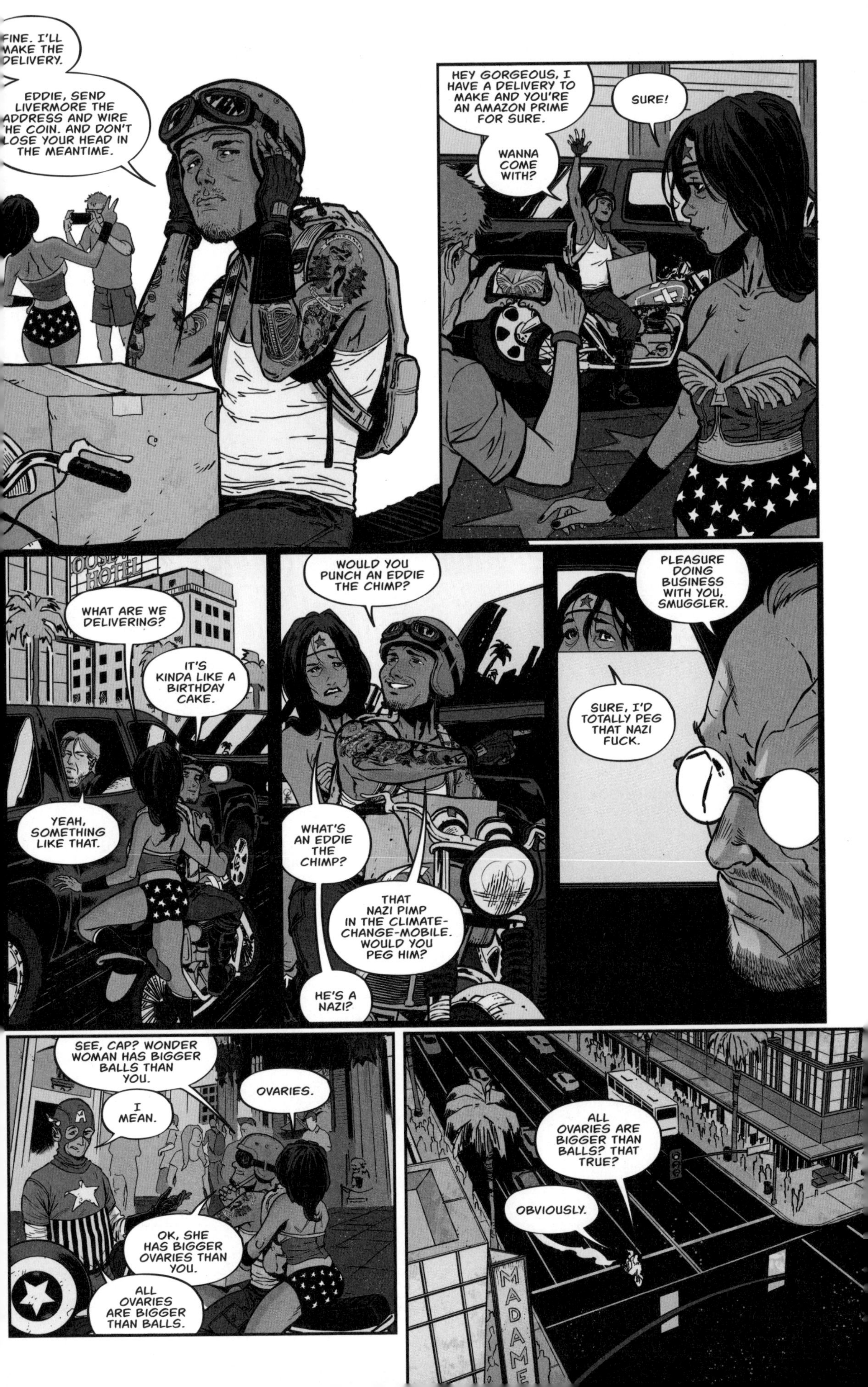
FINE. I'LL MAKE THE DELIVERY.
EDDIE, SEND LIVERMORE THE ADDRESS AND WIRE THE COIN. AND DON'T LOSE YOUR HEAD IN THE MEANTIME.
HEY GORGEOUS, I HAVE A DELIVERY TO MAKE AND YOU'RE AN AMAZON PRIME FOR SURE.
WANNA COME WITH?
SURE!
WHAT ARE WE DELIVERING?
IT'S KINDA LIKE A BIRTHDAY CAKE.
YEAH, SOMETHING LIKE THAT.
WOULD YOU PUNCH AN EDDIE THE CHIMP?
WHAT'S AN EDDIE THE CHIMP?
THAT NAZI PIMP IN THE CLIMATE-CHANGE-MOBILE. WOULD YOU PEG HIM?
HE'S A NAZI?
PLEASURE DOING BUSINESS WITH YOU, SMUGGLER.
SURE, I'D TOTALLY PEG THAT NAZI FUCK.
SEE, CAP? WONDER WOMAN HAS BIGGER BALLS THAN YOU.
I MEAN.
OVARIES.
OK, SHE HAS BIGGER OVARIES THAN YOU.
ALL OVARIES ARE BIGGER THAN BALLS.
ALL OVARIES ARE BIGGER THAN BALLS? THAT TRUE?
OBVIOUSLY.
MADAME

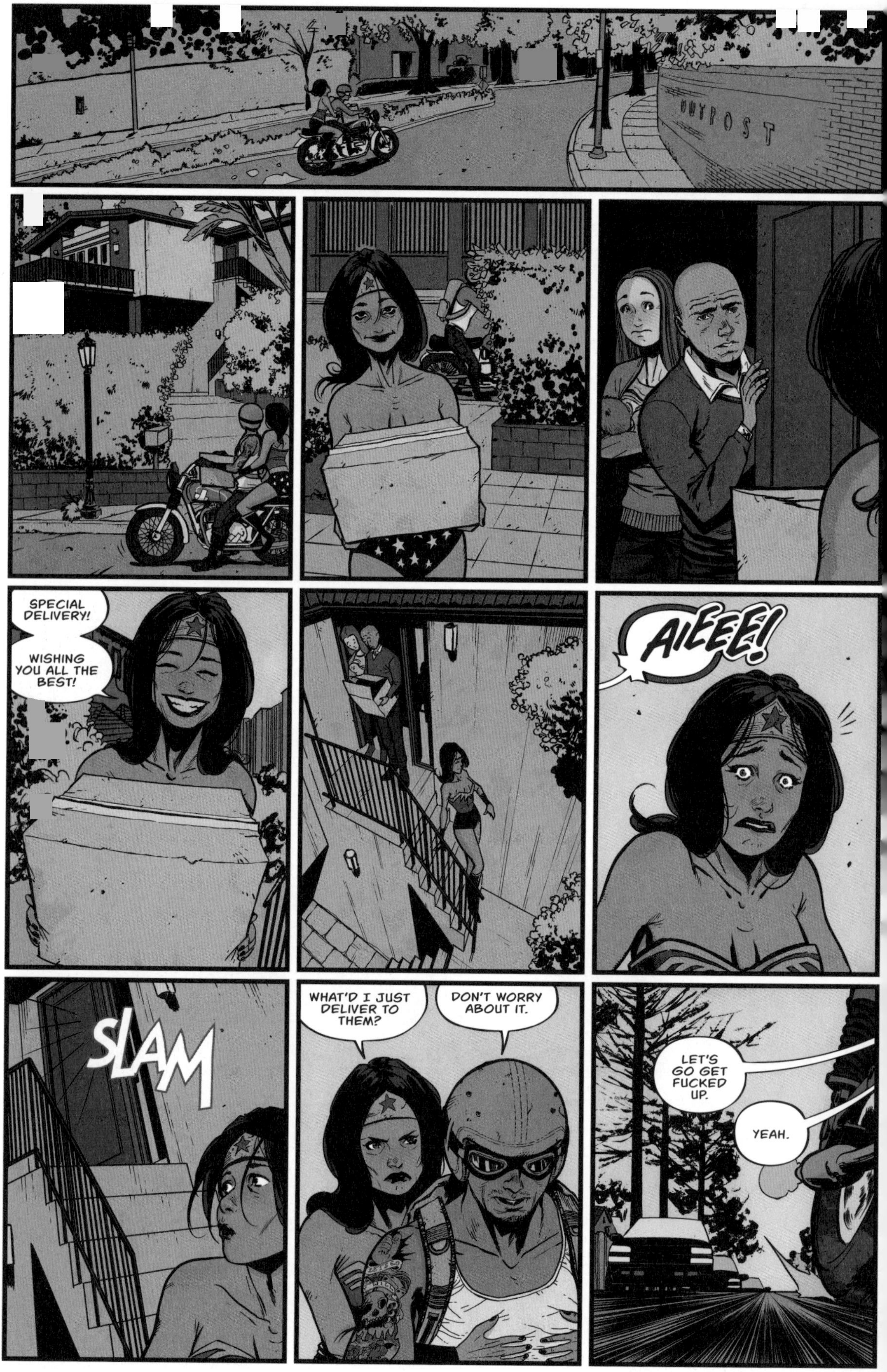
OUTPOST
SPECIAL DELIVERY!
WISHING YOU ALL THE BEST!
AIEEE!
SLAM
WHAT'D I JUST DELIVER TO THEM?
DON'T WORRY ABOUT IT.
LET'S GO GET FUCKED UP.
YEAH.

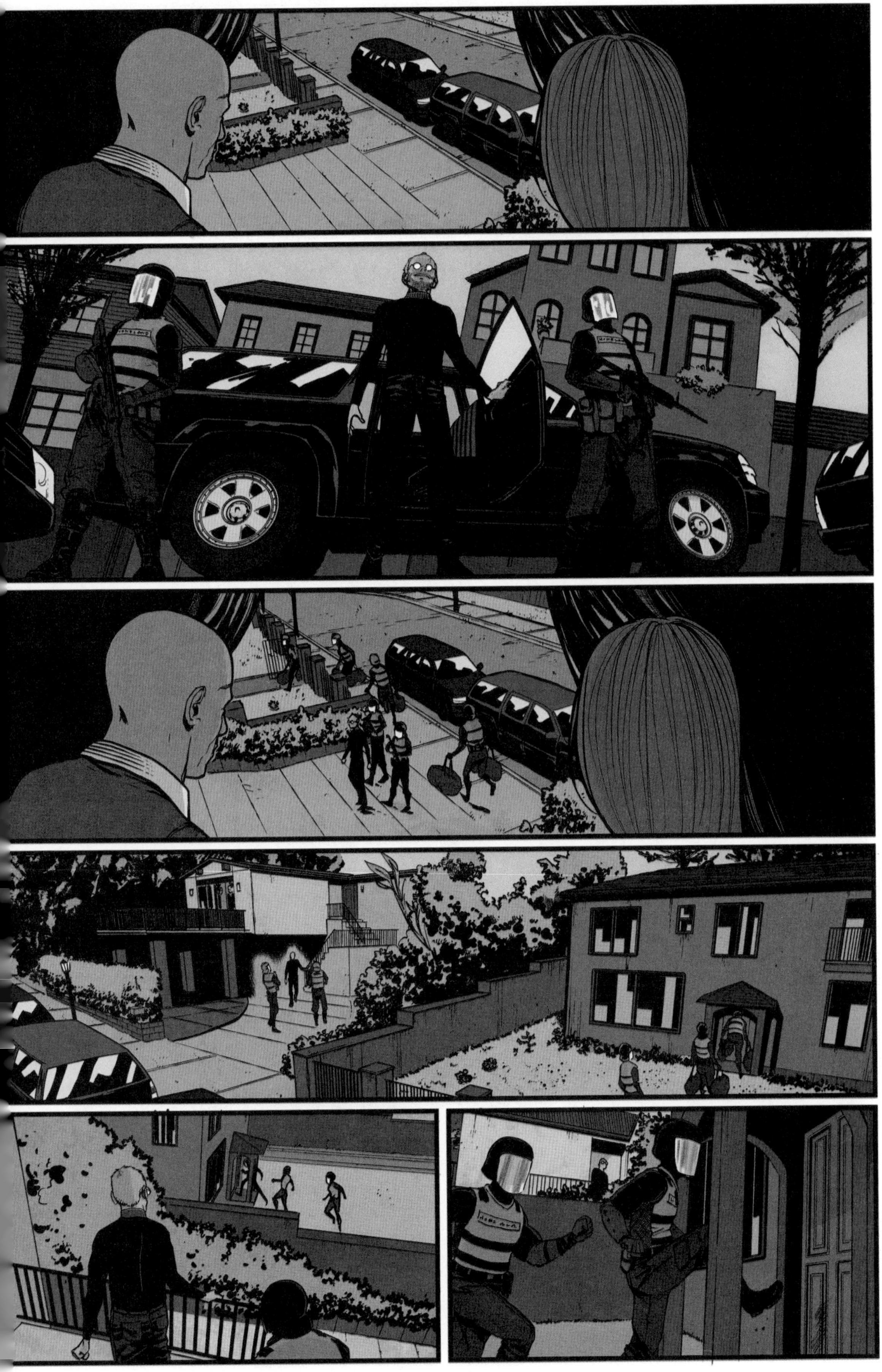

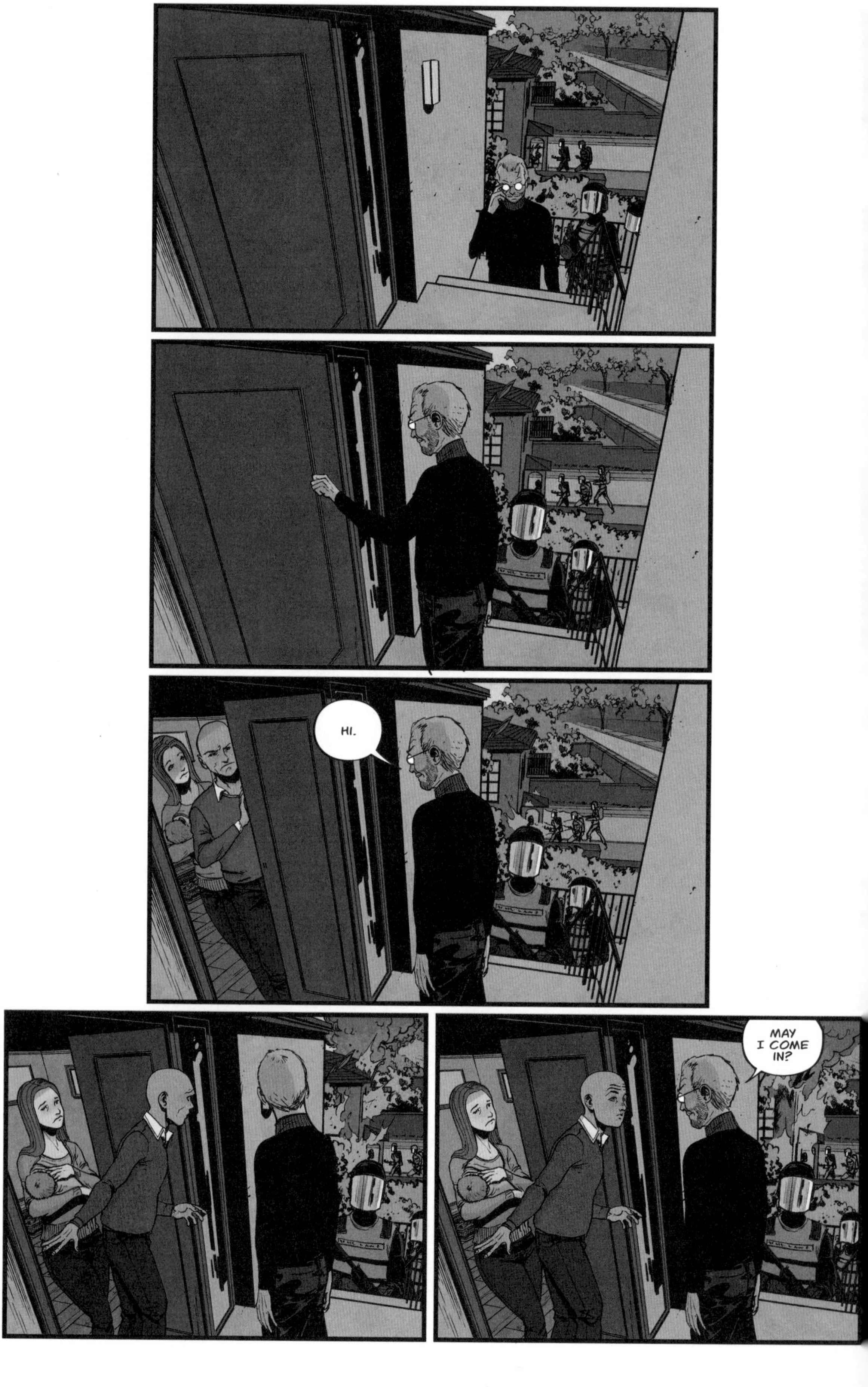
HI.
MAY I COME IN?

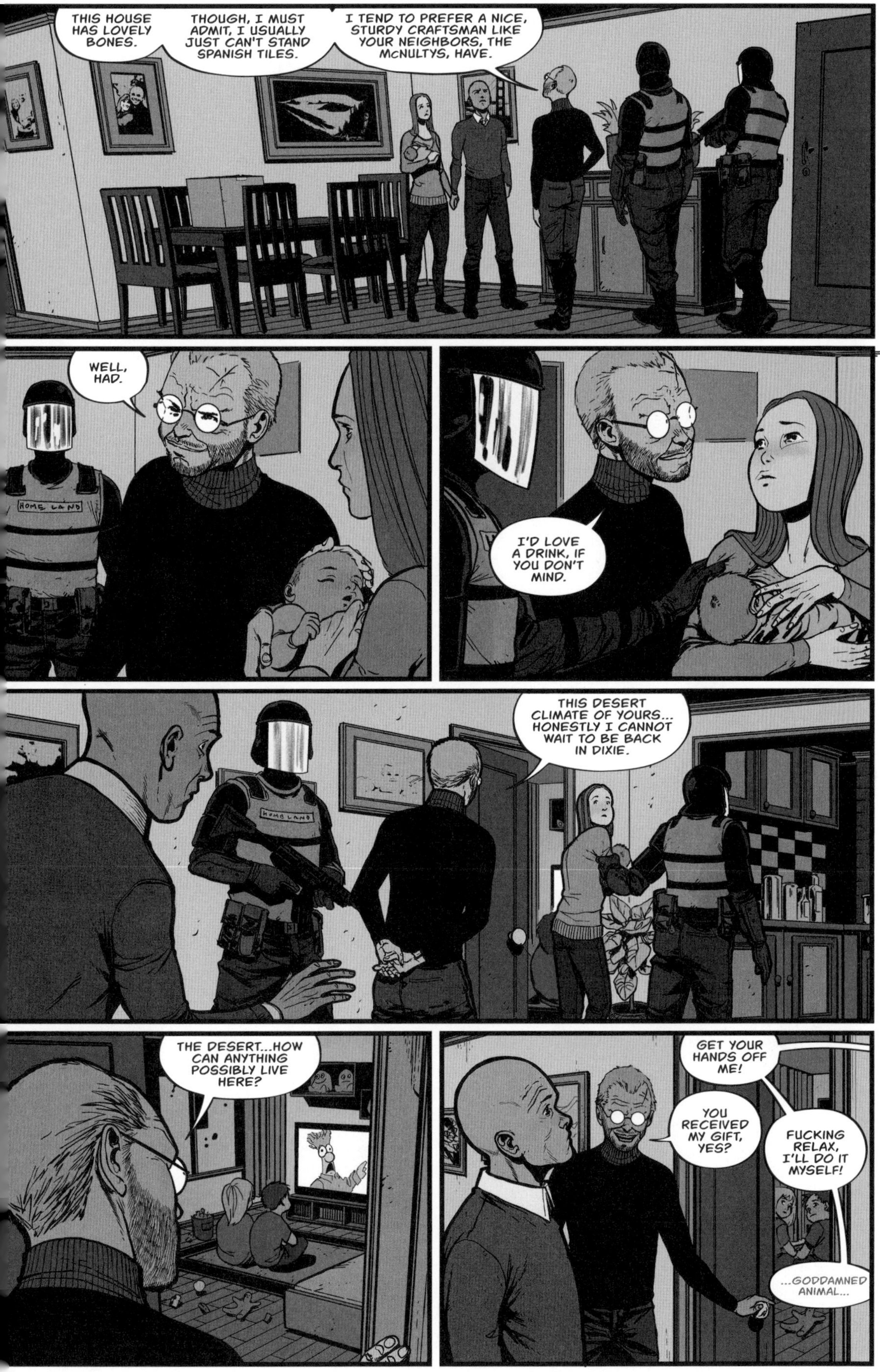
THIS HOUSE HAS LOVELY BONES.
THOUGH, I MUST ADMIT, I USUALLY JUST CAN'T STAND SPANISH TILES.
I TEND TO PREFER A NICE, STURDY CRAFTSMAN LIKE YOUR NEIGHBORS, THE McNULTYS, HAVE.
WELL, HAD.
I'D LOVE A DRINK, IF YOU DON'T MIND.
THIS DESERT CLIMATE OF YOURS... HONESTLY I CANNOT WAIT TO BE BACK IN DIXIE.
THE DESERT...HOW CAN ANYTHING POSSIBLY LIVE HERE?
GET YOUR HANDS OFF ME!
YOU RECEIVED MY GIFT, YES?
FUCKING RELAX, I'LL DO IT MYSELF!
...GODDAMNED ANIMAL...

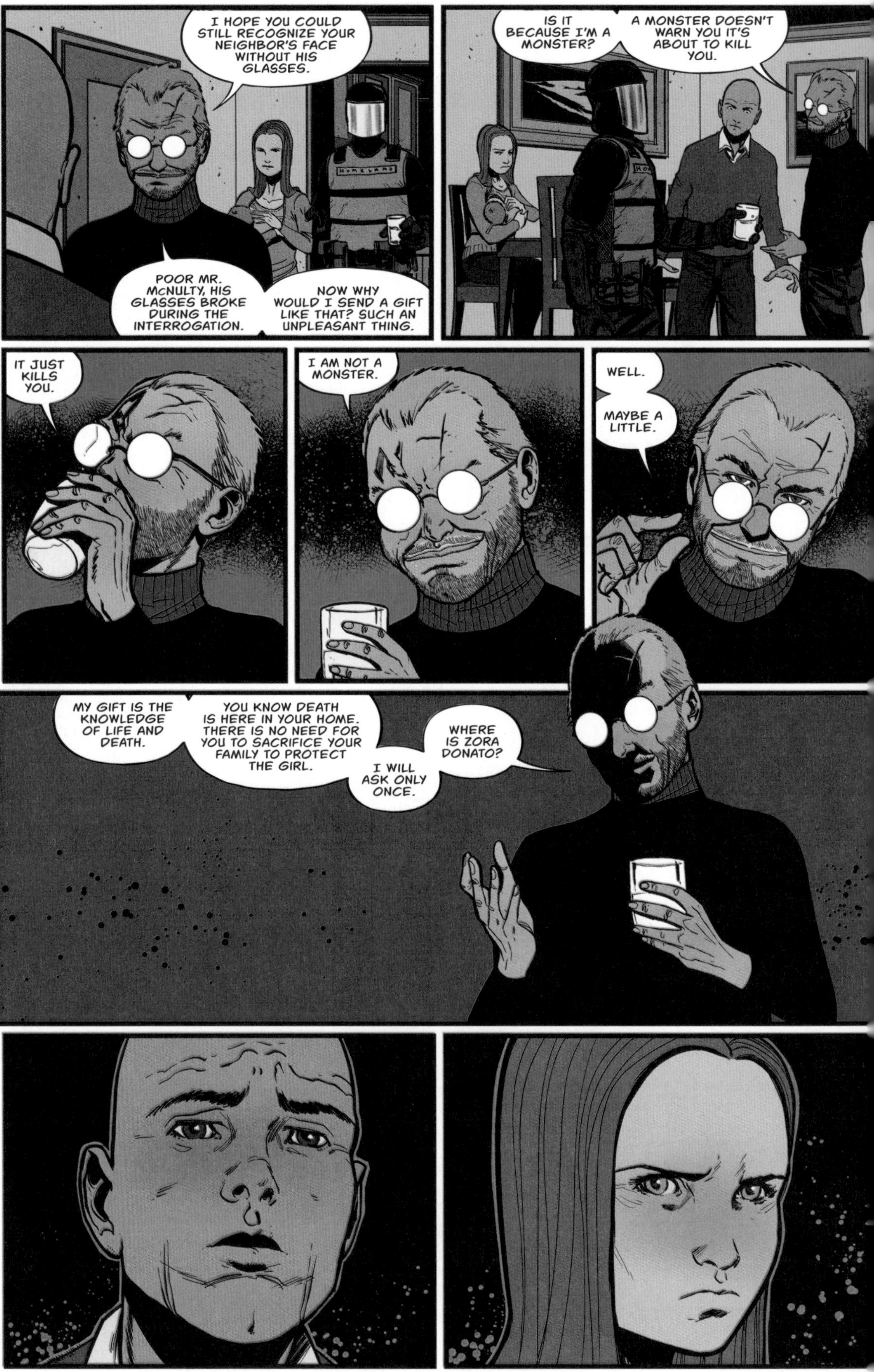

I HOPE YOU COULD STILL RECOGNIZE YOUR NEIGHBOR'S FACE WITHOUT HIS GLASSES.
POOR MR. McNULTY, HIS GLASSES BROKE DURING THE INTERROGATION.
NOW WHY WOULD I SEND A GIFT LIKE THAT? SUCH AN UNPLEASANT THING.
IS IT BECAUSE I'M A MONSTER?
A MONSTER DOESN'T WARN YOU IT'S ABOUT TO KILL YOU.
IT JUST KILLS YOU.
I AM NOT A MONSTER.
WELL.
MAYBE A LITTLE.
MY GIFT IS THE KNOWLEDGE OF LIFE AND DEATH.
YOU KNOW DEATH IS HERE IN YOUR HOME. THERE IS NO NEED FOR YOU TO SACRIFICE YOUR FAMILY TO PROTECT THE GIRL.
I WILL ASK ONLY ONCE.
WHERE IS ZORA DONATO?

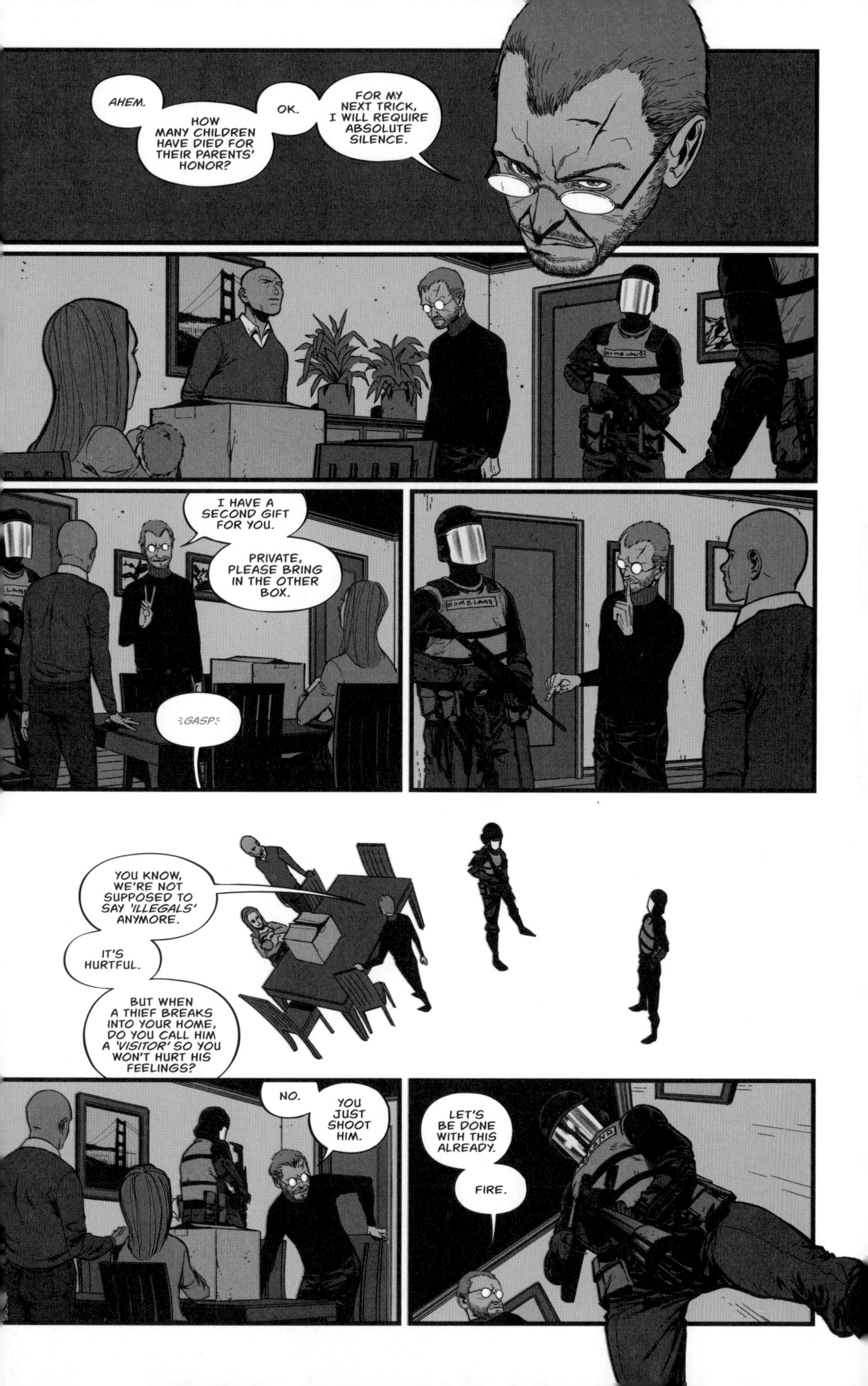
AHEM.
HOW MANY CHILDREN HAVE DIED FOR THEIR PARENTS' HONOR?
OK.
FOR MY NEXT TRICK, I WILL REQUIRE ABSOLUTE SILENCE.
HOMELAND
I HAVE A SECOND GIFT FOR YOU.
PRIVATE, PLEASE BRING IN THE OTHER BOX.
GASP
HOMELAND
YOU KNOW, WE'RE NOT SUPPOSED TO SAY 'ILLEGALS' ANYMORE.
IT'S HURTFUL.
BUT WHEN A THIEF BREAKS INTO YOUR HOME, DO YOU CALL HIM A 'VISITOR' SO YOU WON'T HURT HIS FEELINGS?
NO.
YOU JUST SHOOT HIM.
LET'S BE DONE WITH THIS ALREADY.
FIRE.

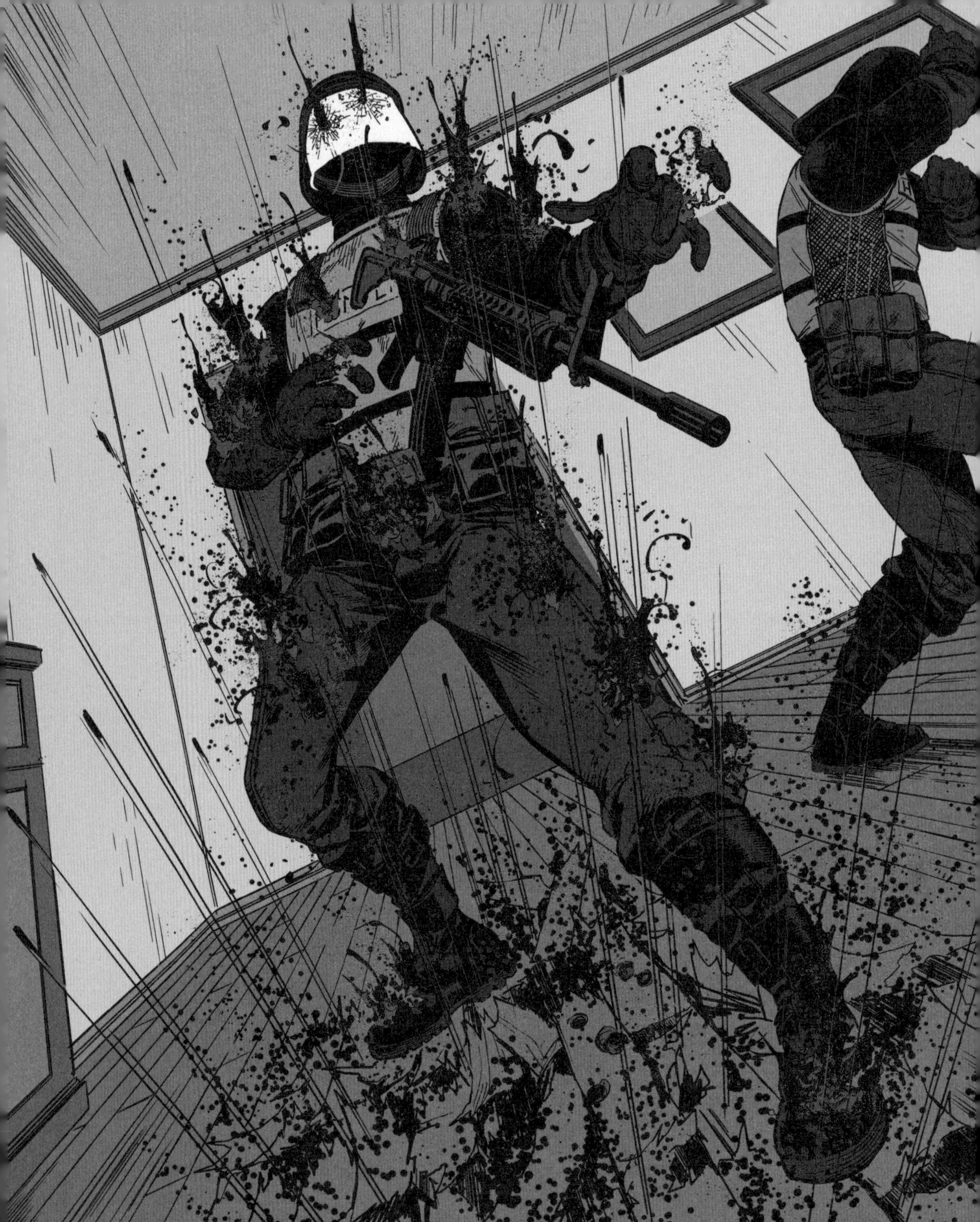

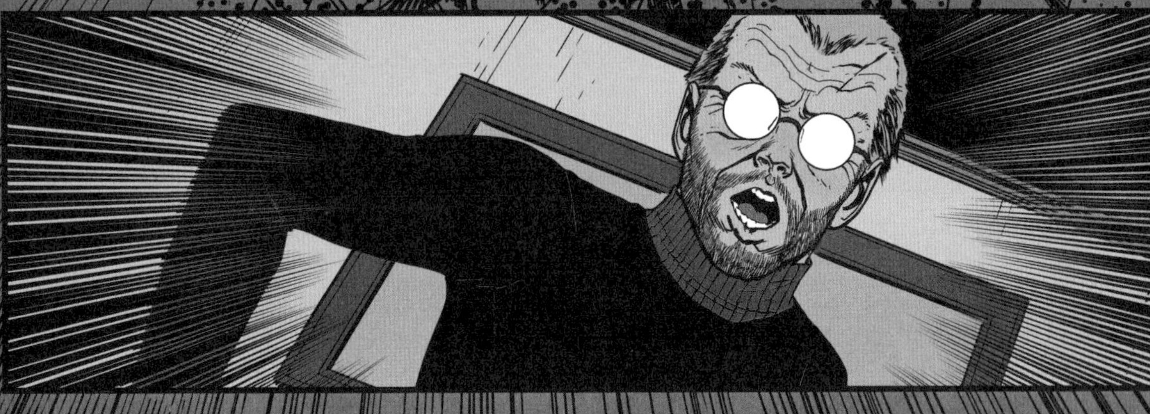

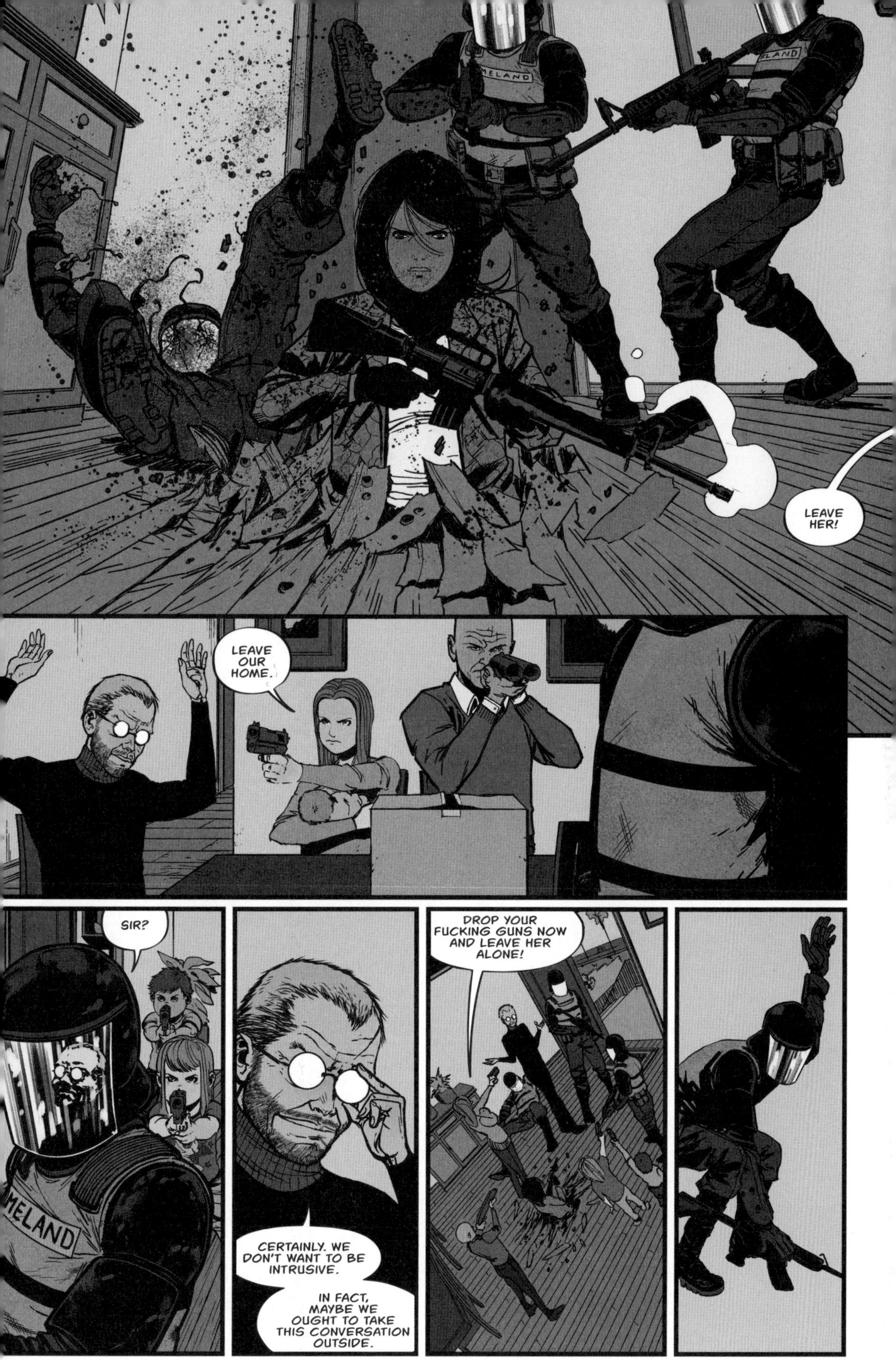
LEAVE HER!
LEAVE OUR HOME.
SIR?
CERTAINLY. WE DON'T WANT TO BE INTRUSIVE.
IN FACT, MAYBE WE OUGHT TO TAKE THIS CONVERSATION OUTSIDE.
DROP YOUR FUCKING GUNS NOW AND LEAVE HER ALONE!

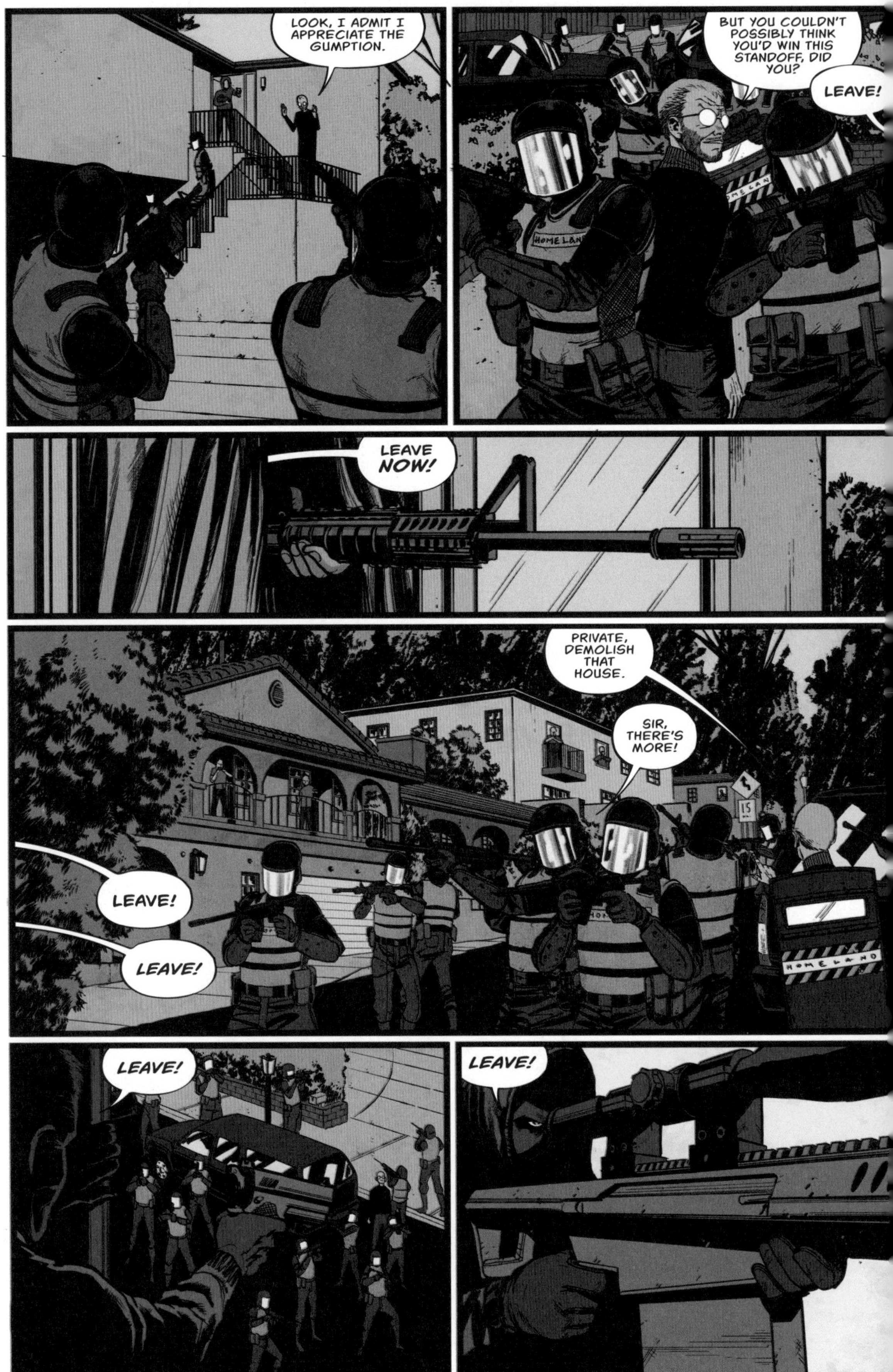
LOOK, I ADMIT I APPRECIATE THE GUMPTION.
BUT YOU COULDN'T POSSIBLY THINK YOU'D WIN THIS STANDOFF, DID YOU?
LEAVE!
LEAVE NOW!
PRIVATE, DEMOLISH THAT HOUSE.
SIR, THERE'S MORE!
LEAVE!
LEAVE!
LEAVE!
LEAVE!

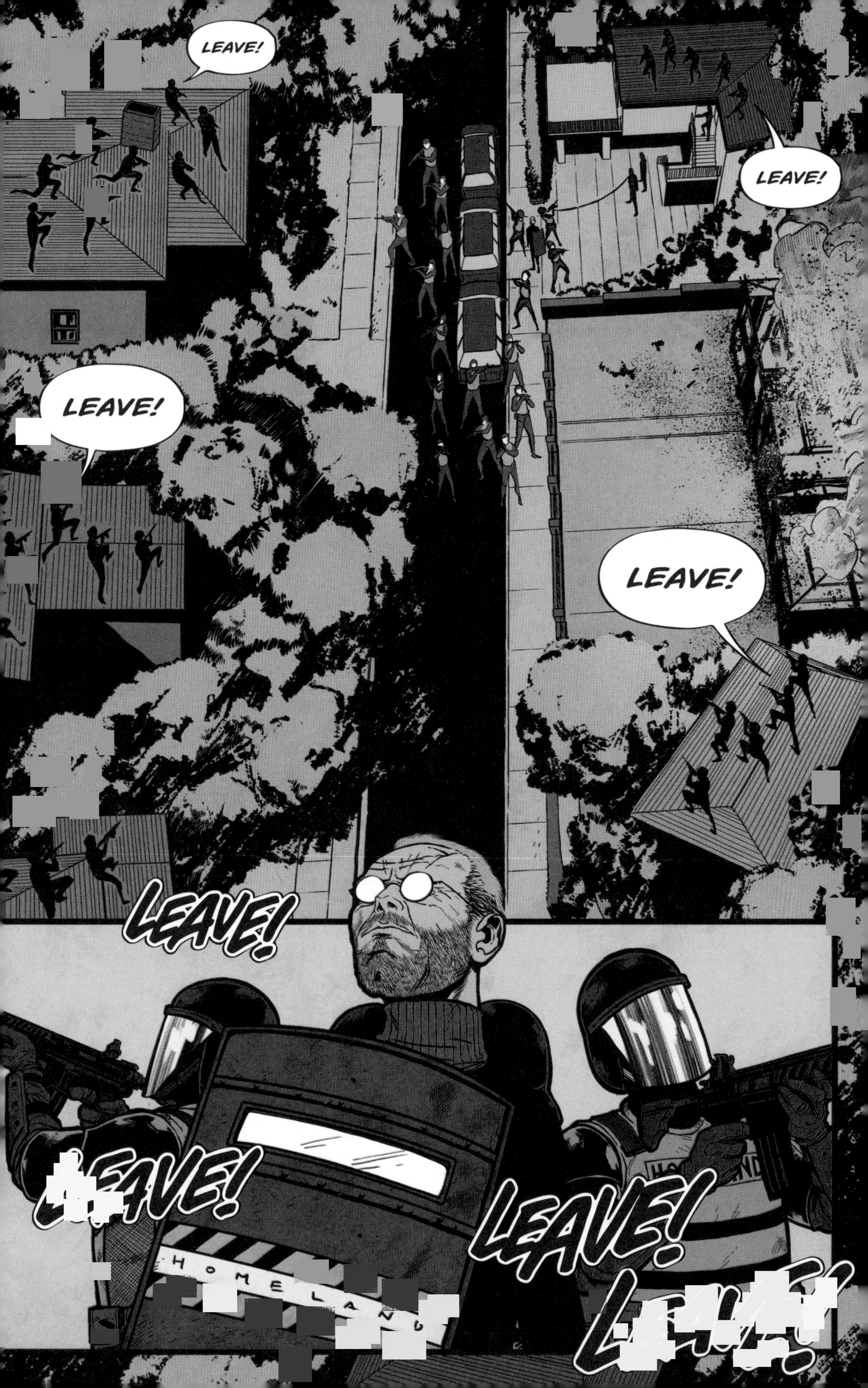
LEAVE!
LEAVE!
LEAVE!
LEAVE!
LEAVE!
LEAVE!

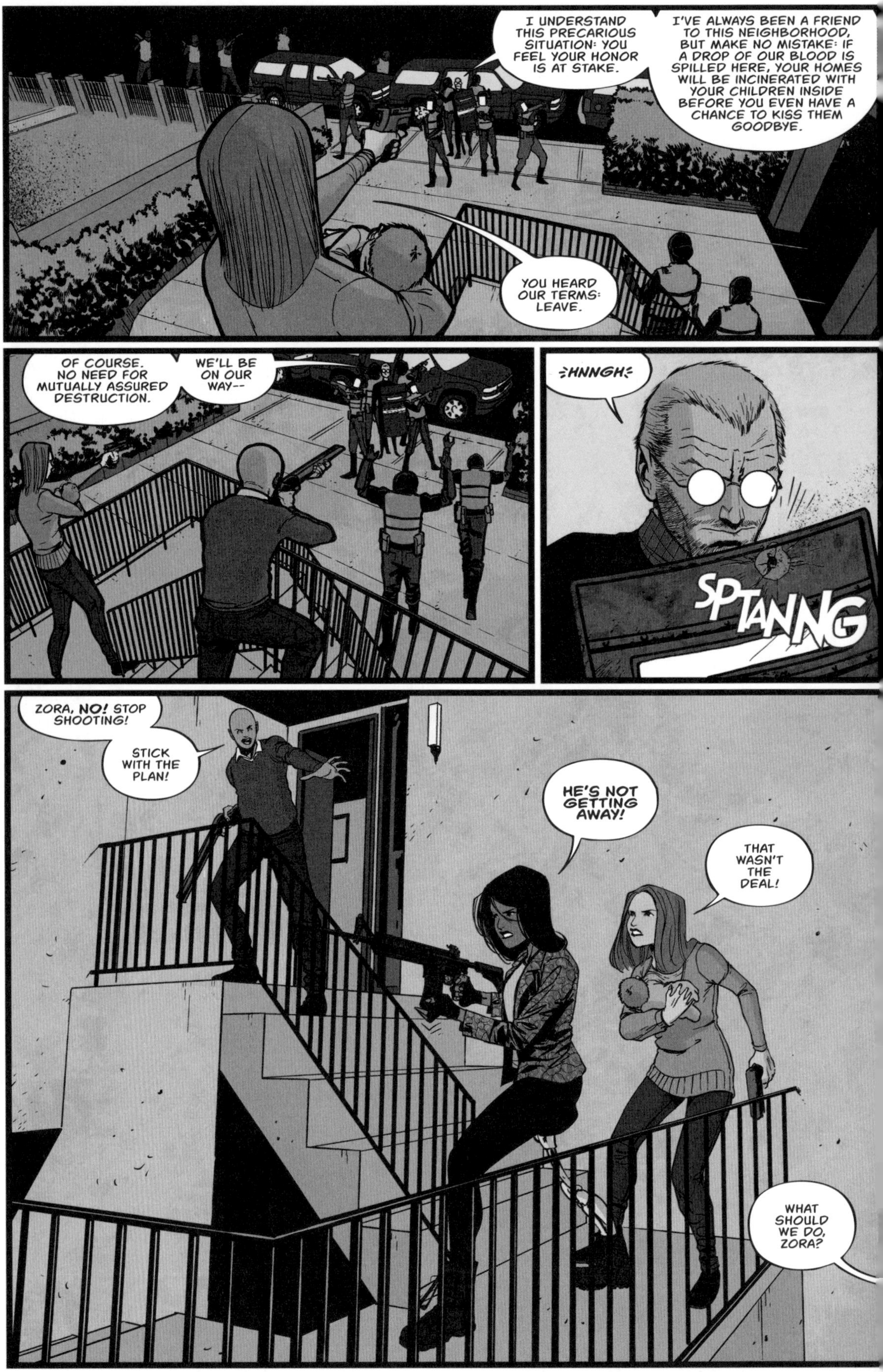
I UNDERSTAND THIS PRECARIOUS SITUATION: YOU FEEL YOUR HONOR IS AT STAKE.
I'VE ALWAYS BEEN A FRIEND TO THIS NEIGHBORHOOD, BUT MAKE NO MISTAKE: IF A DROP OF OUR BLOOD IS SPILLED HERE, YOUR HOMES WILL BE INCINERATED WITH YOUR CHILDREN INSIDE BEFORE YOU EVEN HAVE A CHANCE TO KISS THEM GOODBYE.
YOU HEARD OUR TERMS: LEAVE.
OF COURSE. NO NEED FOR MUTUALLY ASSURED DESTRUCTION.
WE'LL BE ON OUR WAY--
HNNGH
SPTANNG
ZORA, NO! STOP SHOOTING!
STICK WITH THE PLAN!
HE'S NOT GETTING AWAY!
THAT WASN'T THE DEAL!
WHAT SHOULD WE DO, ZORA?

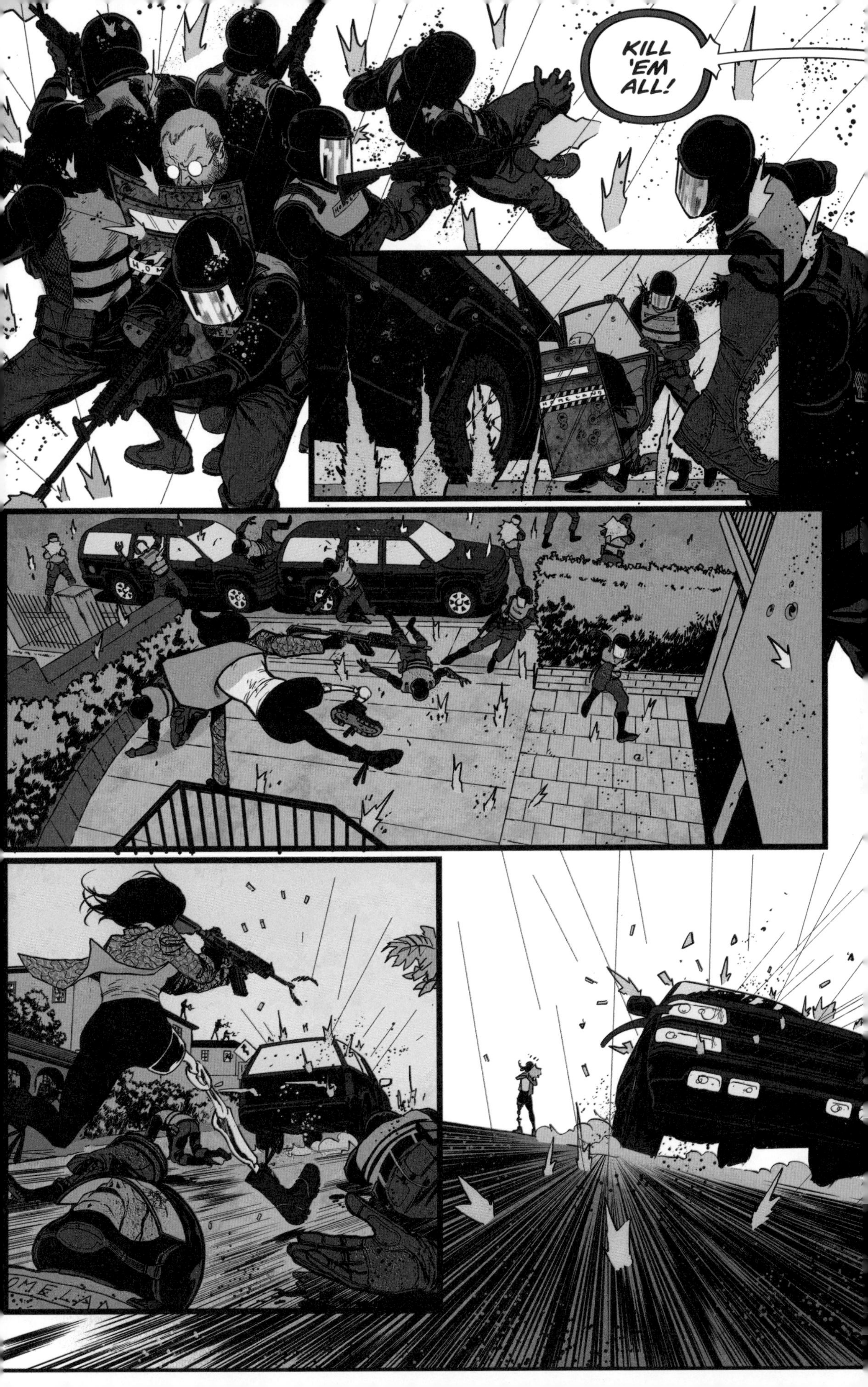
KILL 'EM ALL!

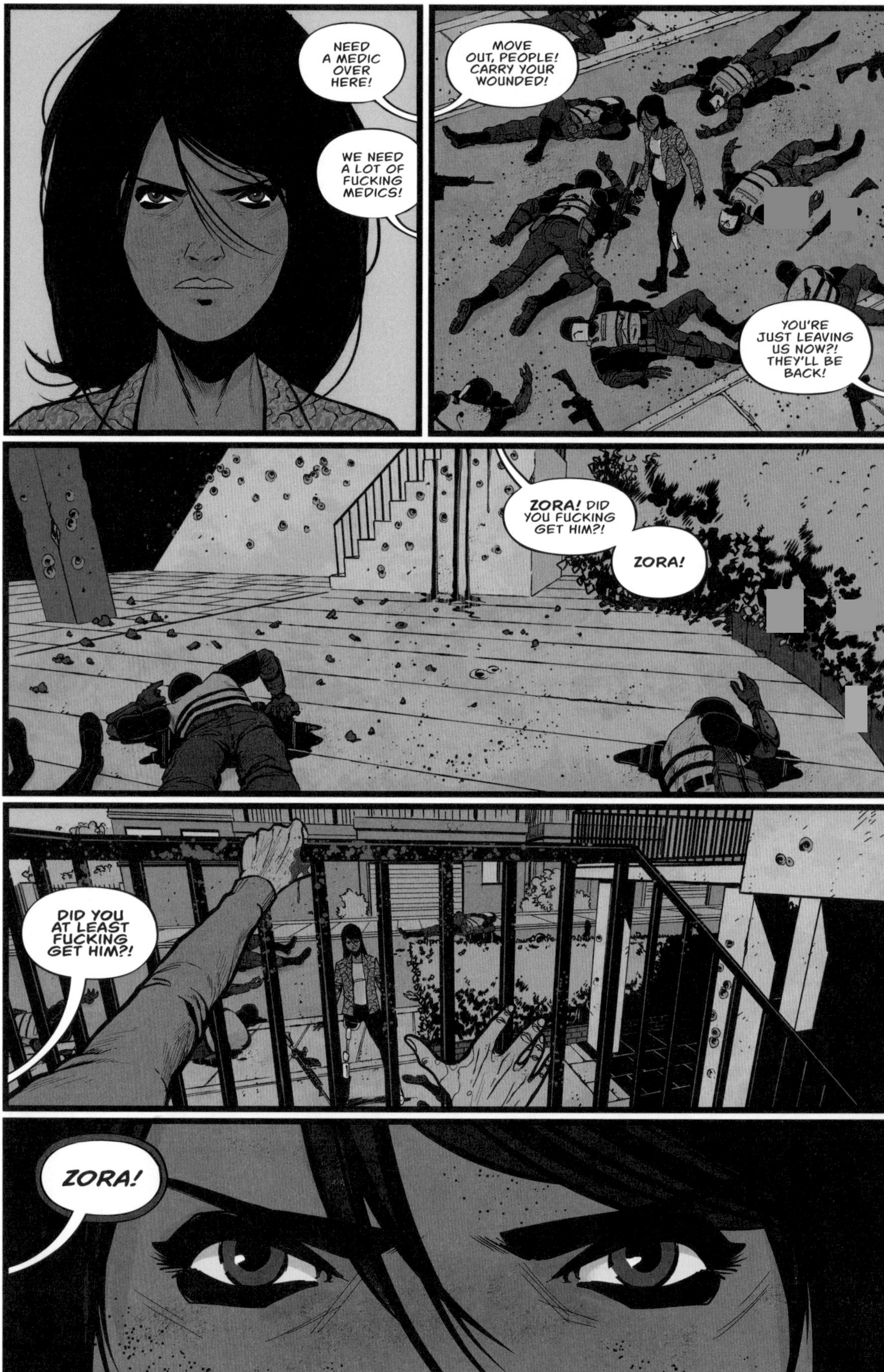
NEED A MEDIC OVER HERE!
WE NEED A LOT OF FUCKING MEDICS!
MOVE OUT, PEOPLE! CARRY YOUR WOUNDED!
YOU'RE JUST LEAVING US NOW?! THEY'LL BE BACK!
ZORA! DID YOU FUCKING GET HIM?!
ZORA!
DID YOU AT LEAST FUCKING GET HIM?!
ZORA!

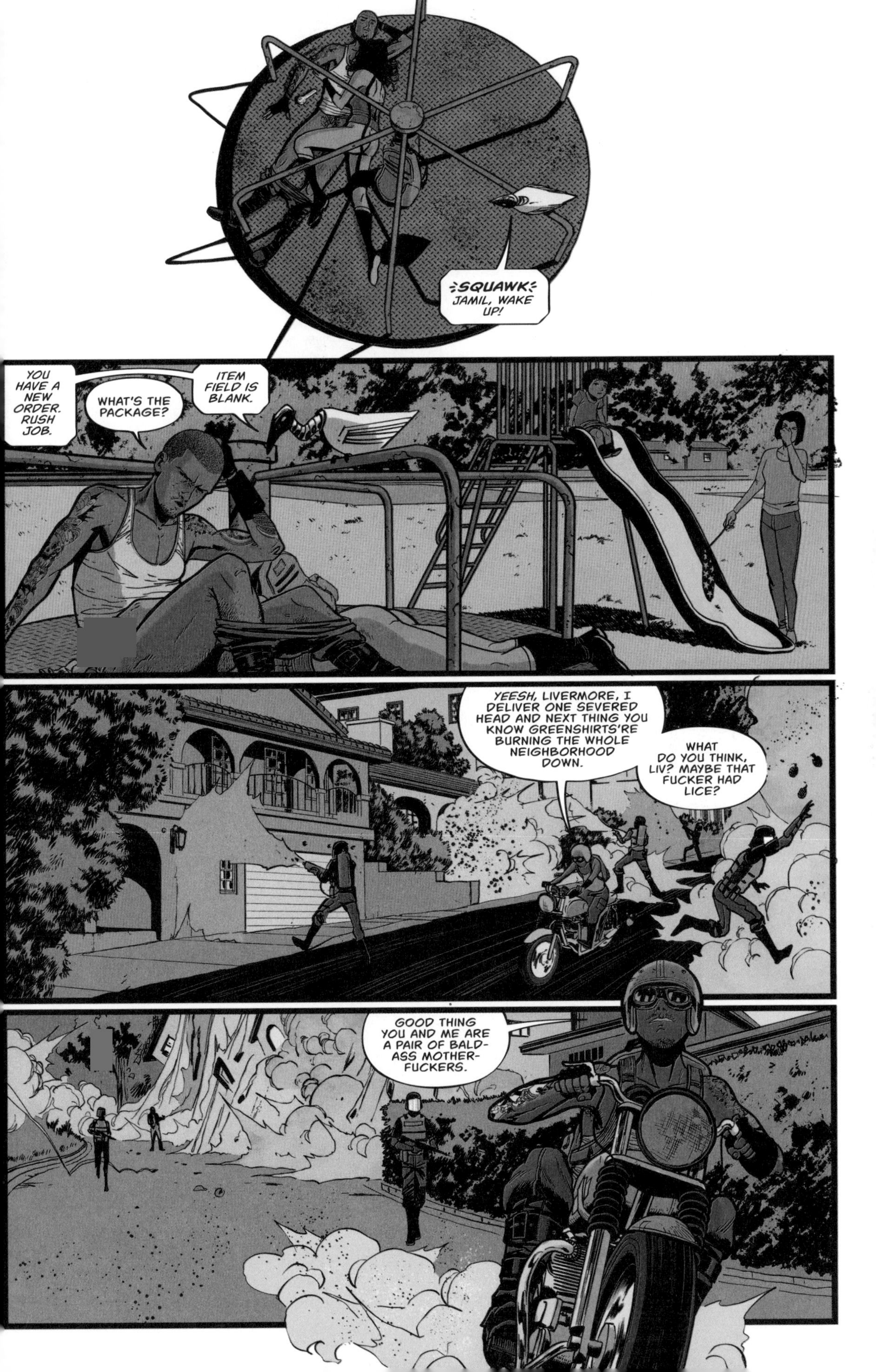
SQUAWK
JAMIL, WAKE UP!
YOU HAVE A NEW ORDER. RUSH JOB.
WHAT'S THE PACKAGE?
ITEM FIELD IS BLANK.
YEESH, LIVERMORE, I DELIVER ONE SEVERED HEAD AND NEXT THING YOU KNOW GREENSHIRTS'RE BURNING THE WHOLE NEIGHBORHOOD DOWN.
WHAT DO YOU THINK, LIV? MAYBE THAT FUCKER HAD LICE?
GOOD THING YOU AND ME ARE A PAIR OF BALD-ASS MOTHER-FUCKERS.

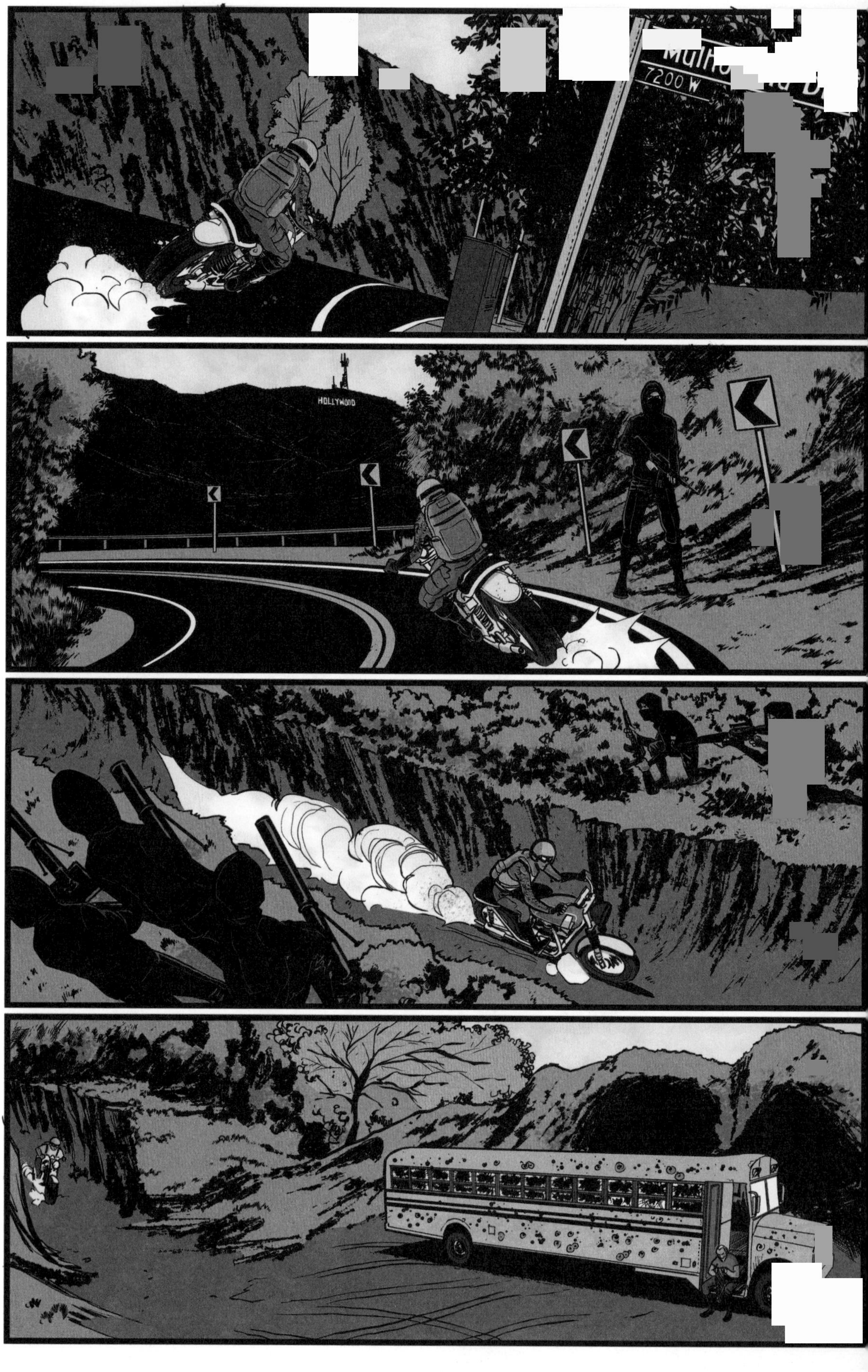
7200 W
HOLLYWOOD

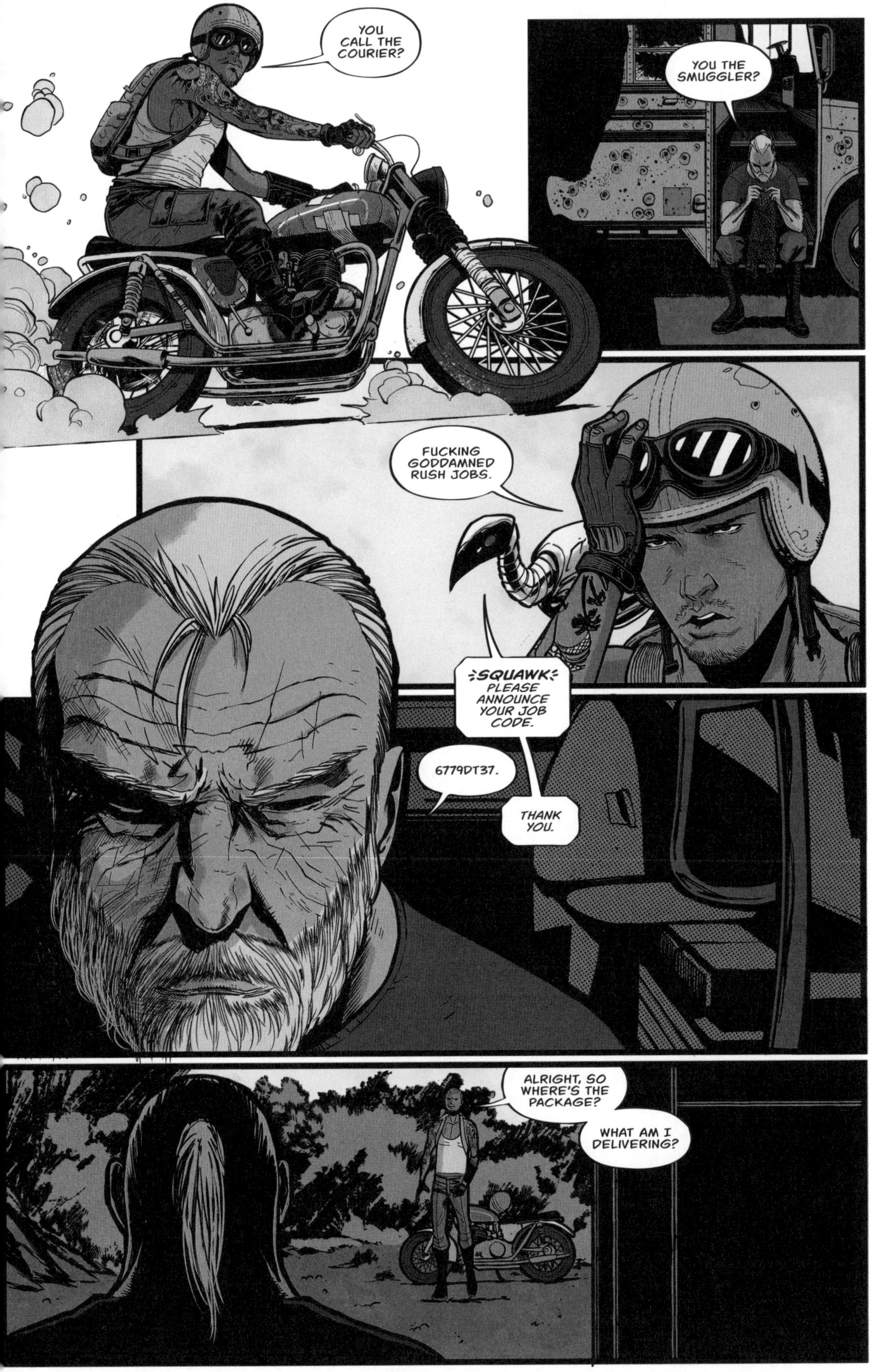
YOU CALL THE COURIER?
YOU THE SMUGGLER?
FUCKING GODDAMNED RUSH JOBS.
SQUAWK PLEASE ANNOUNCE YOUR JOB CODE.
6779DT37.
THANK YOU.
ALRIGHT, SO WHERE'S THE PACKAGE?
WHAT AM I DELIVERING?

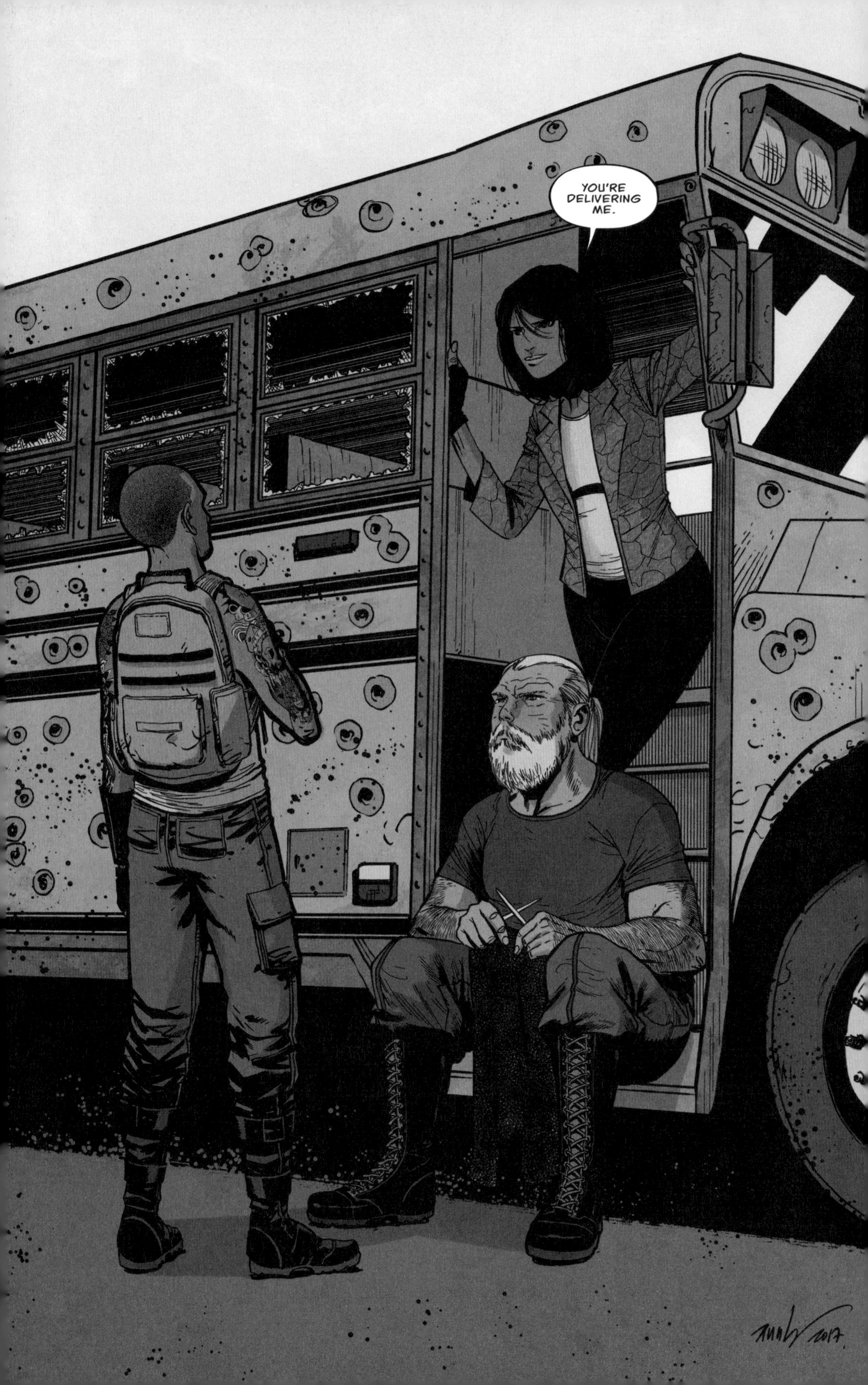
YOU'RE DELIVERING ME.

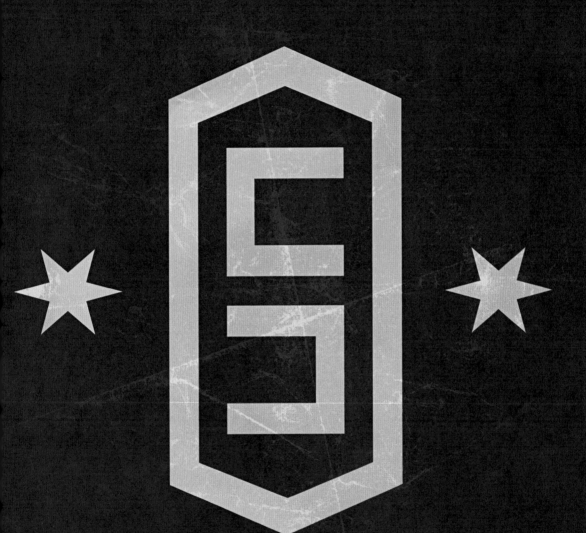

CHAPTER TWO

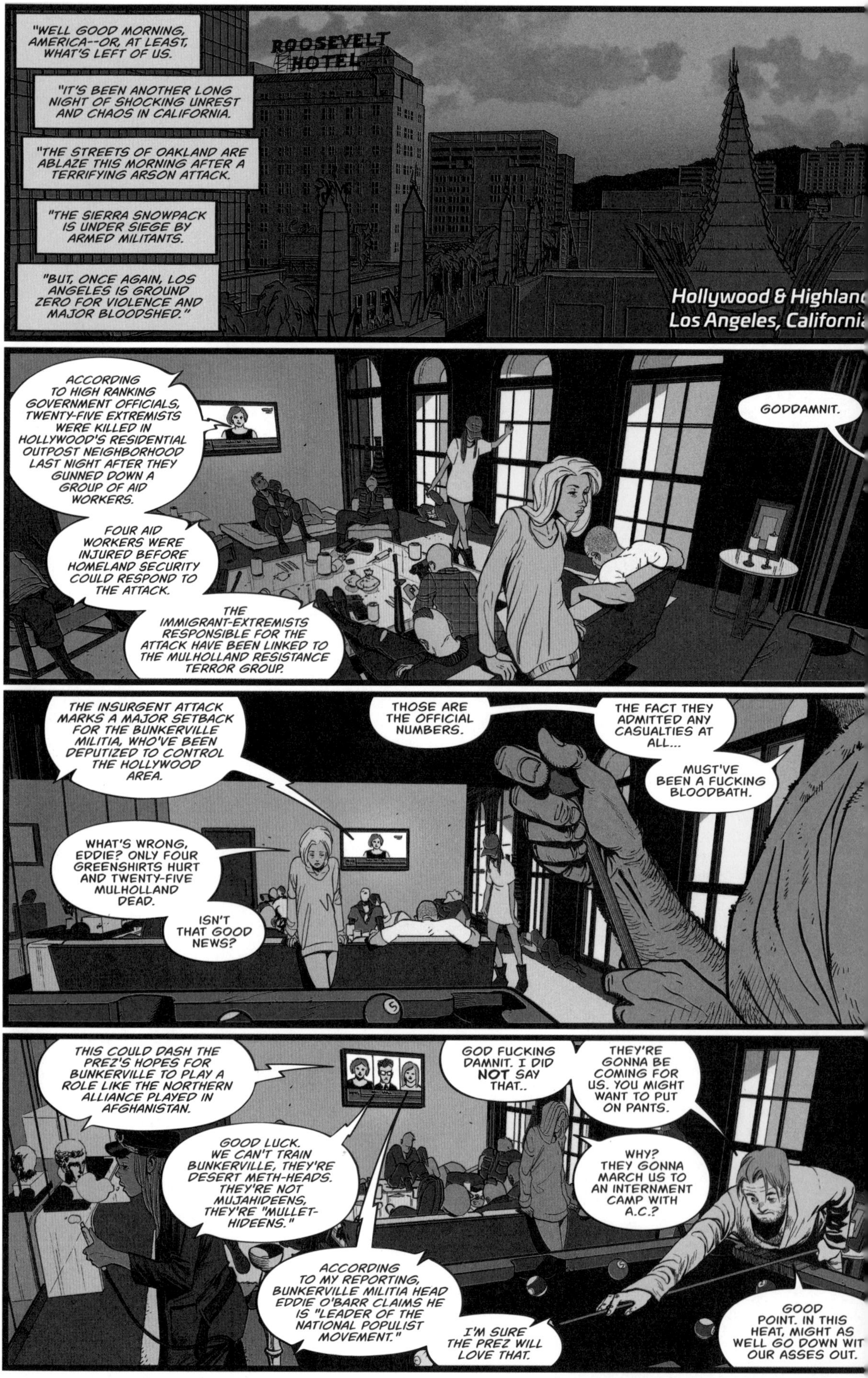
"WELL GOOD MORNING, AMERICA--OR, AT LEAST, WHAT'S LEFT OF US.
ROOSEVELT HOTEL
"IT'S BEEN ANOTHER LONG NIGHT OF SHOCKING UNREST AND CHAOS IN CALIFORNIA.
"THE STREETS OF OAKLAND ARE ABLAZE THIS MORNING AFTER A TERRIFYING ARSON ATTACK.
"THE SIERRA SNOWPACK IS UNDER SIEGE BY ARMED MILITANTS.
"BUT, ONCE AGAIN, LOS ANGELES IS GROUND ZERO FOR VIOLENCE AND MAJOR BLOODSHED."
Hollywood & Highland
Los Angeles, California
ACCORDING TO HIGH RANKING GOVERNMENT OFFICIALS, TWENTY-FIVE EXTREMISTS WERE KILLED IN HOLLYWOOD'S RESIDENTIAL OUTPOST NEIGHBORHOOD LAST NIGHT AFTER THEY GUNNED DOWN A GROUP OF AID WORKERS.
FOUR AID WORKERS WERE INJURED BEFORE HOMELAND SECURITY COULD RESPOND TO THE ATTACK.
THE IMMIGRANT-EXTREMISTS RESPONSIBLE FOR THE ATTACK HAVE BEEN LINKED TO THE MULHOLLAND RESISTANCE TERROR GROUP.
GODDAMNIT.
THE INSURGENT ATTACK MARKS A MAJOR SETBACK FOR THE BUNKERVILLE MILITIA, WHO'VE BEEN DEPUTIZED TO CONTROL THE HOLLYWOOD AREA.
THOSE ARE THE OFFICIAL NUMBERS.
THE FACT THEY ADMITTED ANY CASUALTIES AT ALL...
MUST'VE BEEN A FUCKING BLOODBATH.
WHAT'S WRONG, EDDIE? ONLY FOUR GREENSHIRTS HURT AND TWENTY-FIVE MULHOLLAND DEAD.
ISN'T THAT GOOD NEWS?
THIS COULD DASH THE PREZ'S HOPES FOR BUNKERVILLE TO PLAY A ROLE LIKE THE NORTHERN ALLIANCE PLAYED IN AFGHANISTAN.
GOOD LUCK. WE CAN'T TRAIN BUNKERVILLE, THEY'RE DESERT METH-HEADS. THEY'RE NOT MUJAHIDEENS, THEY'RE "MULLET-HIDEENS."
GOD FUCKING DAMNIT. I DID NOT SAY THAT..
THEY'RE GONNA BE COMING FOR US. YOU MIGHT WANT TO PUT ON PANTS.
WHY? THEY GONNA MARCH US TO AN INTERNMENT CAMP WITH A.C.?
ACCORDING TO MY REPORTING, BUNKERVILLE MILITIA HEAD EDDIE O'BARR CLAIMS HE IS "LEADER OF THE NATIONAL POPULIST MOVEMENT."
I'M SURE THE PREZ WILL LOVE THAT.
GOOD POINT. IN THIS HEAT, MIGHT AS WELL GO DOWN WIT OUR ASSES OUT.

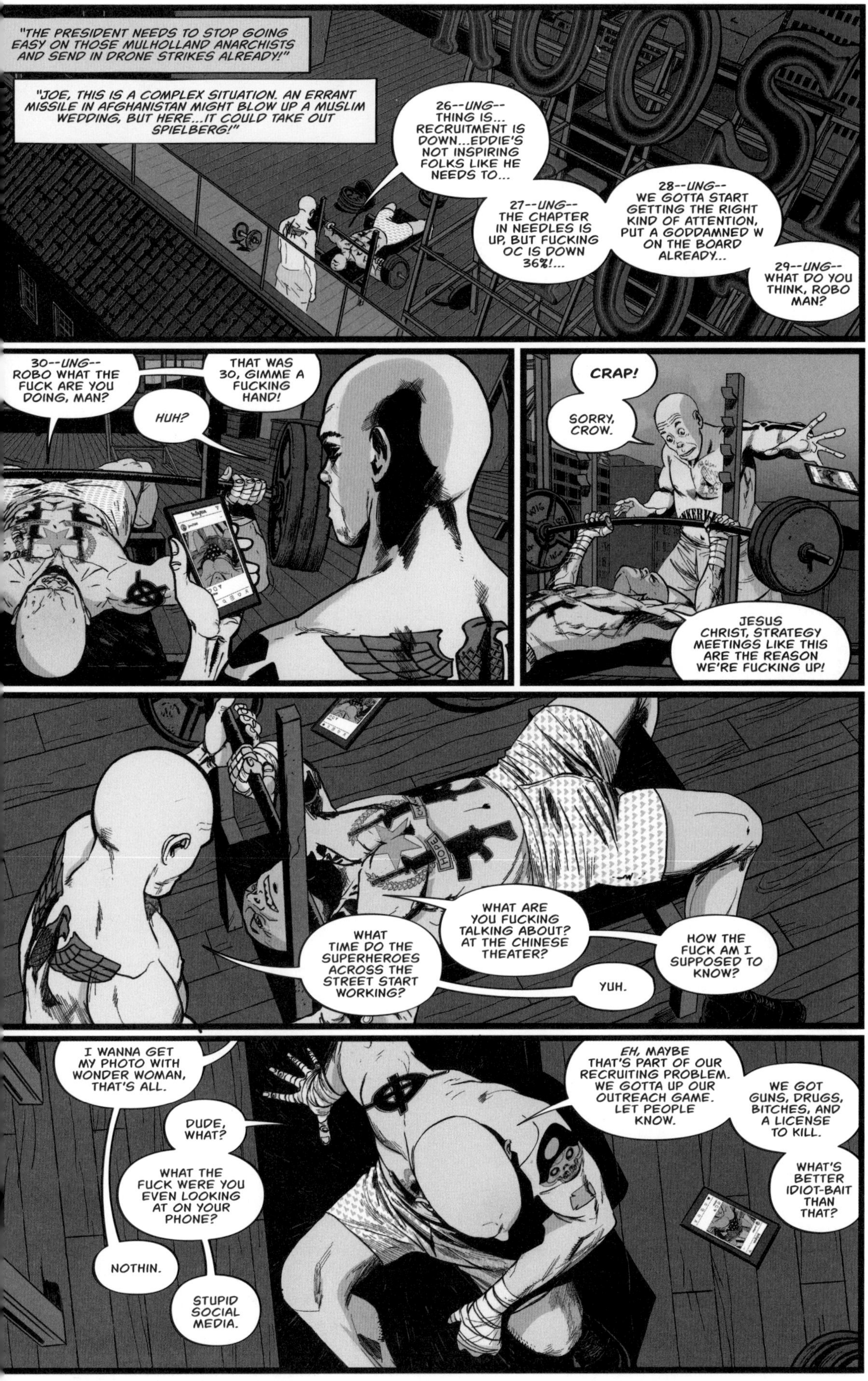
"THE PRESIDENT NEEDS TO STOP GOING EASY ON THOSE MULHOLLAND ANARCHISTS AND SEND IN DRONE STRIKES ALREADY!"
"JOE, THIS IS A COMPLEX SITUATION. AN ERRANT MISSILE IN AFGHANISTAN MIGHT BLOW UP A MUSLIM WEDDING, BUT HERE...IT COULD TAKE OUT SPIELBERG!"
26--UNG-- THING IS... RECRUITMENT IS DOWN...EDDIE'S NOT INSPIRING FOLKS LIKE HE NEEDS TO...
27--UNG-- THE CHAPTER IN NEEDLES IS UP, BUT FUCKING OC IS DOWN 36%!...
28--UNG-- WE GOTTA START GETTING THE RIGHT KIND OF ATTENTION, PUT A GODDAMNED W ON THE BOARD ALREADY...
29--UNG-- WHAT DO YOU THINK, ROBO MAN?
30--UNG-- ROBO WHAT THE FUCK ARE YOU DOING, MAN?
THAT WAS 30, GIMME A FUCKING HAND!
HUH?
CRAP!
SORRY, CROW.
JESUS CHRIST, STRATEGY MEETINGS LIKE THIS ARE THE REASON WE'RE FUCKING UP!
WHAT TIME DO THE SUPERHEROES ACROSS THE STREET START WORKING?
WHAT ARE YOU FUCKING TALKING ABOUT? AT THE CHINESE THEATER?
YUH.
HOW THE FUCK AM I SUPPOSED TO KNOW?
I WANNA GET MY PHOTO WITH WONDER WOMAN, THAT'S ALL.
DUDE, WHAT?
WHAT THE FUCK WERE YOU EVEN LOOKING AT ON YOUR PHONE?
NOTHIN.
STUPID SOCIAL MEDIA.
EH, MAYBE THAT'S PART OF OUR RECRUITING PROBLEM. WE GOTTA UP OUR OUTREACH GAME. LET PEOPLE KNOW.
WE GOT GUNS, DRUGS, BITCHES, AND A LICENSE TO KILL.
WHAT'S BETTER IDIOT-BAIT THAN THAT?

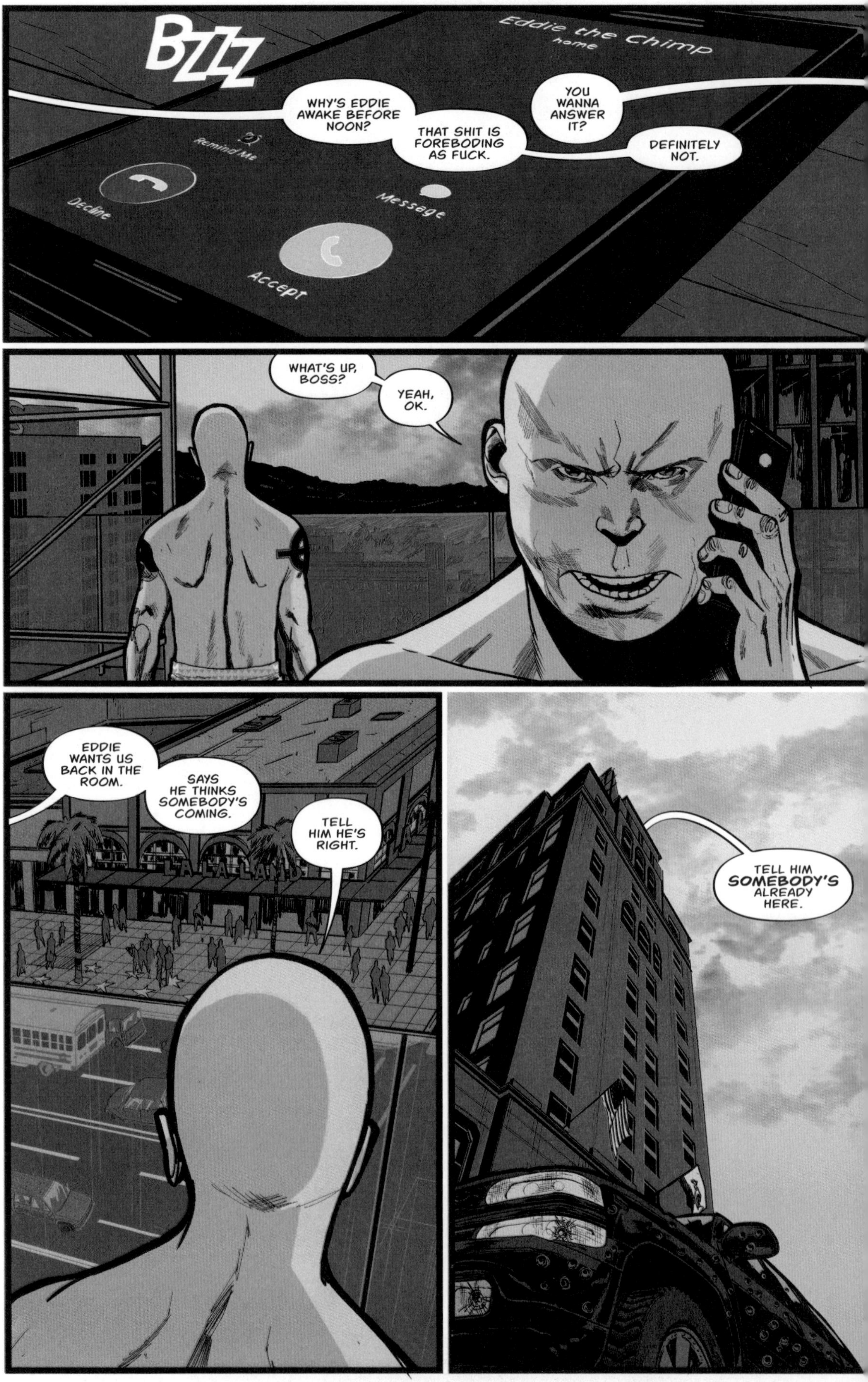
BZZZ
Eddie the Chimp
home
Remind Me
Decline
Message
Accept
WHY'S EDDIE AWAKE BEFORE NOON?
THAT SHIT IS FOREBODING AS FUCK.
YOU WANNA ANSWER IT?
DEFINITELY NOT.
WHAT'S UP, BOSS?
YEAH, OK.
EDDIE WANTS US BACK IN THE ROOM.
SAYS HE THINKS SOMEBODY'S COMING.
TELL HIM HE'S RIGHT.
LA LA LAND
TELL HIM SOMEBODY'S ALREADY HERE.

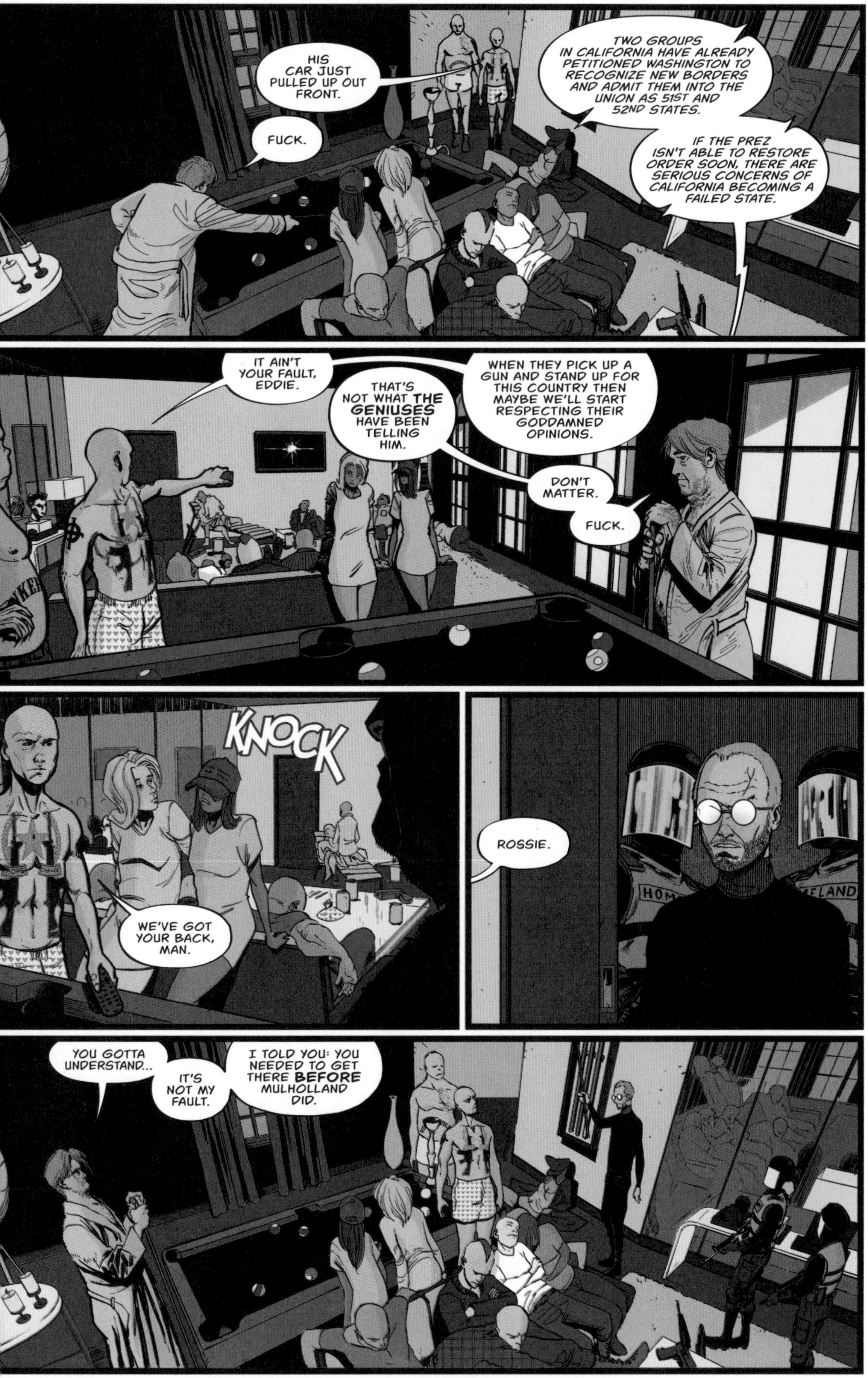
HIS CAR JUST PULLED UP OUT FRONT.
FUCK.
TWO GROUPS IN CALIFORNIA HAVE ALREADY PETITIONED WASHINGTON TO RECOGNIZE NEW BORDERS AND ADMIT THEM INTO THE UNION AS 51ST AND 52ND STATES.
IF THE PREZ ISN'T ABLE TO RESTORE ORDER SOON, THERE ARE SERIOUS CONCERNS OF CALIFORNIA BECOMING A FAILED STATE.
IT AIN'T YOUR FAULT, EDDIE.
THAT'S NOT WHAT THE GENIUSES HAVE BEEN TELLING HIM.
WHEN THEY PICK UP A GUN AND STAND UP FOR THIS COUNTRY THEN MAYBE WE'LL START RESPECTING THEIR GODDAMNED OPINIONS.
DON'T MATTER.
FUCK.
KNOCK
WE'VE GOT YOUR BACK, MAN.
ROSSIE.
YOU GOTTA UNDERSTAND...
IT'S NOT MY FAULT.
I TOLD YOU: YOU NEEDED TO GET THERE BEFORE MULHOLLAND DID.

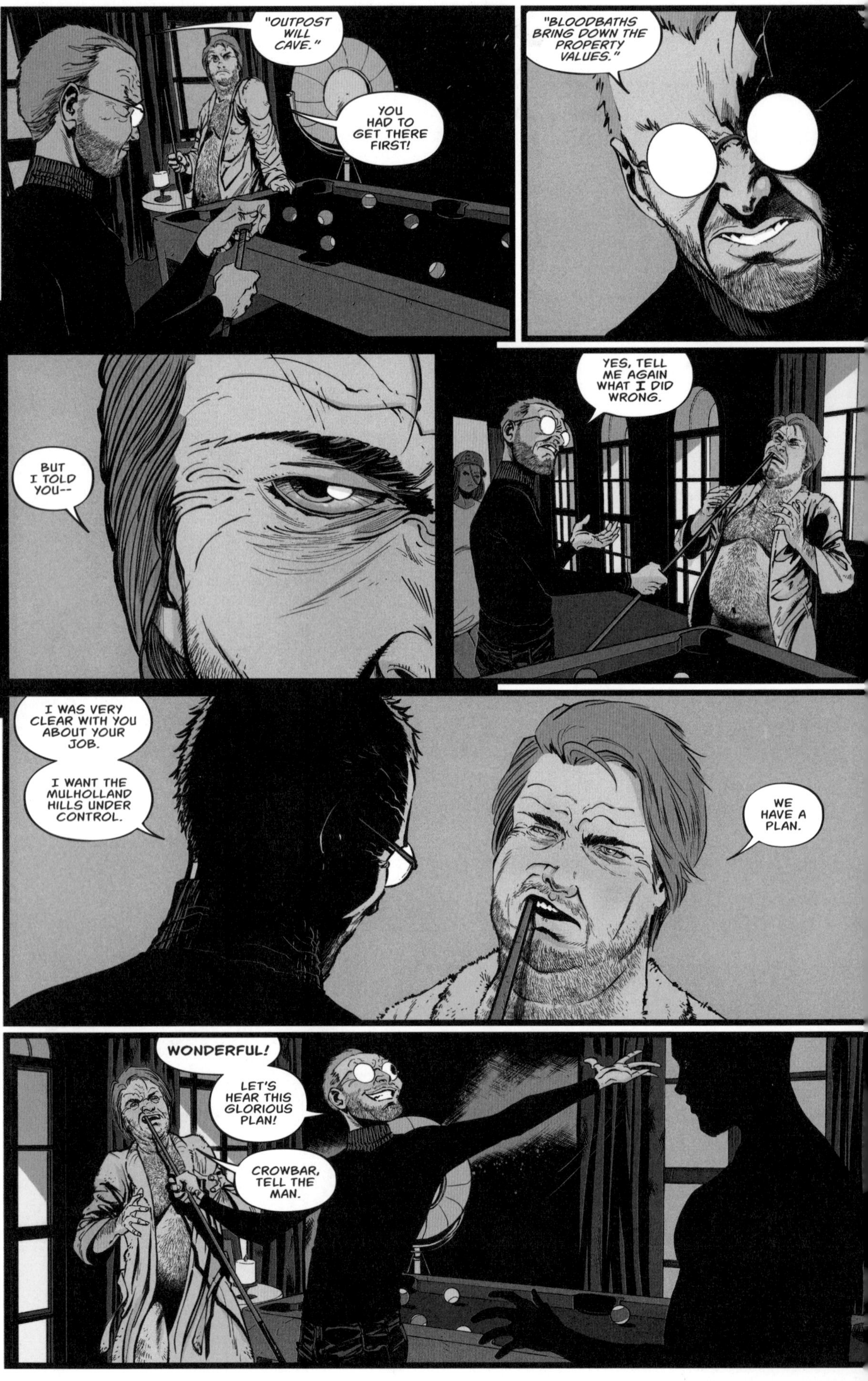
"OUTPOST WILL CAVE."
YOU HAD TO GET THERE FIRST!
"BLOODBATHS BRING DOWN THE PROPERTY VALUES."
BUT I TOLD YOU--
YES, TELL ME AGAIN WHAT I DID WRONG.
I WAS VERY CLEAR WITH YOU ABOUT YOUR JOB.
I WANT THE MULHOLLAND HILLS UNDER CONTROL.
WE HAVE A PLAN.
WONDERFUL!
LET'S HEAR THIS GLORIOUS PLAN!
CROWBAR, TELL THE MAN.

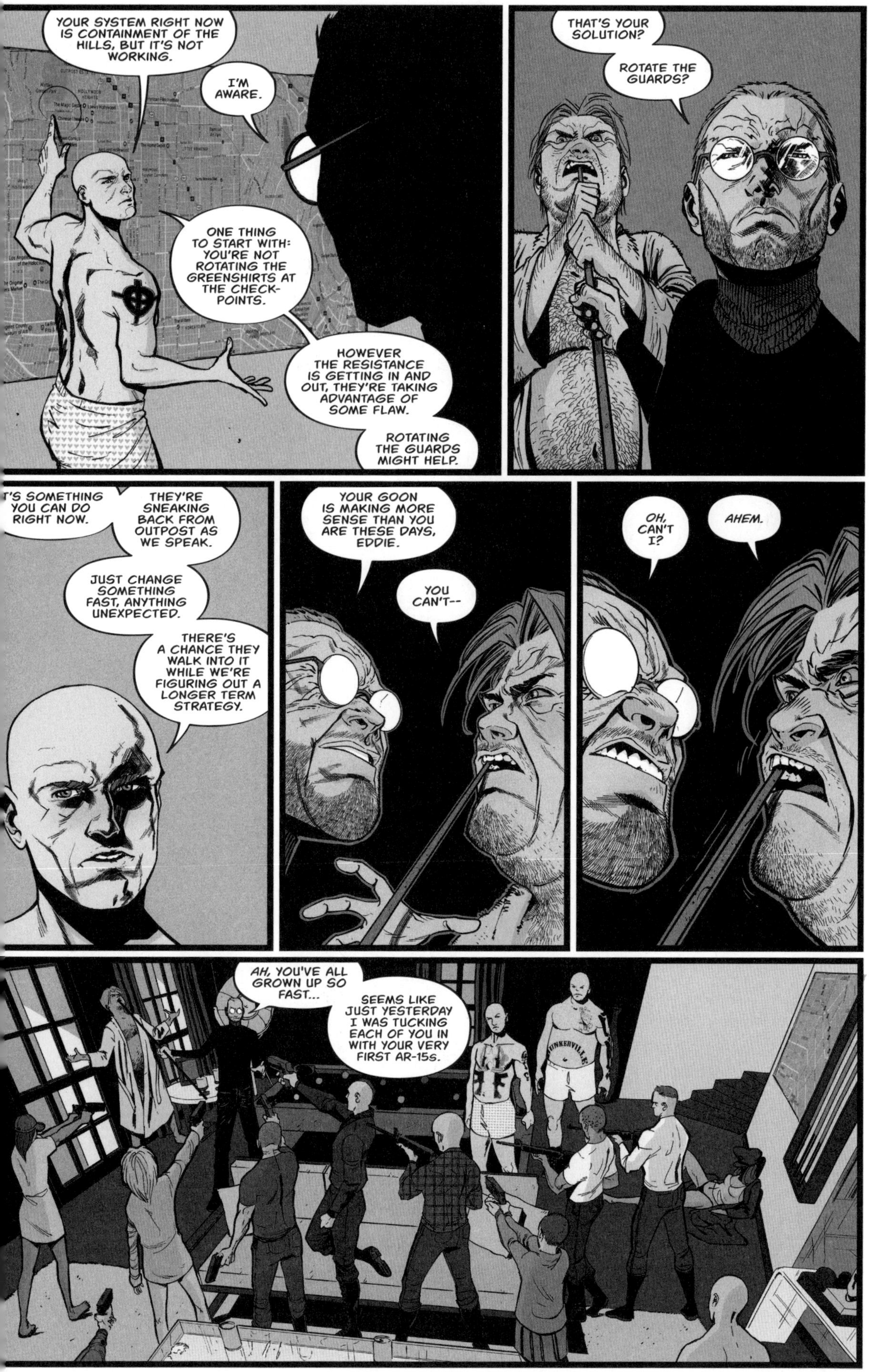
YOUR SYSTEM RIGHT NOW IS CONTAINMENT OF THE HILLS, BUT IT'S NOT WORKING.
I'M AWARE.
ONE THING TO START WITH: YOU'RE NOT ROTATING THE GREENSHIRTS AT THE CHECK-POINTS.
HOWEVER THE RESISTANCE IS GETTING IN AND OUT, THEY'RE TAKING ADVANTAGE OF SOME FLAW.
ROTATING THE GUARDS MIGHT HELP.
THAT'S YOUR SOLUTION?
ROTATE THE GUARDS?
T'S SOMETHING YOU CAN DO RIGHT NOW.
THEY'RE SNEAKING BACK FROM OUTPOST AS WE SPEAK.
JUST CHANGE SOMETHING FAST, ANYTHING UNEXPECTED.
THERE'S A CHANCE THEY WALK INTO IT WHILE WE'RE FIGURING OUT A LONGER TERM STRATEGY.
YOUR GOON IS MAKING MORE SENSE THAN YOU ARE THESE DAYS, EDDIE.
YOU CAN'T--
OH, CAN'T I?
AHEM.
AH, YOU'VE ALL GROWN UP SO FAST...
SEEMS LIKE JUST YESTERDAY I WAS TUCKING EACH OF YOU IN WITH YOUR VERY FIRST AR-15s.

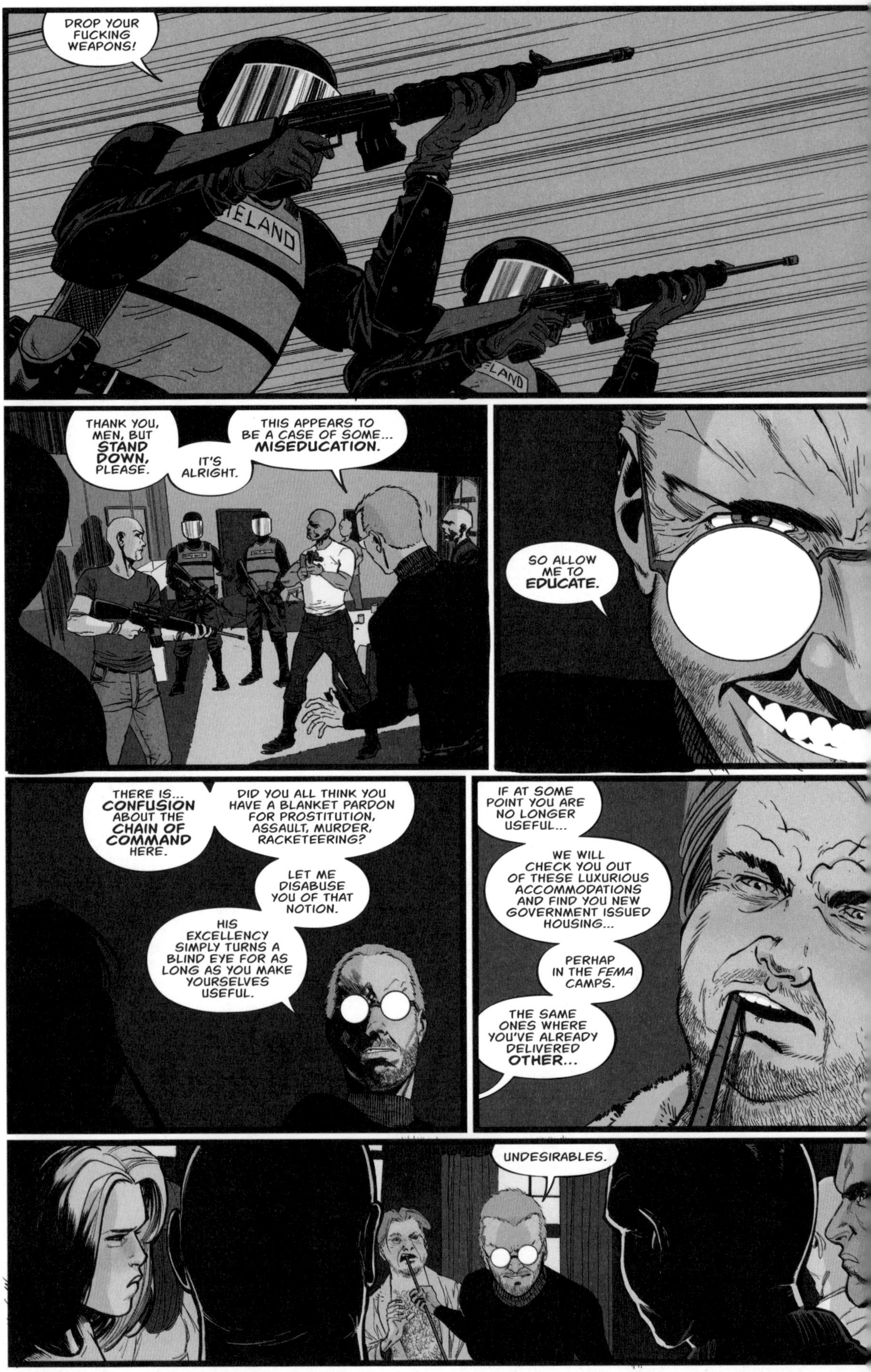
DROP YOUR FUCKING WEAPONS!
THANK YOU, MEN, BUT STAND DOWN, PLEASE.
IT'S ALRIGHT.
THIS APPEARS TO BE A CASE OF SOME... MISEDUCATION.
SO ALLOW ME TO EDUCATE.
THERE IS... CONFUSION ABOUT THE CHAIN OF COMMAND HERE.
DID YOU ALL THINK YOU HAVE A BLANKET PARDON FOR PROSTITUTION, ASSAULT, MURDER, RACKETEERING?
LET ME DISABUSE YOU OF THAT NOTION.
HIS EXCELLENCY SIMPLY TURNS A BLIND EYE FOR AS LONG AS YOU MAKE YOURSELVES USEFUL.
IF AT SOME POINT YOU ARE NO LONGER USEFUL...
WE WILL CHECK YOU OUT OF THESE LUXURIOUS ACCOMMODATIONS AND FIND YOU NEW GOVERNMENT ISSUED HOUSING...
PERHAP IN THE FEMA CAMPS.
THE SAME ONES WHERE YOU'VE ALREADY DELIVERED OTHER...
UNDESIRABLES.

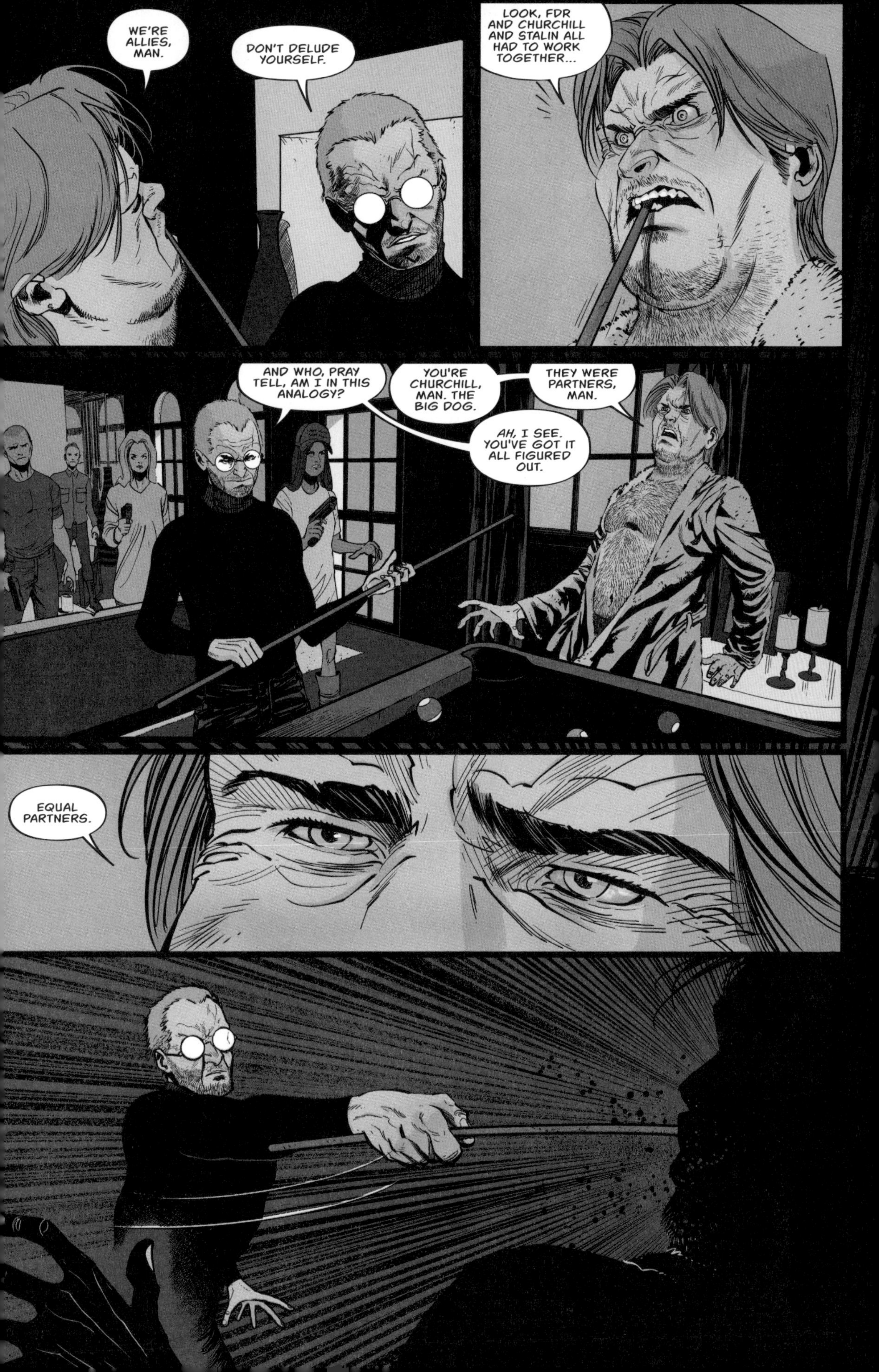
WE'RE ALLIES, MAN.
DON'T DELUDE YOURSELF.
LOOK, FDR AND CHURCHILL AND STALIN ALL HAD TO WORK TOGETHER...
AND WHO, PRAY TELL, AM I IN THIS ANALOGY?
YOU'RE CHURCHILL, MAN. THE BIG DOG.
THEY WERE PARTNERS, MAN.
AH, I SEE. YOU'VE GOT IT ALL FIGURED OUT.
EQUAL PARTNERS.

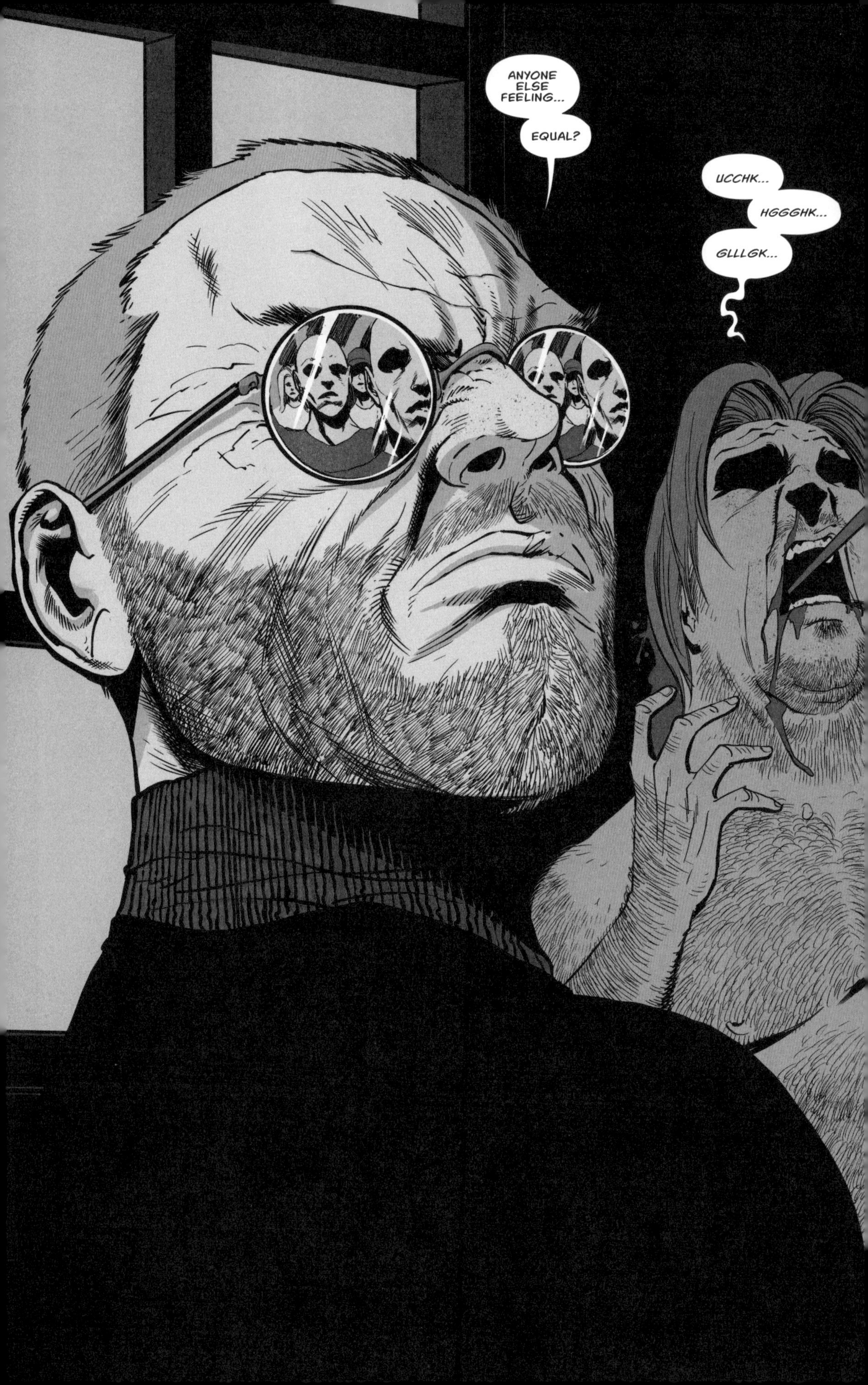
ANYONE ELSE FEELING...
EQUAL?
UCCHK...
HGGGHK...
GLLLGK...

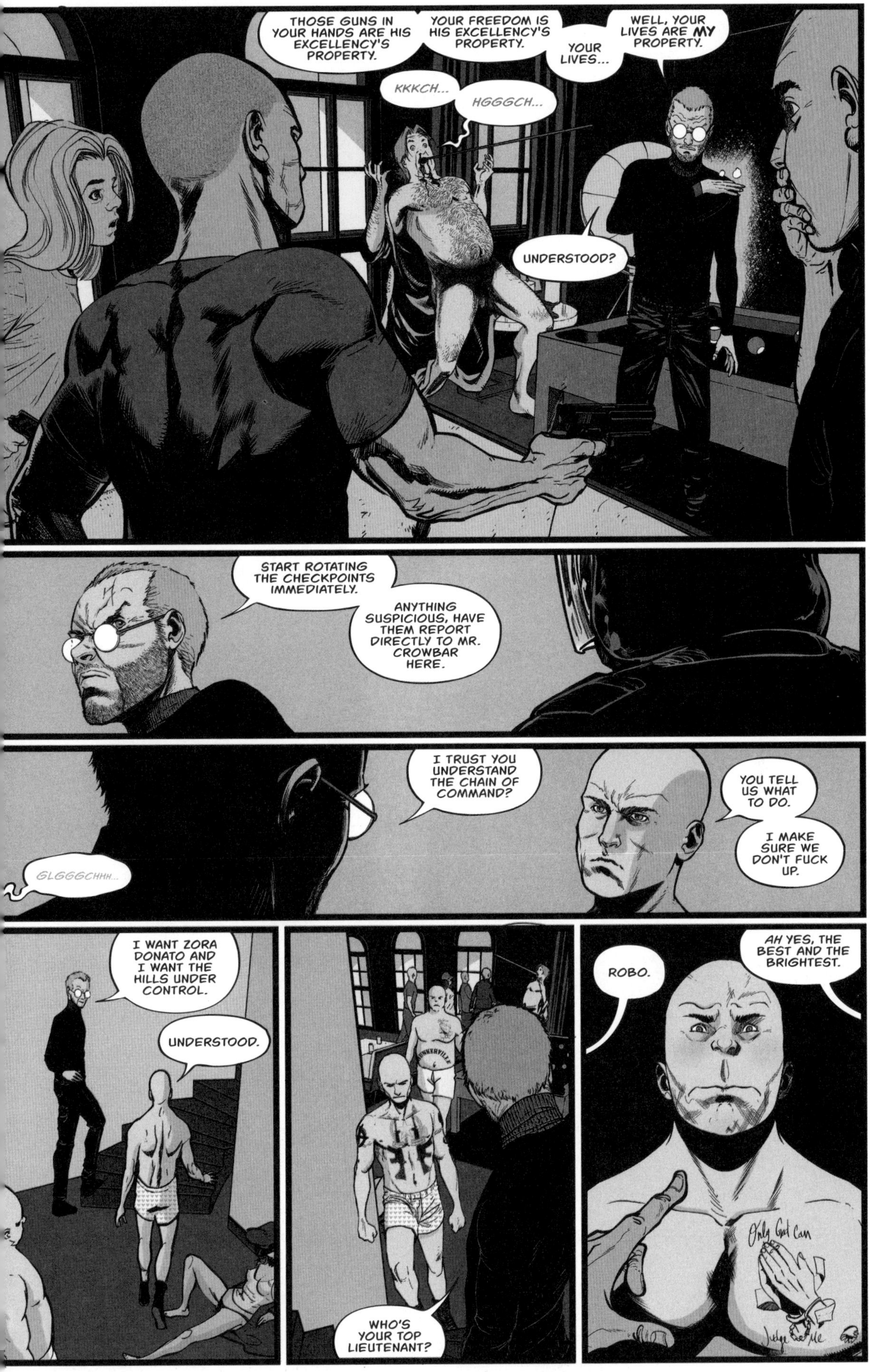
THOSE GUNS IN YOUR HANDS ARE HIS EXCELLENCY'S PROPERTY.
YOUR FREEDOM IS HIS EXCELLENCY'S PROPERTY.
YOUR LIVES...
WELL, YOUR LIVES ARE MY PROPERTY.
KKKCH...
HGGGCH...
UNDERSTOOD?
START ROTATING THE CHECKPOINTS IMMEDIATELY.
ANYTHING SUSPICIOUS, HAVE THEM REPORT DIRECTLY TO MR. CROWBAR HERE.
I TRUST YOU UNDERSTAND THE CHAIN OF COMMAND?
YOU TELL US WHAT TO DO.
I MAKE SURE WE DON'T FUCK UP.
GLGGGCHHH...
I WANT ZORA DONATO AND I WANT THE HILLS UNDER CONTROL.
UNDERSTOOD.
WHO'S YOUR TOP LIEUTENANT?
ROBO.
AH YES, THE BEST AND THE BRIGHTEST.

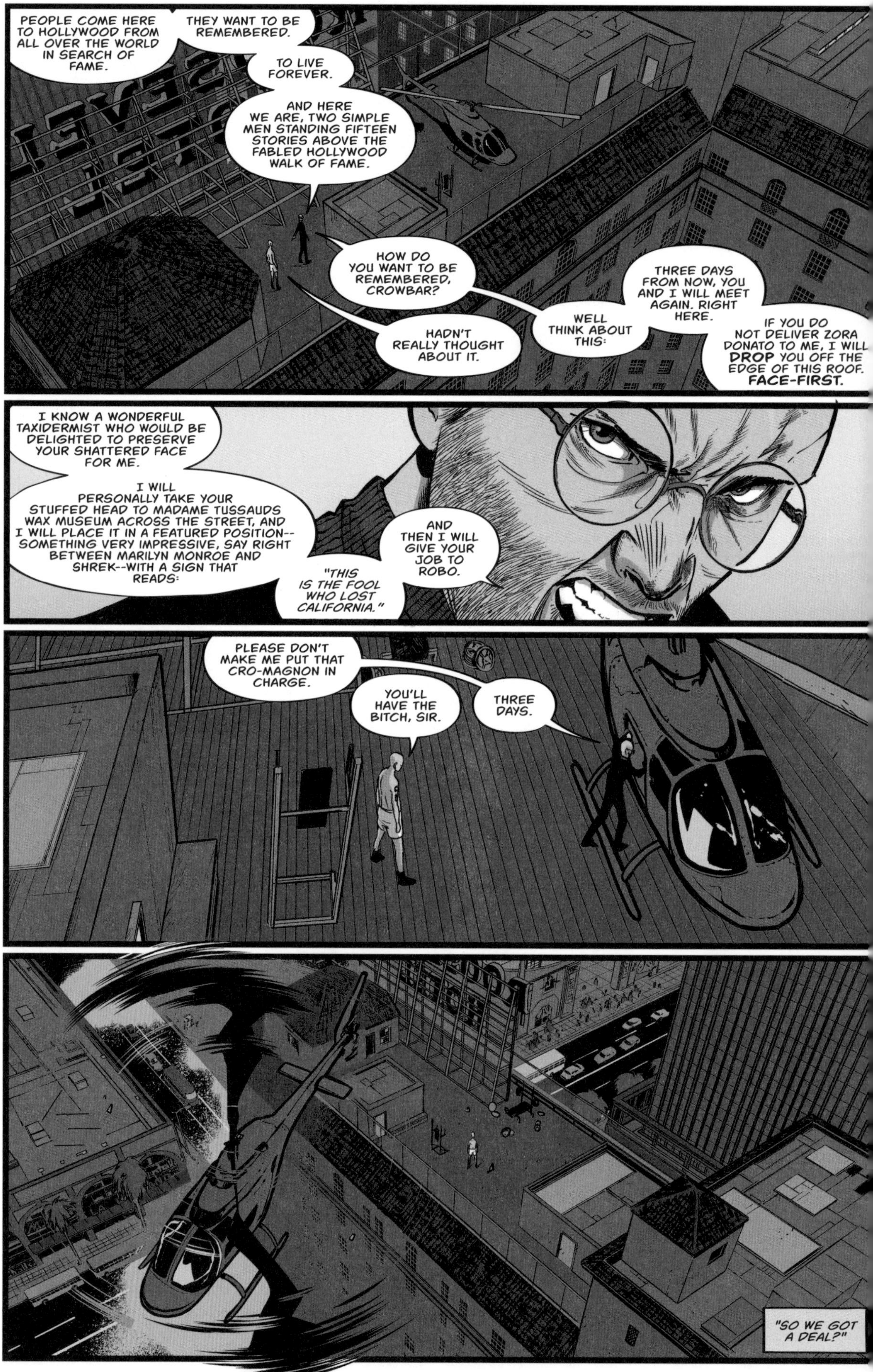
PEOPLE COME HERE TO HOLLYWOOD FROM ALL OVER THE WORLD IN SEARCH OF FAME.
THEY WANT TO BE REMEMBERED.
TO LIVE FOREVER.
AND HERE WE ARE, TWO SIMPLE MEN STANDING FIFTEEN STORIES ABOVE THE FABLED HOLLYWOOD WALK OF FAME.
HOW DO YOU WANT TO BE REMEMBERED, CROWBAR?
HADN'T REALLY THOUGHT ABOUT IT.
WELL THINK ABOUT THIS:
THREE DAYS FROM NOW, YOU AND I WILL MEET AGAIN. RIGHT HERE.
IF YOU DO NOT DELIVER ZORA DONATO TO ME, I WILL **DROP** YOU OFF THE EDGE OF THIS ROOF. **FACE-FIRST.**
I KNOW A WONDERFUL TAXIDERMIST WHO WOULD BE DELIGHTED TO PRESERVE YOUR SHATTERED FACE FOR ME.
I WILL PERSONALLY TAKE YOUR STUFFED HEAD TO MADAME TUSSAUDS WAX MUSEUM ACROSS THE STREET, AND I WILL PLACE IT IN A FEATURED POSITION--SOMETHING VERY IMPRESSIVE, SAY RIGHT BETWEEN MARILYN MONROE AND SHREK--WITH A SIGN THAT READS:
"THIS IS THE FOOL WHO LOST CALIFORNIA."
AND THEN I WILL GIVE YOUR JOB TO ROBO.
PLEASE DON'T MAKE ME PUT THAT CRO-MAGNON IN CHARGE.
YOU'LL HAVE THE BITCH, SIR.
THREE DAYS.
"SO WE GOT A DEAL?"

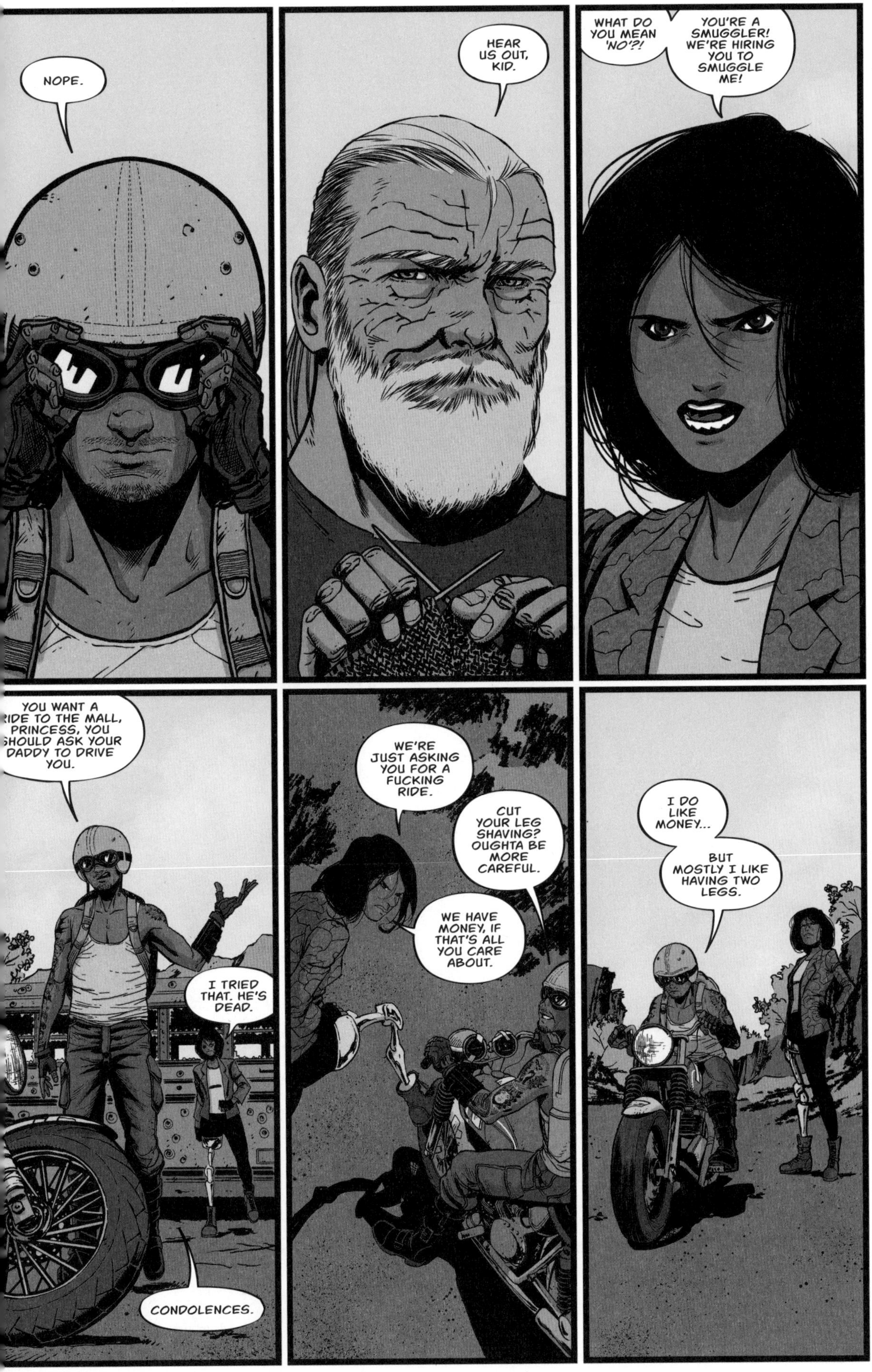
NOPE.
HEAR US OUT, KID.
WHAT DO YOU MEAN 'NO'?!
YOU'RE A SMUGGLER! WE'RE HIRING YOU TO SMUGGLE ME!
YOU WANT A RIDE TO THE MALL, PRINCESS, YOU SHOULD ASK YOUR DADDY TO DRIVE YOU.
I TRIED THAT. HE'S DEAD.
CONDOLENCES.
WE'RE JUST ASKING YOU FOR A FUCKING RIDE.
CUT YOUR LEG SHAVING? OUGHTA BE MORE CAREFUL.
WE HAVE MONEY, IF THAT'S ALL YOU CARE ABOUT.
I DO LIKE MONEY...
BUT MOSTLY I LIKE HAVING TWO LEGS.

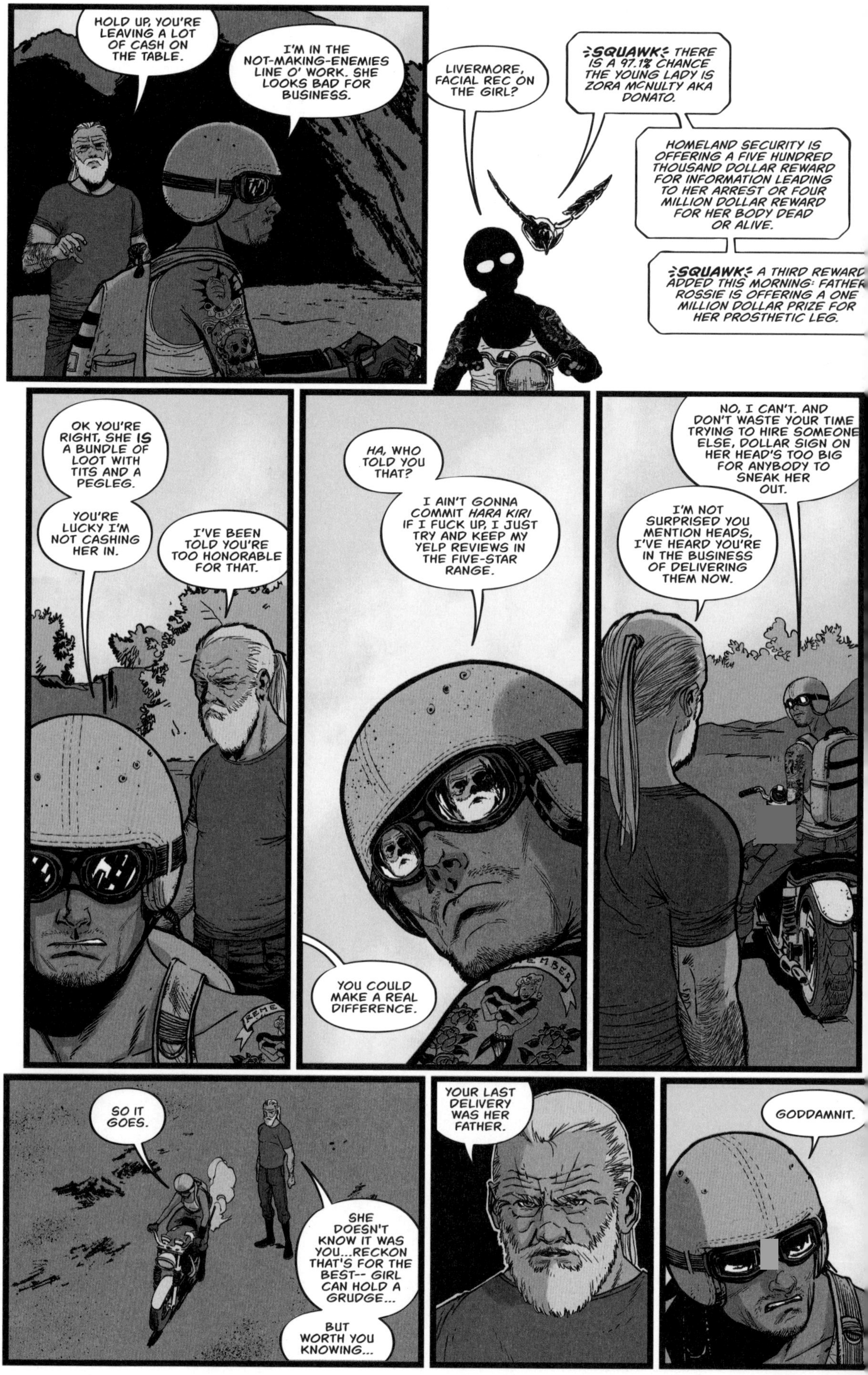
HOLD UP, YOU'RE LEAVING A LOT OF CASH ON THE TABLE.
I'M IN THE NOT-MAKING-ENEMIES LINE O' WORK. SHE LOOKS BAD FOR BUSINESS.
LIVERMORE, FACIAL REC ON THE GIRL?
SQUAWK THERE IS A 97.1% CHANCE THE YOUNG LADY IS ZORA McNULTY AKA DONATO.
HOMELAND SECURITY IS OFFERING A FIVE HUNDRED THOUSAND DOLLAR REWARD FOR INFORMATION LEADING TO HER ARREST OR FOUR MILLION DOLLAR REWARD FOR HER BODY DEAD OR ALIVE.
SQUAWK A THIRD REWARD ADDED THIS MORNING: FATHER ROSSIE IS OFFERING A ONE MILLION DOLLAR PRIZE FOR HER PROSTHETIC LEG.
OK YOU'RE RIGHT, SHE IS A BUNDLE OF LOOT WITH TITS AND A PEGLEG.
YOU'RE LUCKY I'M NOT CASHING HER IN.
I'VE BEEN TOLD YOU'RE TOO HONORABLE FOR THAT.
HA, WHO TOLD YOU THAT?
I AIN'T GONNA COMMIT HARA KIRI IF I FUCK UP, I JUST TRY AND KEEP MY YELP REVIEWS IN THE FIVE-STAR RANGE.
YOU COULD MAKE A REAL DIFFERENCE.
NO, I CAN'T. AND DON'T WASTE YOUR TIME TRYING TO HIRE SOMEONE ELSE, DOLLAR SIGN ON HER HEAD'S TOO BIG FOR ANYBODY TO SNEAK HER OUT.
I'M NOT SURPRISED YOU MENTION HEADS, I'VE HEARD YOU'RE IN THE BUSINESS OF DELIVERING THEM NOW.
SO IT GOES.
SHE DOESN'T KNOW IT WAS YOU...RECKON THAT'S FOR THE BEST-- GIRL CAN HOLD A GRUDGE...
BUT WORTH YOU KNOWING...
YOUR LAST DELIVERY WAS HER FATHER.
GODDAMNIT.

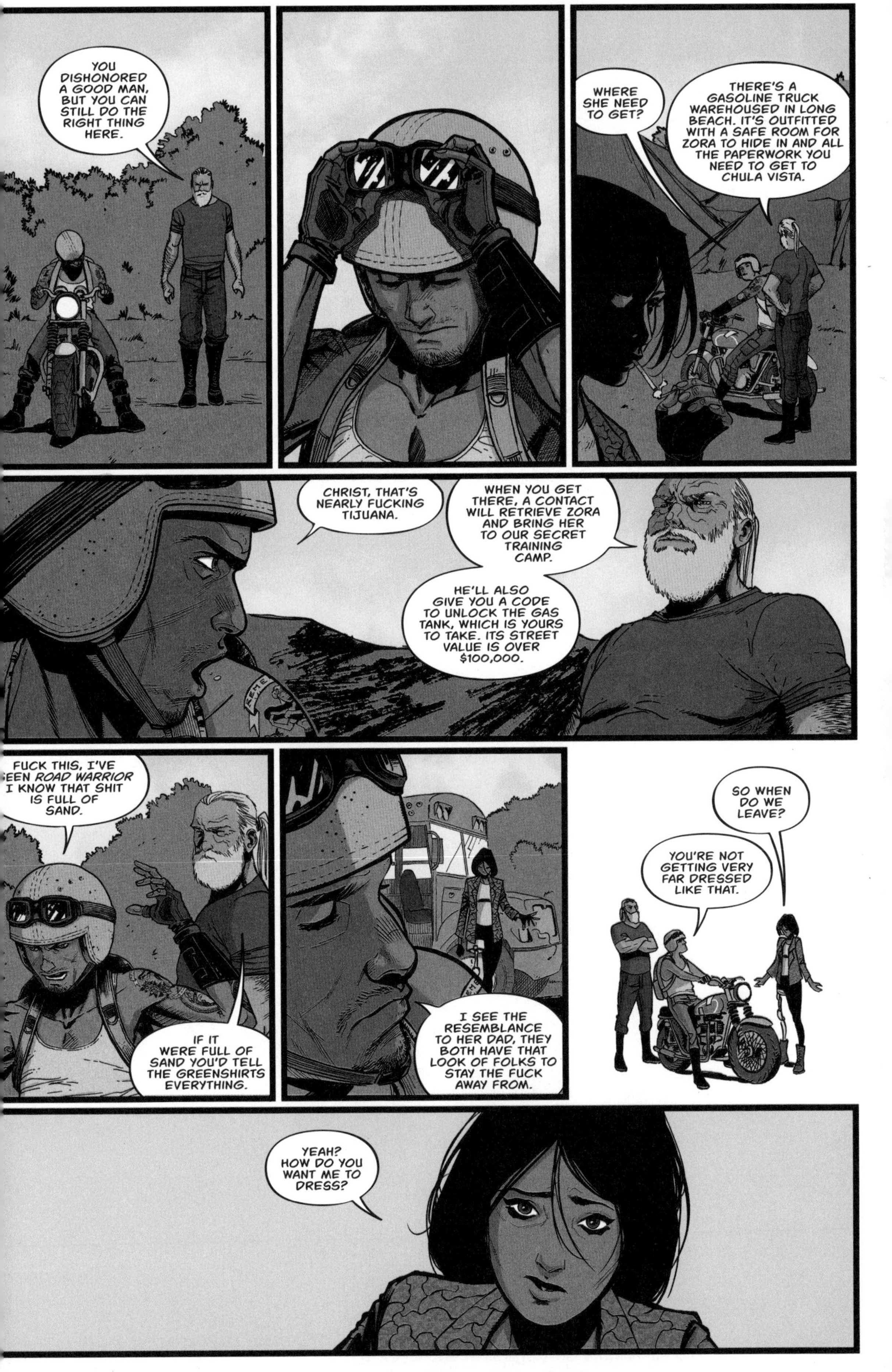
YOU DISHONORED A GOOD MAN, BUT YOU CAN STILL DO THE RIGHT THING HERE.
WHERE SHE NEED TO GET?
THERE'S A GASOLINE TRUCK WAREHOUSED IN LONG BEACH. IT'S OUTFITTED WITH A SAFE ROOM FOR ZORA TO HIDE IN AND ALL THE PAPERWORK YOU NEED TO GET TO CHULA VISTA.
CHRIST, THAT'S NEARLY FUCKING TIJUANA.
WHEN YOU GET THERE, A CONTACT WILL RETRIEVE ZORA AND BRING HER TO OUR SECRET TRAINING CAMP.
HE'LL ALSO GIVE YOU A CODE TO UNLOCK THE GAS TANK, WHICH IS YOURS TO TAKE. ITS STREET VALUE IS OVER $100,000.
FUCK THIS, I'VE SEEN ROAD WARRIOR I KNOW THAT SHIT IS FULL OF SAND.
IF IT WERE FULL OF SAND YOU'D TELL THE GREENSHIRTS EVERYTHING.
I SEE THE RESEMBLANCE TO HER DAD, THEY BOTH HAVE THAT LOOK OF FOLKS TO STAY THE FUCK AWAY FROM.
SO WHEN DO WE LEAVE?
YOU'RE NOT GETTING VERY FAR DRESSED LIKE THAT.
YEAH? HOW DO YOU WANT ME TO DRESS?

BLACK MASK STUDIOS PRESENTS

CALEXIT

CHAPTER 2: MOMENTS LIKE THIS NEVER LAST

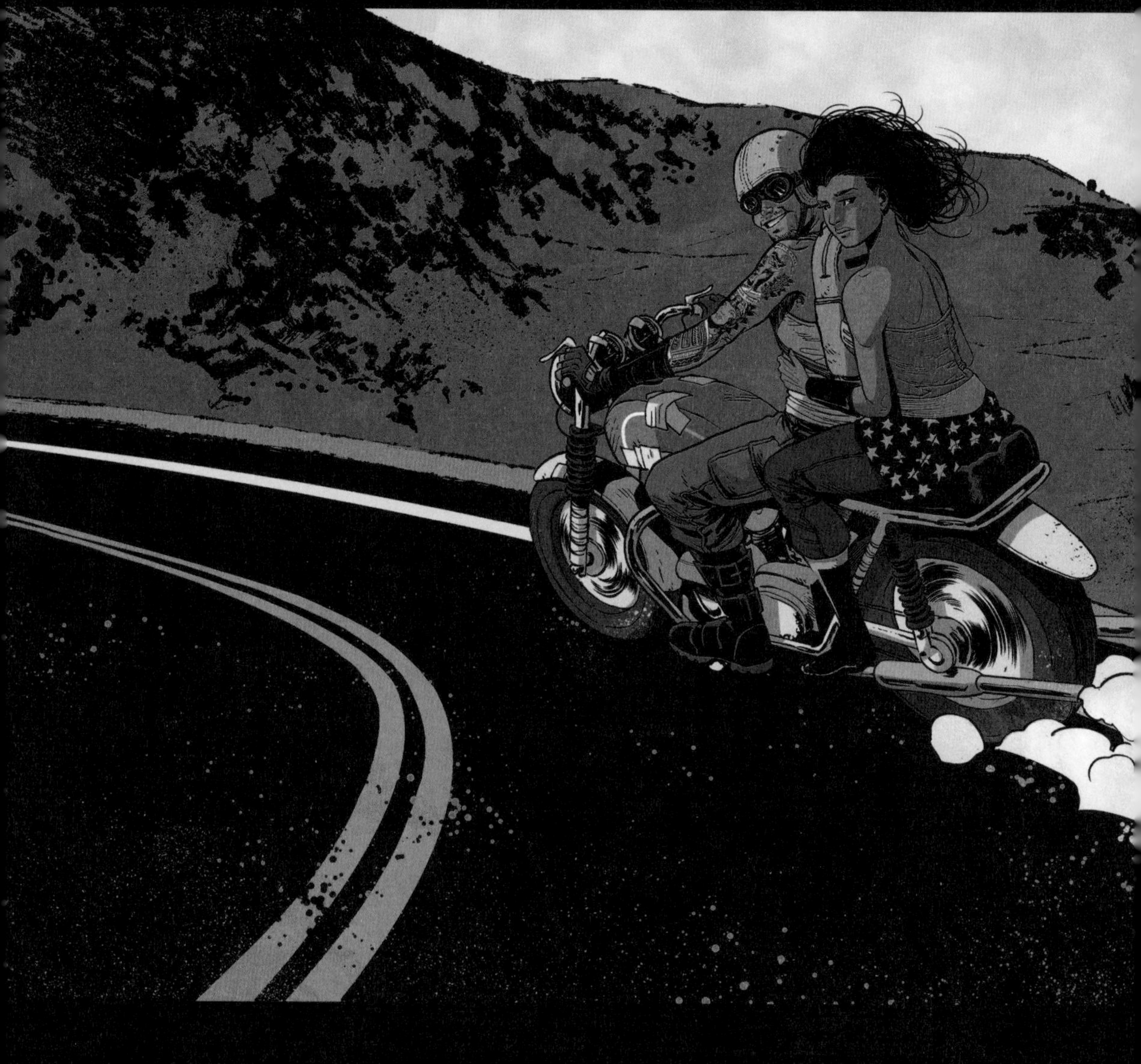

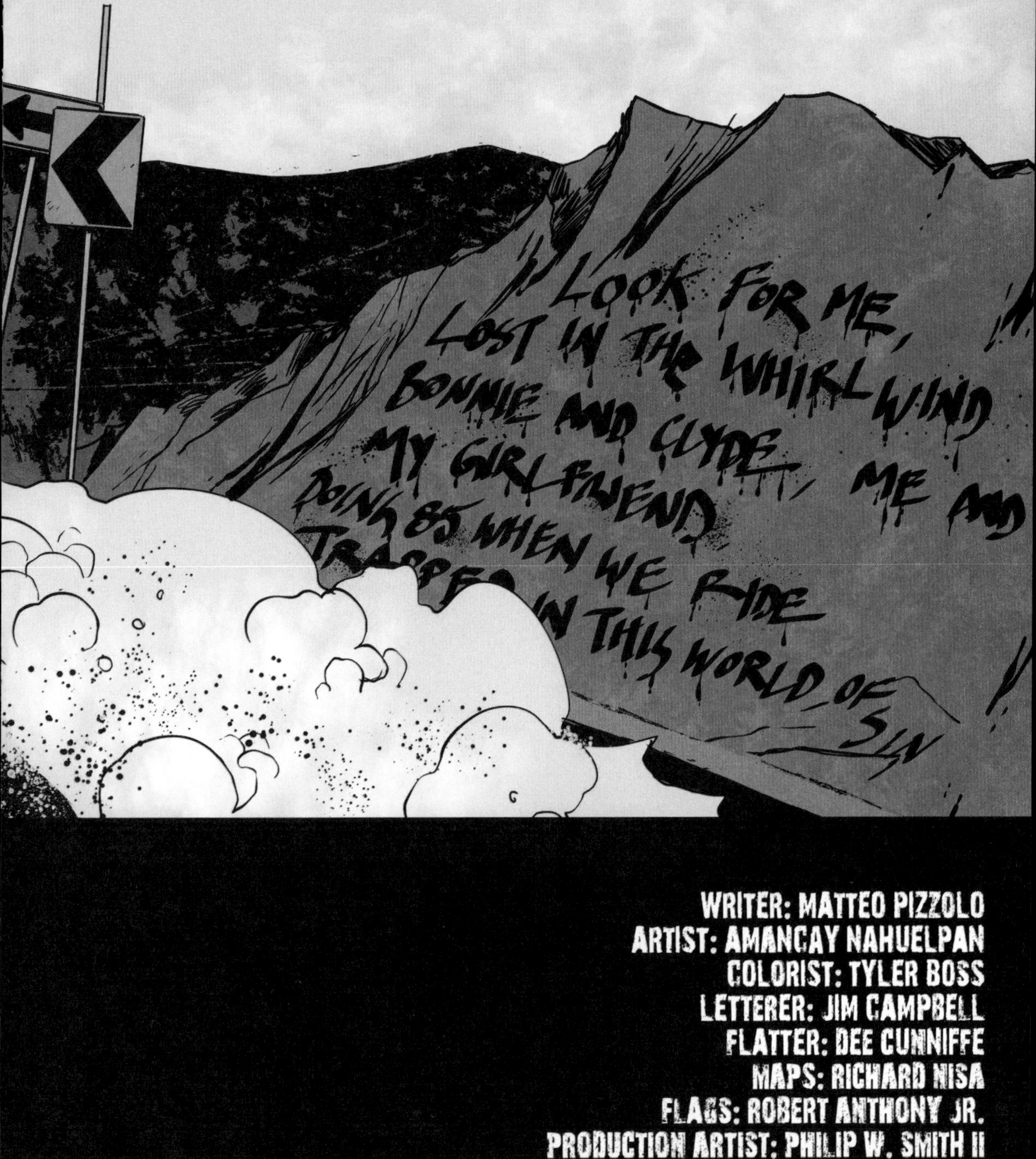
LOOK FOR ME,
LOST IN THE WHIRLWIND
BONNIE AND CLYDE ME AND
MY GIRLFRIEND
DOING 85 WHEN WE RIDE
TRAPPED IN THIS WORLD OF SIN

WRITER: MATTEO PIZZOLO
ARTIST: AMANCAY NAHUELPAN
COLORIST: TYLER BOSS
LETTERER: JIM CAMPBELL
FLATTER: DEE CUNNIFFE
MAPS: RICHARD NISA
FLAGS: ROBERT ANTHONY JR.
PRODUCTION ARTIST: PHILIP W. SMITH II

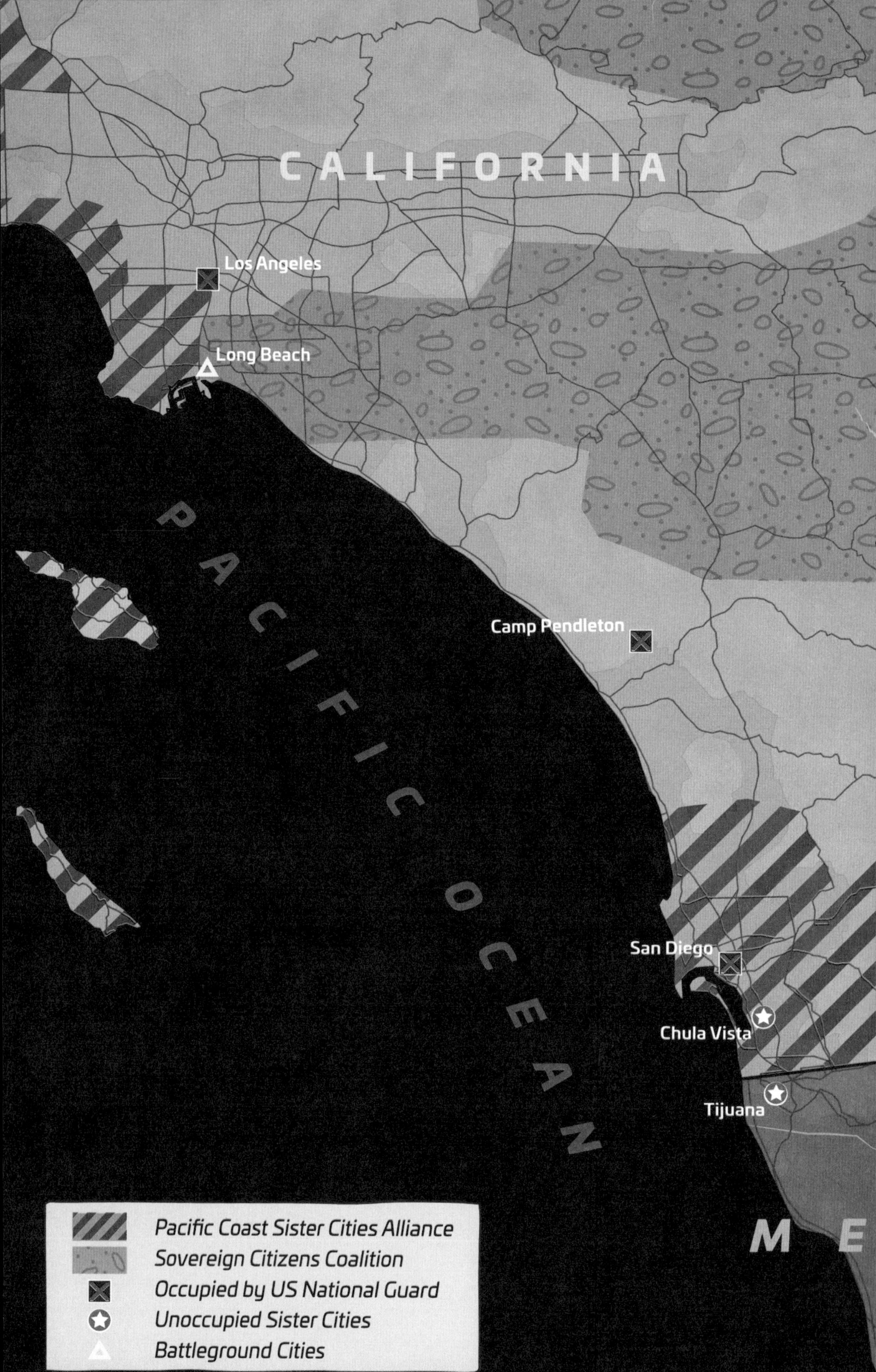
CALIFORNIA
Los Angeles
Long Beach
PACIFIC OCEAN
Camp Pendleton
San Diego
Chula Vista
Tijuana
M E
Pacific Coast Sister Cities Alliance
Sovereign Citizens Coalition
Occupied by US National Guard
Unoccupied Sister Cities
Battleground Cities

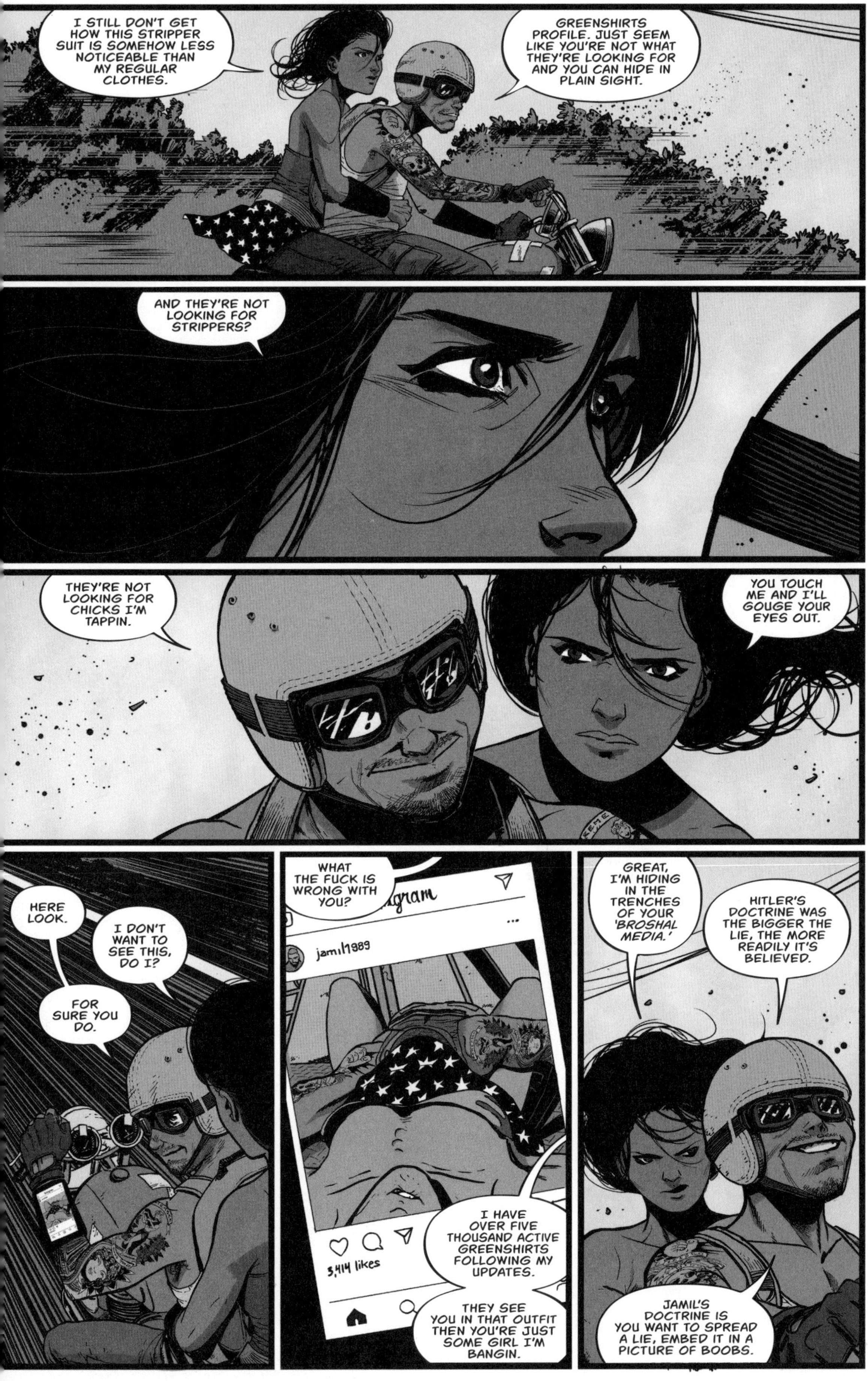
I STILL DON'T GET HOW THIS STRIPPER SUIT IS SOMEHOW LESS NOTICEABLE THAN MY REGULAR CLOTHES.
GREENSHIRTS PROFILE. JUST SEEM LIKE YOU'RE NOT WHAT THEY'RE LOOKING FOR AND YOU CAN HIDE IN PLAIN SIGHT.
AND THEY'RE NOT LOOKING FOR STRIPPERS?
THEY'RE NOT LOOKING FOR CHICKS I'M TAPPIN.
YOU TOUCH ME AND I'LL GOUGE YOUR EYES OUT.
HERE LOOK.
I DON'T WANT TO SEE THIS, DO I?
FOR SURE YOU DO.
WHAT THE FUCK IS WRONG WITH YOU?
jamil1989
3,414 likes
I HAVE OVER FIVE THOUSAND ACTIVE GREENSHIRTS FOLLOWING MY UPDATES.
THEY SEE YOU IN THAT OUTFIT THEN YOU'RE JUST SOME GIRL I'M BANGIN.
GREAT, I'M HIDING IN THE TRENCHES OF YOUR 'BROSHAL MEDIA.'
HITLER'S DOCTRINE WAS THE BIGGER THE LIE, THE MORE READILY IT'S BELIEVED.
JAMIL'S DOCTRINE IS YOU WANT TO SPREAD A LIE, EMBED IT IN A PICTURE OF BOOBS.

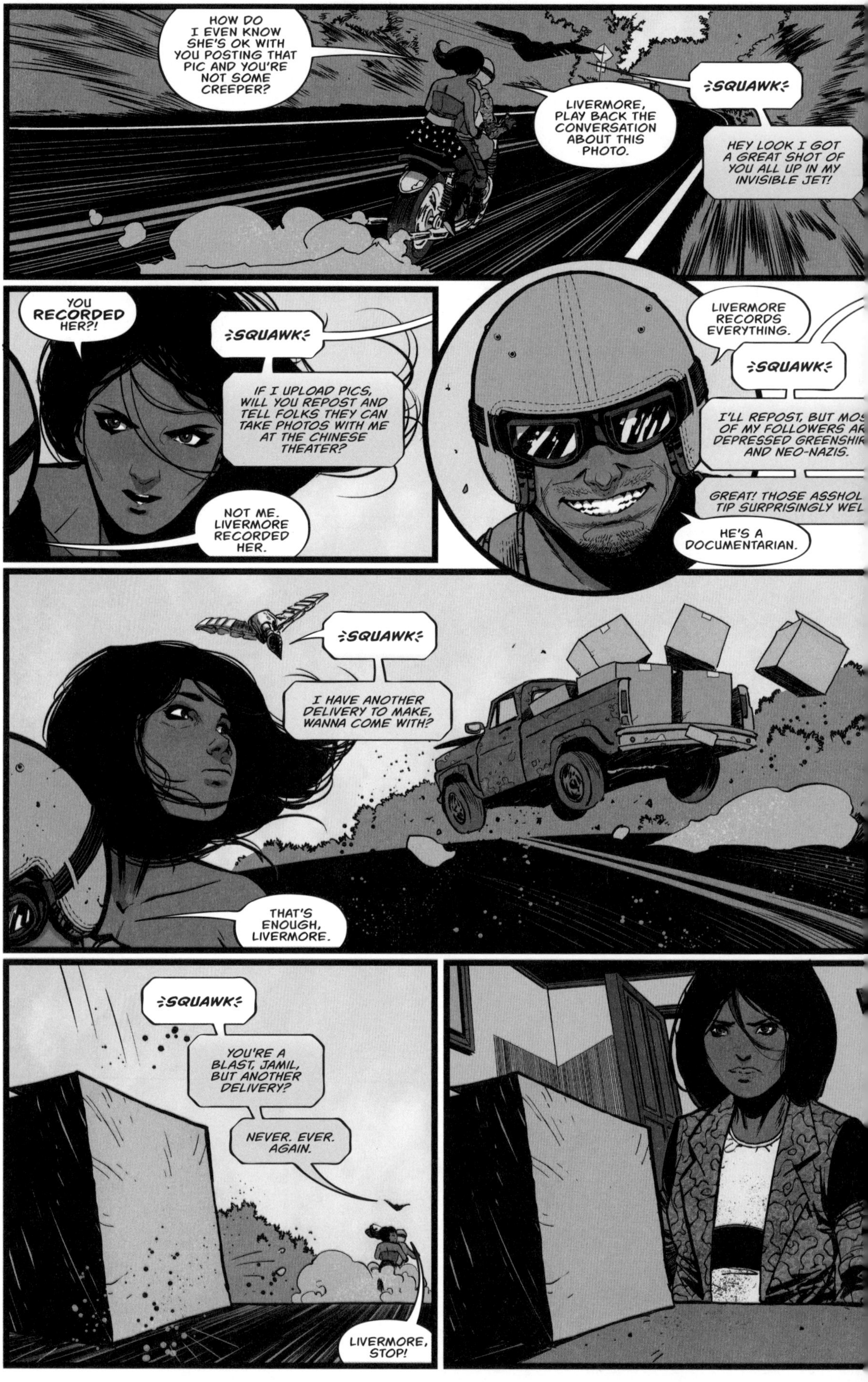
HOW DO I EVEN KNOW SHE'S OK WITH YOU POSTING THAT PIC AND YOU'RE NOT SOME CREEPER?
LIVERMORE, PLAY BACK THE CONVERSATION ABOUT THIS PHOTO.
SQUAWK
HEY LOOK I GOT A GREAT SHOT OF YOU ALL UP IN MY INVISIBLE JET!
YOU RECORDED HER?!
SQUAWK
IF I UPLOAD PICS, WILL YOU REPOST AND TELL FOLKS THEY CAN TAKE PHOTOS WITH ME AT THE CHINESE THEATER?
NOT ME. LIVERMORE RECORDED HER.
LIVERMORE RECORDS EVERYTHING.
SQUAWK
I'LL REPOST, BUT MOS OF MY FOLLOWERS AR DEPRESSED GREENSHIR AND NEO-NAZIS.
GREAT! THOSE ASSHOL TIP SURPRISINGLY WEL
HE'S A DOCUMENTARIAN.
SQUAWK
I HAVE ANOTHER DELIVERY TO MAKE, WANNA COME WITH?
THAT'S ENOUGH, LIVERMORE.
SQUAWK
YOU'RE A BLAST, JAMIL, BUT ANOTHER DELIVERY?
NEVER. EVER. AGAIN.
LIVERMORE, STOP!

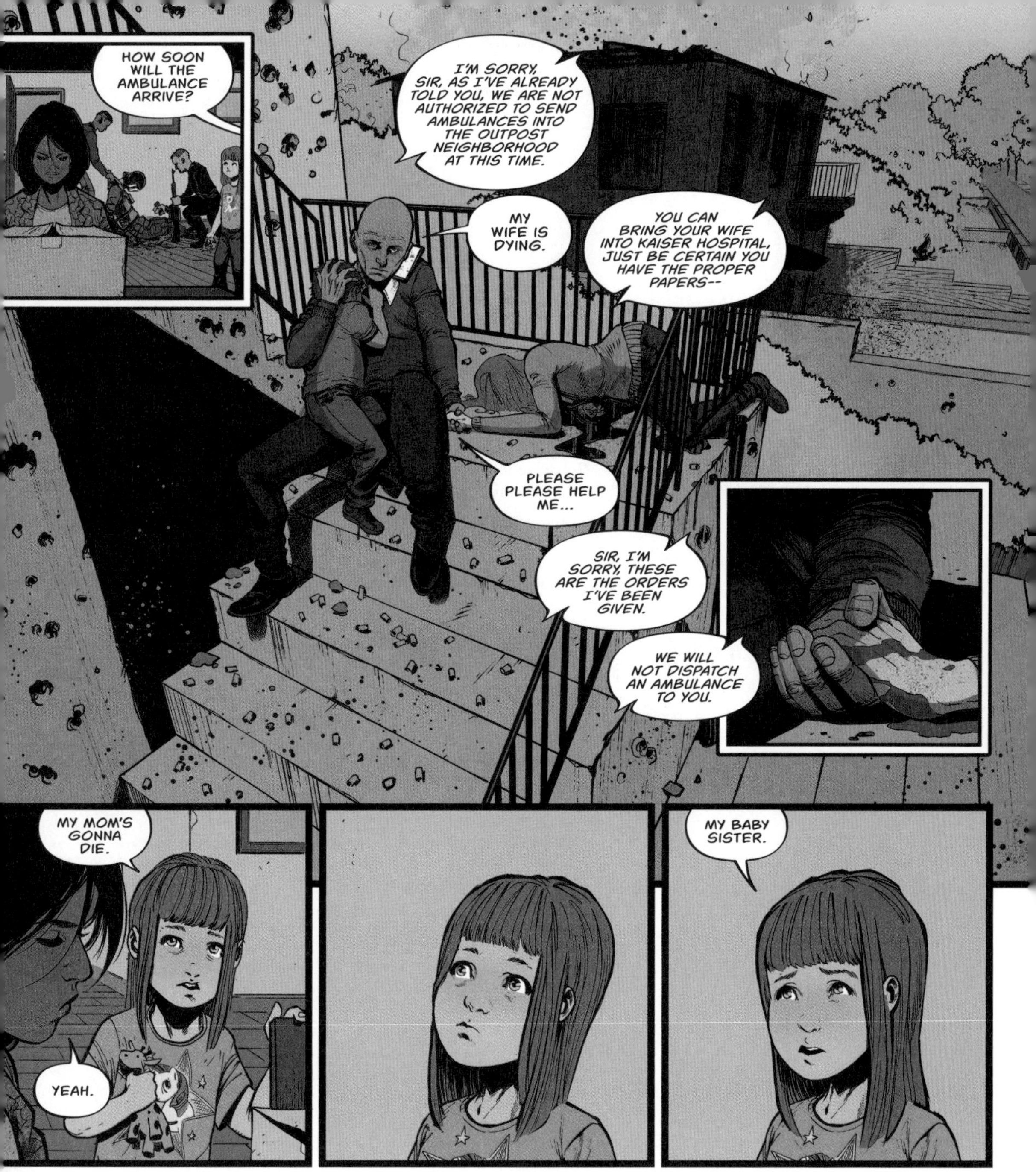
HOW SOON WILL THE AMBULANCE ARRIVE?
I'M SORRY, SIR, AS I'VE ALREADY TOLD YOU, WE ARE NOT AUTHORIZED TO SEND AMBULANCES INTO THE OUTPOST NEIGHBORHOOD AT THIS TIME.
MY WIFE IS DYING.
YOU CAN BRING YOUR WIFE INTO KAISER HOSPITAL, JUST BE CERTAIN YOU HAVE THE PROPER PAPERS--
PLEASE PLEASE HELP ME...
SIR, I'M SORRY, THESE ARE THE ORDERS I'VE BEEN GIVEN.
WE WILL NOT DISPATCH AN AMBULANCE TO YOU.
MY MOM'S GONNA DIE.
YEAH.
MY BABY SISTER.

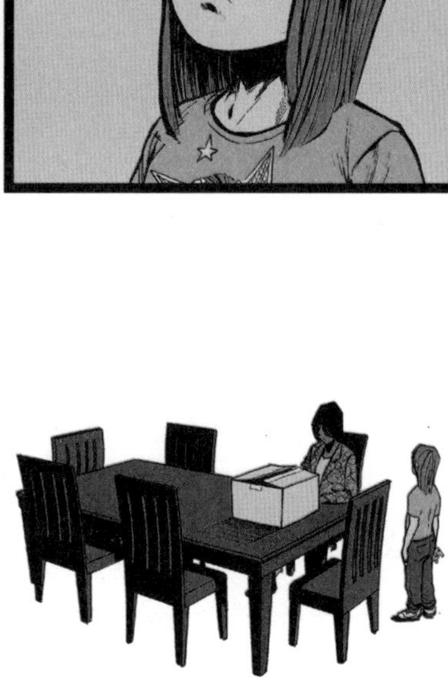

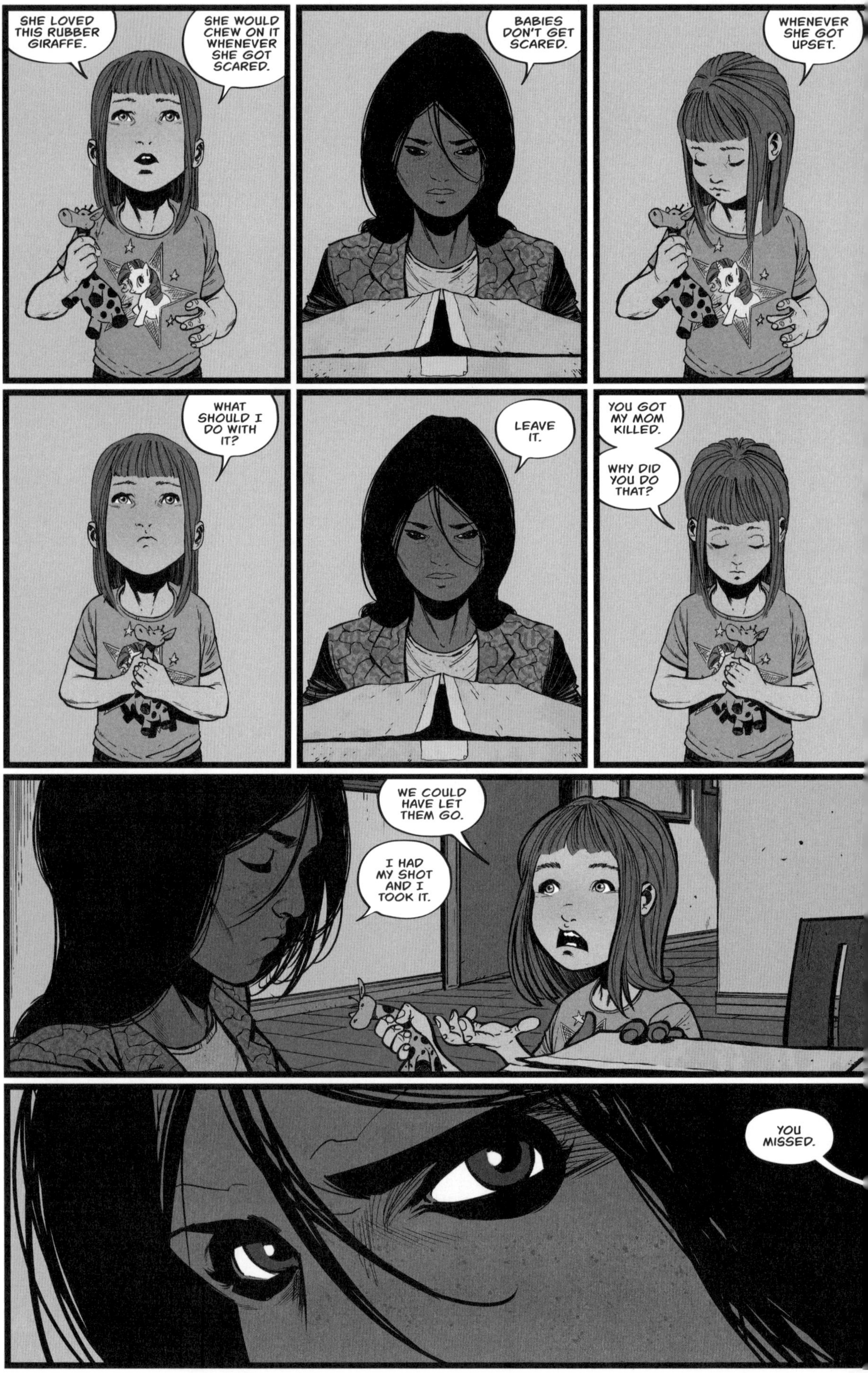
SHE LOVED THIS RUBBER GIRAFFE.
SHE WOULD CHEW ON IT WHENEVER SHE GOT SCARED.
BABIES DON'T GET SCARED.
WHENEVER SHE GOT UPSET.
WHAT SHOULD I DO WITH IT?
LEAVE IT.
YOU GOT MY MOM KILLED.
WHY DID YOU DO THAT?
WE COULD HAVE LET THEM GO.
I HAD MY SHOT AND I TOOK IT.
YOU MISSED.

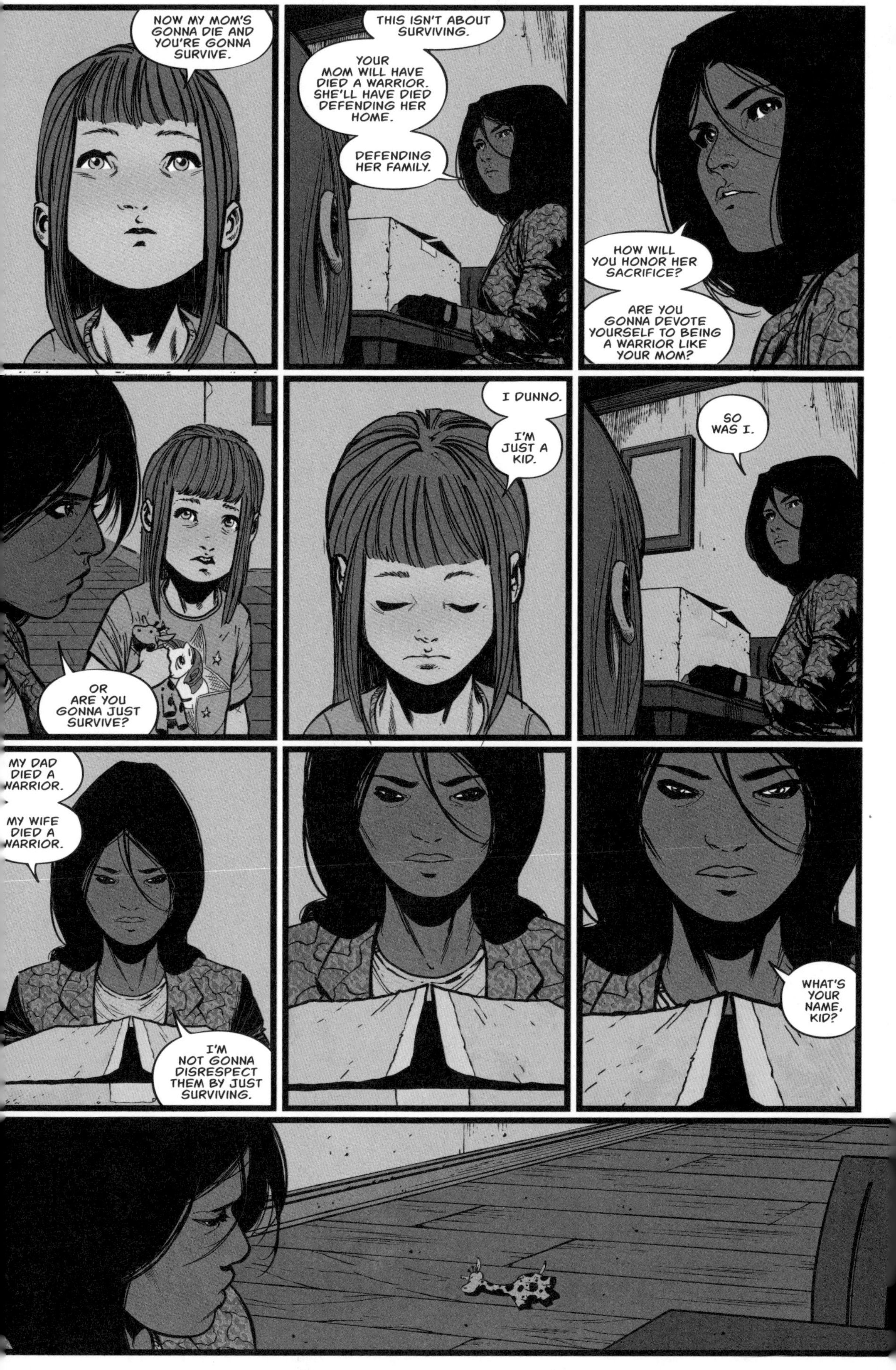
NOW MY MOM'S GONNA DIE AND YOU'RE GONNA SURVIVE.
THIS ISN'T ABOUT SURVIVING.
YOUR MOM WILL HAVE DIED A WARRIOR. SHE'LL HAVE DIED DEFENDING HER HOME.
DEFENDING HER FAMILY.
HOW WILL YOU HONOR HER SACRIFICE?
ARE YOU GONNA DEVOTE YOURSELF TO BEING A WARRIOR LIKE YOUR MOM?
OR ARE YOU GONNA JUST SURVIVE?
I DUNNO.
I'M JUST A KID.
SO WAS I.
MY DAD DIED A WARRIOR.
MY WIFE DIED A WARRIOR.
I'M NOT GONNA DISRESPECT THEM BY JUST SURVIVING.
WHAT'S YOUR NAME, KID?

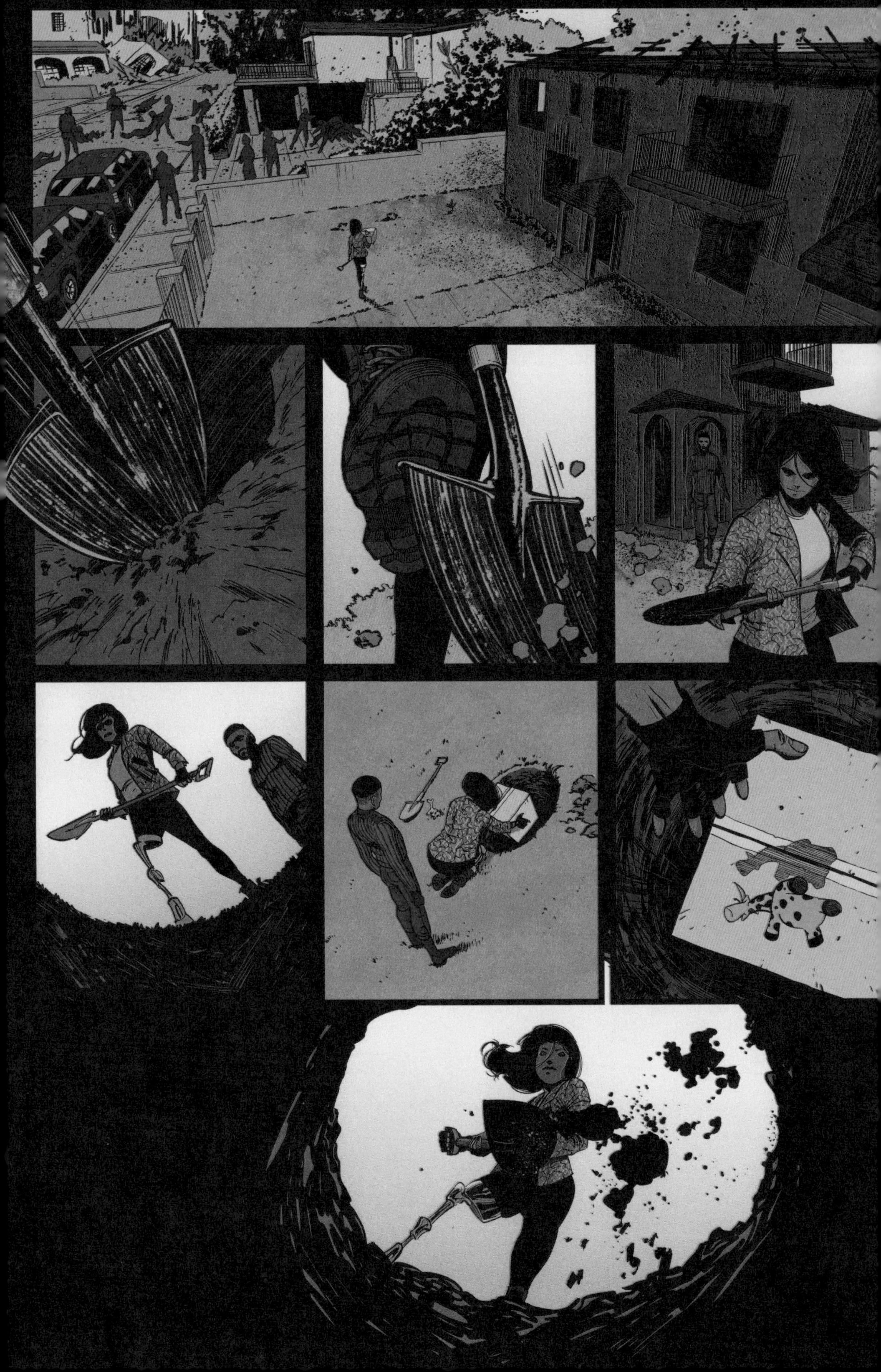

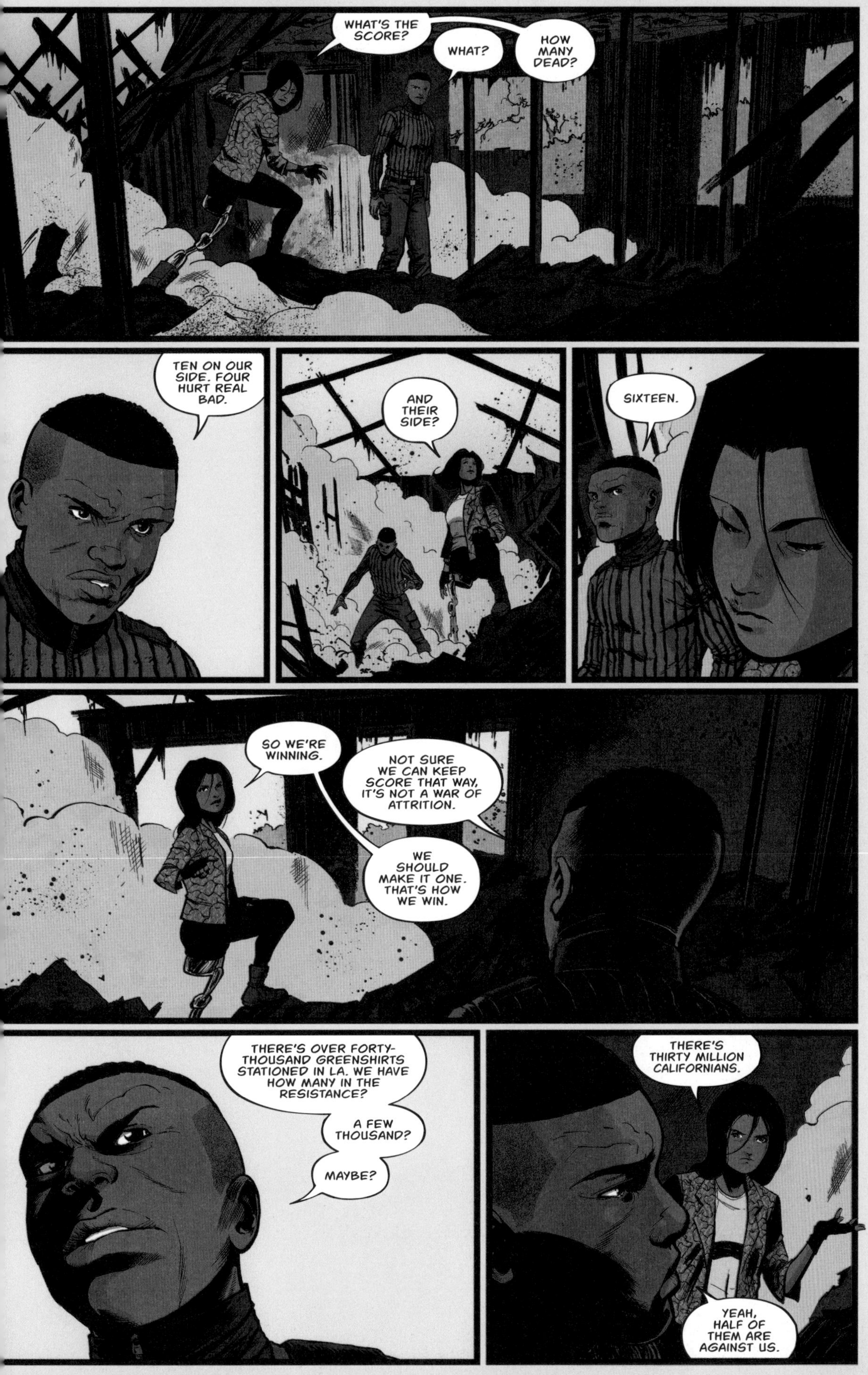
WHAT'S THE SCORE?
WHAT?
HOW MANY DEAD?
TEN ON OUR SIDE. FOUR HURT REAL BAD.
AND THEIR SIDE?
SIXTEEN.
SO WE'RE WINNING.
NOT SURE WE CAN KEEP SCORE THAT WAY, IT'S NOT A WAR OF ATTRITION.
WE SHOULD MAKE IT ONE. THAT'S HOW WE WIN.
THERE'S OVER FORTY-THOUSAND GREENSHIRTS STATIONED IN LA. WE HAVE HOW MANY IN THE RESISTANCE?
A FEW THOUSAND?
MAYBE?
THERE'S THIRTY MILLION CALIFORNIANS.
YEAH, HALF OF THEM ARE AGAINST US.

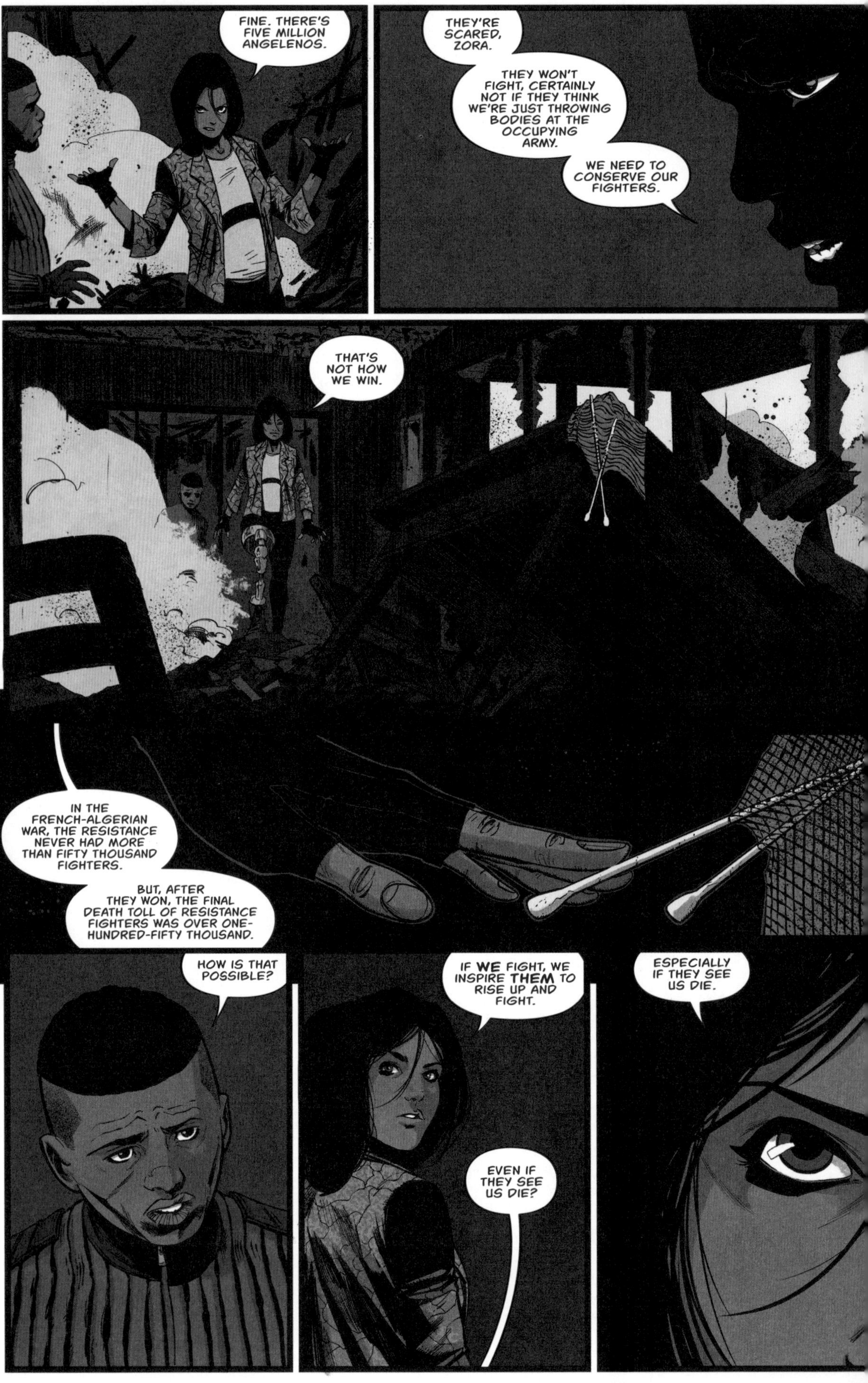
FINE. THERE'S FIVE MILLION ANGELENOS.
THEY'RE SCARED, ZORA.
THEY WON'T FIGHT, CERTAINLY NOT IF THEY THINK WE'RE JUST THROWING BODIES AT THE OCCUPYING ARMY.
WE NEED TO CONSERVE OUR FIGHTERS.
THAT'S NOT HOW WE WIN.
IN THE FRENCH-ALGERIAN WAR, THE RESISTANCE NEVER HAD MORE THAN FIFTY THOUSAND FIGHTERS.
BUT, AFTER THEY WON, THE FINAL DEATH TOLL OF RESISTANCE FIGHTERS WAS OVER ONE-HUNDRED-FIFTY THOUSAND.
HOW IS THAT POSSIBLE?
IF **WE** FIGHT, WE INSPIRE **THEM** TO RISE UP AND FIGHT.
EVEN IF THEY SEE US DIE?
ESPECIALLY IF THEY SEE US DIE.

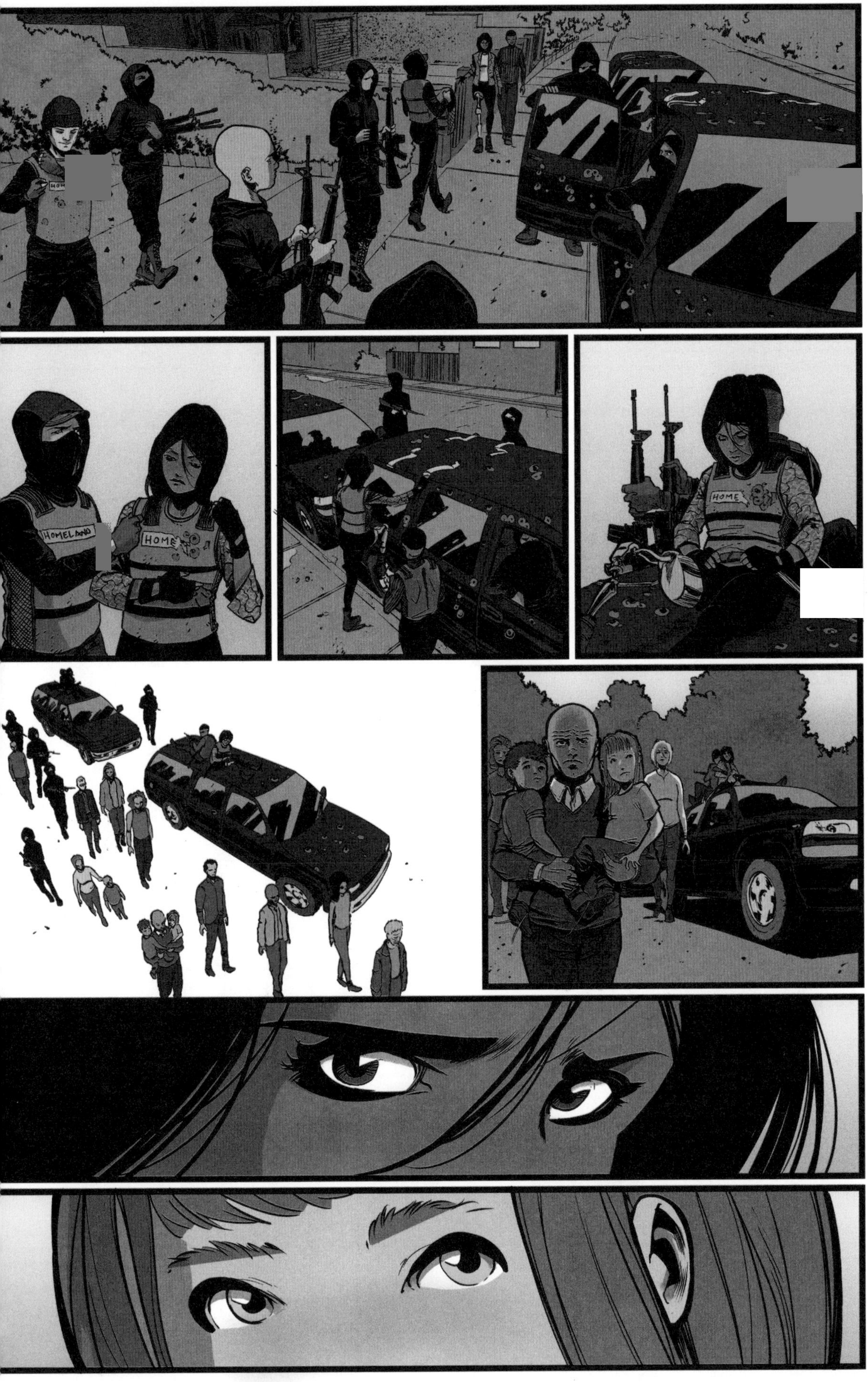
HOMELAND
HOME
HOME

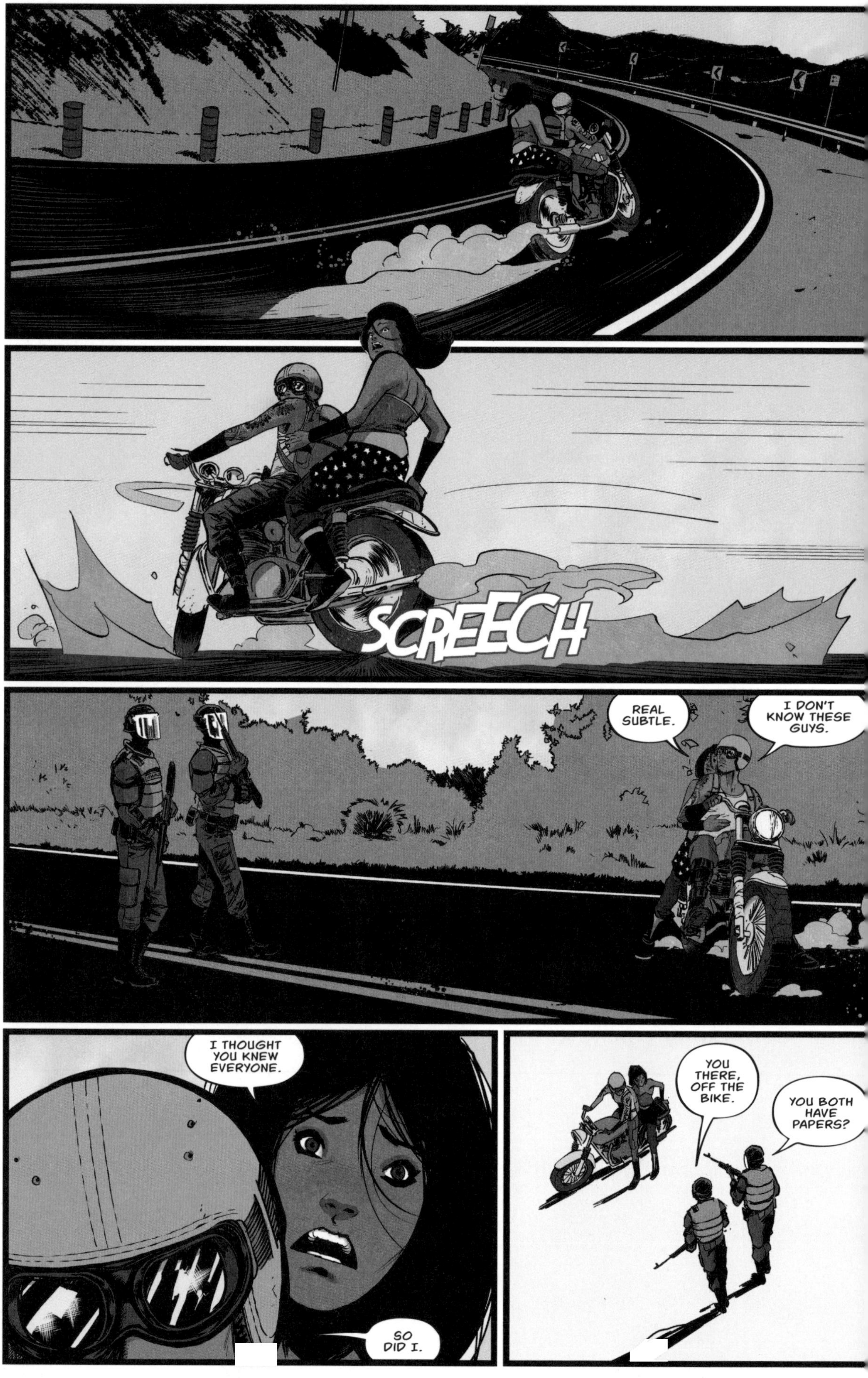
SCREECH
REAL SUBTLE.
I DON'T KNOW THESE GUYS.
I THOUGHT YOU KNEW EVERYONE.
SO DID I.
YOU THERE, OFF THE BIKE.
YOU BOTH HAVE PAPERS?

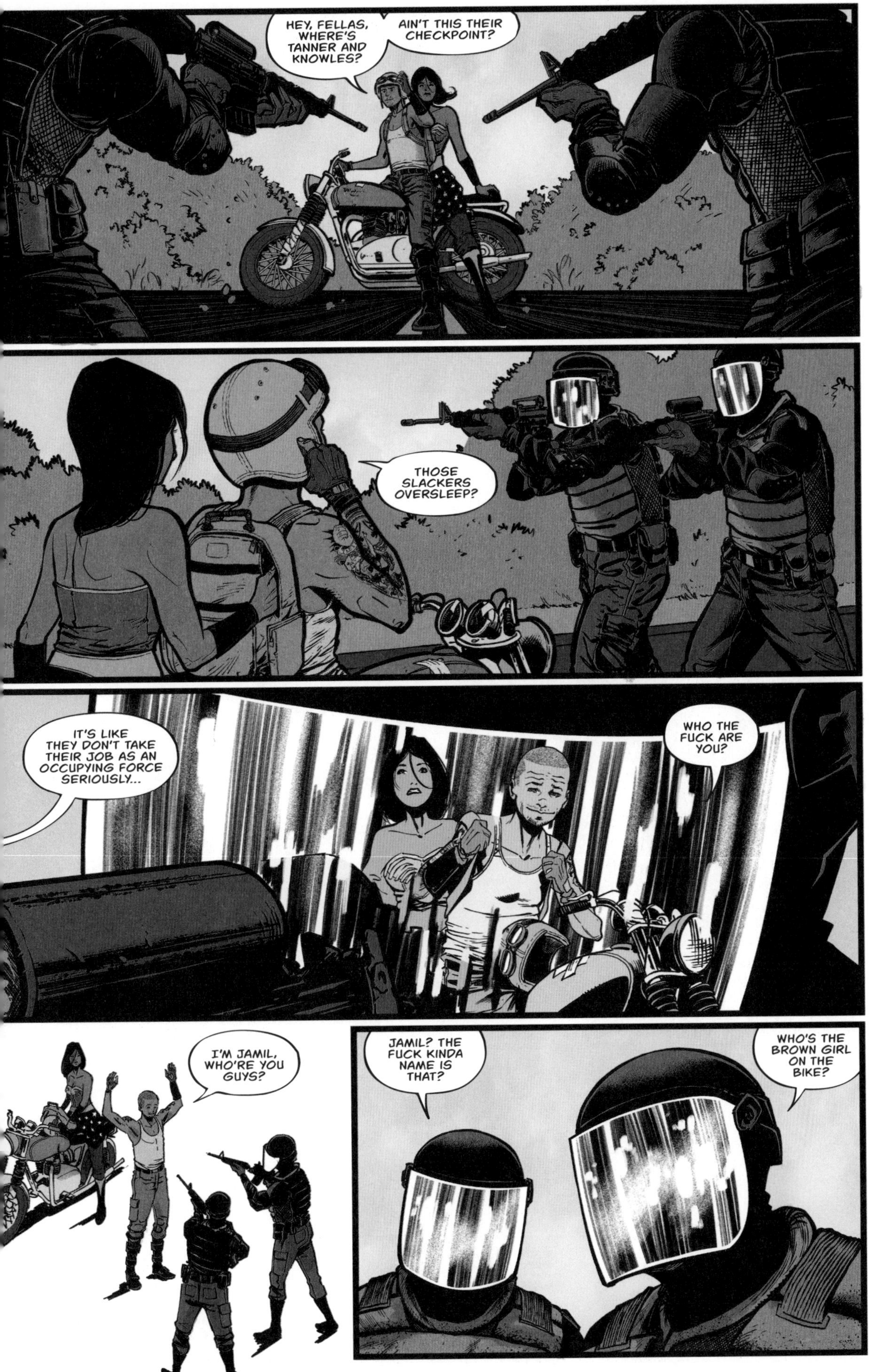
HEY, FELLAS, WHERE'S TANNER AND KNOWLES?
AIN'T THIS THEIR CHECKPOINT?
THOSE SLACKERS OVERSLEEP?
IT'S LIKE THEY DON'T TAKE THEIR JOB AS AN OCCUPYING FORCE SERIOUSLY...
WHO THE FUCK ARE YOU?
I'M JAMIL, WHO'RE YOU GUYS?
JAMIL? THE FUCK KINDA NAME IS THAT?
WHO'S THE BROWN GIRL ON THE BIKE?

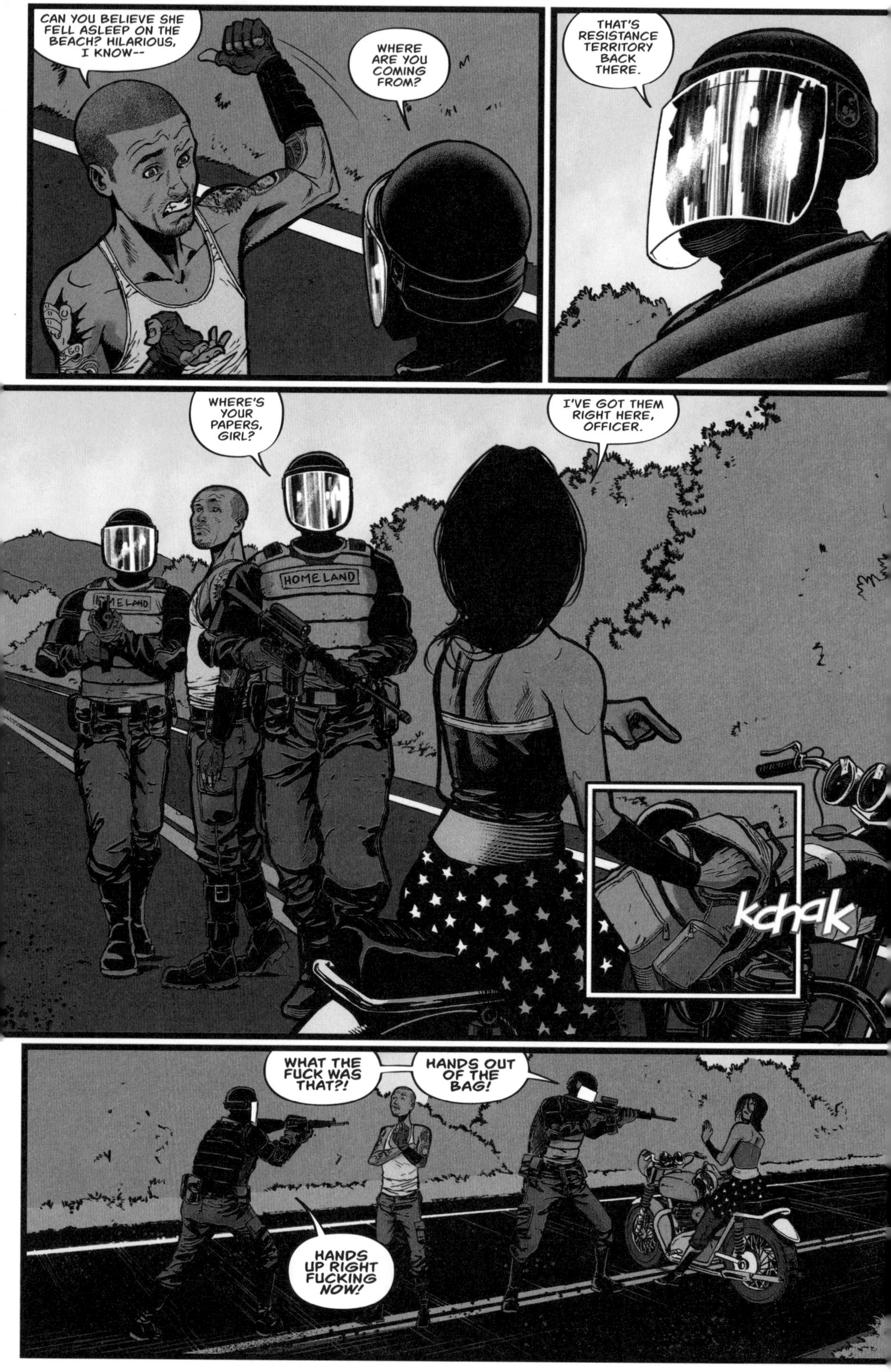
CAN YOU BELIEVE SHE FELL ASLEEP ON THE BEACH? HILARIOUS, I KNOW--
WHERE ARE YOU COMING FROM?
THAT'S RESISTANCE TERRITORY BACK THERE.
WHERE'S YOUR PAPERS, GIRL?
I'VE GOT THEM RIGHT HERE, OFFICER.
HOME LAND
HOME LAND
kchak
WHAT THE FUCK WAS THAT?!
HANDS OUT OF THE BAG!
HANDS UP RIGHT FUCKING NOW!

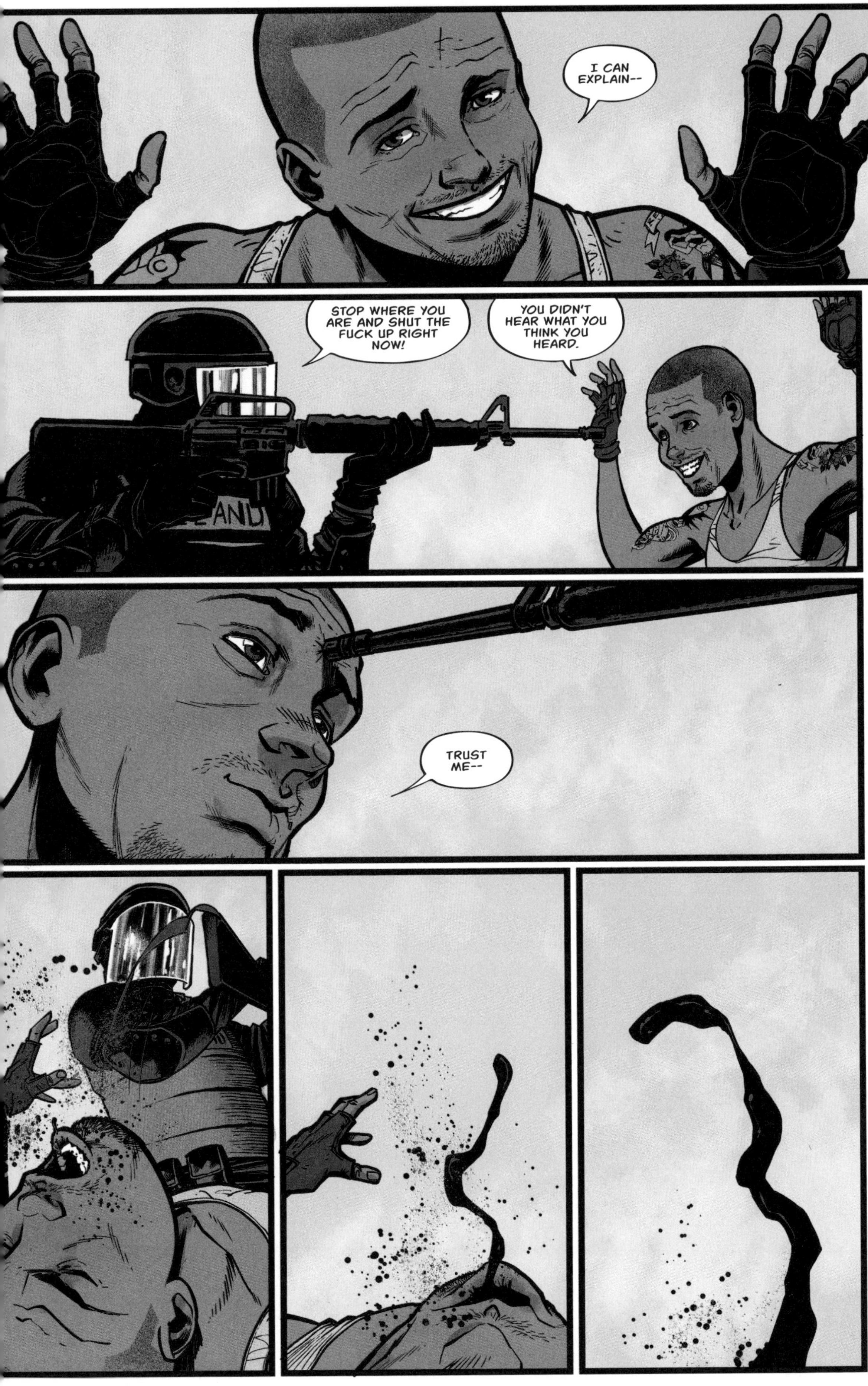
I CAN EXPLAIN--
STOP WHERE YOU ARE AND SHUT THE FUCK UP RIGHT NOW!
YOU DIDN'T HEAR WHAT YOU THINK YOU HEARD.
TRUST ME--

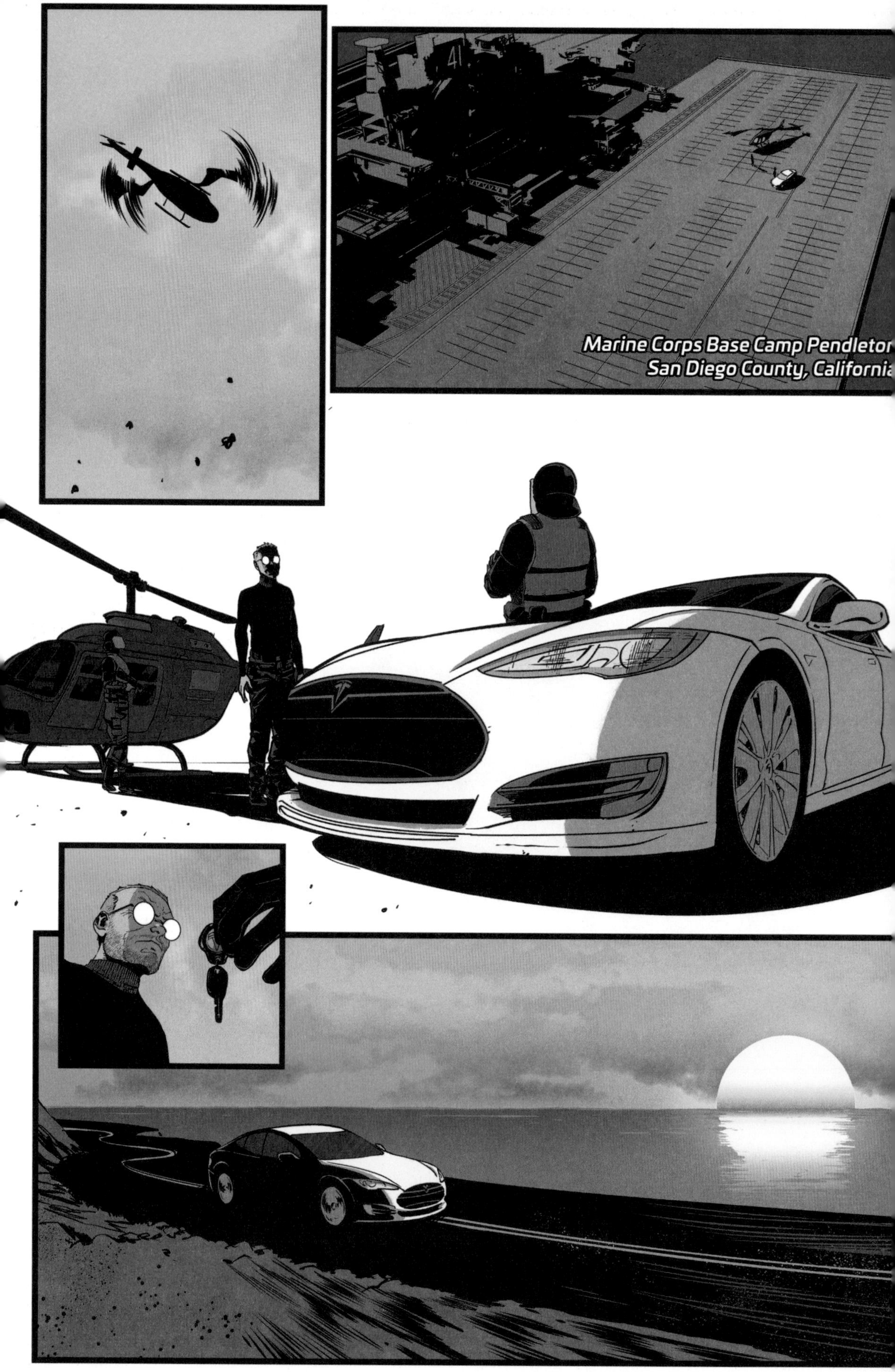
Marine Corps Base Camp Pendleton
San Diego County, California

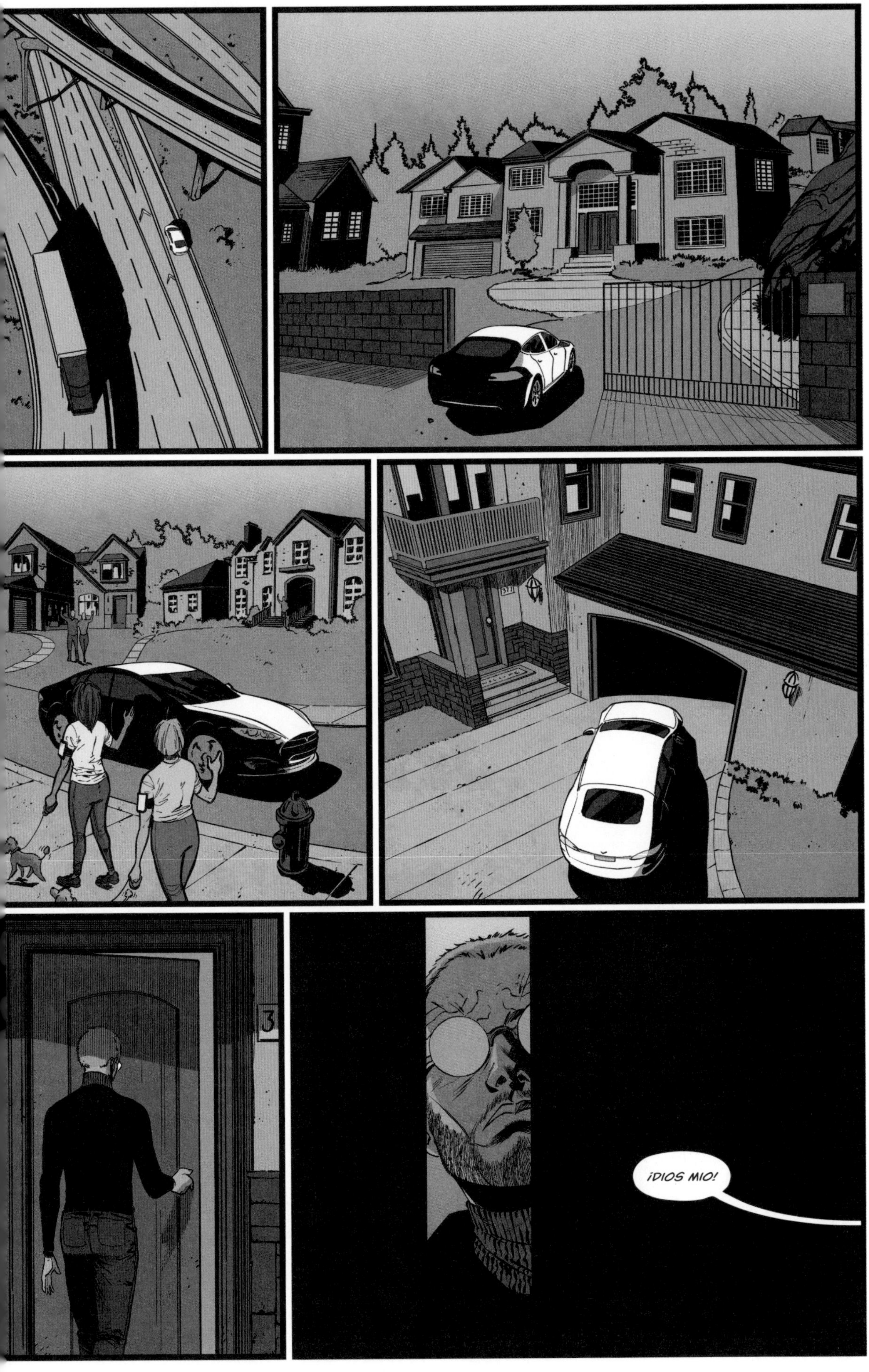
¡DIOS MIO!

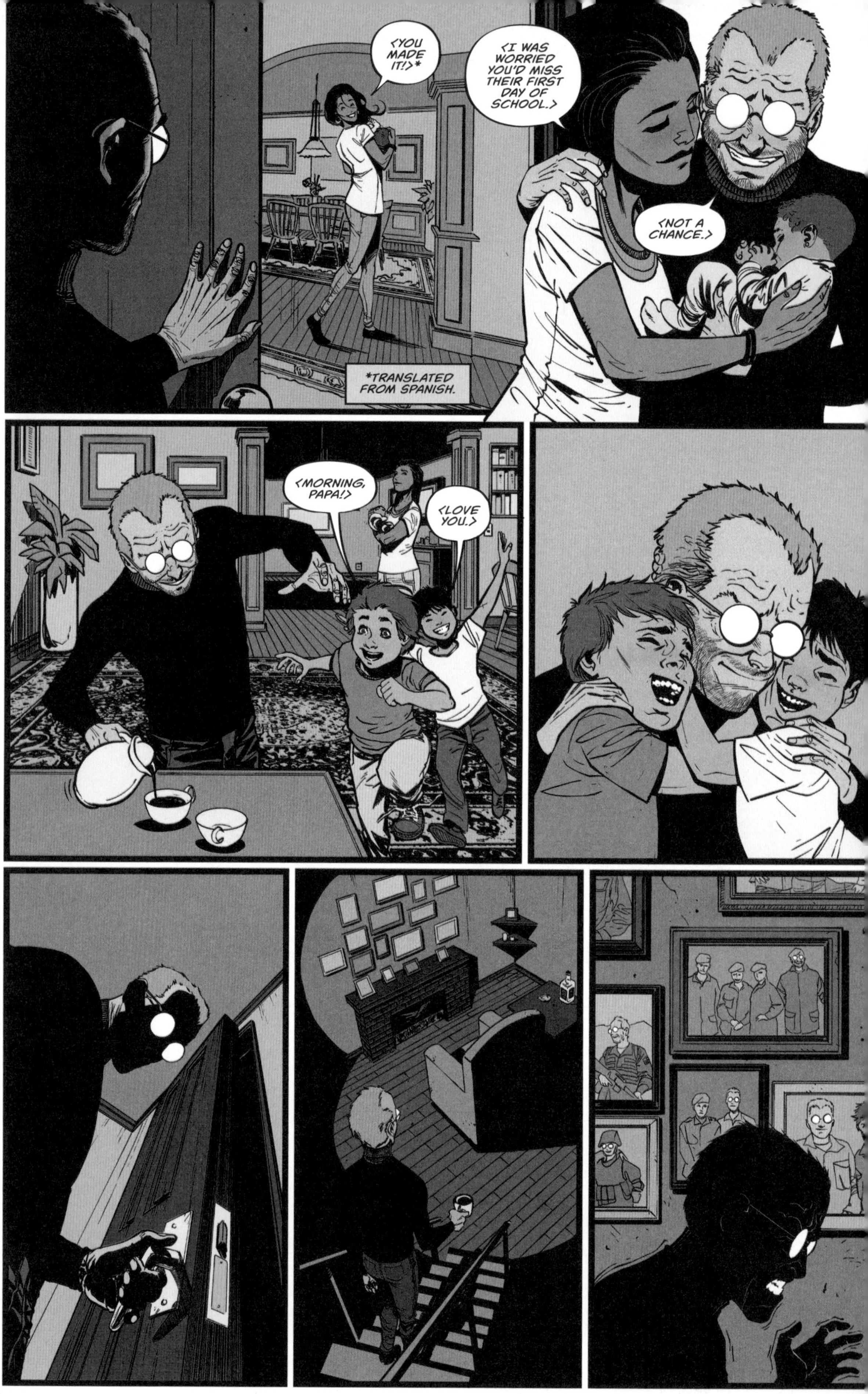

<YOU MADE IT!>*
<I WAS WORRIED YOU'D MISS THEIR FIRST DAY OF SCHOOL.>
<NOT A CHANCE.>
*TRANSLATED FROM SPANISH.
<MORNING, PAPA!>
<LOVE YOU.>

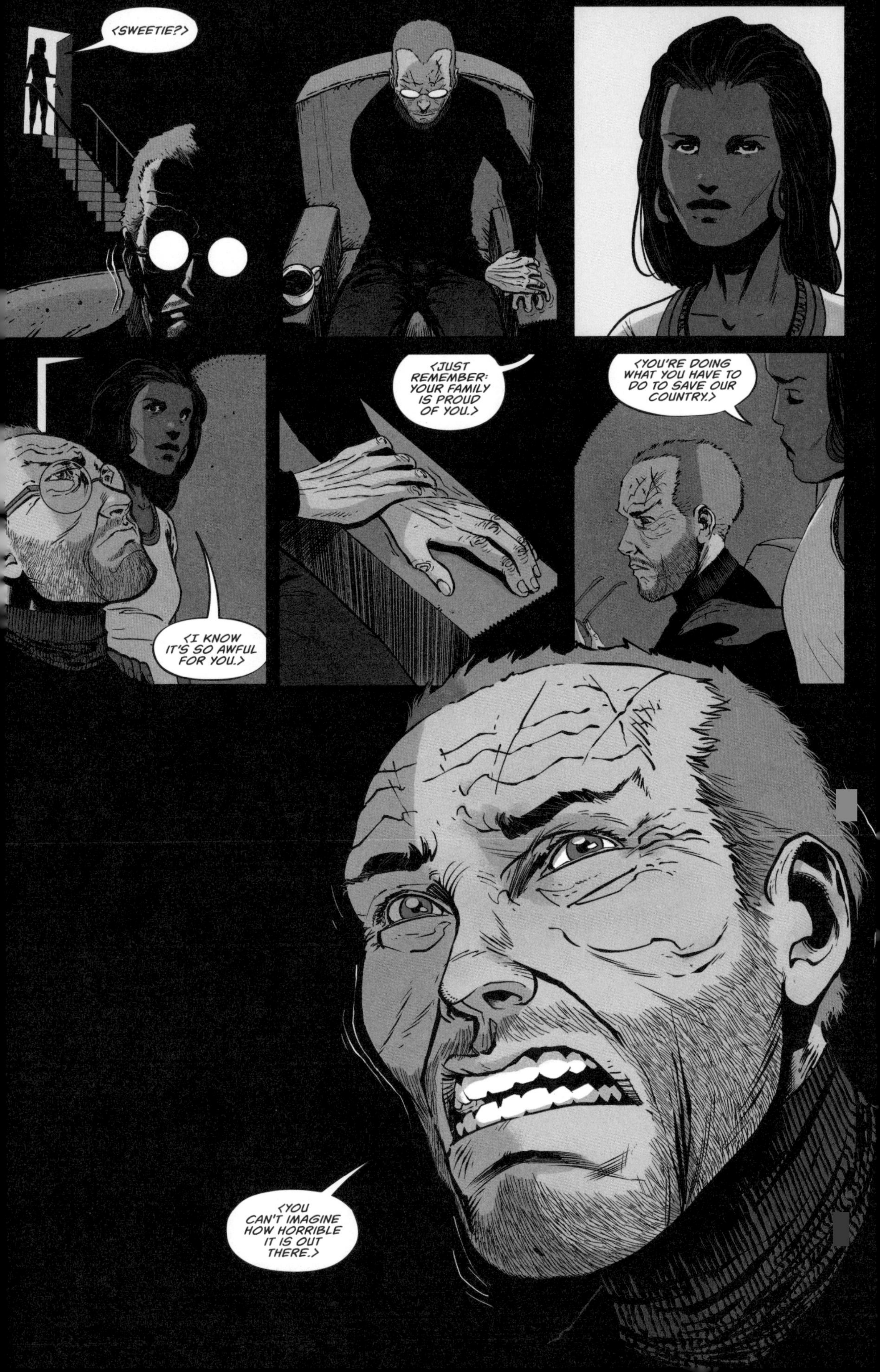
<SWEETIE?>
<I KNOW IT'S SO AWFUL FOR YOU.>
<JUST REMEMBER: YOUR FAMILY IS PROUD OF YOU.>
<YOU'RE DOING WHAT YOU HAVE TO DO TO SAVE OUR COUNTRY.>
<YOU CAN'T IMAGINE HOW HORRIBLE IT IS OUT THERE.>

89007

CHAPTER THREE

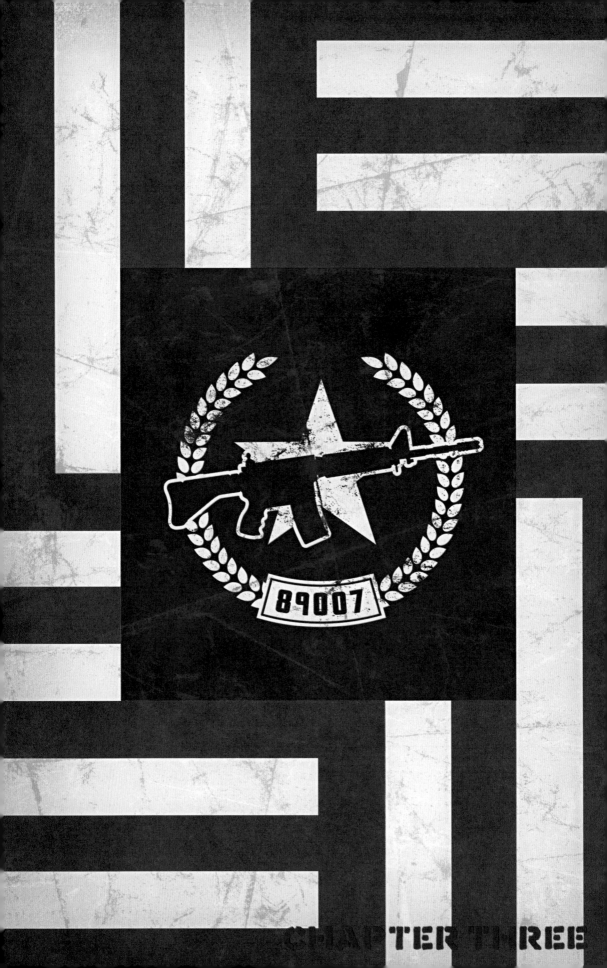

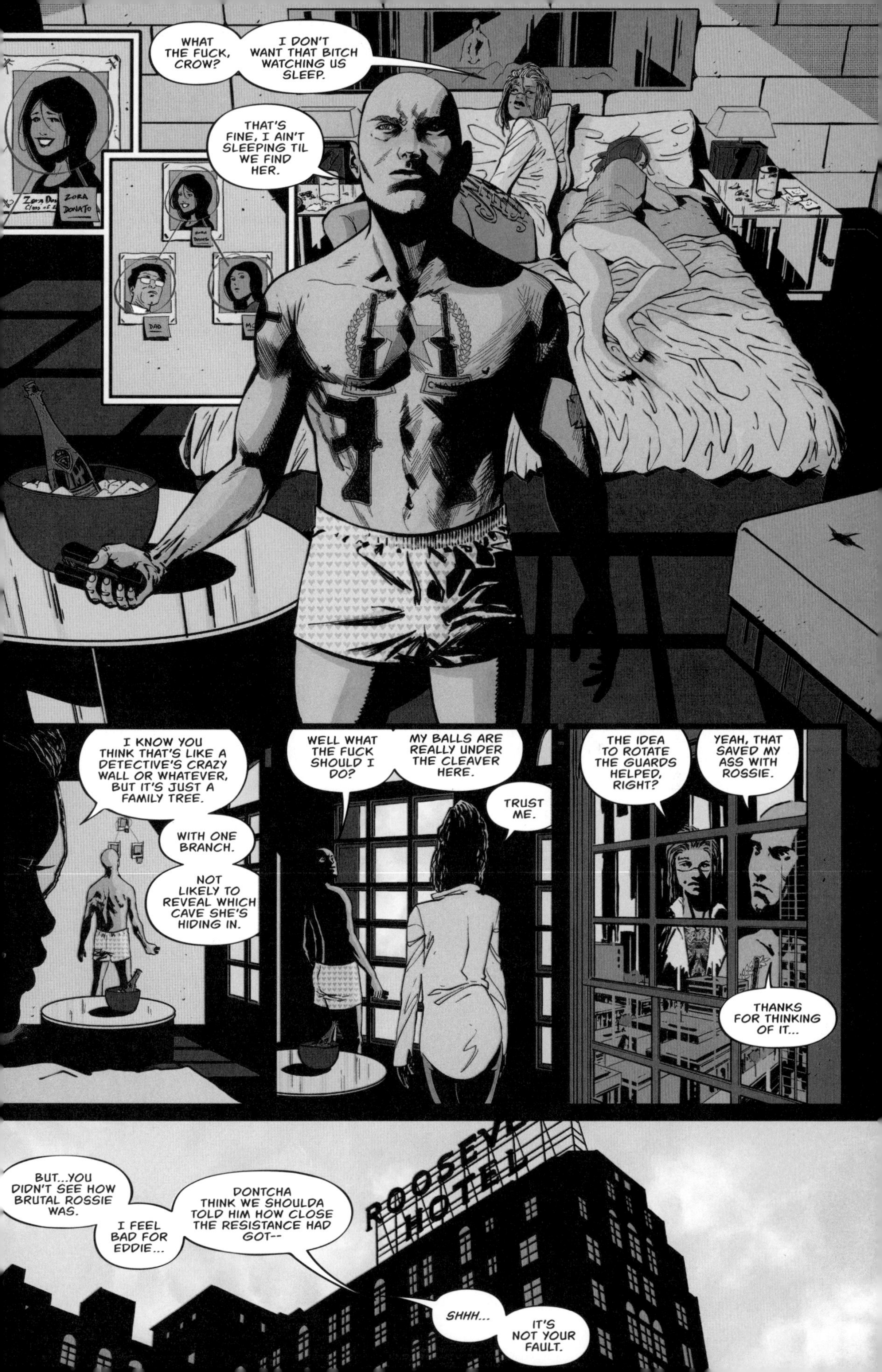
WHAT THE FUCK, CROW?
I DON'T WANT THAT BITCH WATCHING US SLEEP.
THAT'S FINE, I AIN'T SLEEPING TIL WE FIND HER.
ZORA DONATO
DAD
I KNOW YOU THINK THAT'S LIKE A DETECTIVE'S CRAZY WALL OR WHATEVER, BUT IT'S JUST A FAMILY TREE.
WITH ONE BRANCH.
NOT LIKELY TO REVEAL WHICH CAVE SHE'S HIDING IN.
WELL WHAT THE FUCK SHOULD I DO?
MY BALLS ARE REALLY UNDER THE CLEAVER HERE.
TRUST ME.
THE IDEA TO ROTATE THE GUARDS HELPED, RIGHT?
YEAH, THAT SAVED MY ASS WITH ROSSIE.
THANKS FOR THINKING OF IT...
BUT...YOU DIDN'T SEE HOW BRUTAL ROSSIE WAS.
I FEEL BAD FOR EDDIE...
DONTCHA THINK WE SHOULDA TOLD HIM HOW CLOSE THE RESISTANCE HAD GOT--
SHHH...
IT'S NOT YOUR FAULT.

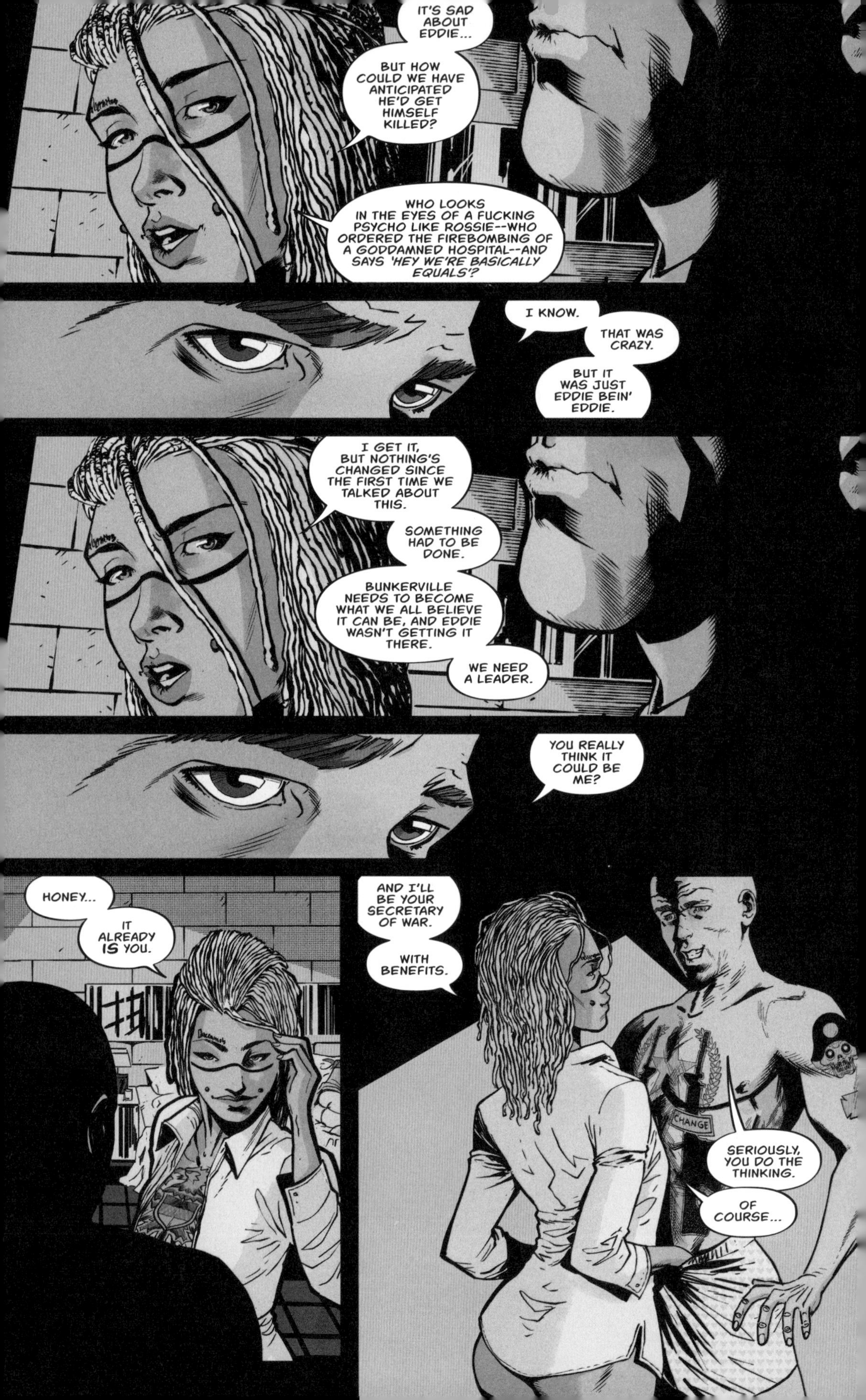
IT'S SAD ABOUT EDDIE...
BUT HOW COULD WE HAVE ANTICIPATED HE'D GET HIMSELF KILLED?
WHO LOOKS IN THE EYES OF A FUCKING PSYCHO LIKE ROSSIE--WHO ORDERED THE FIREBOMBING OF A GODDAMNED HOSPITAL--AND SAYS 'HEY WE'RE BASICALLY EQUALS'?
I KNOW.
THAT WAS CRAZY.
BUT IT WAS JUST EDDIE BEIN' EDDIE.
I GET IT, BUT NOTHING'S CHANGED SINCE THE FIRST TIME WE TALKED ABOUT THIS.
SOMETHING HAD TO BE DONE.
BUNKERVILLE NEEDS TO BECOME WHAT WE ALL BELIEVE IT CAN BE, AND EDDIE WASN'T GETTING IT THERE.
WE NEED A LEADER.
YOU REALLY THINK IT COULD BE ME?
HONEY...
IT ALREADY **IS** YOU.
AND I'LL BE YOUR SECRETARY OF WAR.
WITH BENEFITS.
CHANGE
SERIOUSLY, YOU DO THE THINKING.
OF COURSE...

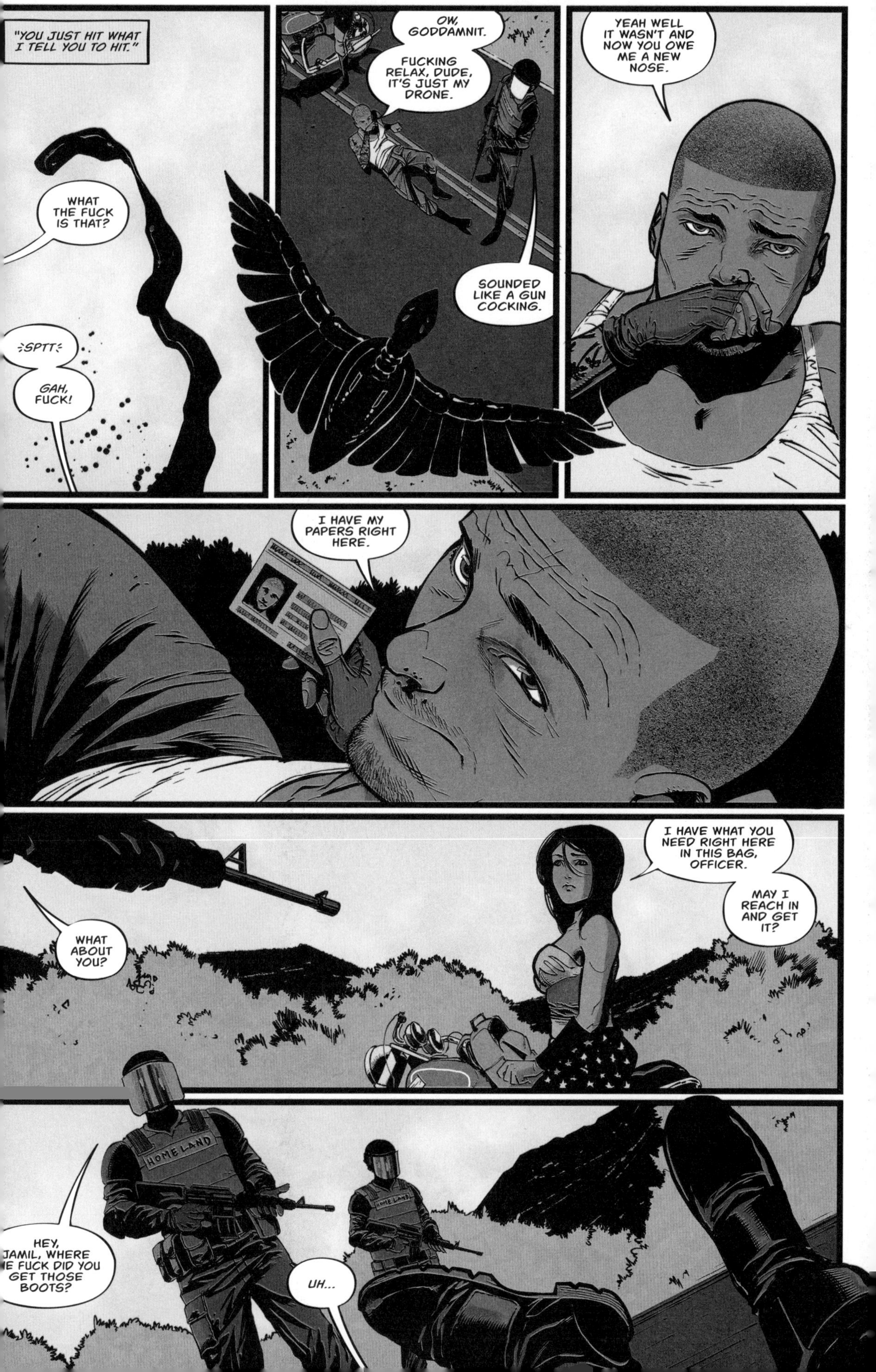
"YOU JUST HIT WHAT I TELL YOU TO HIT."
WHAT THE FUCK IS THAT?
SPTT
GAH, FUCK!
OW, GODDAMNIT.
FUCKING RELAX, DUDE, IT'S JUST MY DRONE.
SOUNDED LIKE A GUN COCKING.
YEAH WELL IT WASN'T AND NOW YOU OWE ME A NEW NOSE.
I HAVE MY PAPERS RIGHT HERE.
WHAT ABOUT YOU?
I HAVE WHAT YOU NEED RIGHT HERE IN THIS BAG, OFFICER.
MAY I REACH IN AND GET IT?
HOMELAND
HOMELAND
HEY, JAMIL, WHERE E FUCK DID YOU GET THOSE BOOTS?
UH...

BLACK MASK STUDIOS PRESENTS

CALEXIT

CHAPTER 3: YOU HIDE YOUR LOOKS BEHIND THESE SCARS

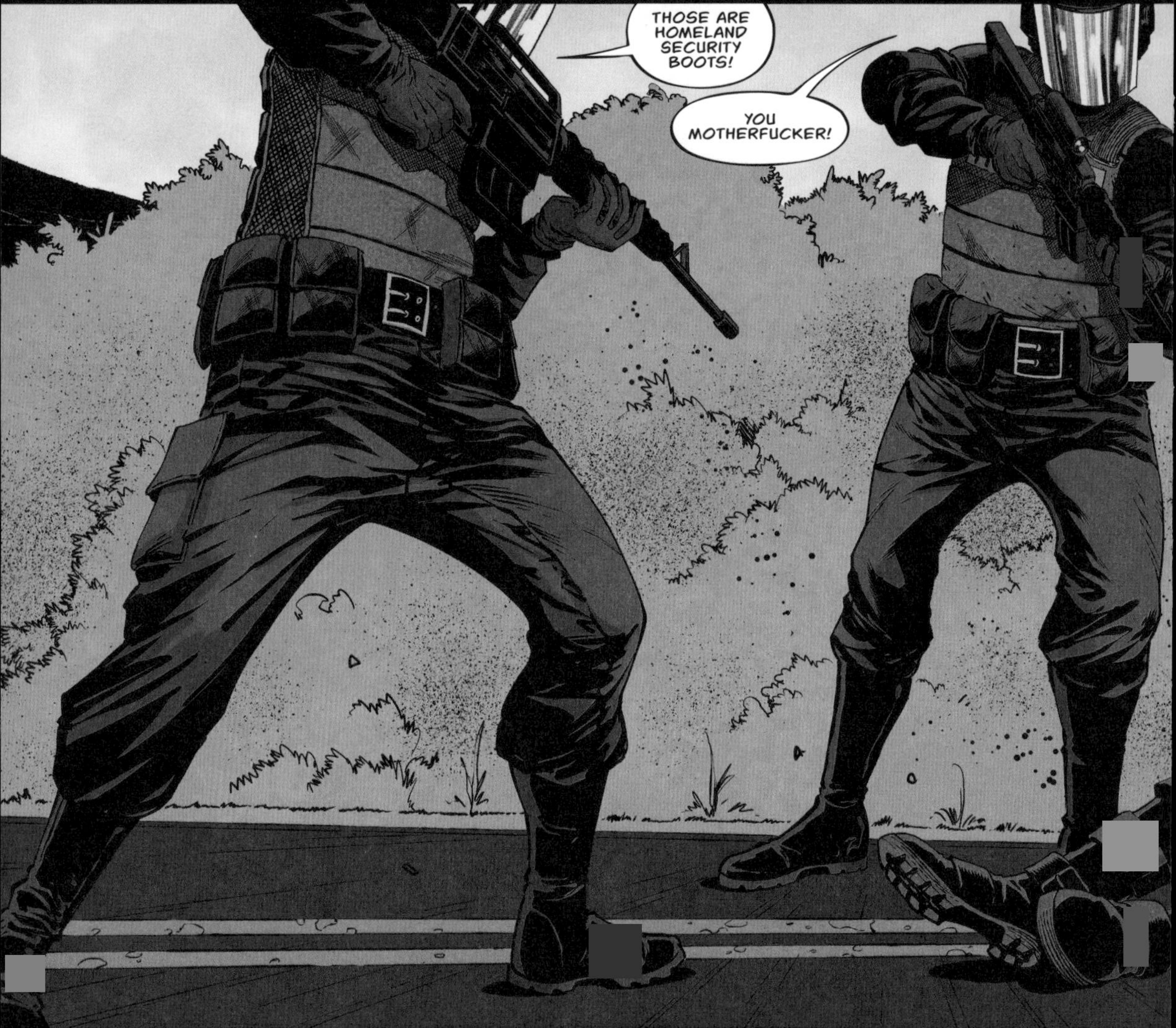
THOSE ARE HOMELAND SECURITY BOOTS!
YOU MOTHERFUCKER!

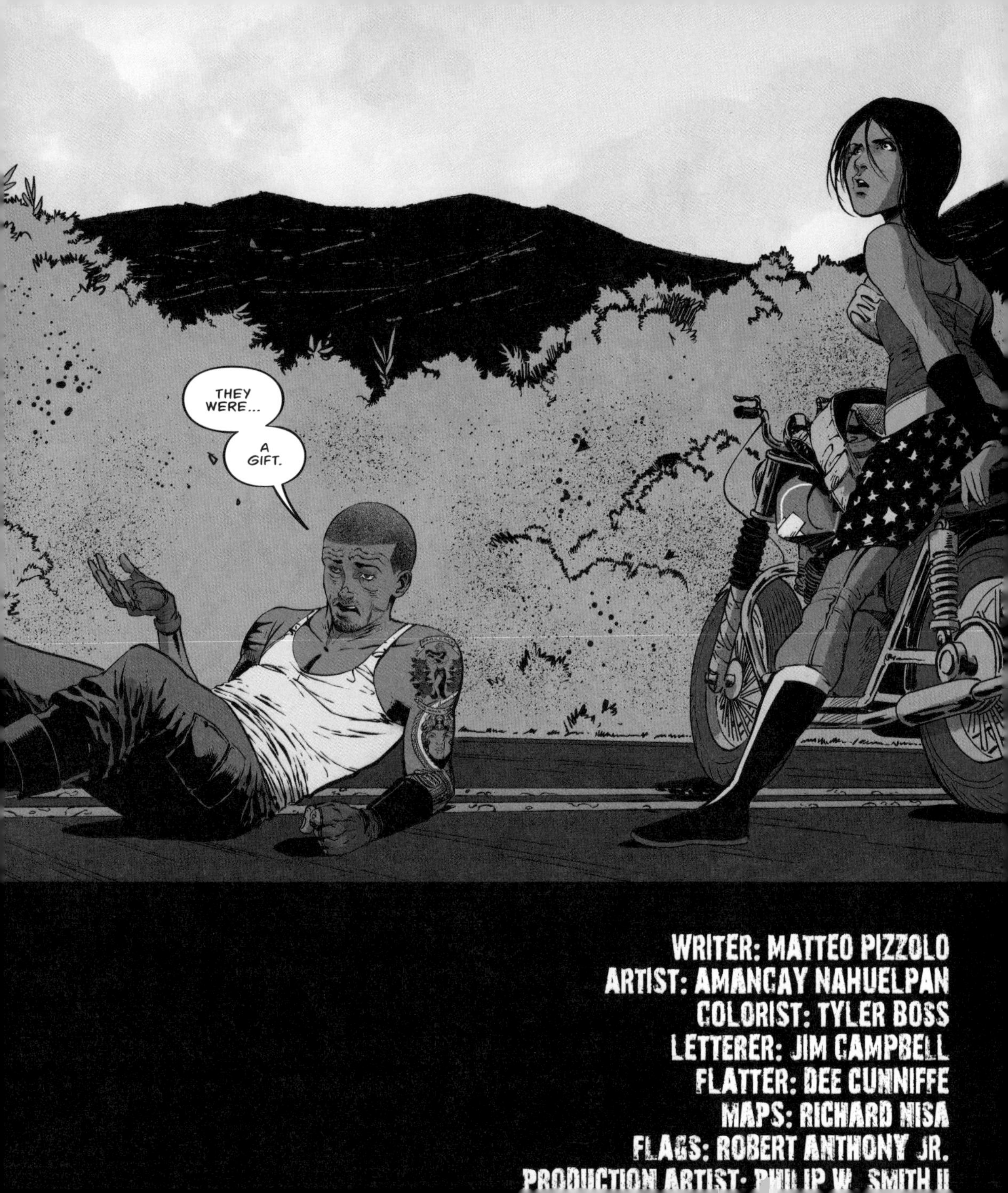
THEY WERE...
A GIFT.

WRITER: MATTEO PIZZOLO
ARTIST: AMANCAY NAHUELPAN
COLORIST: TYLER BOSS
LETTERER: JIM CAMPBELL
FLATTER: DEE CUNNIFFE
MAPS: RICHARD NISA
FLAGS: ROBERT ANTHONY JR.
PRODUCTION ARTIST: PHILIP W. SMITH II

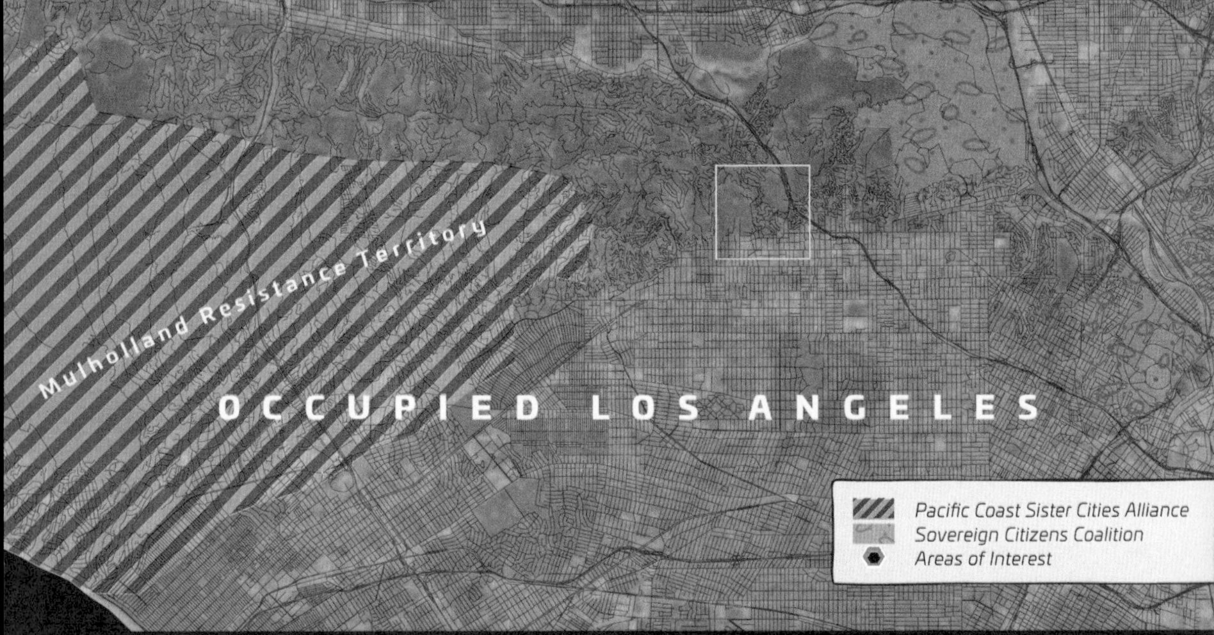
Mulholland Resistance Territory
OCCUPIED LOS ANGELES
Pacific Coast Sister Cities Alliance
Sovereign Citizens Coalition
Areas of Interest

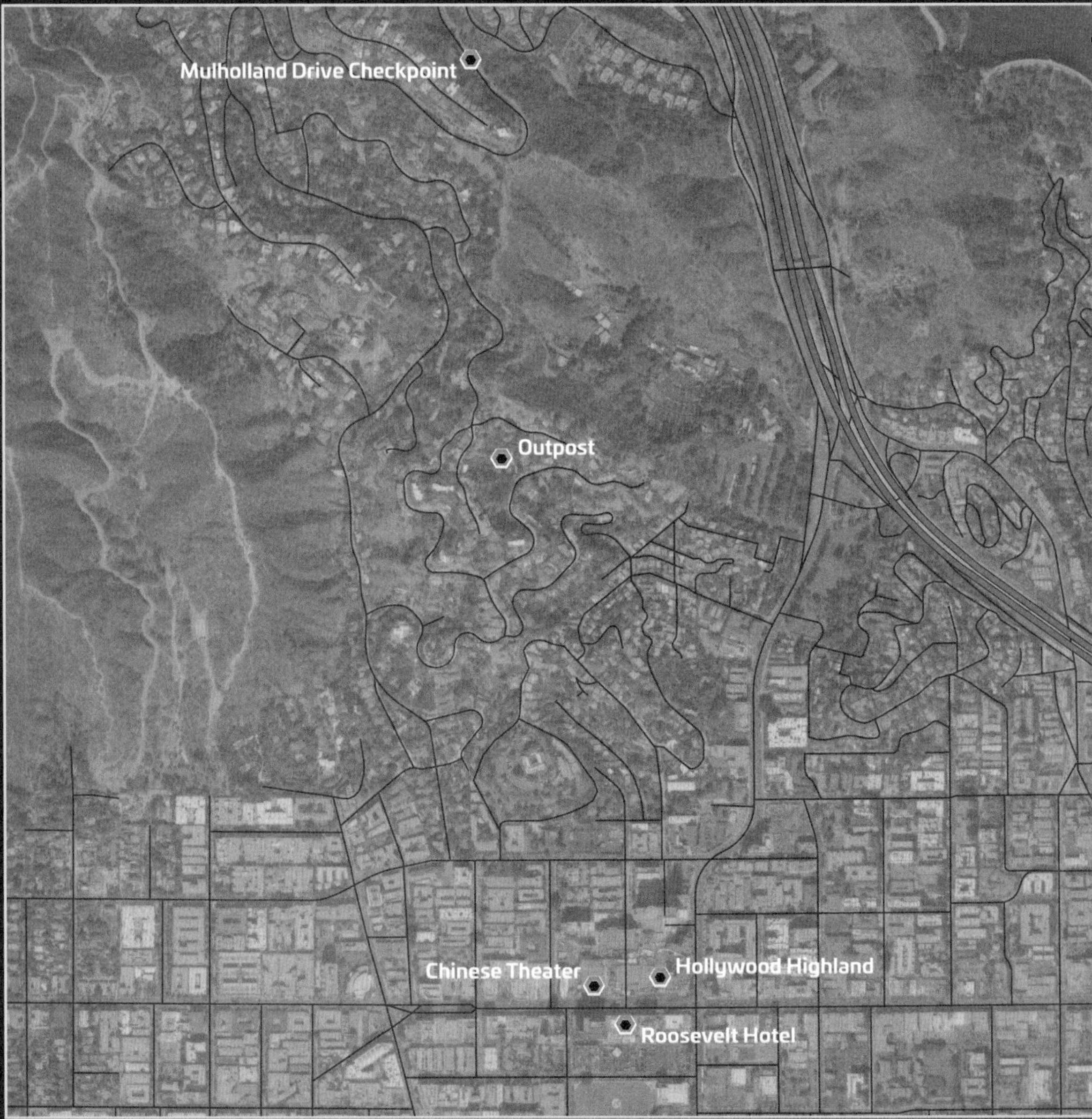
Mulholland Drive Checkpoint
Outpost
Chinese Theater
Hollywood Highland
Roosevelt Hotel

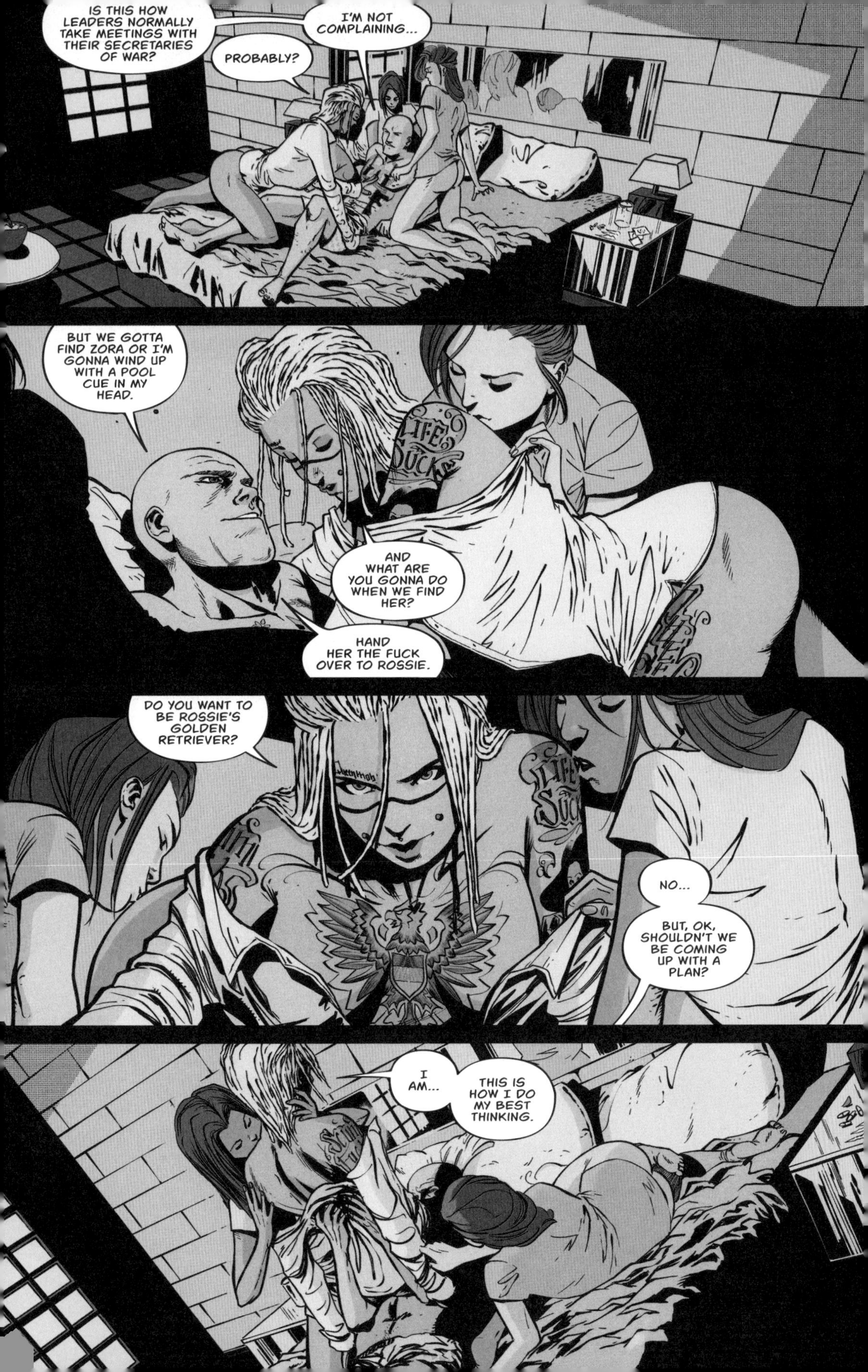
IS THIS HOW LEADERS NORMALLY TAKE MEETINGS WITH THEIR SECRETARIES OF WAR?
I'M NOT COMPLAINING...
PROBABLY?
BUT WE GOTTA FIND ZORA OR I'M GONNA WIND UP WITH A POOL CUE IN MY HEAD.
AND WHAT ARE YOU GONNA DO WHEN WE FIND HER?
HAND HER THE FUCK OVER TO ROSSIE.
DO YOU WANT TO BE ROSSIE'S GOLDEN RETRIEVER?
NO...
BUT, OK, SHOULDN'T WE BE COMING UP WITH A PLAN?
I AM...
THIS IS HOW I DO MY BEST THINKING.

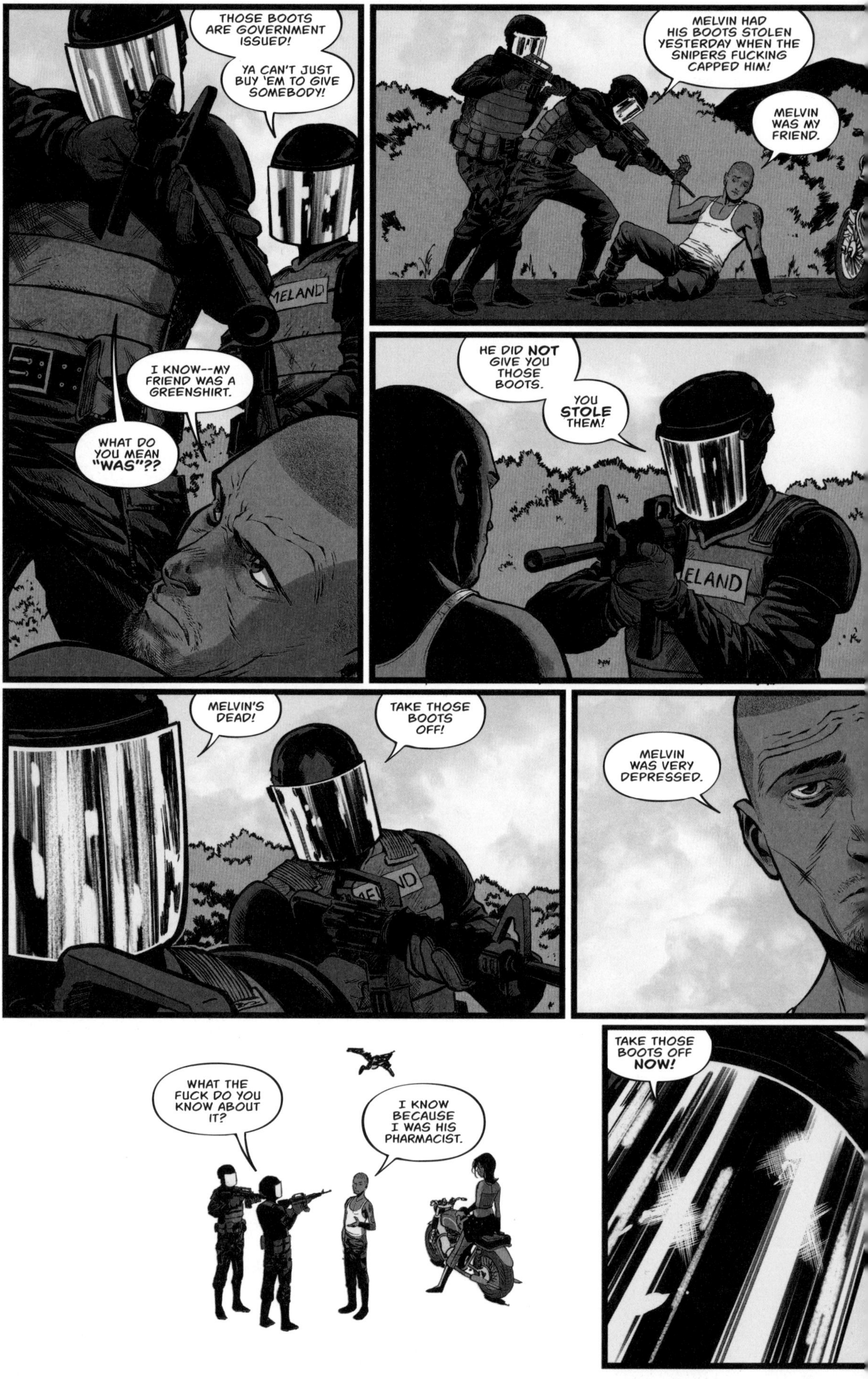
THOSE BOOTS ARE GOVERNMENT ISSUED!
YA CAN'T JUST BUY 'EM TO GIVE SOMEBODY!
MELAND
I KNOW--MY FRIEND WAS A GREENSHIRT.
WHAT DO YOU MEAN "WAS"??
MELVIN HAD HIS BOOTS STOLEN YESTERDAY WHEN THE SNIPERS FUCKING CAPPED HIM!
MELVIN WAS MY FRIEND.
HE DID NOT GIVE YOU THOSE BOOTS.
YOU STOLE THEM!
ELAND
MELVIN'S DEAD!
TAKE THOSE BOOTS OFF!
MELVIN WAS VERY DEPRESSED.
WHAT THE FUCK DO YOU KNOW ABOUT IT?
I KNOW BECAUSE I WAS HIS PHARMACIST.
TAKE THOSE BOOTS OFF NOW!

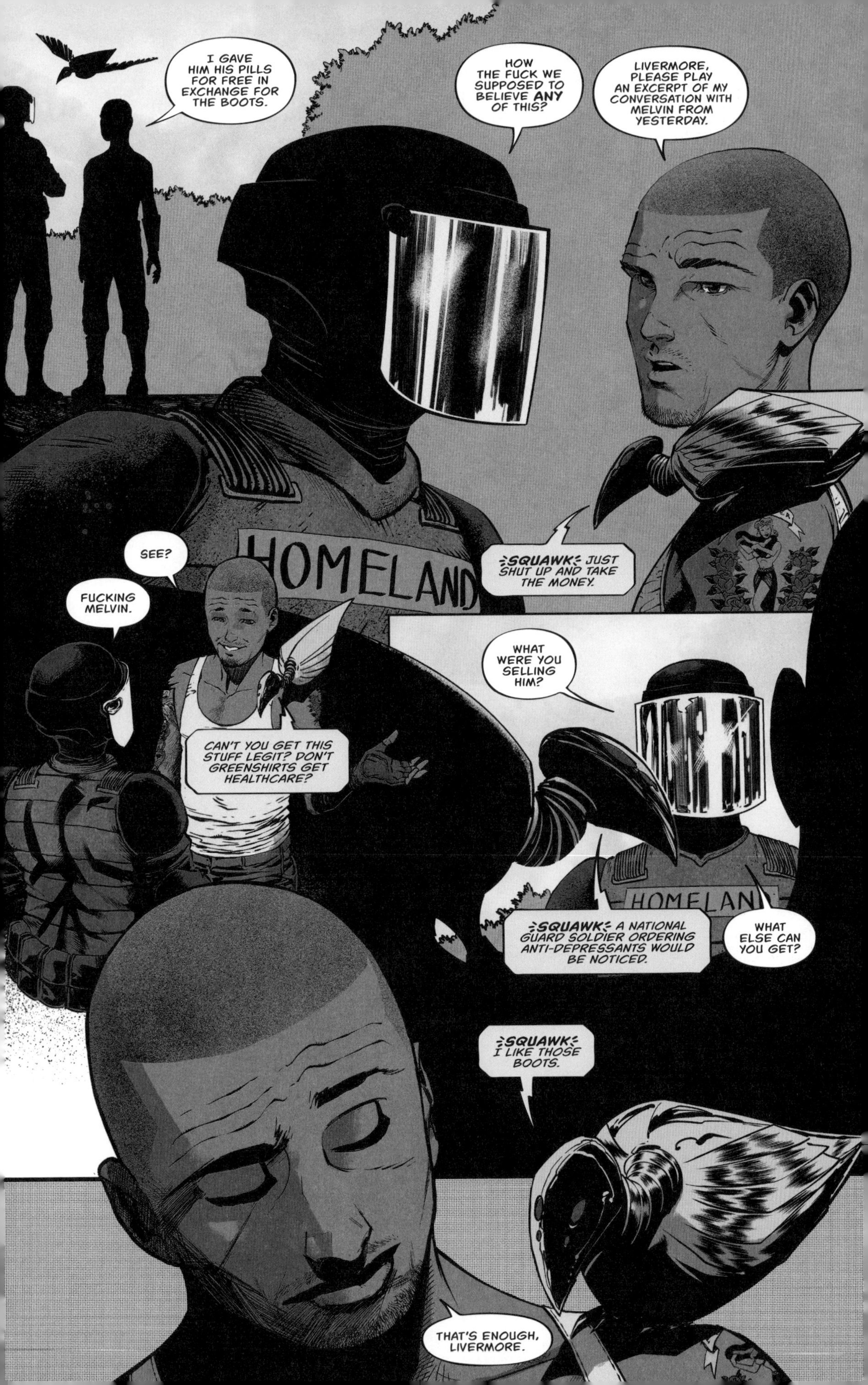
I GAVE HIM HIS PILLS FOR FREE IN EXCHANGE FOR THE BOOTS.
HOW THE FUCK WE SUPPOSED TO BELIEVE ANY OF THIS?
LIVERMORE, PLEASE PLAY AN EXCERPT OF MY CONVERSATION WITH MELVIN FROM YESTERDAY.
HOMELAND
SEE?
FUCKING MELVIN.
SQUAWK JUST SHUT UP AND TAKE THE MONEY.
WHAT WERE YOU SELLING HIM?
CAN'T YOU GET THIS STUFF LEGIT? DON'T GREENSHIRTS GET HEALTHCARE?
HOMELAND
SQUAWK A NATIONAL GUARD SOLDIER ORDERING ANTI-DEPRESSANTS WOULD BE NOTICED.
WHAT ELSE CAN YOU GET?
SQUAWK I LIKE THOSE BOOTS.
THAT'S ENOUGH, LIVERMORE.

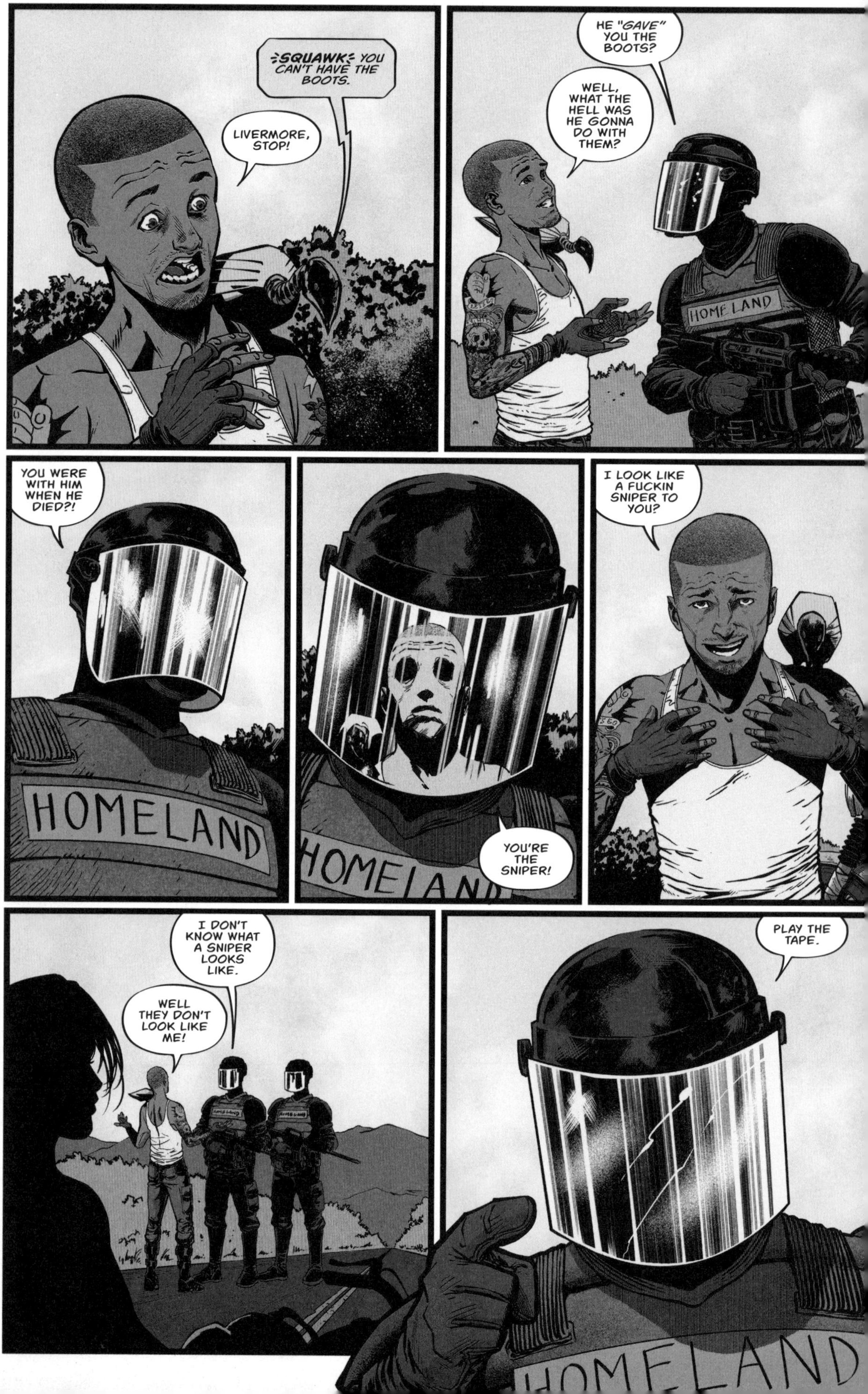

LIVERMORE, STOP!
SQUAWK YOU CAN'T HAVE THE BOOTS.
HE "GAVE" YOU THE BOOTS?
WELL, WHAT THE HELL WAS HE GONNA DO WITH THEM?
HOMELAND
YOU WERE WITH HIM WHEN HE DIED?!
HOMELAND
YOU'RE THE SNIPER!
HOMELAND
I LOOK LIKE A FUCKIN SNIPER TO YOU?
I DON'T KNOW WHAT A SNIPER LOOKS LIKE.
WELL THEY DON'T LOOK LIKE ME!
PLAY THE TAPE.
HOMELAND

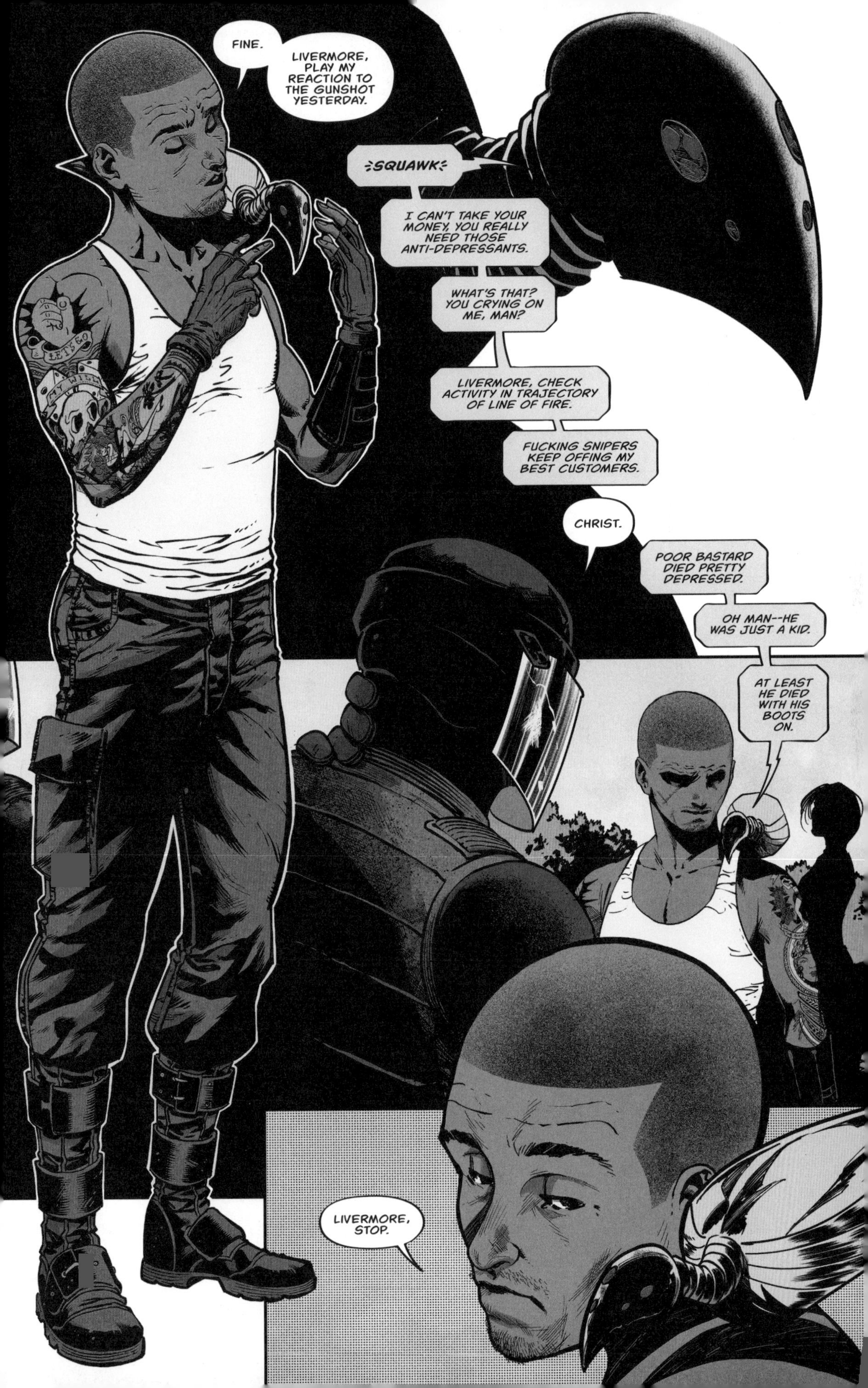
FINE.
LIVERMORE, PLAY MY REACTION TO THE GUNSHOT YESTERDAY.
SQUAWK
I CAN'T TAKE YOUR MONEY, YOU REALLY NEED THOSE ANTI-DEPRESSANTS.
WHAT'S THAT? YOU CRYING ON ME, MAN?
LIVERMORE, CHECK ACTIVITY IN TRAJECTORY OF LINE OF FIRE.
FUCKING SNIPERS KEEP OFFING MY BEST CUSTOMERS.
CHRIST.
POOR BASTARD DIED PRETTY DEPRESSED.
OH MAN--HE WAS JUST A KID.
AT LEAST HE DIED WITH HIS BOOTS ON.
LIVERMORE, STOP.

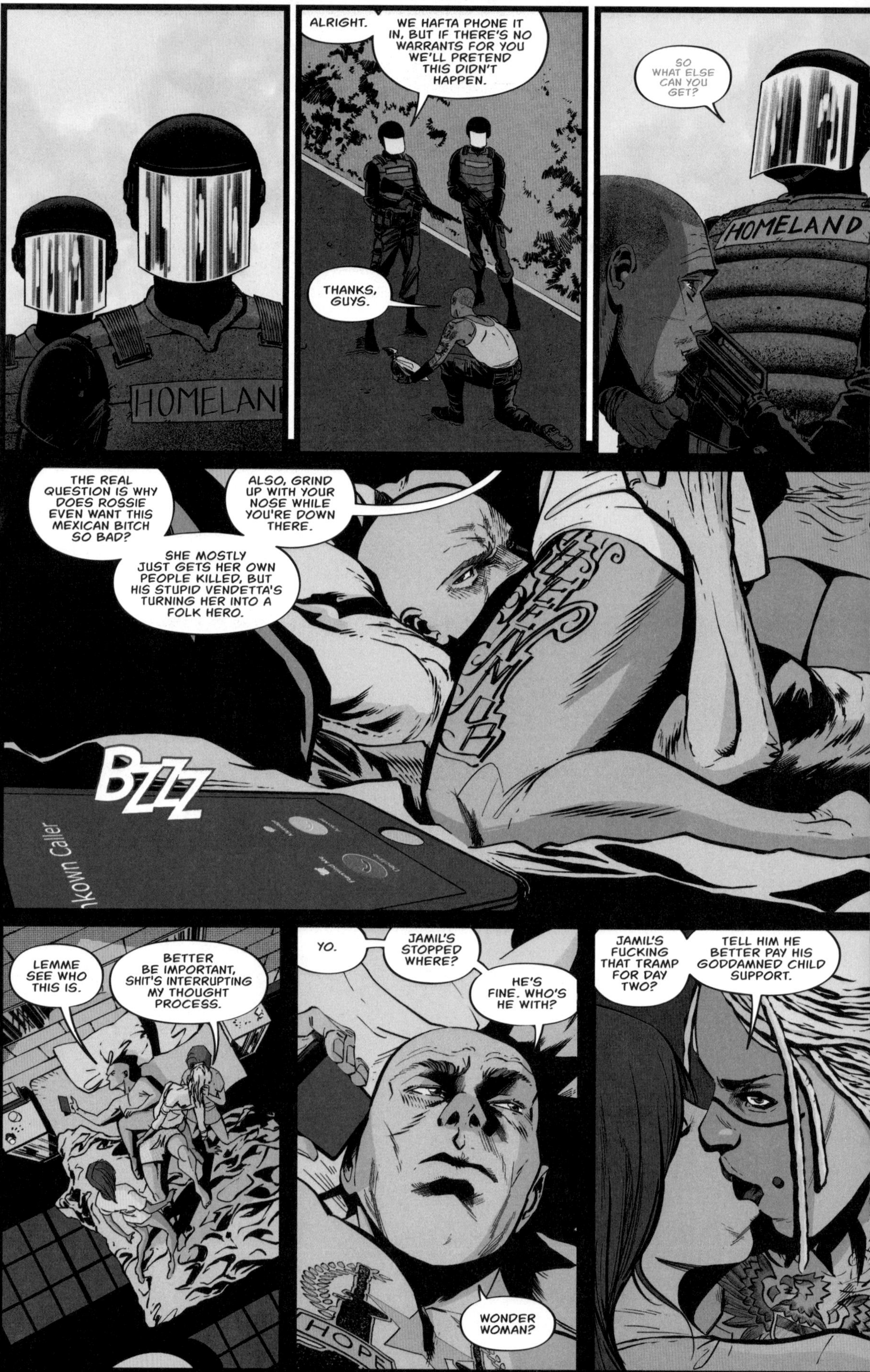

ALRIGHT.
WE HAFTA PHONE IT IN, BUT IF THERE'S NO WARRANTS FOR YOU WE'LL PRETEND THIS DIDN'T HAPPEN.
THANKS, GUYS.
HOMELAND
SO WHAT ELSE CAN YOU GET?
HOMELAND
THE REAL QUESTION IS WHY DOES ROSSIE EVEN WANT THIS MEXICAN BITCH SO BAD?
ALSO, GRIND UP WITH YOUR NOSE WHILE YOU'RE DOWN THERE.
SHE MOSTLY JUST GETS HER OWN PEOPLE KILLED, BUT HIS STUPID VENDETTA'S TURNING HER INTO A FOLK HERO.
BZZZ
nkown Caller
LEMME SEE WHO THIS IS.
BETTER BE IMPORTANT, SHIT'S INTERRUPTING MY THOUGHT PROCESS.
YO.
JAMIL'S STOPPED WHERE?
HE'S FINE. WHO'S HE WITH?
WONDER WOMAN?
JAMIL'S FUCKING THAT TRAMP FOR DAY TWO?
TELL HIM HE BETTER PAY HIS GODDAMNED CHILD SUPPORT.

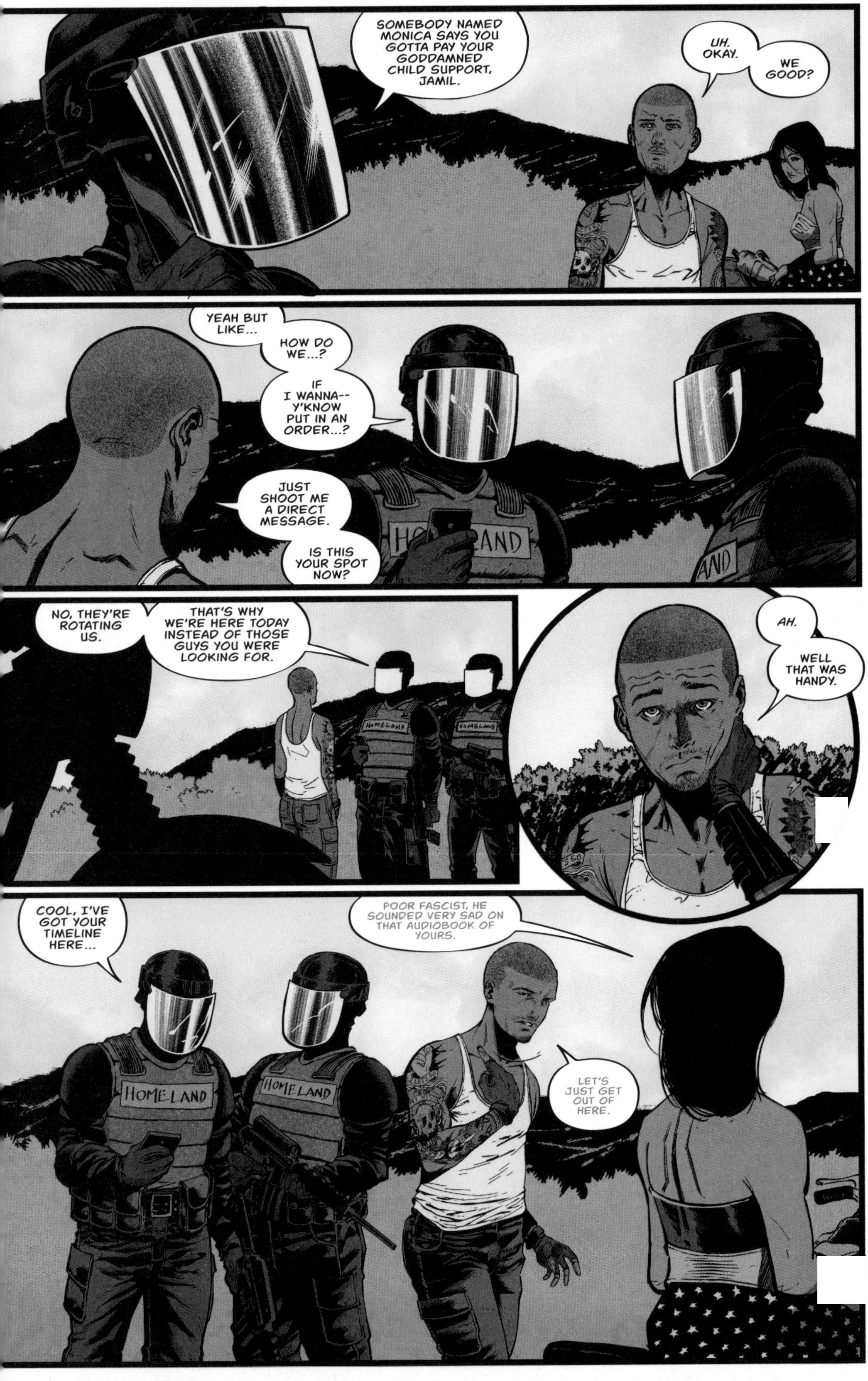
SOMEBODY NAMED MONICA SAYS YOU GOTTA PAY YOUR GODDAMNED CHILD SUPPORT, JAMIL.
UH. OKAY.
WE GOOD?
YEAH BUT LIKE...
HOW DO WE...?
IF I WANNA-- Y'KNOW PUT IN AN ORDER...?
JUST SHOOT ME A DIRECT MESSAGE.
IS THIS YOUR SPOT NOW?
HOMELAND
NO, THEY'RE ROTATING US.
THAT'S WHY WE'RE HERE TODAY INSTEAD OF THOSE GUYS YOU WERE LOOKING FOR.
AH.
WELL THAT WAS HANDY.
COOL, I'VE GOT YOUR TIMELINE HERE...
POOR FASCIST, HE SOUNDED VERY SAD ON THAT AUDIOBOOK OF YOURS.
HOMELAND
HOMELAND
LET'S JUST GET OUT OF HERE.

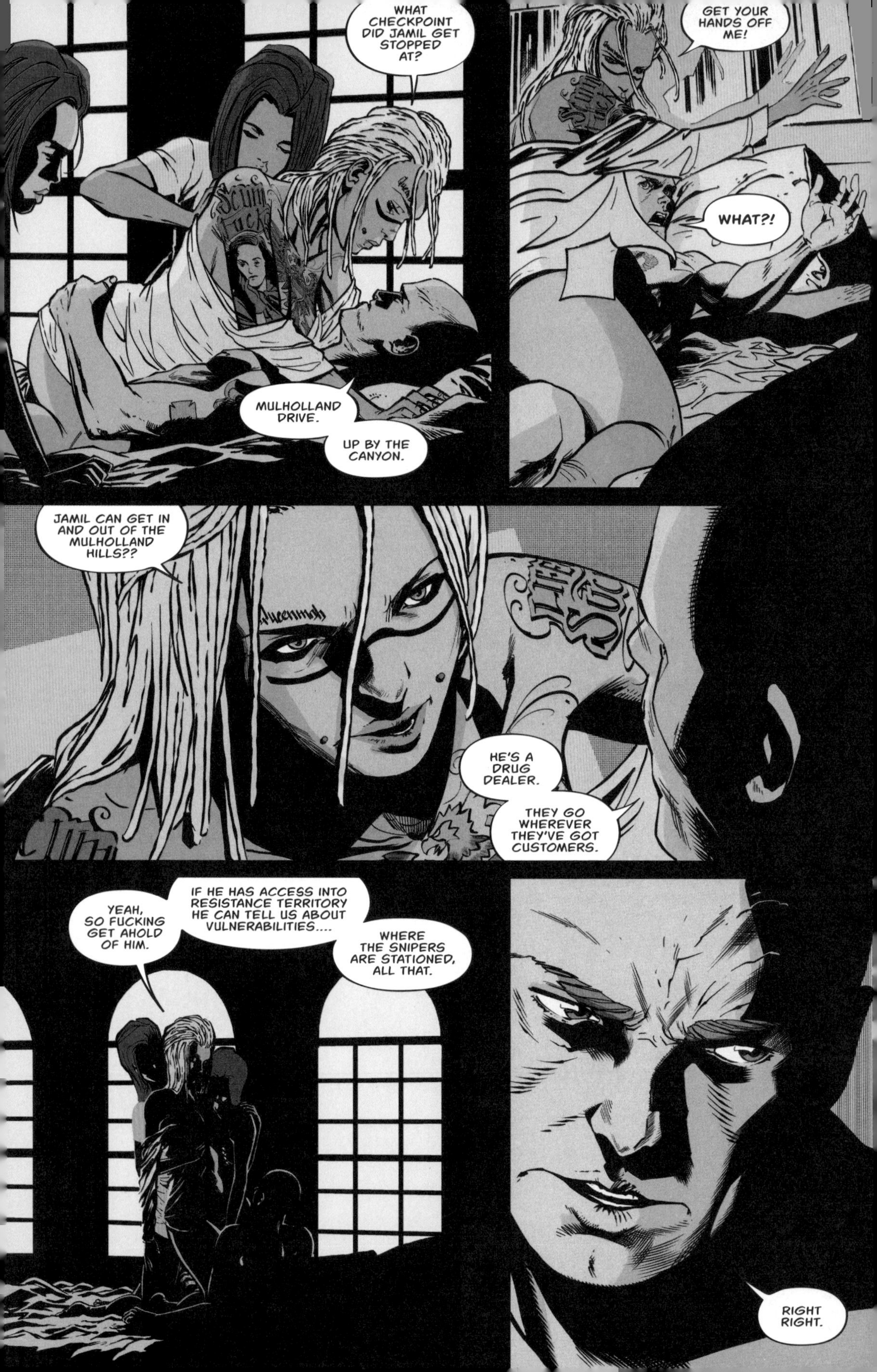
WHAT CHECKPOINT DID JAMIL GET STOPPED AT?
MULHOLLAND DRIVE.
UP BY THE CANYON.
GET YOUR HANDS OFF ME!
WHAT?!
JAMIL CAN GET IN AND OUT OF THE MULHOLLAND HILLS??
HE'S A DRUG DEALER.
THEY GO WHEREVER THEY'VE GOT CUSTOMERS.
YEAH, SO FUCKING GET AHOLD OF HIM.
IF HE HAS ACCESS INTO RESISTANCE TERRITORY HE CAN TELL US ABOUT VULNERABILITIES....
WHERE THE SNIPERS ARE STATIONED, ALL THAT.
RIGHT RIGHT.

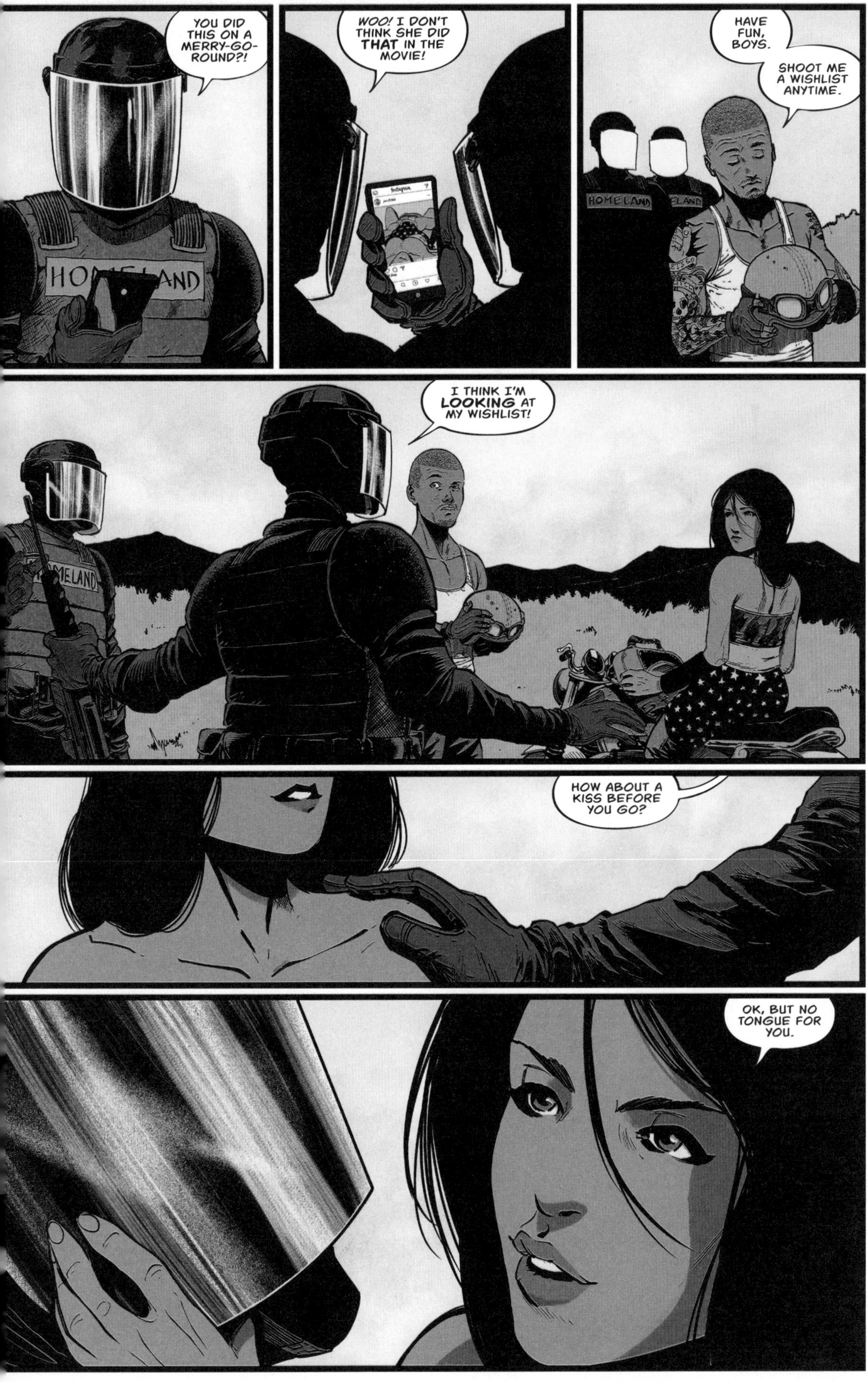

YOU DID THIS ON A MERRY-GO-ROUND?!
WOO! I DON'T THINK SHE DID **THAT** IN THE MOVIE!
HAVE FUN, BOYS.
SHOOT ME A WISHLIST ANYTIME.
HOMELAND
I THINK I'M **LOOKING** AT MY WISHLIST!
HOW ABOUT A KISS BEFORE YOU GO?
OK, BUT NO TONGUE FOR YOU.

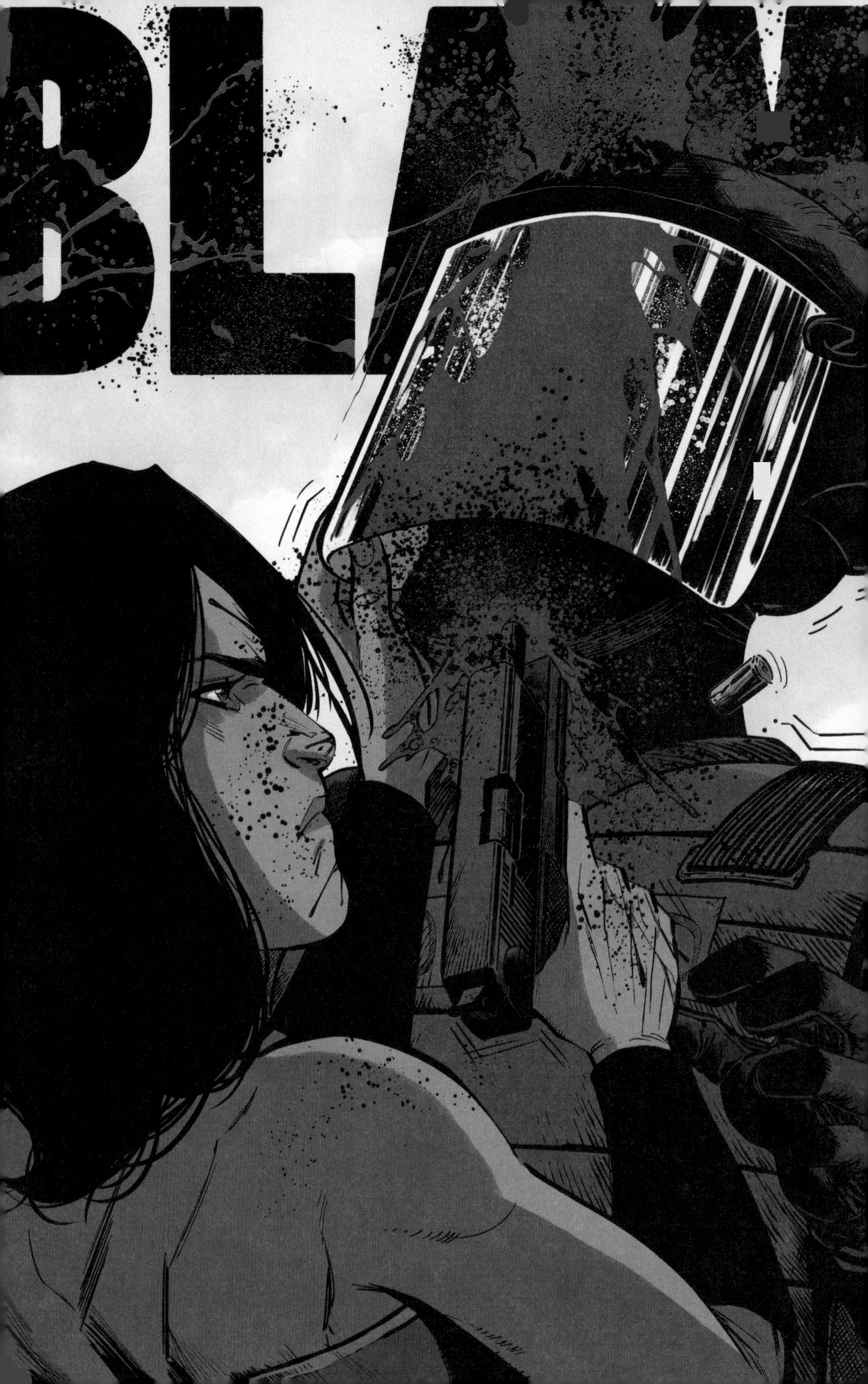
BLA

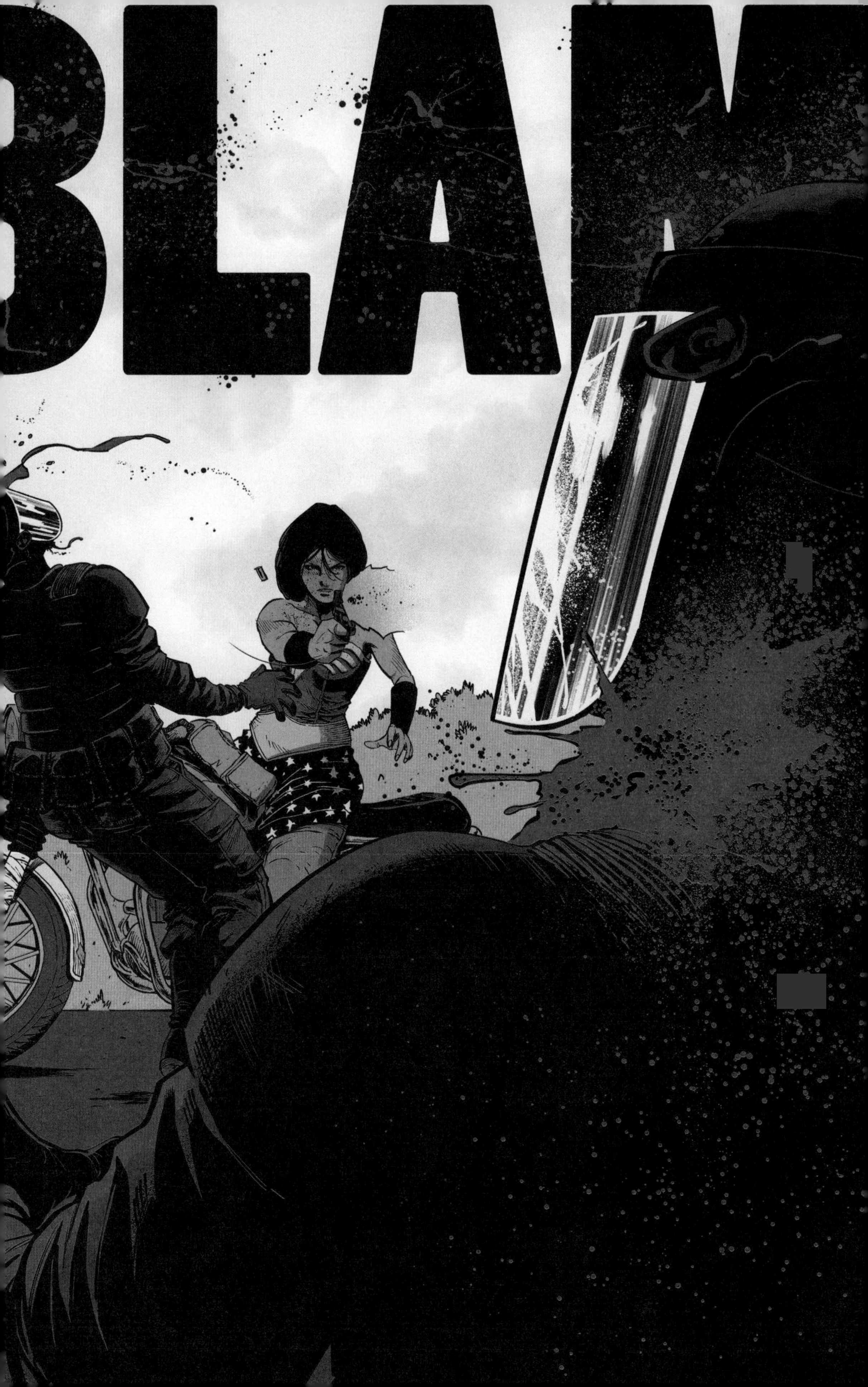
BLAM

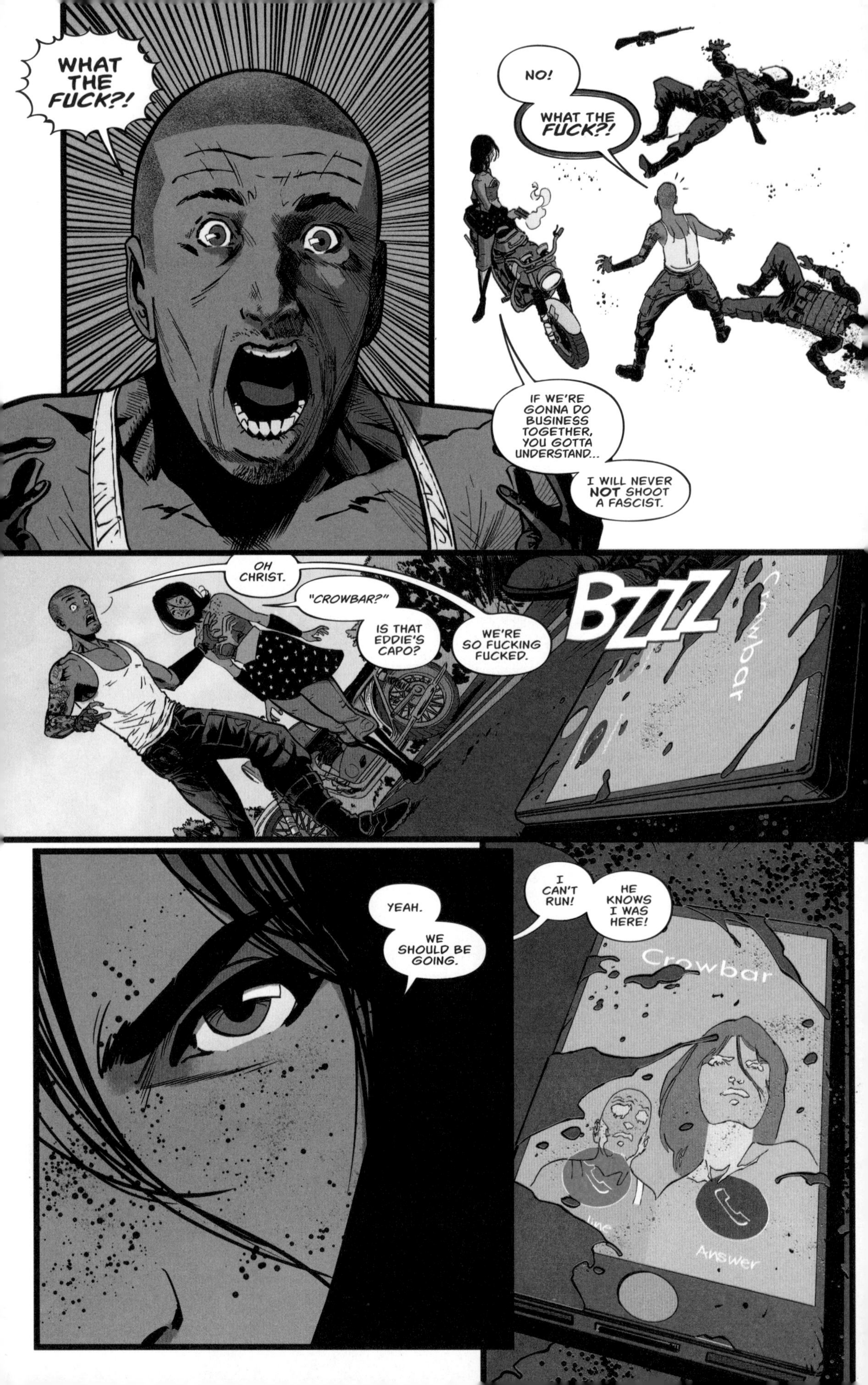

WHAT THE FUCK?!
NO!
WHAT THE FUCK?!
IF WE'RE GONNA DO BUSINESS TOGETHER, YOU GOTTA UNDERSTAND...
I WILL NEVER NOT SHOOT A FASCIST.
OH CHRIST.
"CROWBAR?"
IS THAT EDDIE'S CAPO?
WE'RE SO FUCKING FUCKED.
BZZZ
Crowbar
YEAH.
WE SHOULD BE GOING.
I CAN'T RUN!
HE KNOWS I WAS HERE!
Crowbar
Answer

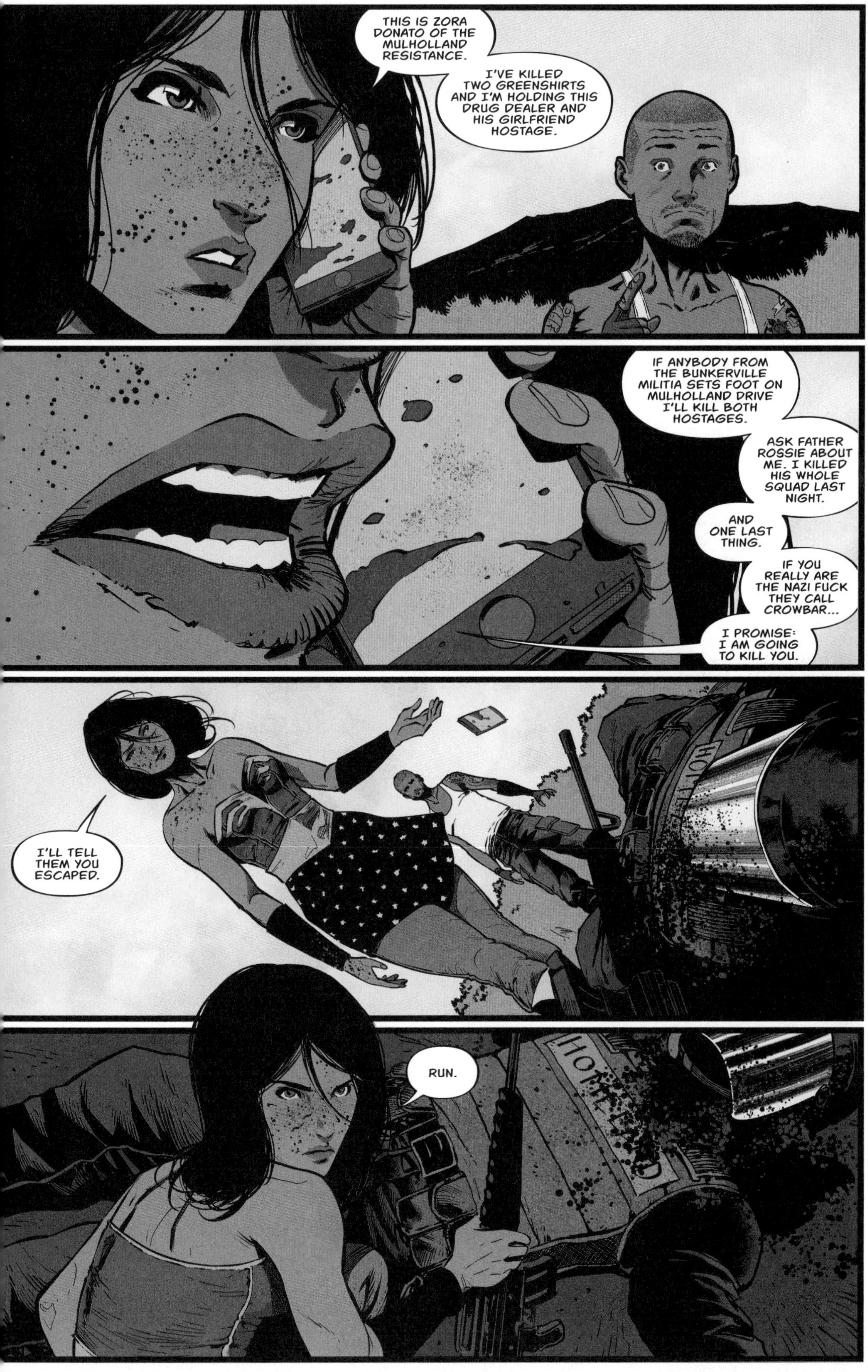

THIS IS ZORA DONATO OF THE MULHOLLAND RESISTANCE.
I'VE KILLED TWO GREENSHIRTS AND I'M HOLDING THIS DRUG DEALER AND HIS GIRLFRIEND HOSTAGE.
IF ANYBODY FROM THE BUNKERVILLE MILITIA SETS FOOT ON MULHOLLAND DRIVE I'LL KILL BOTH HOSTAGES.
ASK FATHER ROSSIE ABOUT ME. I KILLED HIS WHOLE SQUAD LAST NIGHT.
AND ONE LAST THING.
IF YOU REALLY ARE THE NAZI FUCK THEY CALL CROWBAR...
I PROMISE: I AM GOING TO KILL YOU.
I'LL TELL THEM YOU ESCAPED.
RUN.

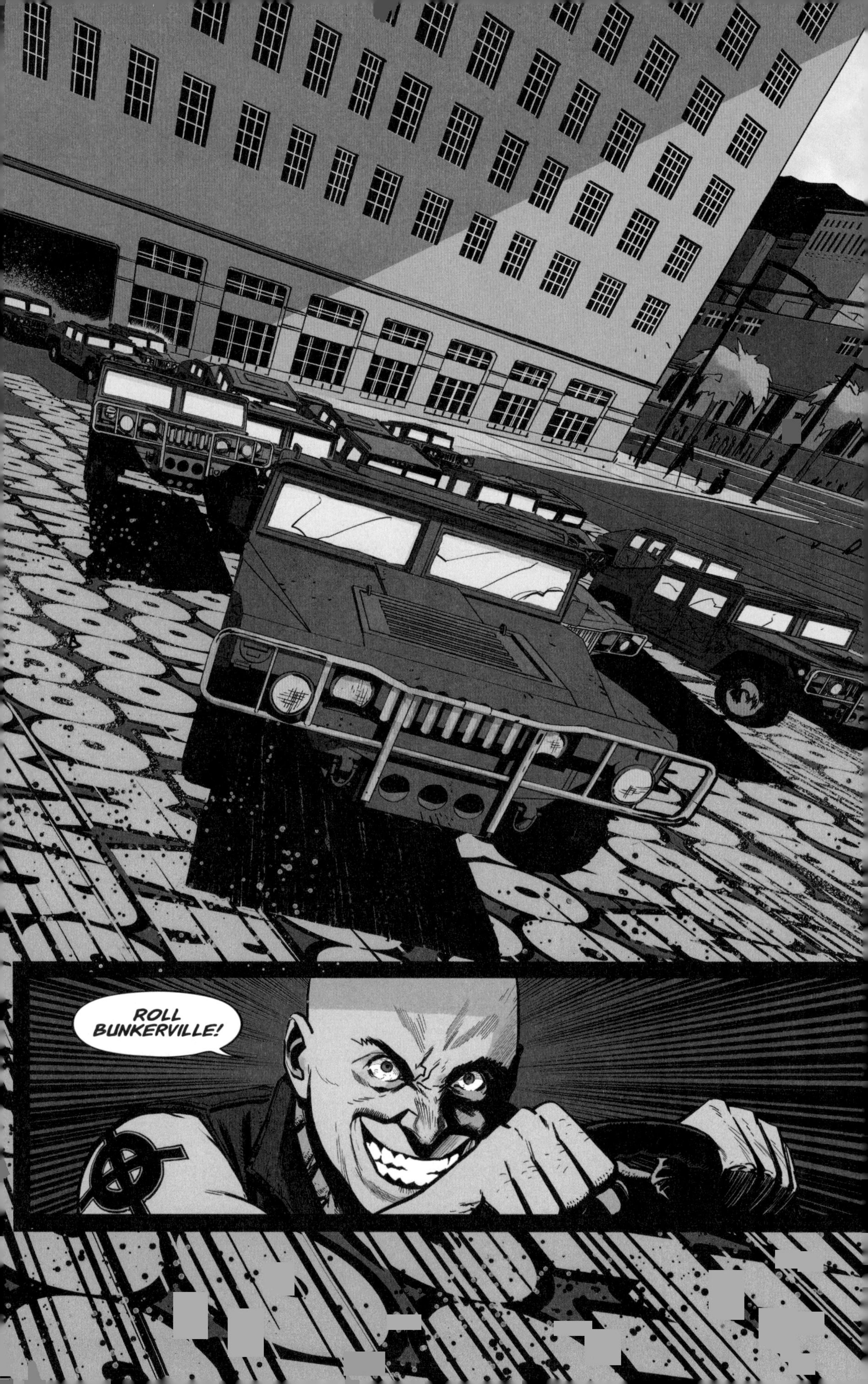
ROLL BUNKERVILLE!

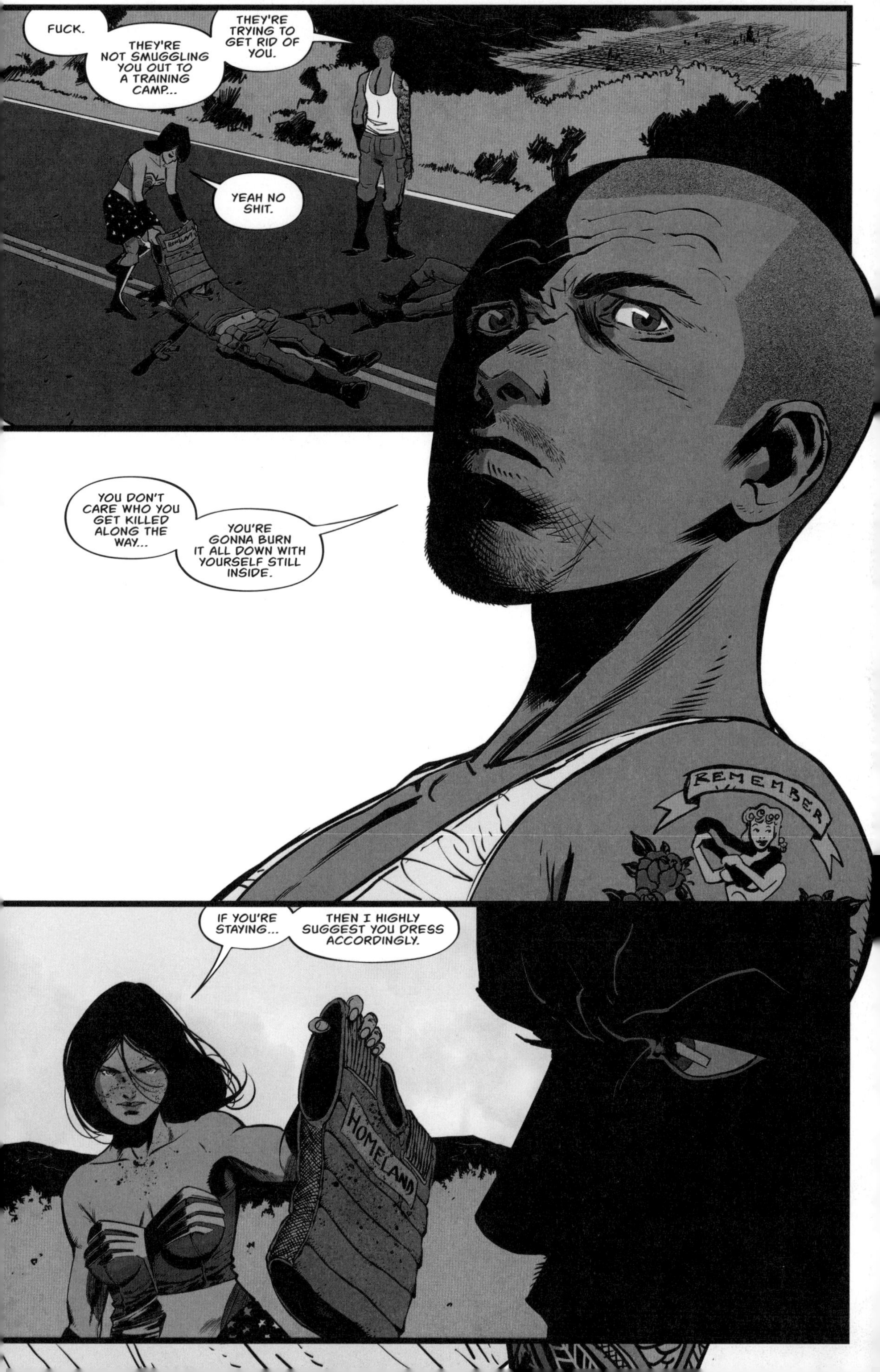
FUCK.
THEY'RE NOT SMUGGLING YOU OUT TO A TRAINING CAMP...
THEY'RE TRYING TO GET RID OF YOU.
YEAH NO SHIT.
YOU DON'T CARE WHO YOU GET KILLED ALONG THE WAY...
YOU'RE GONNA BURN IT ALL DOWN WITH YOURSELF STILL INSIDE.
REMEMBER
IF YOU'RE STAYING...
THEN I HIGHLY SUGGEST YOU DRESS ACCORDINGLY.
HOMELAND

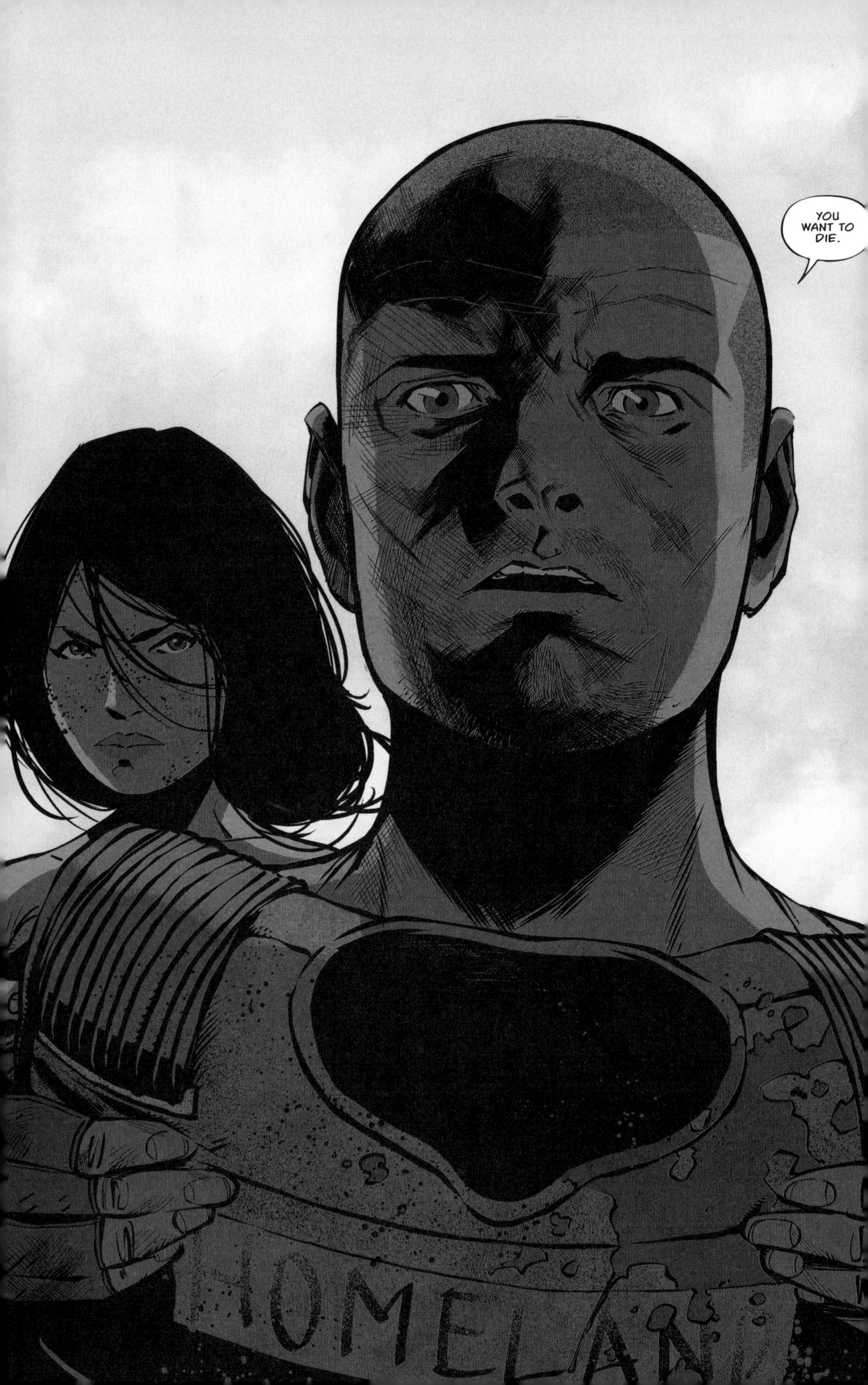
YOU WANT TO DIE.
HOMELAN

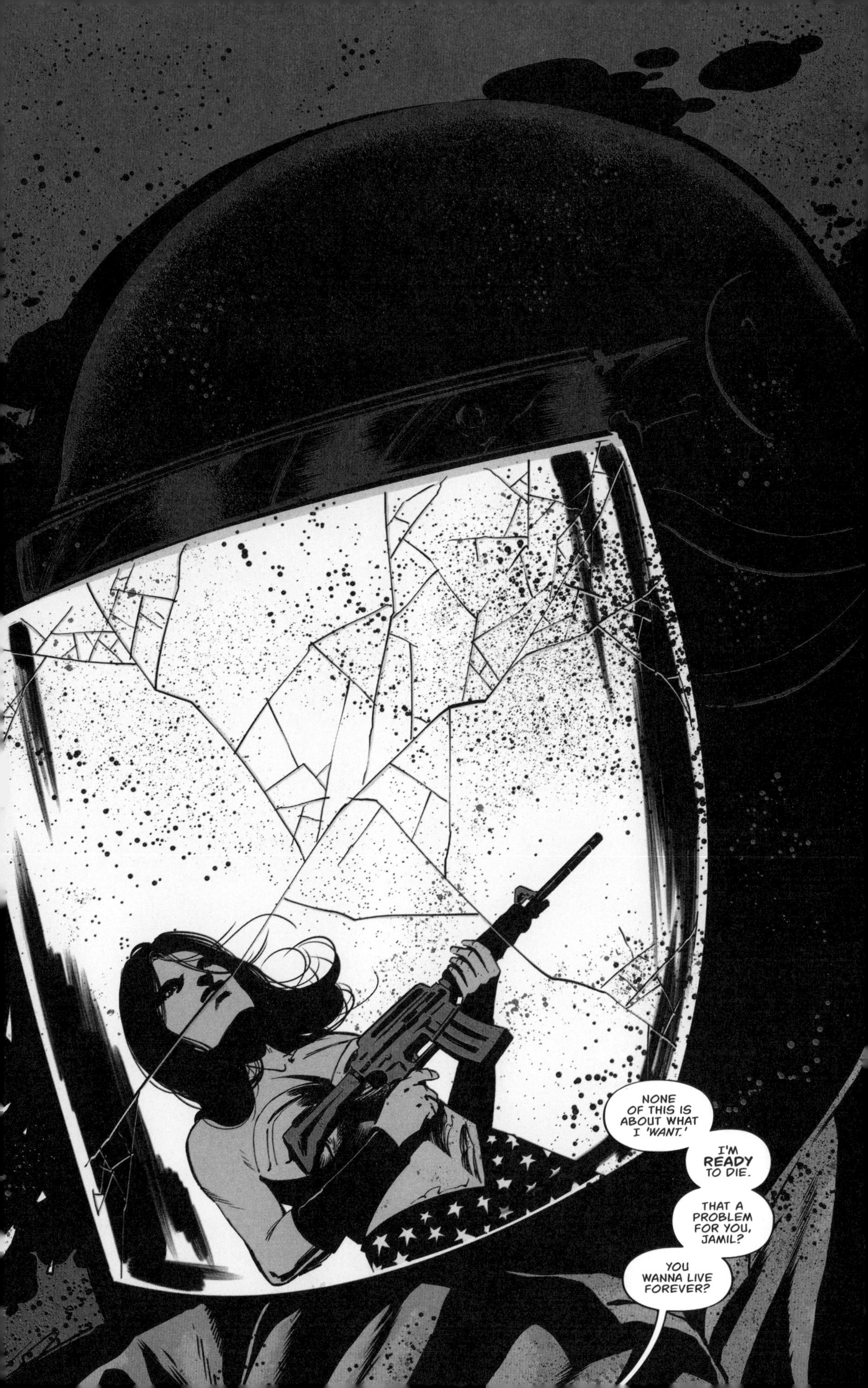
NONE OF THIS IS ABOUT WHAT I 'WANT.'
I'M **READY** TO DIE.
THAT A PROBLEM FOR YOU, JAMIL?
YOU WANNA LIVE FOREVER?

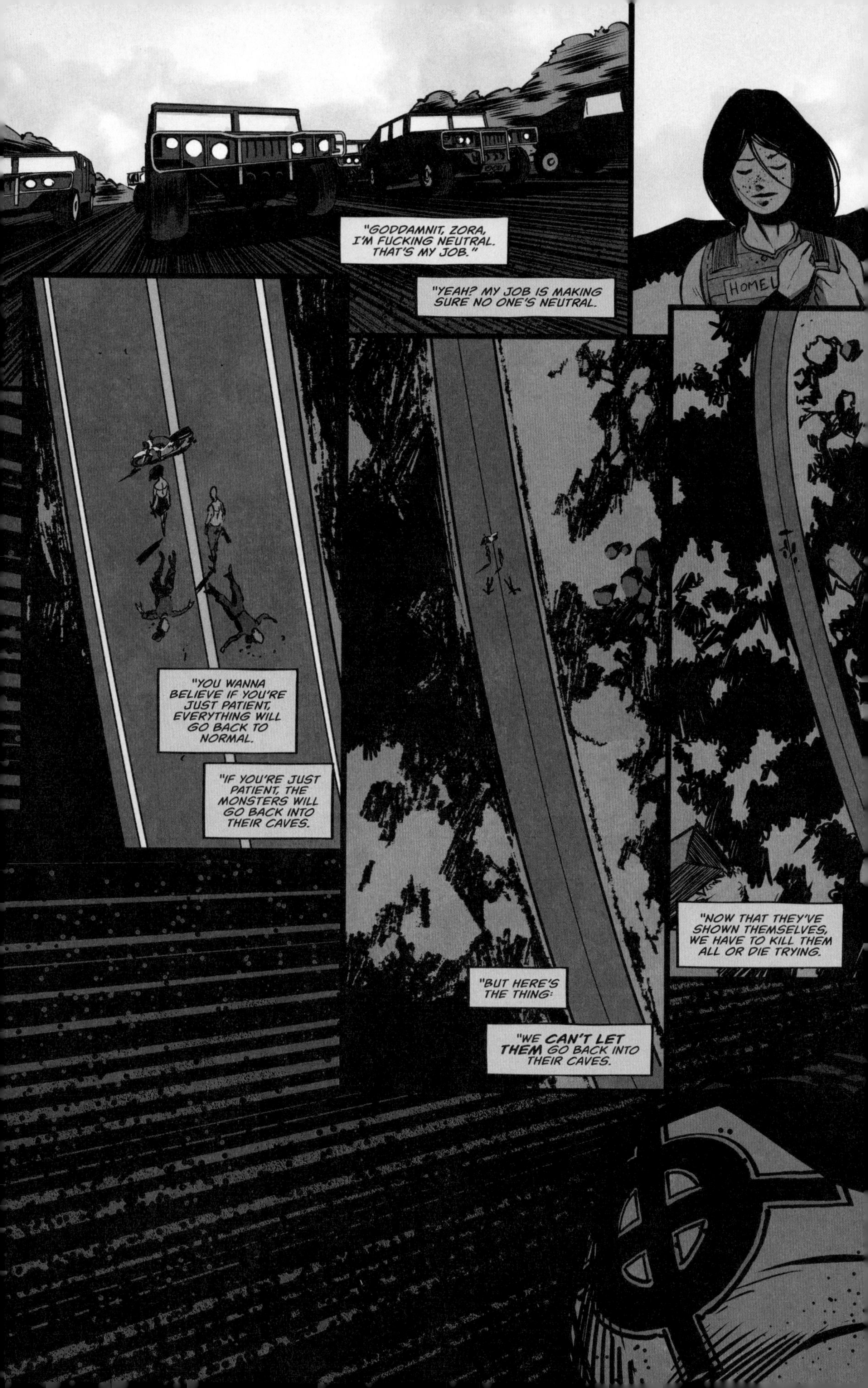
"GODDAMNIT, ZORA, I'M FUCKING NEUTRAL. THAT'S MY JOB."
"YEAH? MY JOB IS MAKING SURE NO ONE'S NEUTRAL.
HOMEL
"YOU WANNA BELIEVE IF YOU'RE JUST PATIENT, EVERYTHING WILL GO BACK TO NORMAL.
"IF YOU'RE JUST PATIENT, THE MONSTERS WILL GO BACK INTO THEIR CAVES.
"BUT HERE'S THE THING:
"WE CAN'T LET THEM GO BACK INTO THEIR CAVES.
"NOW THAT THEY'VE SHOWN THEMSELVES, WE HAVE TO KILL THEM ALL OR DIE TRYING.

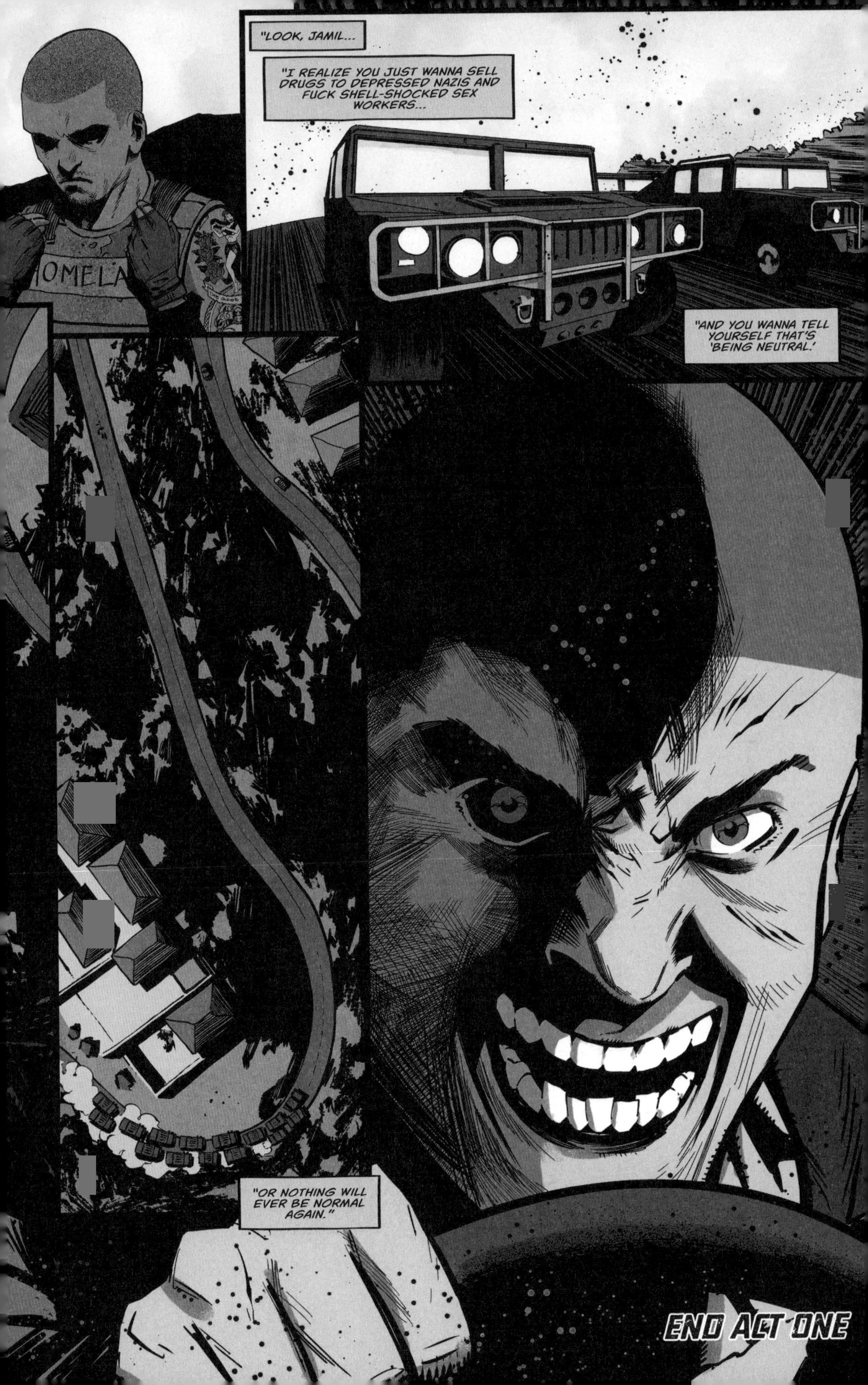
"LOOK, JAMIL...
"I REALIZE YOU JUST WANNA SELL DRUGS TO DEPRESSED NAZIS AND FUCK SHELL-SHOCKED SEX WORKERS...
"AND YOU WANNA TELL YOURSELF THAT'S 'BEING NEUTRAL.'
"OR NOTHING WILL EVER BE NORMAL AGAIN."
END ACT ONE

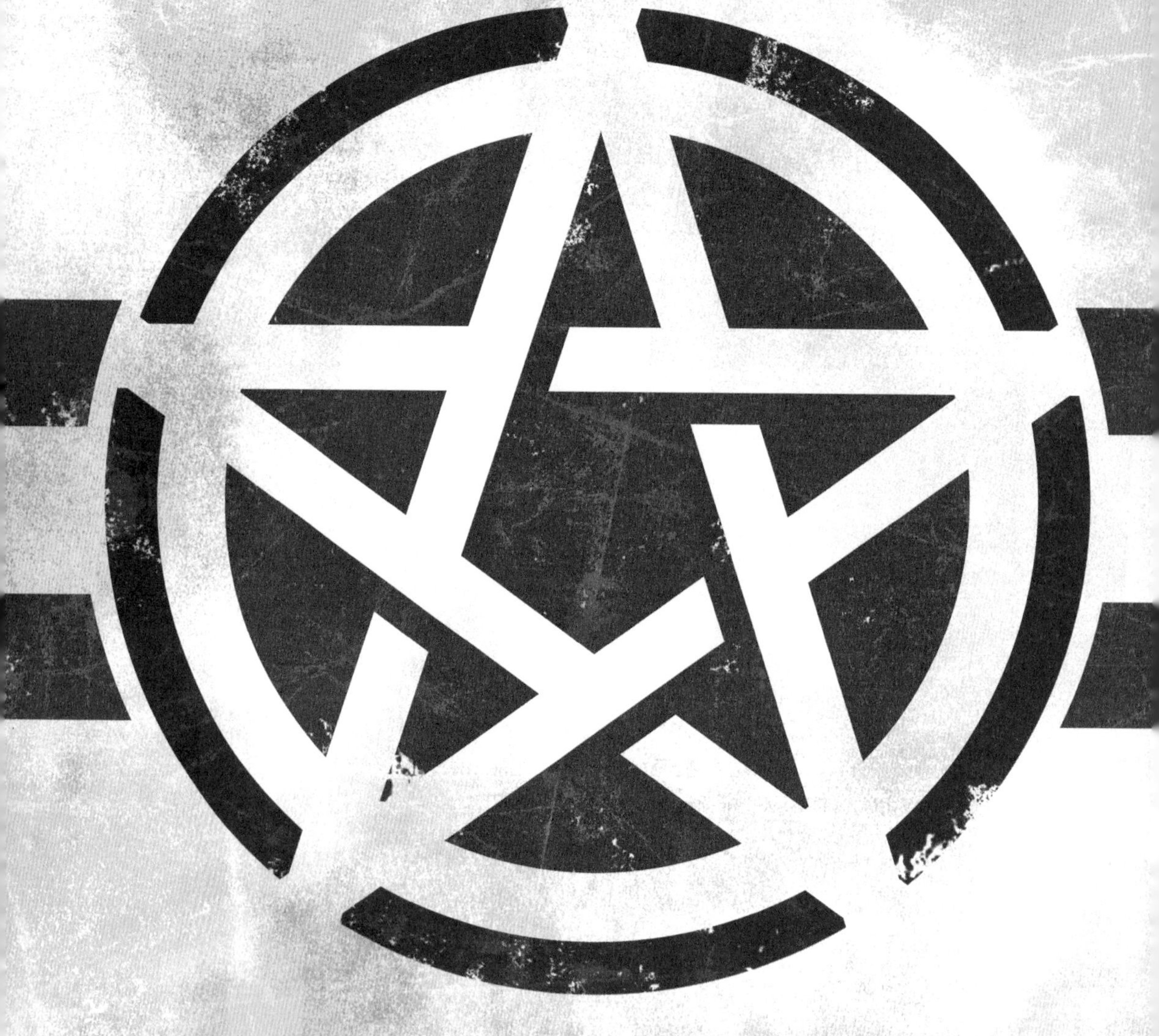

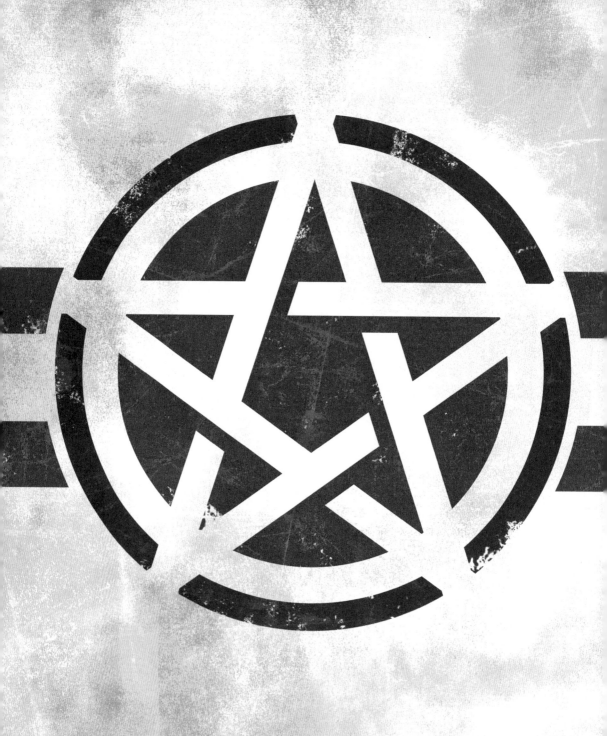

This material originally ran in Paste Magazine July 18, 2017.
To read the article online visit ***www.paste.com***

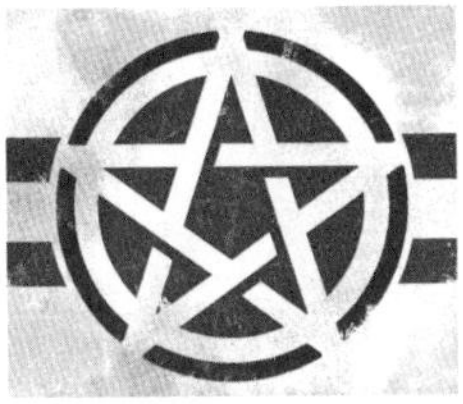

BEHIND THE SCENES

FLAGS OF OUR FACTIONS

artwork by **Robert Anthony Jr.** • *source material written by* **Matteo Pizzolo**
flag designs by **Anthony Jr.** and **Pizzolo**

Symbolism and iconography are critical to any political movement, government, or military force, and so we set out to design emblems and flags for each faction in CALEXIT.

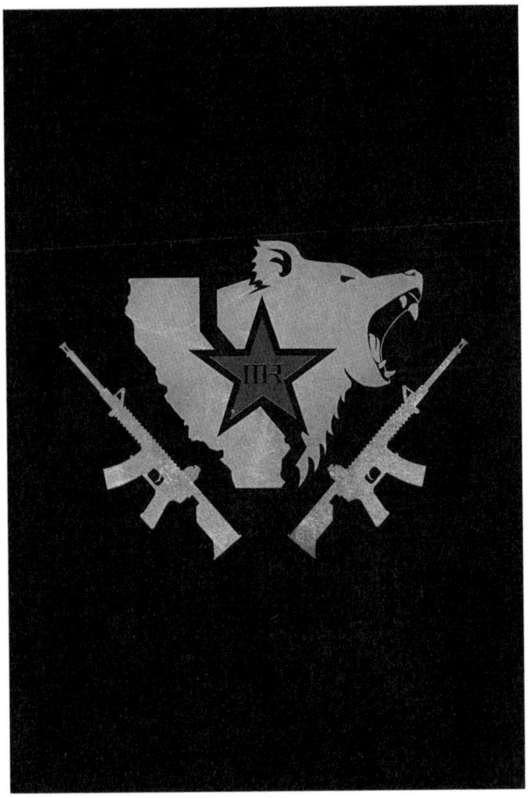

MULHOLLAND RESISTANCE

Mulholland Resistance is an insurgent group fighting back against the occupying forces of US Homeland Security.

MR originally formed in the Mulholland hills north of Hollywood, where caverns were expanded by the US military following the bombing of Pearl Harbor. MR has retained its locally inspired name even as its movement spreads throughout the occupied zones of California.

In terms of the designing, obviously you've got the bear from the Bear Flag Revolt right here, but fiercer than the bear we've come to know from the popular California Republic flag. That flag is from a time when California seceded from Mexico, so the bear harkens back to California's revolutionary ethos from an era before it was even a part of the USA. We felt the ferocious bear is intrinsic to the DNA of California's rebel spirit, and so an extremist rebel group like the Mulholland Resistance would take a great deal of inspiration from it.

The inclusion of assault rifles represents their willingness to engage in armed struggle, inspired by the flags of groups like FARC and Red Army Faction, the red star was also inspired by RAF and the black background representing the group's black bloc/antifa origins.

SOVEREIGN CITIZENS COALITION

Sovereign Citizens Coalition is one of the first factions to break off in the history behind CALEXIT. The initial sequence of events is that the US President passes an executive order to deport all immigrants, the California government in Sacramento refuses to enforce the law and declares California a sanctuary state, and then a set of suburban, rural and exurb regions rebel against Sacramento, declaring themselves the Sovereign Citizens Coalition and cutting off water and agriculture to Los Angeles and San Francisco.

Contrasting the ferocity of the Mulholland Resistance, SCC's emblem is colder and more intimidating. They don't need to engage in armed struggle, they control their own resource-rich land and they can exert their will on others simply by standing firm.

The design of the SCC emblem is inspired by various nativist groups, who tend to use stark graphic lines that signify strength and conviction. The S is formed by the two Cs which conveys that each citizen's sovereignty is derived by the force of their own wills and dedication to the coalition.

PACIFIC COAST SISTER CITIES ALLIANCE

When the SCC forms and cuts off resources to Los Angeles and San Francisco, the Pacific Coast Sister Cities Alliance is founded. Initially running from Chula Vista to Seattle, the PSCSA runs supply lines into Los Angeles and San Francisco, as well as an underground railroad to sneak immigrants out. When Vancouver and, most crucially, Tijuana join the PCSCA, the President feels he can no longer tolerate what is becoming an international conflict and decides he must invade California.

The emblem itself repurposes the Crescent and Star into an S. The Crescent and Star is often considered an Islamic symbol, although it goes back to antiquity. In this case we utilized it to represent the Moslem immigrants who are among the first to be targeted under the President's executive order on immigration, and also as a nod to Battle Of Algiers which was very influential on Calexit.

THE BUNKERVILLE MILITIA

The Bunkerville Militia is an armed resistance group formed in solidarity with the SCC in direct opposition to the Mulholland Resistance. While the Federal Government's Homeland Security forces are focused on holding the cities, executing counter-insurgency operations, and coercing local authorities to implement immigration law, TBM engages in aggressive armed strikes on Mulholland Resistance and PCSCA positions.

The TBM design merges traditional American patriotism with the trappings of Fascism, with the assault rifle demonstrating TBM's fearlessness in using deadly means to achieve their ends. The violent image wrapped in olive branches denotes TBM's mantra of peace through militancy.

HOMELAND OCCUPATION

The Homeland Occupation flag is used by Homeland Security in rebel cities the US Government is holding with an occupying force. The single star held in place by red stripes indicates the Federal Government's assertion that California remains a state under its control.

EDITORIAL ESSAY *by* **Matteo Pizzolo**

You don't have to live in California very long before you wind up in conversations about secession. Even though California is a reliable "blue state," it's deeply diverse—so whenever there's a new Presidential election, regardless of who wins, there's always chatter that California should secede. "*We have the sixth largest economy in the world, we'd be bigger than France!,*" etc. And, hell, there's some good arguments for it.

But, from my point of view, any secession would likely lead to a civil war *within* California before the US military could even get their boots on.

Lots of people think about California strictly in terms of the (generally liberal) metropolitan cities, but that's a geographically tiny portion of the state. Political views get more complicated as you leave those major cities and head into the parts of the state with all the water and pipelines and agriculture that the cities rely on. Add immigration into the mix? Powderkeg. Political passion/rage is as bipartisan in California as it is in the rest of the country.

In fact, California might just be a pretty good microcosm of the country as a whole.

And that's the premise we were working from when we cooked up the idea of CALEXIT back in the halcyon days of 2016.

We didn't know the winning Presidential candidate would lose California by nearly 2-to-1, a margin of almost 3.5 million votes.

We didn't know the day after the President took office, the largest mass demonstration in history would occur, and the state with the largest turnout would be California.

We didn't know that California's two major international airports, LAX and SFO, would be blockaded by furious protesters.

We didn't know there would be an actual CALEXIT movement, that it would be exposed as a Russian scam, or that it would respawn and launch again under new leadership.

We didn't know the US would pull out of the Paris Climate Accord and California would respond by forming an alliance with other states, signing a climate deal direct with China.

Or that the President would threaten to deputize the National Guard.

I think one thing we can all agree on is that shit's been hurtling into the fan at an accelerated pace lately.

So, as we work on the comic, it's also constantly being recontextualized in real time. Our key responsibility is to serve the story and follow our characters, but this is all happening in a historical time and place of real significance.

We don't want anyone to put this book down more depressed than they picked it up, so we put together a backmatter section that aims to be more constructive and inspiring by talking to folks we consider fascinating and asking them what they're doing, what's inspiring them, and what do they see as actions people can take right now to effect change.

I reached out to a lot of people with the question: "can I interview you for the back of a comic book called Calexit that's about California going to war against the US government?" Shockingly, some people said yes and I'm extremely grateful to them for it.

Because I really enjoy long, deep-dive conversations, the interviews ran too long to publish in their entirety here—so we are pulling excerpts for publication in the comic and we will post the complete transcripts online at calexitcomic.com

This isn't a place where I'm trying to shove a bunch of political rhetoric down readers' throats, but I do feel comics are such a unique community that the back of a book like this can be a cool and unique place to open a dialogue. If you have an opinion on the book and/or the backmatter that you'd like to share, you can email us at calexit@blackmaskstudios.com.

Onward! -Pizzolo

Editorial and Interview section Design, Layout and Book Production by **Phil Smith**

CONVERSATIONS WITH PEOPLE I FIND INTERESTING

This conversation has been lightly edited and excerpted from a much longer interview.
For the complete, unabridged interview please visit ***www.calexitcomic.com***

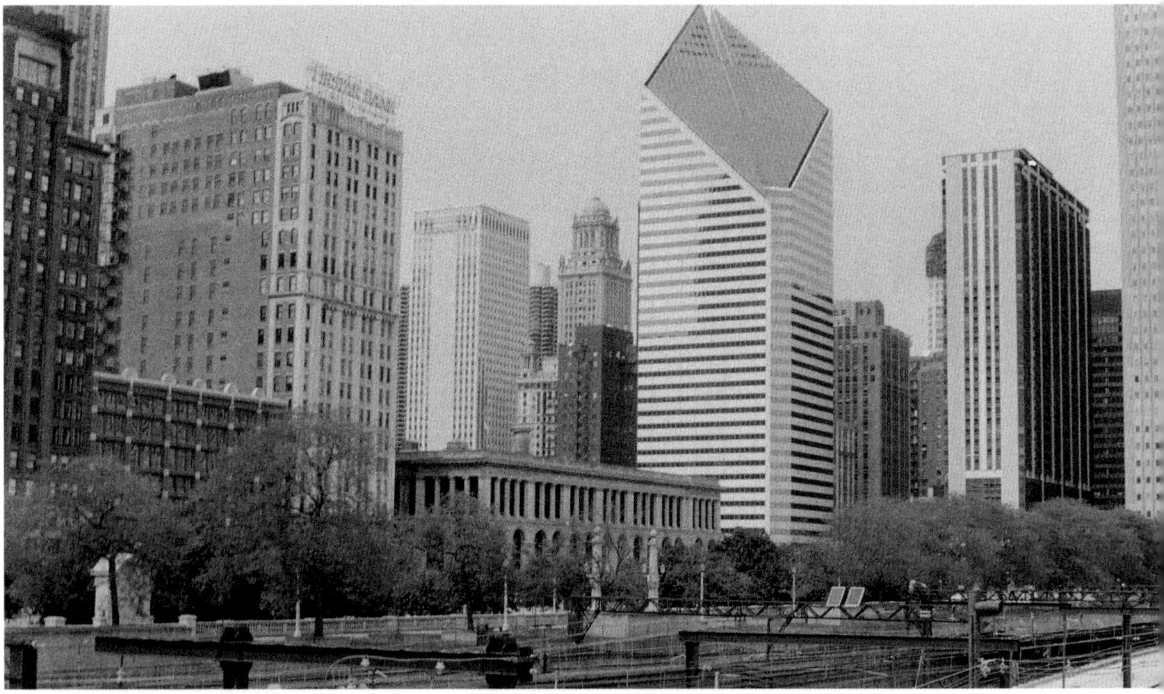

CONVERSATIONS WITH PEOPLE I FIND INTERESTING

AMANDA WEAVER

Interview by **Matteo Pizzolo**

"I was not political at all until my last year o grad school. I found these organizers and went to this training, and I came back furious.

Pizzolo: Can you start by telling us what Reclaim Chicago is and how you became involved with it?

Amanda Weaver: Sure, Reclaim Chicago is a people-led grassroots movement. It's devoted to reclaiming Chicago and Illinois governments from the grip of corporate interests and the very wealthy. It was formed with the support of an organization called The People's Lobby and National Nurses United.

The partnership and Reclaim launched primarily to have an effect in the 2015 Chicago municipal election and our plan at that time was to affect ward levels-- in Chicago we have alderman who are connected to wards that usually span one neighborhood sometimes two, and there's fifty of them in the city.

So we endorsed a bunch of candidates, and the way that we work is we activate members of the union, nurses, and c grassroots communities to knock on doors and get out to ta about the issues and the vision that we have for our city, a to connect a politician with that vision, and we talk about w we believe the politician or elected official is going to work that vision.

I started as a student organizer running a campaign agair the administration where I was going to grad school. It w around the cost of meal plans and how that was directly ti to low-income students being forced to give their scholarsh money to this corporation Aramark for a term's worth of fo that they likely weren't going to eat. And that was somethin care a lot about because I am a first-generation college gra grew up really low income in New Hampshire, college me was always the way I was going to escape and do bet than my parents did... and instead what I ended up with is ures in student loan debt.

have a hundred-fifty thousand dollars in college debt, and got activated into organizing as a grad student because I arted reading Saul Alinsky and I was there in the birthplace modern organizing… and I was just really angry. I wanted do something about it and try and work with students so at they maybe would get a little less screwed than I felt like ad been.

P: So with the protest you organized around the meal plan, hat was the process?

W: I was not political at all until my last year of grad school. ound these organizers and I went to this training run by a tional organization called People's Action, and I came back rious.

e core methodology that I was trained in is that *you share ur story and ask other people about theirs,* we call them ne-to-ones.'

said to the team that I was working with at the time that I as going to go do forty of these conversations, these one-to-es, in a month's time. So when I sat down on campus and I d these forty one-to-ones, in more than half of them people ought up the meal plan and how it was going to devastate e plan that they had for how to pay for college because it as going to cost them up to five thousand dollars more than ey were planning. If you were a freshman or sophomore, t only were you required to live on campus (so you couldn't en find cheaper housing), but since you lived on campus u were required to have this unlimited-access meal plan at nobody actually wanted. For some students, especially w-income students, it was going to cost them almost their tire scholarships.

ter hearing this time and time again, I got all the folks who ere really angry about this into a room together and we ked about why this is happening, we talked about the fact at the university had cut a deal with Aramark, which is a very g corporation who was making money off of us and making oney especially from the low-income students. We were ally angry about that, and so we started a campaign at that int. There were about twenty-five people in the room, half those folks formed a core team. We did several different ngs, we didn't win… what I learned very quickly from this mpaign was just how much corporate power is entrenched our college campuses. The contract had already been gned before students even got wind of it. But we got a lot news coverage, we got the community involved, and the dents we organized went on to continue protesting and hieved some pretty significant victories on campus after me there.

P: And after graduating you joined Reclaim Chicago? What as that transition like?

V: I started doing very similar things, but on more community-sed issues. I organized the Section 8 in the neighborhood at I live in and I was working to form a Tenants Association, ich was also just a really cool way to screw with corporate wer because it was public housing being run by a private rporation, so we were able to target them and target some the State Board—and we were able to get people's broken oves replaced, get working locks and security cameras, t things people needed for basic living conditions. We've so been working on some statewide policy, and I was ing direct actions like recruiting membership and building ders, doing some lobbying around state revenue bills. And en, after my first year of organizing, we started doing direct

political work.

We started a 501(c)4, which gave us the legal entity to be able to endorse and work for candidates. And that's the first time I ever worked on an electoral campaign, first time I ever knocked doors, and for me it was just contagious. I loved it. I loved being able to connect with people and have a deep conversation in five minutes, and talk about vision and values and either try and recruit them or at least get their vote.

And so that's when I started moving more into doing electoral work, which is primarily what I do now: recruiting grassroots leadership to actually run for local and state office.

MP: Were you using the same skillsets to organize on the community level that you'd learned from campus organizing?

AW: Yeah, it's sitting down with people and asking about their concerns--immediately connected to their housing but also getting to know them, and where they came from and what are their visions for themselves and their family. And what do they wish their community had.

Really our main push is getting to know people, and I think society just beats us down to believe that we're not leaders and we're not smart enough or good enough to be in the public arena. So a lot of an organizer's jobs is to hear people's stories, share our story, and push people to take up space in the public arena and actually become a leader.

That can mean you organize your block, you organize your building, maybe you organize your entire ward and run for alderman. No matter what the level is, we want people to have power and to be building it and to be heard in our organization and be heard in society at large.

MP: And now you work as part of a 501(c)4 and also a PAC, how do you organize on those levels?

AW: Our organization and a few others just did a two hundred mile march from Chicago to our state capital in Springfield to call attention to the fact that Illinois hasn't had a budget in two years--which is a record for the country--and the true cost on people's lives of that. And then we did a seven-hundred person takeover of the capitol, and thirty-five were busted for civil disobedience, shutting down the governor's office. So we're still doing all of that, and even though we're electing people, we're still holding them accountable when they get into office. Because we don't do all this work to have you sell us out, and for the most part the people that we're electing are great and co-conspiring with us. We're still doing the deep relationships, the direct action, shutting shit down when it takes that. Elections are the newest tool in the toolbox of what we've been doing over the last five years.

MP: The door knocking thing is so interesting to me. I mean, I don't even like answering my own door, let alone walking up to a stranger's door and knocking. What was it like the first you did it?

AW: Yeah, the first time I did it was really terrifying.

I think it's really scary because overwhelmingly people don't want to answer their doors or knock on stranger's doors. But after the first good conversation, it almost becomes addictive. The first good conversation where someone engages with you, when it's like *'yes I'm totally down with your vision, I'm totally down with your candidate,'* it's just a mini-victory and I feel like right now we're in it for the long haul, so every little mini victory feels great.

I grew up in New Hampshire, I'm white, I grew up in an

overwhelmingly white community. And the first election that I knocked doors was in the south suburbs, which is mostly middle-class African-American families. So it was really transformative for me, to be knocking on doors talking about issues that connected us. Like around gun violence, because the community I can afford to live in has a lot of gun violence. And we connected on budget and food stamps... and I had to take big risks to say that my family grew up on food stamps, and then to have people saying *'wow.'* I think that there's this assumption based on the dominant narrative that white people don't use food stamps, so I just like taking those risks and having conversations and people moving and then seeing some of those people show up to volunteer because of conversations and invitations I was offering them. It felt like, *'okay this isn't just something we're saying works, I'm seeing it happen in front of me'* and those relationships were really meaningful for me. So I just kept doing it even though it was really uncomfortable.

We're aiming for a five to eight minute conversation, whereas typically an electoral campaign will tell you to do a two-minute conversation. They really want you to get the talking points out and get the idea of how is the person voting, but we're trying to build permanent infrastructure and a permanent organization for people to be a part of.

I think there's this "Savior Candidate" dynamic out there. Like, *'we have one great progressive idealistic person, if we elect them then everything's going to be great.'* And that's not the reality.

So it's really important for us to have a longer conversation and start the politicizing process of *'here's what's wrong with our state'* or *'here's what's wrong with our city, do you agree? how is that showing up in your life?'* Like here's some things we can do about it and one of them is electing this person, but there's like three other things that you can be a part of, because we are going to elect this person--that's the goal for these six months--but once we elect them, we have to support them and be in the streets and rallying support for the stuff that you know overwhelmingly the majority of people in elected office don't agree with... we have to make sure we're gonna keep them in office, so we have to keep our neighbors understanding that this person is fighting the fight but it's a long way away. And then we have to elect more people like them, so they can actually start passing stuff we care about.

So for us that's why we do the five to ten minute conversation, because there's a longer term goal than just electing one person.

MP: I know that a lot of organizing focuses on down-ballot elections and midterms and you mentioned aldermans etc. Why are those smaller, less glamorous elections important?

AW: Yeah, I think it's the only way that we can change anything. I think it's very very important. It's absolutely how we got to the place that we did now in our elections. There was a planned-out strategy to take over local seats and to build a bench to have what we have now--which isn't working for people. We can't take forty years to get there, but we have to be planning four and six and eight years out, so that we're recruiting people who can build enough power to combat the big money.

You can't just like run for Congress one day--I know people do that, but overwhelmingly those people aren't successful. It's usually people being a part of a system and moving up, and I think many of us want to create the world where people can run for Congress based on their values and merit and experience and just get in, but for right now I think we have to live in the world as it is and it takes building up yo credentials and building up your people power.

And also, those down-ballot elections absolutely affect o lives. Much of the legislation in this very turbulent world tha being overturned at the federal level will affect us, but, f example, the minimum wage is something that you can affe at your state level, actually many municipalities have t ability to do it.

I think that's a big thing: that we need to elect people to schc boards and library boards and local councils, because it's t only way we're going to be able to guard against privatizati of every public good.

And it's also winnable. It's really hard to knock as many doc and to raise enough money to get in everybody's mailbox, b if you're building your network and running for school coun and now everybody in that school knows who you are and y build a reputation, then it becomes a little bit easier and mc feasible in two years to run for your state representative alderman. So we're doing candidate training fairly frequent and it's very little about how to run a campaign but more li *'let's look at what you currently have as far as a network, a what can you build by the next election to run for somethi you can actually win.'*

MP: If someone is new to organizing and they haven't be super politically active before but now they suddenly feel t need to participate, what do you think are the best first ste for them?

AW: I think finding the thing that's mostly in your backya has been the best for me. I got to organize on my campus was comfortable there, I knew people and I got to know a more people.

Find a good meeting that's local and that is connected to doi something after the meeting. Because there's lots of plac to talk about the crisis, but I think the thing that is giving r hope is that we're moving, so we're not just having meetin to talk about how bad things are or what we think we shou do. We're having meetings that are about the work, and th we're going out to do the work. So I think the more you c find a place that provides that for you, once you take the fi risk of showing up it just starts becoming a routine and a lit bit contagious.

In addition to getting plugged in, for me... I grew up in pove and now I'm in all this debt because of the way that the wo works, and it's not working for me and that's why I get and I do this work. I think it's really important to find wc that's connected to your personal stories, because we all g busy--all of us have other things to do when it all gets rea overwhelming, but if you're doing something that's rea connected to what you're angry about in your gut... it's goi to keep you going to that meeting or picking up the clipboar If you can say *'this is a thing that's directly impacting me an have to fight back,'* I think that's the most important thing. T reason why I love working with this organization so much because I've been angry for a long time and now I get to something about that.

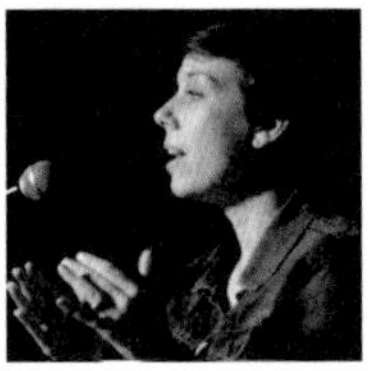

Amanda Weaver is a political activist and commu organizer based in Chicago. For more informat follow her on Twitter **@weavermanda**

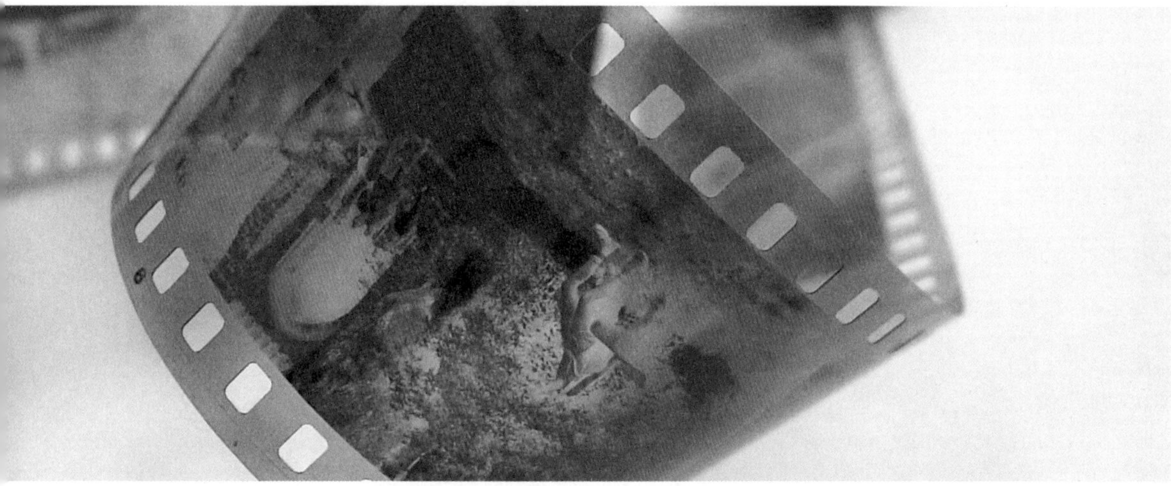

CONVERSATIONS WITH PEOPLE I FIND INTERESTING

LEXI ALEXANDER

***Interview by* Matteo Pizzolo**

"In history, no oppression has ever changed until eople got really angry and did something."

izzolo: So I know a lot of your activism takes place on social edia and interpersonally as opposed to making overtly olitical movies, but do you feel your politics influence your t subtextually?

exi Alexander: Well there's really two sides to being a mmaker: when I'm a hired gun, my political point of view oesn't really matter. I mean, I can influence it… for example ith *The Punisher*. When I went on my second meeting for *he Punisher*, we were discussing the vision and what it nould be like with both Marvel and Lionsgate. Well, the day efore, The Virginia Tech shooting happened. And I happened see a news report where the shooter had a Punisher poster his room.

nd I think I even mentioned it to them, that doesn't mean at anybody in a suit now doesn't want to make the movie, nd even I didn't think we shouldn't make this movie, but what as important to me is that it wasn't a grounded, *'oh this could appen like right here, next door'* type movie. Because also, me, that wasn't what the Punisher comic books were about. ney were so over the top. The violence is so over the top. I ept saying to people *'you can't actually break somebody's ce with a fist,'* and I would know!

o the fact that we put this over-the-top, almost cartoonish olence in it--which wasn't something I invented, a lot of the ames were taken right out of the comic book--but that choice was I think my political influence in terms of *'listen, there's no way I'm going to make the Punisher a documentary-style shoot-em-up,'* especially not after seeing a guy shoot up an entire school.

But on things like *Supergirl*, the showrunner is the boss, really the person who decides what's written in the script. It's nothing I complain about, it's kind of nice sometimes to be the person that brings in a kind of cool stylish way to interpret somebody else's work.

In movies, when it's a studio movie like *The Punisher*, that was obviously based on something so it's also the case that I'm not going to make it completely political in my point of view. I would say *Green Street* definitely, that was more of a writer-director kind of job that came from my history, something I grew up with, but also I was very young at the time, politically I had no idea that there was this much racism and gender discrimination in liberal Hollywood. So to me, I was making a film about a bunch of white guys because that's who I happened to grow up with in Germany, even as an Arab girl. It was not far-fetched, I think if you would ask me to do that now it would be much more difficult.

MP: It seems Twitter has become a really effective platform for you to share your political views?

LA: Yeah I mean let's be very honest, I always tell people:

oftentimes I have helpers, it's not actually only me running my account. A couple of years ago a bunch of women directors really fought for this ACLU EEOC investigation. And I was part of that group who tried to become more political about gender equality within directors. It did become a big government investigation that still goes on now.

During that time, we wanted to do social media and everybody kind of looked at me, because for some reason I had the biggest following--and that came because of *Green Street* and *Punisher*. So I had these two young film student girls helping run my Twitter account during the time we needed it, and then I felt like it would be really unfair to stop paying them so I just let it keep going.

MP: And was the social media component really effective for the campaign?

LA: Oh no doubt, 100% Twitter--which I can't always stand, because the owners and people who run it are often the worst people themselves. So it's a little bit of all of us kind of thinking *"oh my god, why hasn't somebody good actually come up with a platform like this so that we don't have a bad conscience being on it."* But in terms of what it has done for us, you have to understand nobody wants to give voice to any marginalized or oppressed people, nobody ever gives these groups a soapbox or microphone or spotlight, and all of a sudden there was social media and now they can't shut us up.

MP: I've been talking to a few traditional political organizers recently, and one of the core tactics of organizers is to knock on doors and engage strangers in political conversations. It seems that what you've been doing on Twitter is essentially knocking on thousands of doors?

LA: Completely. And in my case it's really interesting because I've done such violent male-dominated movies and genre work, there's these guys that have been following me--I mean, look there's many guys that followed me that then unfollow me because they can't stand it--but there's been some guys who say *'you've totally opened my eyes on what goes on with women, what goes on with racism'* and so I feel like this is the power you should use, and so that's my little lucky place that I have as a woman director.

But in general, even if you don't have any kind of following, it's a soapbox--that is what it's like. It always reminds me of Hyde Park where people would stand on soapboxes. You are kind of like a street preacher, and once in a while people pass by and they're like *'wait a minute that actually made a lot of sense what she said.'*

And all of a sudden you have this crowd around you. And it can turn into an echo chamber, but you know I don't think that really matters because essentially that echo chamber goes to a Thanksgiving dinner and talks about it with other people. Yes, usually like-minded people listen to you, but if it's something that gets retweeted hundreds of thousands of times, it potentially lands in front of somebody's eyes who is neither here nor there on an issue and simply thinks about it for the first time.

So it is the best thing that has ever been invented for us. It would be a shame to lose it. And that's why in so many countries, like Turkey and Egypt, they're shooting all of the social media down because they know that it can bring a government down.

MP: It's interesting when you say it's like a soapbox. The way you're describing it as people walking by and hearing a street preacher--it does sound more like a mob than an

organizing tool. But you've also talked about using Twitter t target and take down a TV show that has misrepresentatio or appropriation [see full interview at **www.calexit.com**]. Tha seems more coordinated than just a mob, no?

LA: Well, I think you want to put it in a more pleasing politica tone, because "mob" to you sounds like maybe a bad thing. love history and a mob has oftentimes been the only thing tha saved humanity, talking about the French Revolution and th pitchforks… I don't mind forming a mob.

In history, no oppression has ever changed until people go really angry and did something. Nobody's ever said *'hey yo know what, these quiet people over there--they're so quiet oppressed, we should change their circumstances.'*

I was fifteen when the Wall fell, and that has affected m tremendously. I drove with my friends five hours to the Wa and watched people who'd never had freedom running acros a Wall that fell because of the power of the people. Thes people coming down across the Wall with tears streaming this really affected me as a teenager. I'm not sure what peopl have against mobs, I definitely think we should be a mob.

MP: When I'm using the term "mob" I'm trying to describ something like a force that wouldn't be sustainable… but I se your point about revolutions coming from mobs that are sort formed in like a pressure cooker…

LA: It *is* a pressure cooker. That's exactly what it is, an by the way that's how the Wall fell. And oddly it started i churches, which was kind of mind-blowing to me. Ther are always people who have to light up the passion in othe people… there's this saying someone once told me, *"peop don't change unless it's too painful not to,"* and I think what yo have to do as a leader is point out how painful it is. Becaus a lot of people, they grow numb to it and they're in denial. It really true that people don't change unless it's too painful n to, so you have to point it out to them that they are in pain, tha the situation is really bad and it's going to get worse.

That's what I mean by soapbox, and yeah by really incitin them up. I think you are absolutely in the right to incite a mo for the good. When it's the Nazis it's a different thing. I gre up in a country that had hate speech laws, which I kno Americans are weird about. Okay, but 32 democracies hav them because what they want to avoid is for people like th Nazis in Germany to become a mob, and what hate speec laws do is they always protect the weak from the bullies. S when you are an oppressed group or a minority group, wh you say can never really be laid out against you. But the othe way around, for a bunch of Germans to say *"Jews need go,"* that is a crime in most Western democracies except America.

So I would definitely incite a mob if it's for the good of th people. If I have to incite a mob to have people not lose heal insurance, I will happily do that.

Born in Mannheim, Germany to Palestinian father and German moth **Lexi Alexander**, a former Wo Kickboxing Champion, worked h way up from stunt woman to Osc nominated director with her live acti short film Johnny Flynton. She h helmed feature films including t SXSW Jury & Audience Award winni drama *Green Street Hooligans*, Marve *Punisher: War Zone*, and *Lifted*. S has directed an episode of the CW's show *Arrow* as well as CBS' *Superg* and *Limitless*. For more informati follow her on Twitter @Lexialex

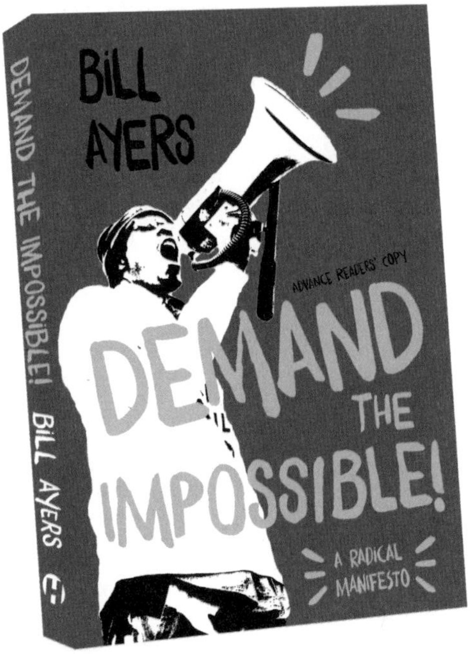
BILL AYERS
ADVANCE READERS' COPY
DEMAND THE IMPOSSIBLE!
A RADICAL MANIFESTO
DEMAND THE IMPOSSIBLE! BILL AYERS

CONVERSATIONS WITH PEOPLE I FIND INTERESTING

BILL AYERS

***Interview by* Matteo Pizzolo**

"It seems to me that as long as we're staying inside the boundaries of the possible, we're being dictated to..."

izzolo: Your most recent book is called *Demand The npossible: A Radical Manifesto.* What's the core idea behind ?

ill Ayers: The idea of it is very simple; I started by thinking wanted to write a pamphlet and what was in my mind was at progressives, radicals, revolutionaries, are pretty good at aming and critiquing the system as it is, but we're not always good about saying what we want or what we're fighting for nd frankly I think that our struggles go off the track and also se momentum unless we have an evolving vision of what it we want or what it is we're trying to achieve.

nd so I set out to write a pamphlet and I was very taken ith the kind of contradiction in this phrase that appeared l over the walls of Paris in 1968 and the phrase was, *"Be realistic: demand the impossible."* It seems to me that as long as we're staying inside the boundaries of the possible, we're being dictated to and we can have all kinds of spirited debate that gives us the illusion of free thinking, but as long as the frame of that debate is as narrow as, for example, between Obamacare and the Republican Health Care Plan... or, on another issue, if the debate is between invading and occupying countries as opposed to strangling them economically... those aren't the debates I want to have. I want to change the frame.

And so this is a book that attempts to make an argument that we unleash our most radical imaginations, rethink what's possible on the big issues of the day, and try to build and forge a social movement that has energy and creativity at its heart--that's what "demand the impossible" is.

MP: It seems like, coming out of the 2016 election, for better and for worse in some ways, people have been more inspired to be doing that--to be taking social action.

BA: Yeah, the book was published in August 2016 so it was well underway before Trump. Michael Moore's movie *Where To Invade Next* preceded Trump, Naomi Klein's recent book No Is Not Enough preceded Trump. So it's not Trump per se, but what the Trump election does is it gives energy to this idea that the choice before us is not just between fascism or neoliberalism with all of its austerity and permanent war and mass incarceration. We have to find another alternative, we have to create the possibility.

Now, Trump doesn't come out of nowhere, and this is part of why we're in a unique situation, because the Democrats--the leaders of the Democratic Party--are struggling to try to keep up with the spontaneous resistance that's on the ground. They're trying to claim that they *are* the resistance, but that's not true. For 40 years it's been a bipartisan effort that's gotten us into a place of permanent war, mass incarceration, the destruction of the public space including public education, and a health care system that is riddled with predatory capitalism all over it, and the destruction of the environment. That's all bipartisan.

We have to find a third way, we have to find a way out of that and in many ways that's what my book is trying to do, it's trying to say *"let's reframe every issue: not 'Obamacare versus the Republican Health Care Plan' but 'universal health care for all;' not 'should we bomb and invade countries or should we strangle them' but 'let's put an end to war;' 'let's abolish the prisons;' 'let's tax the filthy extractors until it hurts;' and 'let's create an environment that we can live in;'"* and on and on.

MP: We're in a very intense political climate right now but probably not as contentious as it was in the days of The Weather Underground, how do you feel it's different or similar between then and now?

BA: I think what was unique at that time was the Black Freedom Movement, that iteration of the Black Freedom Movement, was defining the moral compass of the nation. And the United States plunged into an aggressive imperialist war in Vietnam that united so many progressive elements, and so we had a movement that came together around furthering the agenda of the Black Freedom Movement *and* around opposing American military recklessness in Vietnam and genocide. That was a unique moment.

And one of the things that made it unique for people like us is that we actually believed that we were going to win. It wasn't like we were doing it simply as an exercise in self-righteousness or something, we actually thought that the days of the empire were numbered.

Now, we were wildly mistaken, but I think what's exciting about now is that the Black Freedom Movement has another iteration--a modern iteration--that is as compelling and as sweeping and as comprehensive as anything I've ever seen and that's the Black Lives Matter group, which is not a group exactly but it's a sentiment all over the country and it's finding ways to organize itself into a movement.

We also have today not only the Queer Movement, which has been remarkably successful, and the Women's Movement, which continues to find new ways to define a way forward for equality, but we have Undocumented And Unafraid, we have Standing Rock, and these things are on the ground and happening.

So, to the extent that we can find a way to unite, and we ca[n] build a program of unity that we take to the people as a[n] alternative to Trump or Clinton, or as an alternative to fascis[m] and neoliberalism, I think that we're in a very strong positio[n]. And I'm more excited than I've been in a long long time t[o] think that the impossible is becoming possible.

MP: I'm curious in your long history of being part o[f] movements, what have you seen to be some of the mor[e] effective tactics?

BA: Well, I'm really not a tactician. I think tactics flow fro[m] strategy and strategy flows from principle and princip[le] flows from having an ethical stance. And so what I think i[s] remarkable, and I think it's more remarkable today than eve[r] is the ways in which the arts and activism come together t[o] create something new.

Here we are in a situation where *The Daily Show* an[d] Stephen Colbert and John Oliver are the main commentato[rs] on the political scene today. That's both remarkable and kin[d] of wonderful because humor and art is generous in a wa[y] that didactics is never generous, and so--I'm not funny an[d] I'm not particularly artistic, but I hang out with young poe[ts] and young artists and some of them graffiti artists but man[y] of them playwrights and novelists and painters and I thir[k] that what we're seeing is an absolute explosion of art on th[e] street, on the ground, in the schools, that's redefining what [is] possible.

I don't know if you participated in the Women's Marc[h] anywhere on January 21st, but I was in DC and I had th[e] most remarkable several days in DC but it culminated wi[th] the Women's March. And to see the creativity, the genuir[e] inventiveness and the generosity of spirit that broug[ht] people into the streets in costume, with different banne[rs] and slogans, representing different things, coming togeth[er] intersectionally, it was breathtaking. And it didn't happen wi[th] the national leadership or a national organization, it happene[d] because people were pissed off and they found each other. but they weren't just pissed off, and this is another them[e] incidentally from my book, there's a bumper sticker I love th[at] says, *"if you're not pissed off, you're not paying attentio[n]"* and that draws our attention to the fact that you have to ope[n] your eyes in order to understand the state of the world. Bu[t I] always want to put a bumper sticker next to that that says, *["if] you're only pissed off, you're not going to stay in the strugg[le] and you're not going to get where we need to go,"* you hav[e] to kind of combine being pissed off with generosity, creativit[y,] imagination and love.

And it seems to me that that's what I'm seeing right now [in] Chicago on the ground, these Black Lives Matter activists a[re] not only in the streets protesting police violence and poli[ce] occupation, but they've got a plan to rebuild communitie[s,] to rebuild schools, and they do it a lot through the arts ar[d] through poetry and through song and through music. So, I'[m] not making a comparison with the 60s, but I'm saying we'[re] in an upsurge right now that everyone should embrace ar[d] dive into with a smile on your face and a song in your hea[rt] because this is it.

MP: I was talking to Amanda Weaver who is an organiz[er] with Reclaim Chicago, and it was really fascinating; sh[e] was talking about everything from knocking on doors [to] participating in a Political Action Committee, and what wa[s] interesting to me was she was talking about it on multip[le] levels: electoral campaigns and also direct action.

BA: I think in order to make real change and in order to bri[ng] about fundamental progressive change, you need to nev ose sight of the fact that masses of people, workers, ordinary people have to constantly be mobilized--you can never let go of that aspect of it, there has to be independent mobilization of masses of people.

And yes, occasionally, well not occasionally--but there has to be some turning toward regular politics. The problem we have in this country is what we call 'regular politics,' elections become such a dark hole in space, they suck all the energy out of the movement and we then end up with a false narrative which is, *'if we would just elect the right person, our problems will be solved.'* But that's not true, even a brief glance at history shows you that Lyndon Johnson passed the most far-reaching civil rights legislation since Reconstruction and he was not part of the Black Freedom Movement. Franklin Roosevelt wasn't part of the Labor Movement and Lincoln wasn't part of the Abolitionist Movement, it's fire from below that changes something and that's where we should spend most of our energy, collectively, in building that kind of fire.

MP: I'm curious what you think about direct action at protests, specifically anti-fascist groups and there was the whole thing about Richard Spencer getting punched and more broadly about the perception that peaceful protests are ruined when property is destroyed.

BA: In terms of the ethical question, in my view, if I'm asked by the young anarchists, and I often am asked, *'what should we do tactically?'* My answer is very simple, which is: you should act, and then you should doubt. And the measure of your evaluation of what your action did should always be, *'did I educate people and did I educate myself?'*

Now a lot of people will say breaking windows doesn't educate people, I disagree. I've seen breaking windows educate people a lot in all directions, so I am loath to lecture people on what they should and shouldn't do. When I look at the demonstrations, for example, recently in Berkeley, some bank windows were broken but meanwhile thousands of people were being murdered by our government all over the world, I can't make a comparison.

But I want activists to be in the business of educating and mobilizing and organizing, I don't want to be in the business of posing and posturing and performing, that's not the important part. But I think a lot of lecturing of the anarchists is wasted energy, and I think it serves the status quo.

So what happened during Occupy--listen, this is true my whole life incidentally, everything I've ever done, from sit-ins to being arrested at demonstrations to the Weather Underground--there's always a scold standing in the sideline saying, *'that's not the right way to do it.'* Well then you come and do it the right way, you show me the right way. So I was told that I shouldn't sit-in at the draft board because that would turn people off, it turns out that scold was wrong; we turned people on, we showed people what commitment looked like. I was told that we shouldn't go to Washington and rampage through the streets, turns out we were right to do it and we educated people there too. So I don't buy that.

I'm not really in the business to say the tactic of breaking windows is never right or the tactic of doing this is always right, I don't agree. I think sometimes different things are required. What was required when the Germans were rounding up the Jews in Austria? What was required when the troops were moving on Native Americans? What was required during slavery; was it okay that Harriet Tubman carried a pistol? I think it was okay. Was it okay that John Brown raided the arsenal at Harpers Ferry? Yes it was. And so I don't think we should get stuck in tactics, we should always be talking about larger strategy, we should also always base that strategy in a moral framework.

MP: What are you optimistic about these days?

BA: I should say I'm not optimistic but nor am I pessimistic because optimists and pessimists share a sense of determinism; that is, they know what's coming--I have no fucking idea what's coming. And because I have no idea, I'm a hopeful person. Because I choose to be hopeful. I choose to wake up in the morning saying maybe today we'll be able to move this thing a notch forward or maybe even overthrow capitalism, maybe today. And then I go to bed every night disappointed at what we didn't do, but that doesn't diminish the possibility that we could do it tomorrow. As long as we're living and breathing, as long as human beings are here, we have the possibility of coming to our senses and remaking the world in a way that's sustainable, survivable, peaceful, just, filled with joy and justice, we can do that.

And I'll tell you another thing, existentially, that makes me hopeful, and it's always made me hopeful, is if you put a pillow over a person's head and you try to suffocate them, that person will fight back. And that's in our nature, that's in our biological makeup. And so the fact that a pillow's being put over our head should not completely discourage us because we know we're gonna fight back.

Bill Ayers is a social justice activist, teacher, distinguished professor of education (retired) at the University of Illinois at Chicago, and author of two memoirs, *Fugitive Days* and *Public Enemy*. His most recent book is called *Demand The Impossible: A Radical Manifesto*. For more information, follow him on Twitter **@WilliamAyers**

BRAZIL'S DANCE WITH THE DEVIL
THE WORLD CUP, THE OLYMPICS, AND THE FIGHT FOR DEMOCRACY
DAVE ZIRIN
HOW OWNERS ARE RUINING THE GAMES WE LOVE
BAD SPORTS
DAVE ZIRIN
"[T]he perfect book for our time in sports."
—Christine Brennan, USA Today sports columnist
GAME OVER
HOW POLITICS HAS TURNED THE SPORTS WORLD UPSIDE DOWN
DAVE ZIRIN
FOREWORD BY MICHAEL ERIC DYSON
THE JOHN CARLOS STORY
A PEOPLE'S HISTORY OF SPORTS IN THE UNITED STATES
DAVE ZIRIN

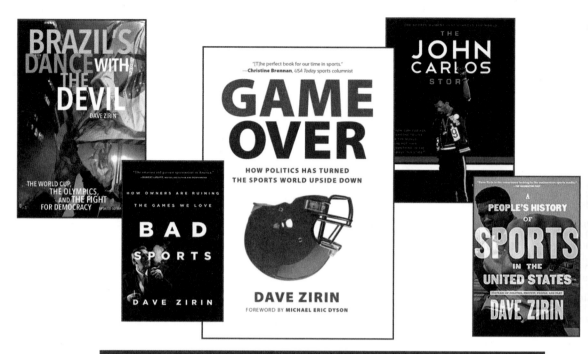

CONVERSATIONS WITH PEOPLE I FIND INTERESTING

DAVE ZIRIN

***Interview by* Matteo Pizzolo**

"You have to start with the question of 'What is our power as fans? And where does that power actually exist?'"

Pizzolo: You're a sports writer and a journalist, but you've also used your platform to do things like call for sports-related political boycotts and you've carved out a very specific thought-leadership role connecting sports and politics, so how did you start doing that? How did you begin using sports journalism in a political context?

Zirin: I grew up an absolutely rabid sports fan, and then in college I was a history major with a strong concentration in issues like social justice history, labor history, and just a history of social movements. I never gave much thought to how these two worlds would mix. So on parallel tracks I was a big sports fan and I was studying all this work about struggle throughout history.

Then in 1996, when I was in college, there was this basketball player named Mahmoud Abdul-Rauf who made the decision to not stand for the national anthem, and, as this story was becoming volcanic in the world of sports, I heard a commentator speak about Rauf as being part of a tradition of activist-athletes and that just turned all kinds of lights on i my head. Because I thought I was this huge sports fan, but didn't know this tradition.

So I really started studying people from Jack Johnson t Billie Jean King and in that process I came upon a book now we're into 1998, 1999, so I'd spent several years just i the woodshed studying this history and then this book cam out in like '99 called *Redemption Song: Muhammad Ali an The Spirit of the 60s* by an author named Mike Marqusee Reading Mike's works was the first time I ever felt like I sa the synthesis between what I thought of as really good sport writing and activist history mixed together.

And that really became my template for trying to not only writ about this history of sports and politics but also apply it to th present day, and I've been doing it pretty much ever since.

Pizzolo: Beyond the writing itself, it's really interesting tha you've also specifically called for boycotts.

Zirin: Absolutely. You have to start with the question of "What our power as fans? And where does that power actually exist?"

Because, far too often, sports--and I love sports--but all too often it's this ideological tool that pushes through a lot of messages which aren't necessarily in the best interests of sports fans themselves, whether you're talking about hundreds of millions of dollars for publicly funding a stadium, whether you're talking about the use of sports to stoke patriotism and militarism, or whether you're talking about using sports to put a wash or a gloss on countries that commit human rights violations, and that goes for the World Cup staging itself in Qatar or it goes for the NBA and the NFL doing tours of Jerusalem and ignoring the plight of Palestinians.

And the boycott is a tool to draw attention to this, to say "hey wait a minute." Sports is not just sports, so why should we the consumer pretend that it is, especially if it's pushing ideas or ideologies that we disagree with.

Pizzolo: In your observation, the athletes that you've written about or that you interact with contemporarily, do they come into their position with a political point of view or, for lack of a better word, a political agenda, or do they tend to discover these issues they're passionate about when they're already established in their field?

Zirin: It depends on the athlete. I've interviewed a lot of athletes who grew up in very political households, so they were going to be political people whether they worked in a library, whether they worked as a sanitation worker, or whether they were an athlete--this is just who they were gonna be.

I've met other athletes who only when they became athletes did they finally understand that they're part of this tradition, and they want to be part of that tradition, and they start learning about people like Muhammad Ali or Kareem Abdul-Jabbar, and they say to themselves "hey, I want to be a part of this." So sometimes it's that way that they come at politics.

But most of the time, the way it happens, and this is frankly true for Ali as well, is that they didn't come into this sport with any kind of a political perspective or as you called it an agenda, instead they become affected by the social movements that are taking place around them. And that's the big difference.

They're inspired by movements in the streets and they feel that, as athletes, particularly as these highly representative figures for different communities--whether it's black, female, LGBT communities--they come to realize that silence is just not an option. Especially if they feel like they're being used to front for political ideas that are detrimental to those communities. Like for example, the women's NCAA basketball team that didn't go to the White House to meet with Donald Trump. They said this is not for us, this is not what we're going to do.

Pizzolo: One of the things that's interesting about the topics you cover is a lot of people might say the athletes are taking a political position in an apolitical sports business, but your point of view is that sports is not an apolitical business?

Zirin: Yeah and I think one would have to be willingly blind to not see a team name like the Washington Redskins or to see the way the Olympics are now being pushed through in Los Angeles, for example, and to not see the political machinations behind that. One would really have to suffer from a willing blindness to not see what these athletes are seeing.

And once you see something, it's very difficult—I mean, let me quote Arundhati Roy, the Indian activist whose writings were also a tremendous influence on Mahmoud Abdul-Rauf, the basketball player I mentioned at the beginning, who said that once you see something, you can't unsee it. It's a hidden war, and then not choosing a side becomes as political an act as choosing a side.

Pizzolo: What's the potential fallout for an athlete who takes a political position? Is there a lot of risk for them?

Zirin: Yes. I mean, you see that with Colin Kaepernick right now, there's a tremendous risk in speaking out. But that's what makes it matter.

You're in Los Angeles and you've got these Hollywood people currently speaking out on a bunch of issues. It's great that they're speaking out, whether you're talking about George Clooney and the Sudan, whether you're talking about Brad Pitt and New Orleans, or whether you're talking about Natalie Portman, Mira Sorvino, Ashley Judd, and the people who've spoken out against sexism and sexual assault in Hollywood. These are brave acts and they should be lauded. But at the same time, these are people who have 20, 30, 40, 50 year careers… and, when you're talking about athletes, you're talking about people who come from very poor, impoverished backgrounds—largely, not entirely but largely—and they have a very narrow time in the spotlight before their career is done.

So when athletes speak out, there's a risk involved that transcends all other areas of culture because the time is so limited. And I think that element of risk is precisely what lends it the gravity that makes people pay attention

Pizzolo: A lot of your work delves into the class relationship between the owners and the players, and I think that also is playing into what you're saying now about the risk factors. For a lot of athletes, the amounts they're paid are pretty gigantic, so how does the class analysis work when you're talking about players who are being paid that amount of money?

Zirin: It's complicated. It certainly has a distorting effect, but there are a couple of factors at play: like, first, when you talk about movements, whether it's against sexism or the Black Lives Matter movement, it's not like money isolates these players from these issues. Like Michael Bennet of the Seattle Seahawks always likes to say "I'm only gonna be a football player for a few more years, but I'm gonna be black the rest of my life."

So, first, whether it's the racism that they themselves are on the receiving end of through life, through social media, or whether their own concerns and fears for their own children, or the communities in which they were born, they're not acting merely out of empathy or distant solidarity, these are their communities and there's a connection there that money does not altogether rid one of. And the idea that money does is actually one of the critiques from the right, like "who are you to say anything about injustice given the amount of money you make," I think that's incredibly short-sighted in our society, particularly given who's in the White House right now. And we see how racism operates at the most official levels of government, that means everybody needs to stand up. And the same is certainly true for sexism and homophobia.

The second thing, though, is the money these athletes make--it's tremendous--but, for most of them, not all of them, but for most of them it's not generational wealth, it's not taking care of their children and their grandchildren.

Because so much of the money either gets taken away by managers, taxes, by poor business decisions, and just by the immaturity that I think many of us would have if we were handed that much money--like I had horrible financial issues between the ages of 22 and 26, but all my financial issues involved like having 50 dollars go out of my bank account. And if that 50 was 500,000, it's not like I would have made better decisions. It's just a fact that most people who make a lot of money in their lives, they're generating that wealth in their 40s and 50s and have a degree of maturity and perspective that most young athletes simply just do not have. That's just a fact.

So when we think about athletes and how they have all this money, some are also a year away from being back where they started. And, unfortunately, we have a lot of evidence that speaks to that.

Pizzolo: You've mentioned Trump a few times, have you seen a shift in the political tenor among athletes since the Trump Administration?

Zirin: Absolutely. There's more and more people who are speaking out because they don't feel like they have a choice but to speak out when you have someone who practices this level of virulent racism, and then also goes after people in the sports world when they dare speak out, and doesn't try to dialogue with them or communicate with them, but curses their names.

People have to understand, Donald Trump is the most irresponsible bastard to ever hold this office, and the reason I say that so strongly is that I know these players who've had to get security officers to walk their kids to school after Donald Trump spoke out against them.

When he speaks out in the way he does, when he does not even grant basic humanity to the people who are protesting against him, he puts their lives at risk. And they know this very clearly.

This is about fear and terror against people who dare dissent. And the fact that he's practiced that is criminal, it's impeachable, and the fact that it's not a bigger issue in official Washington just says something about official Washington.

Pizzolo: Do you feel that it's actually putting the athletes in physical danger when he takes a position against them?

Zirin: It shouldn't have to be physical danger. In theory, maybe you're risking your job, maybe you're risking your livelihood--and frankly those risks are big enough.

But in the hands of this Administration and in the context of 2018, yeah they're risking their physical safety and the safety of their families. And yet they're still speaking out.

Pizzolo: It seems that we're in a golden age of celebrities being able to use their positions to share a political perspective, and, especially with social media, they can organize their fans politically. Is that part of it new, the ability for them to organize their fans, or has that always been there and social media is just the newest tool?

Zirin: Social media has made it much more immediate, without question, and it's changed the relationship of the fan in the passive role taking this in, but we have seen exceptional moments in the past: whether you're talking about the derision and also support received by Tommie Smith and John Carlos when they came back from Mexico City, or the fans who gathered to cheer Jackie Robinson against the haters when he was breaking in... you have seen instances throughout history, Billie Jean King beating Bobby Riggs in the Battle Of The Sexes match, these are big moments.

Pizzolo: Comics would be a small microcosm compared to sports, of course, but it seems like both comic fans and sports fans are reconciling right now with instant social media access to creators and athletes who are vocal about their political perspectives. In comics right now, the temperature really seems to have gone up with vocal backlash against creators taking political positions. Is it similar in sports at the moment?

Zirin: In a weird way it's never been better or safer for an athlete to take a political position, precisely because you have social media and all the people willing to give them support. You also have some movements in the streets that are willing to give them support.

I'll give you one example: in the early 1990s, Bill Clinton violated a promise when he took office that HIV+ Haitian refugees would be taken into the United States, and when he broke that promise a Haitian basketball player named Olden Polynice went on a hunger strike during the NBA season. Now if you go back and you look at the coverage of that at the time, you'll see he was excoriated. Coverage saying that he was actually being selfish, he was hurting his team, that he was grandstanding, that he should stick to sports... all of these things were thrown at him and he eventually gave it up.

I believe that if an athlete right now, for example, went on a hunger strike against Trump calling Haiti and countries from sub-Saharan Africa "shithole countries," there would be hashtags of support all over the place, you would have far going on hunger strikes in solidarity with them, and it woul all be organized through social media and there would be fa fewer articles, if any (outside the right wing echosphere (hell), condemning Olden Polynice for doing it.

And that's another way things have changed, the sport writer fraternity is still not nearly diverse enough, it's st overwhelmingly white and male, but it's less so than it was i the early 90s. And many of these writers now take their cue from what's happening on social media, in terms of readin the pulse of sports fans, when in the early 90s it was almo like they had a button on their back or a string like on thos dollys that talk when you pull them, where it would just b like "Ah stick to sports, stick to sports" y'know? It wouldn matter what Olden Polynice was doing, there would just b that instinct to attack.

So in many ways, even though the opposition is more violer and more vocal, the support is far more vocal as well.

Pizzolo: Where do you see it headed next in terms of politic and sports? Do you see it on the rise?

Zirin: This is where I'm very glad I was a history majc because it helps me answer that question. What we learn i that this kind of sports protest never takes place in a vacuum

The starting point is what's happening outside the stadium So if there aren't big movements outside the stadium, ther won't be more sports protests. It's as simple as that. An anybody who asks "Why aren't more athletes protesting? I'll just respond with "Why aren't more people protesting And why are we asking of athletes what we wouldn't ask c ourselves?"

The other example I give is that Muhammad Ali had no desir to be Muhammad Ali in 1960, he wanted to be Cassius Clay And then the 1960s happened and his life and the worl changed.

Pizzolo: If there's somebody who's reading this and the haven't been involved in activism before but they suddenl feel the desire to get involved, what kind of advice would yo give them?

Zirin: I would say, first of all, when you see athletes takin political positions, support them. Athletes are avid readers c social media and it's a good thing to try to reach out to then and make sure they know you've got their backs if need be.

Another thing is think about how you can become an active sports fan. There's a thing called the Sports Fan Coalition which I'm on the board of (I don't get paid for being on the board, I'm not pumping something here). It was important fo me to do for this very reason, for what's happening right here and right now.

Pizzolo: What has you excited right now?

Zirin: There's so much that's exciting right now and I'm reall pumped about it. I think a lot about the new generation c athletes--even newer than this era with Colin Kaepernick-people like Jaylen Brown and his willingness to speak out openly LGBT players in college football, the women athletes of the last year from the USA Hockey to USA Soccer who are standing up for equal rights... I mean there's so much fomen at this moment that it's something we should take a great dea of solace in. But more than anything it's the influence that this has had on high school athletes, and that just says to me tha this is going to keep coming.

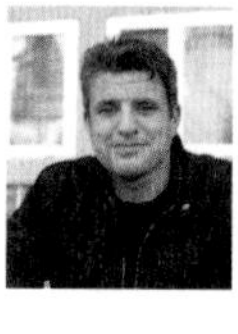

David Zirin is an American political sportswriter. He is the sports editor for The Nation, a weekly progressive magazine dedicated to politics and culture, and writes a blog name Edge of Sports: the weekly sports column by Dave Zirin. Fo more information, follow him on Twitter **@EdgeofSports**

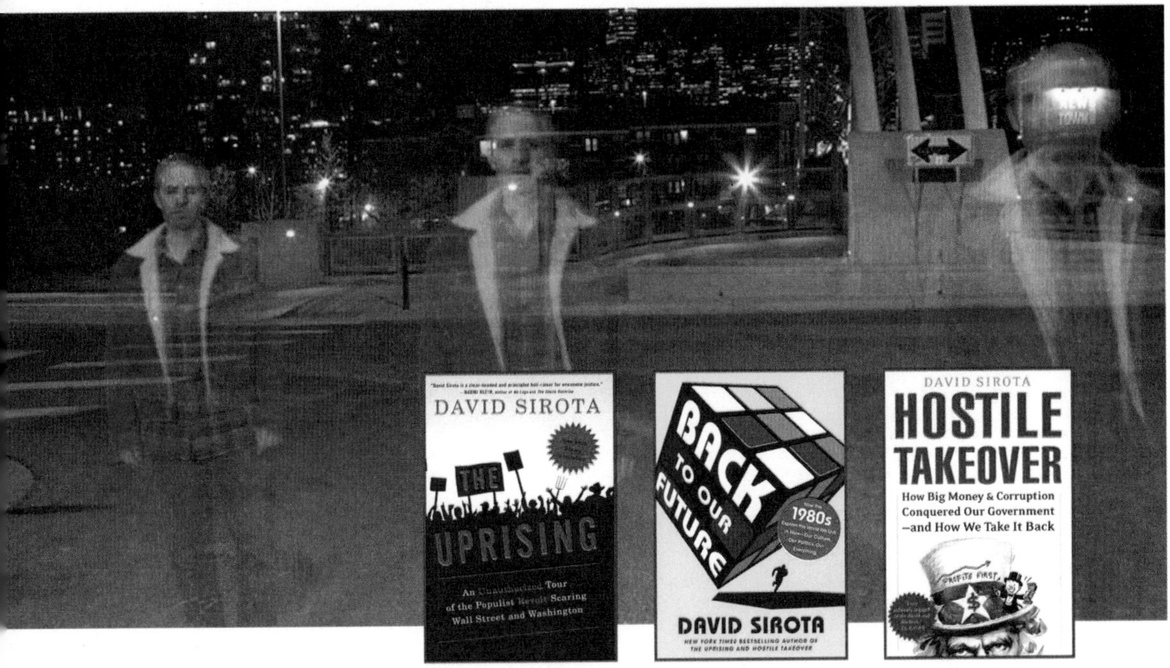
DAVID SIROTA
THE UPRISING
An Unauthorized Tour of the Populist Revolt Scaring Wall Street and Washington
BACK TO OUR FUTURE
1980s
DAVID SIROTA
DAVID SIROTA
HOSTILE TAKEOVER
How Big Money & Corruption Conquered Our Government —and How We Take It Back

CONVERSATIONS WITH PEOPLE I FIND INTERESTING

DAVID SIROTA

Interview by **Matteo Pizzolo**

"If ever there was proof that 80s pop culture has incredible staying power and shapes the way we view our politics: Donald Trump is it."

latt: You're currently an investigative journalist, but you also ave a background in politics, yeah? My awareness of your vork starts mainly with your book *The Uprising*, where you acked the rise of populist movements on both the left and ie right side of politics. In retrospect, it's startlingly prescient. ;ould you get us up to speed on your background and how ou came to write that book?

)avid: Yeah. My first job after college, at least on Capitol Hill nd in major politics, was working for Bernie Sanders as his ress secretary. I worked on Capitol Hill for about five years nd then I moved out to Montana. I'd been working on some ampaigns out there for the guy who was elected governor. 'hen moved out to Denver because my brother was living ere, moved near my family, and did a radio show here in town or about four years, and wrote three books ultimately. One was alled *The Hostile Takeover*, about money in politics and how noney shapes the terms of the political debate in America. And ie second one, as you mentioned, was *The Uprising*, which is about populist movements on both the right and left and how we were headed towards some sort of crescendo on that. And now of course we are kind of living through that.

And then I did a book about how 1980s popular culture helped shape the way we think about major political issues today. So, in a certain sense, all of the books that I wrote ended up coming true in almost cartoonish fashion with Donald Trump. I mean, you've got the influence of money in politics, that was my first book. You've got a guy riding a populist Conservative wave to the Presidency. And you've got a guy who is a 1980s pop culture icon who frames things in many of the cartoonishly 80s pop culture ways. He frames issues and policies in those terms, and plays to a lot of what we were taught during the 1980s about all sorts of issues.

And now I am a full time investigative journalist. I also do a podcast – it's just called *Sirota*. You can find it at patreon.com/sirota. I figured that was just the easiest way for people to find me – where I interview political figures and journalists and the like about the issues of the day. I tend to focus on money and politics, the overlap between how business tries to shape politics and the intersection of money, finance and business is really what I do.

Matt: So when you say that your three books, in different ways, all either predicted or were looking at the drivers that led to the Trump Presidency--is it a scenario where you felt like "Oh this is what I was warning everyone about" or were you as surprised as lots of people were?

David: I was surprised at one level and I was not surprised at another level.

I was surprised that the Democratic Party was so weak that he was able to win. I was surprised that he could win a Republican primary on the sheer force of personality and not necessarily on any specific policy agenda. I mean, he had a specific policy agenda, but you kind of got the feeling that his rise was based on the force of personality.

I was *not* surprised because he really is the culmination of everything that I had been writing about over the last decade, which is a guy who epitomizes the force of money in politics, a guy who understood the Conservative populist uprising that I first reported on way back.

I spent time, for instance, with the Minutemen on the border, the border security activists. I spent time with Lou Dobbs, when Lou Dobbs was this huge deal on CNN. I think a lot of those things I trace in the books were representative of the populist outrage that Trump managed to harness. The thesis of the book was that this populist anger at an economy that many people perceived to be unfair, it was going to be channeled into a Progressive or a Conservative vision. And I think the 2016 election showed that. I don't think Donald Trump and Bernie Sanders have much in common at all, other than the fact that I think they represent the two sides of these populist movements: Bernie being on the Progressive side, Trump channeling the Conservative side.

And then, if I ever need to prove that 80s pop culture is still something that we worship and the prism through which we think about political issues, Donald Trump is quite literally a 1980s pop culture icon. I was actually talking to Adam McKay on my first podcast about this - Donald Trump, if you really trace the history, he was famous in the 1980s and perceived by many to be a very serious and successful businessman. And there were a number of these folks in the 1980s, Lee Iacocca being the best example of this heroic CEO businessman savior. I think Trump - with *The Art Of The Deal* and all that stuff - was perceived to be that way in the 80s.

Now, what's interesting is that by the 2000s, mid and late 2000s, he was famous for having been famous. He wasn't necessarily famous in the 2000s anymore for allegedly being a serious super successful businessman or a super successful corporate manager, he'd gone through the bankruptcies. He'd had these epic failures. He still was successful in the sense of branding himself, but he wasn't somebody who was seen to be this major builder of companies, this heroic icon of capitalism. He still had a business, but it was kind of a branding business - his business was about being famous for having been famous.

It's not like somebody who was Lee Iacocca, who allegedly built up or rebuilt or saved Chrysler, and then based on that record of perceived success was then elected President. Donald Trump was once perceived as that, then that sheen was taken off and he was famous for being famous and in many ways seen as sort of a novelty. And then he was elected to the most powerful office in the world.

If ever there was proof that 80s pop culture has incredible staying power and shapes the way we view our politics: Donald Trump is it. He is the epitome of that.

Matt: Do you feel that it's nostalgia driving it?

David: Well, sure. Nostalgia for a time that probably never in reality actually existed. But, yes nostalgia drives it - you know that because Donald Trump's entire campaign was Make America Great Again.

Matt: I never really thought of that in regards to the 80s, an that's interesting. So you think that that actually harkens bac to the 80s?

David: Well, I think it harkens back to two things.

If we are getting real deep here, I think it harkens back t the 80s and Reagan. I think Donald Trump was appealing t people's view that somewhere in the past things were bette He didn't pinpoint it with an exact year, but I certainly thin to some it was the 80s and this, in many cases, revisioni historical view of the 80s - of this amazing time for everybod And it wasn't an amazing time politically for everybody.

There's that, and then there's also another thing. I have chapter in the book which is about how the 1980s was a tim in which the 1950s was reimagined and idolized in popula culture. You had shows like *Happy Days*, you had this reviva of rockabilly music. I go through a lot of examples in the boo

Ronald Reagan was the sort of iconic 1950s guy, with th slicked hair and he used to be in the movies. And all th people around Reagan, the stars, the celebrities that wer his friends, Frank Sinatra and all these people, they were a 50s icons.

The 80s was this idolization of the 50s as this perfect idyll time. The 1950s, I mean, there were some good parts to i but America was basically an apartheid state. There were a sorts of problems in the 1950s, but I think that the 80s helpe create this idolization of the 50s.

Then, more recently, in the Tea Party there were a bunch o articles that came out where people who had never lived i the 50s were literally talking about how we have to go back t the 50s and how the 50s were great.

So point being, I think Trump was tapping into both a nostalgi potentially for the 80s but also a nostalgia created in the 80 for this past 1950s. He was tapping into all of that.

Matt: That's amazing… because to me, when I see the Mak America Great stuff, in my head it's talking about the 50s bt obviously I wasn't around in the 50s… I mostly know the 80 perception of what the 50s were.

David: Exactly, that was the most fascinating part o researching my book. I had this whole thing about how th ultimate movie to really see that in action is *Back To Th Future*.

Back To The Future is about a suburban kid who is bein chased by Arab terrorists, has to flee this crazy, wil 1980s-out-of-control world into the safety of the 1950s. An the 1950s in that movie is incredibly idealized. It's this tim where the biggest threat is a mean vice principal and a bull named Biff, right?

And I love that movie, but the point is that - I want to be clea about this because one of the things people said about m book there was that the pop culture in the 1980s wasn explicitly political and so there's this idea I must have jus been reading into that myself, but I said: actually that's th political power, political messaging is most powerful when is not perceived to be political at all.

When you see a 30-second political ad on television, there a filter in your brain that says, "I am watching a political a so I'm going to take this with a grain of salt." When you'r taking in sitcoms or movies or music or whatever, that filte isn't there even though the message may be there.

So, in fact, I would argue that popular culture is actually a powerful and, in many ways, more powerful in shaping politica views than explicitly, clearly, overtly political messaging.

Matt: Because it's sublimated into it and you don't realiz you're getting the message.

David: Yeah, you're like "I'm just watching a movie."

ust because you're just watching a movie doesn't mean it's ot transmitting values and ideas and concepts to you that re ideological or political.

att: If the populist movement on the Conservative side is arkening back to the 80s and the 50s, what do you think is riving the populism on the left?

avid: Well, I think that's a frustration with corporate power. I ink it's a frustration with economic inequality. It's a frustration at the current Democratic Party is a collaborator in helping epublicans and corporate forces create a status quo that is conomically unacceptable to millions of people.

att: Obviously one can argue, and people are arguing every ay, over whether or not Trump has an actual opinion on ose matters - but do you feel that the populism on the right n't also driven by a lot of those same factors? By frustration ith corporate forces and an economically unacceptable atus quo?

avid: Let me be clear. I think the populism on left and right, many cases, not all, but in many cases, is driven on an conomic level by the same grievances: corporations have o much power, a feeling of powerlessness, the economy is nfair, inequality is rampant, the rich have too much. I think ose are universal.

here are some differences. I think on the right there is a ostility towards immigrants, a hostility towards diversity. nd I don't think that exists nearly to the same level on the ft, and I don't think the Progressive populist movement is otivated by that. I do think that ethno-nationalism is much ore of a driving force on the right than on the left. But on e economics, I think there's a lot of similarities in terms of e grievance. Where they differ is in terms of what are the roposed solutions.

rogressives want, in general, Medicare for all, a better safety et, higher wages, more regulation on corporate power. I ink, on the right, speaking in broad terms: deregulation, tax uts, get the government out - more of a libertarian kind of conomic program.

you set aside the racial and immigration stuff and focus n the economics, there are similarities. But the racial and nmigration stuff – I don't want to downplay that, that's a eally big part too.

dditionally what's driving the populism on the right, when ou hear people harken back to this sense of nostalgia for e 80s and the 50s, those were eras when white people had ven more disproportionate power than they do now.

latt: Do you feel that the animus you're describing has made e movements on the right more effective?

avid: It's a combination of things. The Conservative populist ovement has the benefit of having its economic program ligned with what corporations actually, in many cases, want so there's more money flowing into it.

latt: You mean like deregulation and tax cuts?

avid: Yeah, what's incredible about that is it's a set of genda items that corporations love, and yet it also has izarrely populist appeal among grassroots Conservatives rho perceive it not as necessarily a corporate giveaway but n actual populist agenda item. That's the whole "What's the latter with Kansas" idea, you have working class people dvocating for policies that are good for the corporations ey purport to be upset with. In some ways the Conservative opulist movement has benefited from more political esources from monied interests. That's not all of it, but that's ome of it.

also think that the Democratic Party has been more effective t suppressing a Progressive populist movement. The nachinery of the Democratic Party and the moneyed interest ehind the Democratic Party just have effectively used their ower to undermine a Progressive populist movement in rays that we haven't seen the Republican Party machine do

to the Conservative populist movement.

I think the reason why the Conservative populist movement is stronger than the Progressive populist movement – part of it has to do with the fact that the Democratic Party is a bigger obstacle to the Progressive movement, and the Republican Party is less of an obstacle to the Conservative movement.

I would even go farther and say the Republican Party is becoming a vehicle for a Conservative populist movement.

Matt: A bunch of years back I had observed a very early Tea Party, and then I went to Zuccotti Park early on with the Occupy movement, and I observed very much what you are describing which is, from an economic point of view, a lot of the signs and arguments were the same, but there were also different cultural and social identity issues on each.

David: Oh yeah, absolutely.

Matt: But then, to your point about the Republican infrastructure becoming a vehicle for the Tea Party, do you feel that the Tea Party managed to take over the infrastructure or that the proto version of the Tea Party was converted into something else?

David: It's a good question… I don't know "take over" is exactly the right thing. There still is a Republican machine that is distinct from the Conservative movement machine, those two things are not exactly the same. But I guess what I mean is that the Republican Party leaders, to control their apparatus, feel much more accountable to the Conservative movement than the Democratic Party power brokers feel like they have to answer to the Progressive movement.

I think Paul Ryan may not be - I'm sure some people will quibble with it, but if you perceive him not to be himself a Tea Party member or leader - I think we can all agree he at least feels he has to answer to and fear and work with and placate the Tea Party. That's a political force in his political calculations. I would argue that the Progressive movement is not as big of a force in the decision-making and calculations of people like Nancy Pelosi and Chuck Schumer.

Matt: In your observation and analysis and research, is that driven by the Tea Party focusing more on going to the town hall meetings and focusing on the electoral process, as opposed to say - and I don't know if you see Occupy and Tea Party as sort of similar populist movements - but the way that Occupy wasn't looking at electoral infrastructure…

David: That's an interesting question. I think the Tea Party was more inherently electorally focused than Occupy. I think that the Tea Party was a political/electoral movement. It had specific electoral goals, targeting individual members of Congress and the like. I've just seen some of that in some primary challenges at the Democratic Party level. Every now and again, you will see a Progressive anti-establishment challenger in a Democratic primary with some real movement backing. I think you saw that this week with Tom Perriello in Virginia. He lost. He got close, but he lost. I think the Tea Party by contrast – you saw that a lot. You saw a lot of primaries and you saw a lot of pressure on elected officials.

The cultural difference between the Democratic and Republican parties is such that… it's hard to put into words other than to say that I think on the left side of the political spectrum, the Democratic side of the political spectrum, you see political, electoral activism primarily by partisans, as opposed to movement folks. I'm not saying you don't see political or electoral activism by movement folks, you do. I'm just saying, there's much more of a Party First mentality on the Democratic side than there is on the Republican side, where you see much more powerful movement forces for instance in Republican Primaries.

On the Democratic side, I would argue there's a much more tribal sensibility of Democrats First. And I think that's at the activist level, and I think it's obviously at the politician level. I think Bernie Sanders and the people behind him have challenged that, and I think that scares a lot of partisan activists on the Democratic side and politicians. I think Sanders and the movement behind him represents something relatively new in the modern era on the Democrat side. New in the sense that it is an explicitly agenda-driven movement that is willing to challenge the party and rejects the Party First mentality. It's not to say those people want to see Democrats lose, but it's clearly a movement based on an agenda as opposed to simply the agenda being 'let's just elect Democrats no matter who the Democrats are.'

The Sanders movement is newer as an electoral force than the Tea Party, obviously. The Tea Party is that same kind of agenda-driven electoral force that isn't necessarily Party First and is willing to challenge the party, that popped up a little earlier. So there's also a catch-up game. I don't necessarily think the Sanders side is going to ever become as powerful inside the Democratic Party as the Tea Party is inside the Republican Party, but what I would say is my book came out – I'm not giving myself credit for this – but my book came out and soon after there was a Tea Party and then soon after that there was a Sanders movement as an electoral force. And now it's going to be, I think, a competition between them.

Matt: The way you're describing all this, it seems like the Tea Party started electorally targeting statewide, local, down-ballot type of elections--

David: The folklore was that it started because of ObamaCare.

Matt: Sure, but I mean, the initial tactics were electoral.

David: Oh yeah.

Matt: Whereas here, because the democrats had the Presidency there wasn't a primary challenge of course, so it would seem the Conservative populist movement engaging electorally first is just how things lined up due to the historical moment in time. If you're looking at the Sanders movement as being a Progressive version of the electoral tactics of the Tea Party, the Progressive side started its electoral strategy on the Presidential level and is only now, maybe, moving to more local elections. Do you think it's important for the Progressive movement to target smaller elections?

David: You're talking about a problem that I've obsessed over for years. I think the Democratic Party activists and Democratic Party voters, in many cases, are more driven by Presidential politics, and what I would call Celebrity Politics, than in many cases Republican political activists.

And, granted, the Republicans elected a celebrity president. But, if we're talking about the Tea Party, I think the Democratic Party and Democratic activists and organizing operations have tended to focus on the highest profile races - Senate races and Presidential races. If the mentality is Party First, and it's not an agenda-driven movement that's fueling your party, then it's kind of a glam contest for the shiny prize.

On the flip side, if you're an agenda-driven movement or if your party is fueled by an agenda-driven movement, the movement wants to implement that agenda at every level. So there's more of a sense of value in not just having your candidate be in the glam office of the Presidency, but you're also interested in and focused on "I want to win state legislative seats, I want to win governorships" and the like. I think the Sanders movement, in a sense because of the psyche of Democratic Party politics, perhaps there needed to be a Presidential candidate to focus that psyche, because that psyche is looking at the top at the Presidential race - not to say the Presidential race isn't important, it obviously is.

I was just at a conference in Chicago where a lot of the activism was about the most local of local races. So I think maybe you needed a Presidential candidate to focus the attention, and now the question is can that movement be driven in a mass way into those local races. And I think you are starting to see that.

I think perhaps the Tea Party didn't necessarily need that, because of the political psyche on the Republican side where the Conservative movement has been operating for 20 or 30 years in a movement way at the state and local level - because it's a fundamentally agenda-driven movement.

Matt: You worked with Sanders in what years?

David: '99 to 2001.

Matt: Were you involved with his campaign?

David: No. I know people who worked on it, but I didn't wo on it.

Matt: Having observed and researched populist movemen on the left and right over decades, what is it about 2016 th enabled two outsider candidates to harness all that energy You've suggested one of the things Trump benefited fro was nostalgia. What about Sanders?

David: I remember in the 1990s and into the 2000s, the really wasn't much space to challenge the Democratic Par in any kind of movement way. I think part of that was th Clinton Presidency, and then Bush unified the party into monolithic "We've just got to stop Bush."

You started to see things sort of start to change in 2006 whe Ned Lamont challenged Joe Lieberman over the Iraq wa That's a campaign I worked on. And I'm not just saying I thir that was a turning point because I worked on it - I think it's th other way around. When I was working in politics, I alway wanted to work on something that I thought could be a turnir point. And I think it really was. It was the first time, in a real high profile way, that a Democrat had been challenged with the Democratic Party over a hugely high profile issue like th Iraq War. By the way, the Democratic Party was still able ' crush that down in 2006.

Matt: Is that where some of your perspective comes fror feeling crushed in that?

David: No, I don't have a –

Matt: I don't mean in a reactionary way, I just mean havir that experience of going up against a machine.

David: Yeah, I guess. I will put it this way: I sort of figured th Bernie would run and the party would have the same amou of power to stop him as it had when it stopped Ned Lamor And Ned put up a great race.

When Ned Lamont ran against Lieberman, Ned knocke him off in the primary and then Lieberman beat him in th general, because Lieberman came back in the general as a independent. When Ned beat Lieberman in the primary it wa seen as a huge thing. But then the party machinery helpe Lieberman and that was it.

And so I thought the same kind of thing would probab happen to Bernie: he'll run a good race and he'll giv some good speeches and there you go. And look, the en result was the same, I mean Bernie lost, he didn't beat th establishment candidate. But he really overperformed wha I thought he would be able to do. And that's not disrespec my expectations weren't low because of him. They wer low because I was like "The party is just too strong." An ultimately it was too strong for him to win, but he got a l closer and formed a bigger movement than I thought h would be able to.

Matt: On the other end of the 2016 election, I know a lot c people who were expecting different results have been pret depressed. I realize you're not an activist, but as a journalis what do you think are some of the most constructive thing coming out of the campaign?

David: Engagement. There's a huge chunk of the count that's a lot more politically engaged than it has ever been my lifetime really. And, by the way, on both sides. Democrac doesn't work unless people are engaged. So that's good.

David Sirota is an American political commentat and radio host based in Denver. He is a national syndicated newspaper columnist, Democrat political spokesperson, and blogger. For mo information, follow him on Twitter @davidsirota

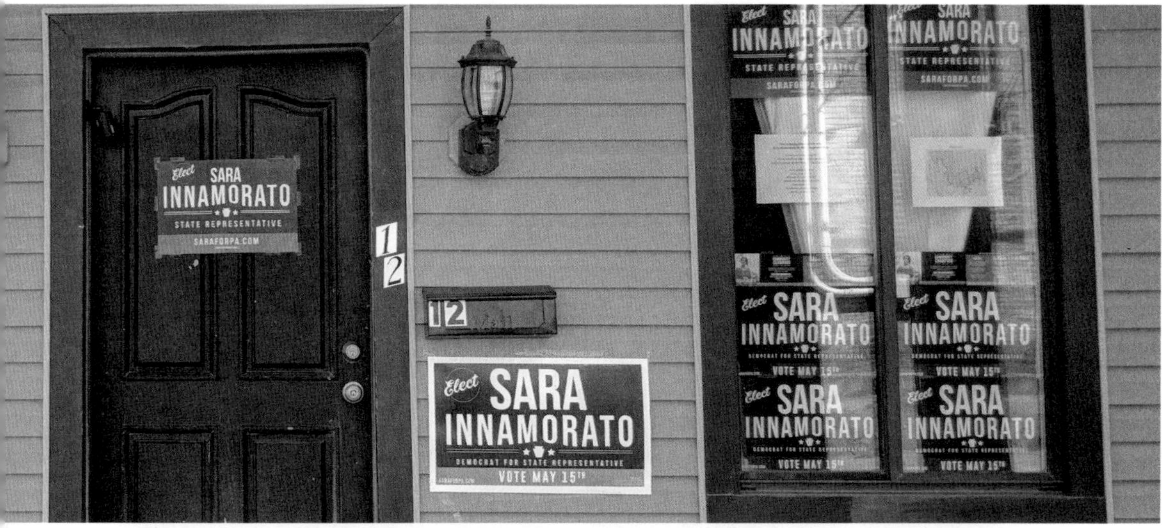
Elect SARA INNAMORATO
STATE REPRESENTATIVE
SARAFORPA.COM
12
Elect SARA INNAMORATO
DEMOCRAT FOR STATE REPRESENTATIVE
VOTE MAY 15TH

CONVERSATIONS WITH PEOPLE I FIND INTERESTING

THE CAMPAIGN TO ELECT SARA INNAMORATO

***Interview by* Matteo Pizzolo**

)18 may well be remembered as the year when the youthful ealism we associate with garage bands, tech startups, and ıerrilla filmmakers took over local politics.

'hile researching grassroots politics for CALEXIT, I was artled to see how many young people are stepping up and nning for office, volunteering on their friends' campaigns, ıd just getting out there and putting together DiY political)erations.

wanted to get a sense of how these indie campaigns are ganized, so I looked for interesting candidates and came)on Sara Innamorato, a young woman running a grassroots ımpaign in Pittsburgh. Sara was kind enough to take time vay from the campaign to talk to me, and provide me with e unique opportunity to interview the entire campaign aff—all three of them (including the candidate herself). ıey were a ragtag group of friends (Sara's Campaign anager, Noah, used to work with her at an Apple Store), but :ould tell right away they were all really sharp, passionate, ıd driven by a desire to help people.

ıra was running against Dom Costa, an incumbent who'd ıld the office for a decade. In that time, Costa had never ıen opposed by a Democrat or a Republican. He's part of political family which holds numerous offices throughout e local government in Sara's region and had never had campaign before. In a kind of anti-Costa solidarity, ıra even held joint events with another insurgent indie ındidate, Summer Lee, who was running against Dom's ıusin Paul Costa, also a longtime incumbent.

ıd y'know what the best part is? Sara and Summer both won their elections! By wide margins, too! Earning 64% and 67% of the vote respectively.

I'm telling you, local politics is the new punk rock!

Read on for an inside look at a young, indie, political campaign that stood up to an entrenched political powerhouse and won.

CANDIDATE
SARA INNAMORATO

Pizzolo: Congratulations on all of the success so far and all the excitement on the campaign.

Sara: Thanks. It's simultaneously draining and invigorating.

Pizzolo: So what inspired you to get involved in the first place to run for office?

Sara: There's a number of reasons, but I think the big picture is that I was working in non-profit-land with a lot of really smart people who are dedicated to solving some of the region's biggest challenges -- whether that was the food bank trying to make sure every single person had enough food to eat, or my local community organization that wanted to keep people in their homes, or the reproductive justice organization I was working in to make sure every woman was able to maintain access to abortion -- there were folks working at all those places who were really passionate and dedicated, and they were fighting really hard... and we had a local Democratic Party that was saying "Well, voter turnout is only 17% in the county, so that means people don't care."

And I'm like, "But they do, people care so much. They've just lost faith in government, that it's there to help and not be so self-serving." I had a big connection to different areas in Pittsburgh and I had a passion to do good work and I had the time to do it, so I decided to throw my hat in the ring.

Pizzolo: Are you from the region originally?

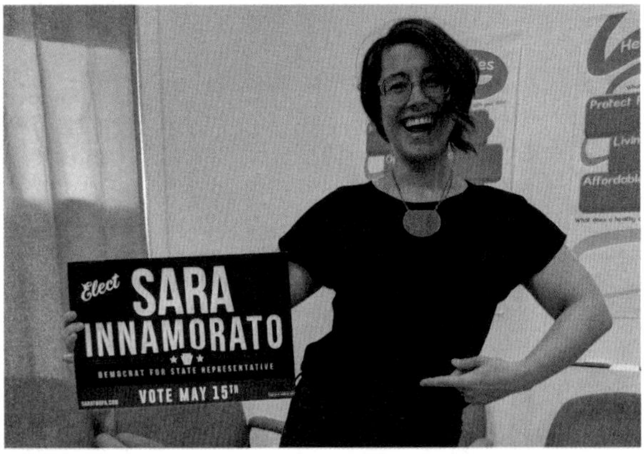
Elect
SARA
INNAMORATO
DEMOCRAT FOR STATE REPRESENTATIVE
VOTE MAY 15TH

Sara: I am. I'm a *yinzer*, I'm a Pittsburgh lifer. I grew up in The Rocks, which is the northern part of the district, it's a suburb that's a couple minutes outside of the city. And then I went to Pitt and have lived in my neighborhood of Lawrenceville for the past decade, and got to buy a home there about three years ago.

Pizzolo: I was reading that the candidate you're running against is part of a political family, is that right? And there's multiple seats held by people from the same family?

Sara: Yes. Yes, they have a lot of family members in different levels of government in the area.

Pizzolo: Are you from a political family?

Sara: I'm probably from the exact opposite of a political family. We were raised in a very apolitical environment.

I remember asking my mom how I should register to vote. I had just attended a John Kerry rally on campus right before I graduated from high school, and I was registering to vote a week or two later, and I asked my mom "Where should I affiliate myself?" She said "Well you should just remain an independent because you should always find the best person for the job, the person who best reflects your values, and not be blindly loyal to a party." While I appreciate that wisdom, in Southwestern PA politics, districts are drawn in a way that the seats mostly go to Democrats, so a lot of the decisions are made in primaries.

In the state of Pennsylvania, those primaries are closed, so you have to be affiliated with a party to be able to vote. At that point I was like, "Well, these Democrats are the folks that at least say they're for the working class, for the underdog, that they're the people who care for women and want to increase diversity in our nation and protect the most vulnerable." So that's who I decided to associate myself with.

Pizzolo: I read that, before running for office yourself, you formed a non-profit that helped other women run for office?

Sara: Yeah, "She Runs." I was in a leadership program with the goal of self-development but also looking outwardly and finding a way to uplift women in Southwestern PA.

Pennsylvania is ranked 49th when it comes to women in office. In Allegheny County, only one woman out of a thirty-eight-person delegation that goes to Harrisburg is a woman. We just have a dearth of women that are in elected office.

So She Runs was to amplify the voices of women wh have been involved in politics -- in either elected offic or running for office or who had worked on campaign whether electoral politics or issue-based campaigns -- ar to get women to just see themselves in a role in politics ar realize they probably already have a skillset that would b really valuable and lend itself to a specific area of politics Southwestern PA.

We wanted to keep it hyper local because we do hav national heroes -- we can look at Elizabeth Warren and w can look at Kirsten Gillibrand -- but to see folks in your ow backyard who ran for School Board and what their journe was like and saying, "Oh, she was just working on her ow business and then she ran for School Board, and she ha enough money to buy one sign and here's what she did do that." That was my friend Elsie, but just to hear that sto and say, "Oh, okay, I didn't even realize School Board cou be a thing that I was involved in," that was really what w wanted to spark with She Runs.

The thing was not to build another training mechanisr because that exists nationally and locally, but to fill in son of the space that needed to be filled in. Just amplifyir voices and bringing together different coalitions of folks talk about policies that could help us achieve gender parit

Pizzolo: What was your first step in being directly involve in politics? Was there a campaign that inspired you to g involved yourself?

Sara: She Runs was my first foray into classic electo politics, but I had worked in the non-profit sector primar with community groups. So you realize that all politics a local, and sitting in a community meeting is a political feat and of itself. But She Runs was the first time I was involve for the races. I worked on my friend Marita's race, she ra for mayor of a municipality in the area. And I worked another local district judge race last year.

Pizzolo: How important do you think local elections are How much do you think people should be paying attentio to them?

Sara: They're extremely important. That's where it all star That's where you build a pipeline for progressive values reach higher office.

And that's also how you get people comfortable with ne ideas, right? If you take third party politics for example, fol running as an Independent or a Libertarian or Green Par if the only time voters see that party affiliation is every fo years during a Presidential Election, it's going to be, "O this is wild." But if they start to see those folks running f School Board or running for City Council or at the municip level, then people can start to become more familiar wi that change and that platform.

And it's a lower risk for people. It's easier to talk to folk because, at the end of the day, it's about the perso representing you. The way that you get to know people is knock on as many doors and to have as many conversatio and make as many phone calls as possible. So when yo have that one on one interaction, you have the luxury building individual trust and then you can represent th broader ideology or platform. But yeah, it all starts local.

Pizzolo: And you feel those local offices really affect peopl

Sara: Oh, absolutely. School boards decide policies that th implement in schools, which could be banning suspensio and detentions for kids under fifth grade, they can deci to spend money on restorative practices, they can alloca funds for nurses as opposed to school officers. There's lot of power in shaping the way that a school district is r through school boards.

With the county or municipal level, that's where you deciding zoning code. So with affordable housing, xample, which is a big issue in Pittsburgh, a lot of the eighborhoods in the district can say, "Okay, developer- If ɔu want to come in, we know that we have a lot of assets offer you, so we're going to mandate that 20% of your nits are below market rate and have to stay so potentially perpetuity or for 50 years" or whatever they can come up ith for the zoning codes they want. That's a very local way ɔu can have an impact on some of these big issues.

ven just getting involved -- if you already have a career nd you're really happy, you could do something like judge n election and you come out once a year when elections e happening and you watch the polls and you make sure at democracy occurs under your watch. You just make ure that everything works for that pool that day. There's lot of different ways to get involved, and I think they're all etty meaningful.

izzolo: What made you decide on this particular office to n for?

ara: Really, with state level government, I love the terconnectedness of the issues. Some of the bigger issues at I care about -- like making sure that every single person as access to healthcare, that we can raise the minimum age to one that is a living wage for all people, and even fordable housing -- I really wanted to work on those vorite issues and see the interconnectedness of them all.

s about a desire and a platform, but it's also about reading e space... reading the citizens that are in that district, oking at who currently holds that office, and looking at nat you could bring to that office given the current climate.

ɔ it was kind of a perfect storm of all of those factors that d me to run for a state level office for the first time.

zzolo: You're challenging an incumbent who has been nopposed the past few elections, and he's part of a political mily. Is it intimidating for you to be going up against that?

ara: Yes, it's intimidating. But you just need to have trust yourself on why you're doing it. And I know why I'm doing it's to serve people.

ɔ anything that comes up that is what I view as superfluous scussion and pretty much rooted in pettiness... I can ways just go back to the core reason of why I'm doing is. And I can look at the people around me, I can have amazing conversation with someone who believes in the ɔrk that they're doing and believes in this campaign and s taken on part ownership of it. It always just refocuses u.

ɔ yeah, it's daunting, but it's easier because there are a lot people involved in it. I don't feel like I'm alone. And I've so built a lot of relationships with other people who are nning across the state, so there's a sense of camaraderie at I think is rare in running campaigns for political office.

zzolo: I saw that you've done joint events with another ɔman who's running for a different office?

ra: Yeah, because she's running for State Rep as well in different district. Her name is Summer Lee, she's running a little town called Braddock, but some of her district erlaps with the city of Pittsburgh as well. And then there's woman Elizabeth Fiedler who's out in the Philadelphia ea, and we've also done joint statewide fundraisers.

zzolo: So do you feel you're part of a community that's ming together to support one another on multiple different mpaigns?

ra: Yeah. Absolutely.

zzolo: I think a lot of people who would be inspired support progressive causes might be scared to put emselves out there and run for office. Is this something u wrestled with at all or was it something that you knew mediately you've always wanted to do?

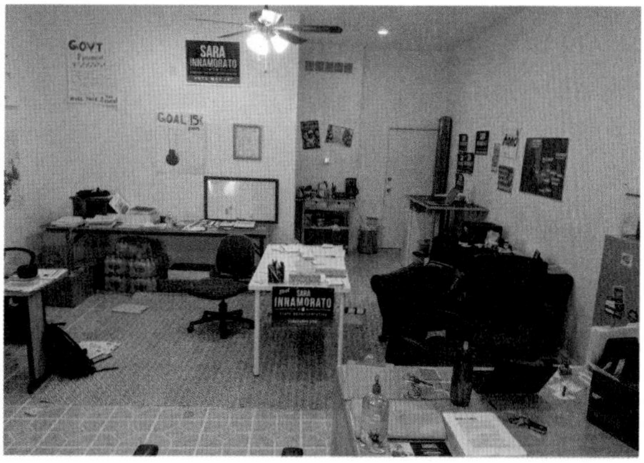
GOVT
SARA INNAMORATO
GOAL
SARA INNAMORATO

Sara: I did not think that I would be running for office. What I knew is that I wanted to do good work, and I wanted to help others do good work. This opportunity came up, and I was like, "This could be the ultimate helper position. We can redefine the way that this will interact with citizens here in the 21st district." And I'm going to be a part of redefining that. It's intimidating.

I don't know if people should aspire to run for office, because if your goal is to run for office then you might do things that will get you to run for a position as opposed to being involved in your community and doing good work and really sensing what's going on around you -- both the really positive things and the needs of that community. If you're in that space and the opportunity comes to run for office, then great. But if you're just driving towards getting into office, then you're maybe not reading the environment as much as you should be. And that should really be what's informing someone to run for office. It shouldn't be a personal motivation of like, "This is where I want to end up." That's my personal opinion. So for me it was the way I feel I can help my community in a very real, big way.

Pizzolo: What is it that you're most personally passionate about that really drives you to go out there and take on a daunting task like this?

Sara: It's my family. You were asking earlier if I come from a political family... I come primarily from a family of women. My mom has three sisters -- so I have three aunts, all of them are divorced, all of them are on their own. I have cousins, none of them went to college, they're all working shift work, they've all been on public assistance on and off throughout the years. I was the rarity, I at least got a degree. I think about them.

And I think about my mom, and how she works at a job that she likes -- she's an office manager for an HVAC company -- and she thinks that she is worth the $10 an hour that she makes. And she's probably going to work there until she can't anymore.

And I think about how I'm supposed to take care of her, and how I can set that up so she can be taken care of. Looking towards the past but then also looking towards the future... what is this world going to look like when I find a partner and when I want to bring kids into this world?

So, it's family. They lived a hard life, they survived abuse, addiction, and I just think that they deserve the best world possible.

Pizzolo: When you decided to take the leap and pursue this, what was the first step you took to put the campaign together?

Sara: It was finding and building that core group of people who would check me, because I feel like with government there is a lack of trust between people who are in elective office and regular old people like me.

I wanted to make sure I had a wide net of accountability, so when I (knock on wood) get elected, there will be a lot of eyes on me to kind of check me and keep me on that course of putting people first.

So the first step was finding my people, finding my crew: who's going to offer advice on how to organize field, who's an expert in educational policy, who were the community leaders that talk to their neighbors all the time… it was just creating a big network, and then it was filling out a lot of paperwork: set up your PAC, and then I started fundraising a little bit. And we started to plan what this campaign would look like, just putting together the tactical things like a website and platforms and things like that.

Because we're a campaign running against the status quo, a lot of it was, "We're going to have to show them that this is possible, as opposed to telling them that this is possible." So we started really early last year, and it was, "I'll talk to the more establishment folks once I have a bunch of money in the bank and we've done a big launch event where we brought hundreds of people out and signed up a ton of people to volunteer so we can be like: This is possible, people are hungry for democracy that is inclusive, they want to feel like they can see themselves in the process and they can take ownership of it." Those were the first steps.

Pizzolo: If people don't live locally, but they're excited about what you're doing, how can they support you?

Sara: Oh my gosh. They can just send me nice messages. [laughs] It's really nice when someone sends you a nice message… sometimes we have rough days, but then it's like, "Oh, but this person thinks that I'm nice."

They could go to SaraforPA.com and there's a donate button, so that is very helpful because we did pledge not to take any money from shady PACs or corporate interests.

And there's ways to help digitally -- writers, content creators, folks who just want to share the campaign and the message through their social network is very helpful. If they want to travel to Pittsburgh and knock some doors for GOTV, that's also super exciting.

So there's a lot of ways, even if you're not a born and raised yinzer, to help out on the campaign.

Pizzolo: What's inspiring you?

Sara: I feel like my whole life is this campaign, but I think what we're doing with the campaign is making it a force for good, right? We've been making it like, "Who do we bring in, who do we train up, who do we give leadership positions that wouldn't normally get a leadership position?" So I'm just really excited about that.

I'm really excited about helping other progressive women run throughout the year and into the future. Locally, we're trying to pass some inclusionary zoning, so that's super exciting.

But yeah, I kind of live, eat, and breathe this campaign. It's a lot of talking to voters, and also a lot of it is sitting down with people who are policy experts in healthcare, in women's health and reproductive rights, in economic justice -- and, just getting access to them and having them talk about what they're working on and saying, "Okay, I'd love to support you," and building those kinds of bridges is really exciting.

CAMPAIGN MANAGER
NOAH LEVINSON

Pizzolo: You're Campaign Manager on Sara Innamorato campaign. Tell me a little about how you got started.

Noah: So this is my first time as a Campaign Manager. I wa brought into the political space right around 2016.

I was always very political, I cared a lot about politics… bu think it was Bernie Sanders that really hit me where it was lik "Oh, it's up to us, isn't it?" So it's sort of a call to action whe it was like, "Alright, let's do it." He talked about the politic revolution, I think this is it. I wouldn't be here without that c to action, so I pushed a lot of my work into politics and ther kind of led me down this path towards different organizatior different projects.

Sara and I had been friends for a long time. She was actua my boss at the Apple Store when I was back in college… s she's still my boss.

We always wanted to do a project together, I just didn't reali the project was going to be running for State Representativ When she shared she was doing that, we stayed in tou and worked a lot on sort of the foundations of the campaig and what this campaign would be about, what this platform about. And then, when it came time to execute, when it can time to act on it, she asked me and I said "Alright, let's do it."

So that's how I got here.

Pizzolo: And what does it mean to be a Campaign Manage What do you do?

Noah: We're trying to talk to as many people as possible. Th district has like 60,000 people in it. So how do we talk to all those people? Well, we don't have enough time and we do have enough people and we don't have enough money to ta to all these people.

People make a science out of how many doors have be knocked, how many e-mails have been sent, how ma contacts have been made. But I think it's a matter of ju managing this energy, right? Like, that feeling when y walk into Pittsburgh and when you talk to someone who's Pittsburgher, that sort of impression of being a neighbor. I thi that is more what I manage than anything else… just creati more of the good energy.

Now, on the day to day, what it involves is… when someo asks "What's going on with the campaign?," that is me. I the living embodiment of it. So every message I get needs response, every email I get needs a response. It's constar talking to people, bringing new people into the fold. Sor Campaign Managers will tell you that the majority of their d

Sara Innamorato is running for State Representative of the 21st District. An experienced nonprofit consultant, Sara plans to bring strong reform to Harrisburg. Her platform includes prioritizing people through Medicare-For-All, comprehensive long-term treatment for the opioid epidemic, affordable housing regulation, and increased transparency and financial integrity in Harrisburg. Learn more at www.saraforpa.com.

; spent raising money. They find where money is, they find who owns money, they find out ways to talk to that money. And will tell you that this is a grassroots operation and that isn't he priority. The priority is that we talk to so many people who ome back to us and want to help. It's my job to figure out how an you help.

A lot of times, the most direct way to talk to someone on a ampaign is just knock on their door and say, "Hi, I'm your eighbor, I wanted to let you know this is happening and it's nportant to me. I'm curious if it's important to you too." Most ften it is.

So that's why we find a lot of the energy goes into going ut and just having conversations. As a first time Campaign Manager who doesn't have the traditional experience of a Campaign Manager, it's a whirlwind. Everyone imagines olitical campaigns to be very all over the place and emotional nd exciting. It's just coming in every day and being like, Alright, how can we talk to as many people as possible? How an we keep the momentum rolling?" I think it's a big wave of hat and eventually it's all going to crash on election day where 's like vote, vote, vote, vote.

My job, in a lot of ways, is: how do I keep that wave going? Like ow do I keep the energy there? And then if the wave gets a bit smaller, how do I make it bigger? When it gets really big, how o I make sure it's still focused on Election Day?

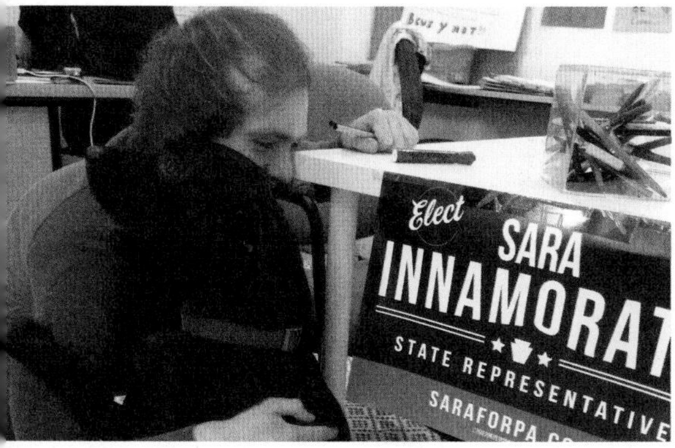
Elect
SARA
INNAMORAT
STATE REPRESENTATIVE

or this campaign we're having wonderful conversations, we're alking about new issues, we're knocking on doors and saying, Hey, Sara supports single payer health care. She supports Medicare for all." And they're like, "Oh, cool." So we're having hese really big conversations and spreading issues, because very time a person talks to another person about something ke that it sticks a little bit more, it makes the issue more real. ny time we can take a concept that someone has heard n TV or in the newspaper or on a blog that sounds scary... ke "socialized medicine," and then actually have someone nteract with the person and be like, "Hey, actually, have you eard of single payer?," those are successful conversations. It as a huge impact.

ut, at the end of the day, whoever has more votes wins. So oting is what we're focused on, it's the north star of this, to get s many votes as we can because all this talk means nothing if e don't have the votes to support it and validate it.

izzolo: So this is your first time campaign managing, have ou worked on campaigns before or are you new to campaigns general?

oah: I have worked on campaigns before. After I had that moment with the Bernie Sanders campaign where I was like, Oh, it's up to us," I immediately pushed forward the Get Out he Vote campaign at my last job. Just trying to get as much oter contact as possible, especially with younger folks. And hile that campaign was rolling with other people, I was able work and help with the Bernie Sanders campaign. I worked ith their digital team and helped them with social media, a unch of digital websites and things like that.

fter the primary, I was on the Creative Council for Hillary Clinton's campaign, which helped with larger creative activations -- especially online videos and things like that. After the election, I helped out with the last burst of the Affordable Care Act marketing, working alongside the White House and some other nonprofit partners to try and get that message out.

So it's sort of weird, because I went from caring about politics to immediately just showing up and asking "How can I help?" They saw my skillset and they're like, "Oh my gosh. Please do this, do that," and it really evolved really quickly where I got a very unique view of elections and seeing campaigns and how they worked.

The next year I started working with candidates all over the country and tried to take everything I learned about YouTubers and internet celebrities and apply those things to the candidates, making them break through the noise through their story, through their message. Taking what was awesome about them and sharing that with the world. But eventually, I wanted to see my theories and my ideas in action.

This campaign was a really awesome way to both, one, help a really good friend who's an incredible, progressive pillar of the community here, and, number two, I wanted to see... like, okay, people talk about running for office, people talk about doing all these things... let's actually put our – not our money, we don't really have that – put our action where our mouth is.

We do have money, it's just not the priority here... we put our action where our talk is. This has been an incredibly illuminating experience because: this is it. I think people all have their own conceptions of things like single payer health care and they have their conceptions of candidates and they have their conceptions of campaigns. And being in it is sort of like, "Oh my gosh, this is exactly how it works, this is insane."

But there's no time to reflect. This is the first time I can stop to be like, "Wow, incredible." There's no time to reflect because it's always... I have a sign on my door that I scribbled in sharpie and it says "Will it get us more votes?" That's the north star, I think. Really, at the end the day, how can we garner support? At the end of the day, the winner has more votes. And not everyone in this country is registered to vote, not everyone in this country has access to information. So there's a lot of work to do just to bring as many people into the fold as possible.

Pizzolo: How big is the campaign? How many people work on the campaign?

Noah: Three, including Sara. And then also a student who works part-time. It reminds me of a startup in a lot of ways. We really have to create an entity that can spread awareness as quickly as possible yet already be spreading that awareness at the same time. So it feels like a sort of startup. It's like a startup from hell, but in a great way. But also what's great about it too is there's an end point. Election day is when the startup business pauses for two years—it's two years here in Pennsylvania for State Rep. But it's a very small crew.

We're running – I wouldn't call it an insurgency campaign exactly – but we're running against a Democratic incumbent in the primary. We aren't getting the sort of institutional support that the standard campaign gets. So, in a lot of ways, we do have to look at each other and be like, "Alright, let's do it."

Pizzolo: If someone was thinking of participating in a campaign or possibly run themselves, do they need to have tons of money beforehand? Do they need to have rich friends or is that not as much part of it in a local election?

Noah: It's so different on a local level versus federal – let's not talk about the President here, because then we're talking about things like press attention that you can't put a value to, brand name that you can't put a value to, things that would exceed the billions of dollars, right? We're not talking about billions of dollars. We're talking about a couple thousand dollars here.

What you really need is a message, a story, and good timing.

But, having that story and timing, it's asking: who is the right person for this time right now that Pittsburgh is in? What is the right kind of message to be saying for the time that Pittsburgh and Southwestern PA is in right now? And I think what's great about this campaign is that we go to the doors, we introduce folks to Sara, and when they look at Sara and then they look at our opposition, our opponent whose campaign is from a decade ago, it's like, "Oh, this is obviously the future of politics." There is this gut feeling that this makes sense. I think vision is what you really need to think about.

So no, I don't think it takes a ton of money. We haven't hired a fundraiser or a Finance Director, that's usually the first hire, someone who brings in more money. The Finance Director often works on commission of how much money they bring in, which is very weird to begin with. We don't have that person.

People say this is a science, but it goes right to the heart because if you have the right message, if you have the right platform, if the story is accurate, the timing is good, you have the vision, you have these things that are not dollars and cents... the money sort of follows it. People will help you.

I think every time we get a donation we look at it like, "Oh my gosh, another donation." It's so validating, it's such a sign of support, whether it's a couple hundred dollars or five dollars, it's just kind of like, "Wow, that person agrees with us on this vision to the point that they'll give us the money they earn from working, the money they spend their time gaining." If you go out there and you give the right reasons, people will support you.

Pizzolo: So your campaign is against an incumbent who's been unopposed in the primary for 10 years, right?

Noah: Yeah. And he hasn't had a Republican opponent. So this is his first campaign in a lot of ways too. May 15th is our election, whoever wins that is pretty much guaranteed. Yeah, so this is it: May 15th is do or die.

Pizzolo: There's a lot of attention on the midterm elections and local elections with progressive candidates coming in to primary against moderate incumbents. And there's also been pushback against that from the Democratic establishment, saying it's risking seats to do that. So in this case with Sara's campaign that's not a problem, but if there had been those risks, would it give you pause? Had there been a Republican opponent who might make a stronger showing against a more progressive candidate, do you think it would be worth the risk?

Noah: I think this is definitely something you should ask Sara too because we've talked about this.

The simple answer there I think is you have to look at a community and determine who is the best person to represent these people. And right now, we don't have a representative that reflects the community and their values. I really do think a lot of us all agree on the same stuff when it comes down to what we want - we want security around health care, we want people really addressing the opioid epidemic in a way that's long term and less about two-term goals thinking, we want more people defending us and not defending corporations or those in power over us.

I think it always makes sense for someone to run for office. I really do. As long as you're pushing the right message and pushing the right issues, there's never a moment when I think anyone should be told "Don't run for office."

Because we need so many more new people running for office that I'd rather risk a couple of potential Democratic strongholds in order to just get new voices into the mix and have new people enter this space. Because if they're told, "Oh, don't do that, the Republicans might win," we don't have time to waste – the Republicans have already won, Donald Trump is President. We can't wait any longer. I don't think anyone really has clear control over any of this stuff. So the only thing you have control over is yourself.

If you want to run for office, run for office and just try and see what happens.

Pizzolo: If somebody wants to get involved for the first time and hasn't been involved in any politics or campaigning before what would you suggest are the best first steps for them?

Noah: Talk to people. Lots of people. Because, when yo want to get involved in politics and want to get involved i campaigns, there's a lot of people who have a vision and the want to see a better future for their community. The realit is, it's never you alone, it's always going to be with so man people. Go to events, sign up to volunteer, just start showin up because then, if you show up in a space, you're guarantee to have conversations when you're there. Just start talking t people and getting to know your community.

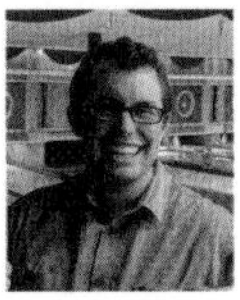

Noah Levinson is the Campaign Manager for Sa Innamorato. Originally from Scranton, PA, Noah is usually strategist working with internet celebrities, memes, and oth fun stuff. But after 2016 ... well ... guess it's up to us! Now h does politics. It's like the same thing but often not as fun.

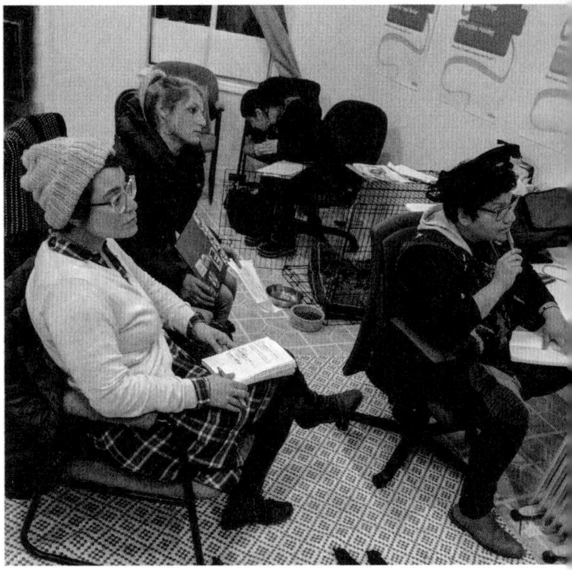

FEILD ORGANIZER DIRECTOR
CELINA NICOLE LOPEZ

Pizzolo: So could you start by explaining what a Fie Organizer Director does?

Celina: A lot. This campaign is to elect Sara Innamorato a a State Rep. So to run a field for State Rep, we want to b able to target our voters and figure out who those voters ar There's a program that lists every registered voter, so w use that to target who we want to talk to. And then we pla out which areas we're going to, when we're going to go, an how many people we need to send out to reach our ultima goal. So it's a lot of planning. A lot of planning and a l of plugging in volunteers, but that's the general spectru I mean, I can go on for hours about what a Field Organiz Director does.

Pizzolo: Are you principally organizing the volunteers wh are going out and knocking on doors and canvassing an stuff like that?

Celina: Yeah. Also we do a lot of recruiting for volunteers. W train them and get them comfortable enough to have casu conversations with their neighbors... to let them know abo an issue-based campaign or focus on a candidate and l them know who is running, when they can vote, stuff li that. We're sending out multiple volunteers a day knocking on doors and talking to voters.

Pizzolo: What brought you to this campaign?

Celina: I worked with someone on a voter registration project and they referred me to Sara Innamorato's campaign. And, before I agree to any campaign, I like to read up on them and then figure out what their expectations are. So what made me say Yes to Sara Innamorato's campaign is that she has a lot of the same values that I do. And one of my huge issues is getting big money out of politics. That's one of the issues she's focusing on, that's what made me say Yes and help organize out here in Pittsburgh.

Pizzolo: When you're putting together the logistics of getting volunteers out into the field, are you looking to recruit people from within those communities or do you have a set of volunteers that you're assigning to communities they haven't been to before?

Celina: Ideally, you want to recruit within the community. A lot of our recruiters are coming from the local universities. Some live within the district and some live outside the district but still believe in what we're doing. You want to recruit within the same area so everyone's familiar with the towns they're going into, and they can help the director know what issues to be focusing on because they'll know more. If you're in the community, you're going to know more about what the communities specifically need.

Pizzolo: Is there a particular attribute you look for in a volunteer when you're recruiting?

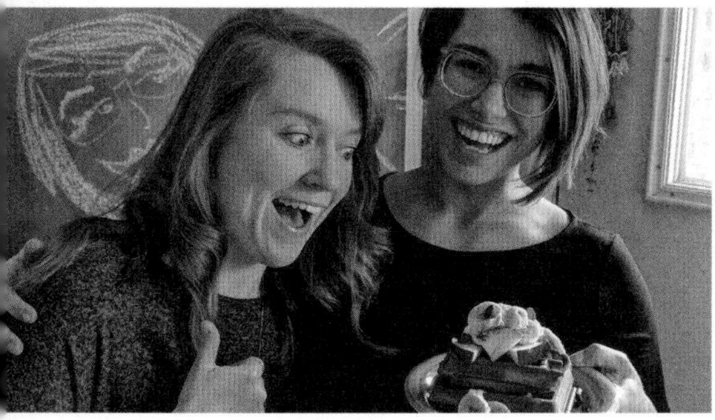

Celina: Anyone that stands out and has a lot of energy, who is really passionate, that's someone you want to bring on. However, a lot of times you don't find that within a person right away, you'll learn it about them from just talking to them throughout the campaign. And you can build up canvassers to get to that level. So you want to just focus on the people that are like "Oh yeah, I want to do this." You want to focus on everyone as a whole, and then build a relationship with them and then see what strengths they have and then you can place them: whether it's canvassing or doing data or phone banking or even helping you in the office put together packets. Whatever their strong attributes are, you'll know where to place them.

Pizzolo: And you started off by canvassing, right? Can you explain what canvassing is?

Celina: Yeah, there's different terms. It's all generally canvassing, but there's door canvassers and then there's street canvassing. Going door to door, you have a list of voters who you want to talk to and either get them to commit to vote or sign a petition. With street canvassing, you don't have a list because you don't know who you're talking to, you're just talking to people that pass by you. Street canvassing is better for fundraising, petition gathering, or even voter registration.

Pizzolo: What kind of canvassing did you get started doing?

Celina: I was on Martin O'Malley's campaign when I first started in 2016 in Iowa. So before the caucuses. And I was just door knocking.

It was the first time I ever knocked on doors. I was actually at a farmer's market in Iowa and a recruiter approached me and told me who Martin O'Malley was, that he was running for President, so I was interested in helping him out. I've always wanted to do some kind of grassroots and non-profit work, so I seized the opportunity.

I was naturally a shy person, so it took me a while to get used to knocking on strangers' doors. But I enjoyed it, because I got to see my community that I was living in. I got to have really good, positive conversations with people that have the same ideas as me. And empowering them to either commit to vote or even volunteer, it all evolved from there.

Pizzolo: Have you had an experience where you started talking to someone and it seemed like it was going to go bad, but then by the end of the conversation you felt like you made a real impact on them?

Celina: Yeah. That happens a lot. When someone comes to the door, you can read their body language and sometimes it can get a little intimidating. But then once you start talking about why you're doing what you're doing or focusing on a specific issue, a lot of the time an issue that you mention sticks to them and then they kind of warm up a little bit and become more receptive.

For example, one time I was talking about clean air. An older gentleman answered the door, he had this kind of body language, "What do you want?" I started talking about who Sara Innamorato is, what she is doing, and then I touched on clean air and water. It turned out this one specific voter works in an organization that tests the quality of water and air. And so he became more responsive because we're talking about something that he's familiar with. You don't know that about someone when you're at the door knocking, it's all by chance.

Pizzolo: When things get tough, is there any one experience that was so awesome you always remember and it keeps you going?

Celina: Yeah. Unfortunately, Martin O'Malley didn't get too far, so that campaign ended very quickly. So I immediately got recruited to an issue-based campaign in Iowa focusing on child care, living wage, paid sick days, paid family leave, and pay equality. Because it was non-partisan, we spoke to both parties, both Democrats and Republicans.

A lot of people aren't talking about how hard it is to pay for childcare. And then here comes this one person knocking on your door asking if you had any issues with childcare, and then a lot of people just spill their guts out. I don't have any children so I don't need childcare, but knowing how many people are struggling on this one specific issue and then mobilizing people to act on it and speak to their legislators… that's something I always keep in the back of my mind… just knowing the amount of people that got organized to go to the State House and talk to their legislators, that's always something I keep thinking about.

Pizzolo: If somebody is new to politics and activism but they're suddenly feeling very inspired to get involved, what advice would you give them?

Celina: Just be proud of yourself. Because any kind of activism, whether it's door knocking or entering data or even just coming into the office to staple packets or whatever, just know that you're part of the movement that you believe in. And it's really rewarding to see how far a campaign gets… knowing that, because of your efforts, we were able to talk to so many people or commit so many people to vote for a candidate or to vote for an issue. Just own what you do.

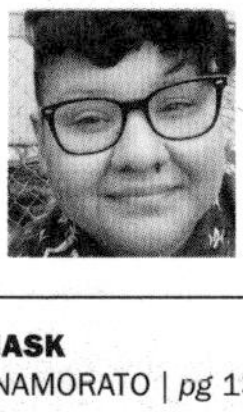

Celina Nicole Lopez has worked on nine campaigns since getting started as a canvasser for Make It Work in Des Moines, Iowa in 2016. Celina ran recruitment, scheduling, briefings, and canvass for a voter registration project in Cleveland, Ohio that registered 17,036 new and updated citizens in Cuyahoga County. Celina is currently Field Organizer Director on the Sara For PA campaign.

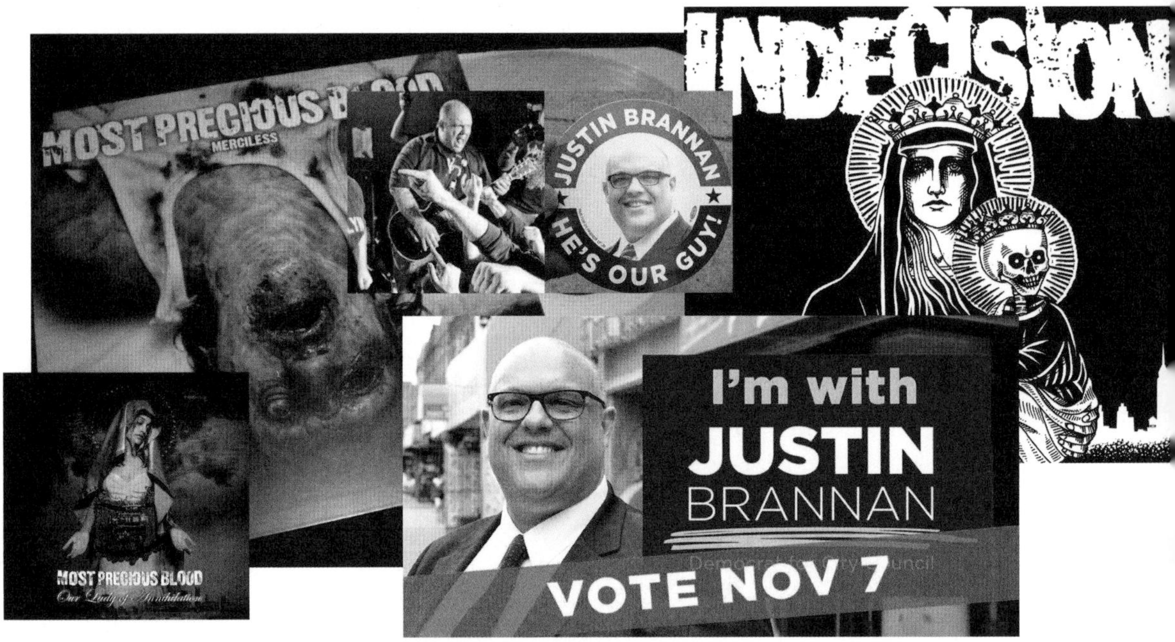
MOST PRECIOUS BLOOD
MERCILESS
JUSTIN BRANNAN
HE'S OUR GUY!
INDECISION
MOST PRECIOUS BLOOD
I'm with
JUSTIN
BRANNAN
VOTE NOV 7

CONVERSATIONS WITH PEOPLE I FIND INTERESTING

JUSTIN BRANNAN

Interview by **Matteo Pizzolo**

"Just because I'm not a lawyer or just because never studied political science, like, none of that stuf mattered. It was just I cared about helping people."

Pizzolo: Hey, Justin. Could you start by introducing yourself to the readers?

Justin: Okay. My name is Justin Brannan. I'm a member of the New York City Council representing the 43rd district, which encompasses a bunch of neighborhoods in southwest Brooklyn including the neighborhood where I grew up, Bay Ridge. I'm one of 51 members of the City Council, and we serve as a co-equal legislative branch of government, which serves to check on the executive branch, which is the Mayor.

Growing up, I wanted to be a member of the Ramones, not a member of the City Council. I definitely got an early start as a teenager in activism doing a lot of animal rights activism, environmental activism, sort of caught the tail-end of the first real AIDS activism in New York City. So, I was involved in a lot of that, but never really was all that interested in politics because I felt like it was all basically a bunch of bullshit, and it was all a bunch of old white guys with white hair talking about stuff that didn't affect my life. Because when your rent is due on the first and when you gotta decide between whether you'r gonna pay your electric bill or buy groceries, it's hard to real get yourself to care about what the President is talking abou -- at least back then it was, now it's different.

But anyhow I toured the world in a couple of hardcore band and I think absence made the heart grow fonder for th neighborhoods and the community where I grew up, so, afte we were done touring, I decided I wanted to get more involve in my neighborhood. So I joined a couple of civic groups, an some of them were welcoming, some of them weren't... there' a mentality, I think anywhere, where sort of like, "Who's th new guy? What does he want?" That kind of thing. So, it too some time and I actually ended up starting my own Democrat club and I started my own non-profit, mainly because the othe groups weren't interested in bringing me onboard. So, I sai I'll just start my own thing, because that's kind of all I ever kne was how to start my own thing.

And I got really involved in my community and I became like

go-to guy when people had problems, whether they were big or small. I took a job working with the council member that I would end up replacing 10 years later, and I worked my way up in his office and just learned the system, learned how to help people, learned how to leverage relationships and learned who to call and how to get things done and that kind of stuff and I just kind of took it and ran with it. I realized that I will always love helping people, and I kind of felt that politics was sort of a means to an end -- like, if I was here for the public service, at least in this field, you had to do the politics, but that's still what draws me is just being able to help people and that was my story.

I ran for office. Never in a million years would I have thought I would ever run for office. I ran, I ended up beating 10 people to get to where I am now. It's like a gauntlet and here I am. So, it's pretty exciting.

Pizzolo: How much did your background in activism inform the process for you? Did it affect the way that you campaigned and the ways you feel passionate about making change?

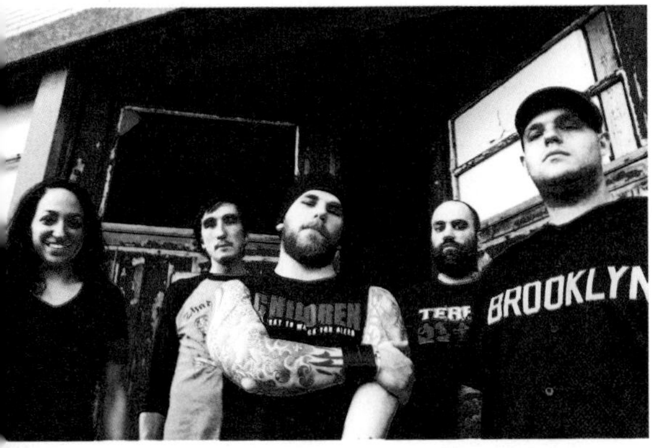
BROOKLYN

Justin: Absolutely. In a million ways, I really think that coming up as an activist and, probably more so, being in a punk rock hardcore band, sleeping on floors and having to sort of be your own manager, your own booking agent, and really all the DiY stuff that we embraced a million years ago before it was co-opted by like Home Depot. It was sort of like, well, you want something done, you got to figure out how to do it, because there was no one else who could do it for you or you couldn't afford to have someone else do it for you or no one else had done what you wanted to do, so there was no blueprint. And I think that I can really draw a straight line from point A to point B from sleeping on floors and touring all over 50 something countries and 5 continents and whatever the hell we did... I can draw a straight line from that to where I am now, because I think it gives you a real fearlessness that you feel that you can truly accomplish anything. If you really set your mind to it, you can really do it, because you've already kind of done it.

And I think it's a hustle... the same way I handed out flyers for a show when we were playing at CBGBs, I would sit outside the subway and hand out palm cards with my face on it saying Vote For Justin. So, it's the same kind of hustle. It's trying to get the word out there, get your message out there, get people to know your name. It's no different from starting a band and putting out a demo.

I was an activist, I'll always be an activist at heart, but I think especially now there's a very important space for activism and activists to move the needle and get politicians to listen and to shape the narrative. But for me, it was like, "Alright, instead of me throwing rocks at the building, let me try to find a way inside the building and effect change from the inside out." It's kind of like the Saul Alinsky playbook of, like: cut your hair, put on a suit and try to infiltrate the system with your own ideas, and that's kind of what I ended up doing.

Just because I'm not a lawyer or just because I never studied political science, like, none of that stuff mattered. It was just I cared about helping people, I cared about my neighborhood, I was able to get things done. I was like, "Well, why the hell shouldn't I just try it to run for office?"

But it was definitely local government that was really the place that I fell in love with, because I felt that that was the one place where you could really get results for real people in real time. It wasn't some of these pie in the sky things that you see coming to DC and some of the arguments and discussions they have where it doesn't feel immediate. It doesn't feel like it affects my life right now. The pace of that process can leave you feeling very disillusioned and disaffected. So, local government was where I felt like, okay, here's where I can really accomplish stuff.

Pizzolo: We all give so much attention to national politics, but it seems that even the perfect President wouldn't really be able to accomplish anything if there is not the infrastructure at the local level and the support from the grassroots. What's been your observation in terms of the importance of local government and focusing there on making change?

Justin: Well, I think, thankfully, change comes from the bottom up -- it doesn't come from the top down. Thank God, right?

I think that this is where you can really make a difference, and this is where you can build from the bottom up. You have to make sure that, if you really do want to take back the House, you have to make sure that you have a solid foundation. I think with Obama, it was probably the first time where people saw that the President can't just do whatever the hell he wants. This is why you have a Senate and a Congress, right? These are the checks and balances. So it showed that you have to have folks who are willing to do the work and willing to compromise and that kind of stuff or else nothing's going to get done, and it will go on and on like ping-pong.

On the local level, I think with New York City now we've sort of taken this "We've got to take care of our own" kind of mentality, because we don't know what's coming next from DC. So it's making sure that the city is taken care of, and that immigrants here feel safe and feel protected, and making sure there's relationships with the police and with ICE and keeping an eye on this kind of thing, and making sure these folks feel safe here and feel at home here.

So, in order to do that, you have to have good people who are those lower-level representatives who are holding the fort down.

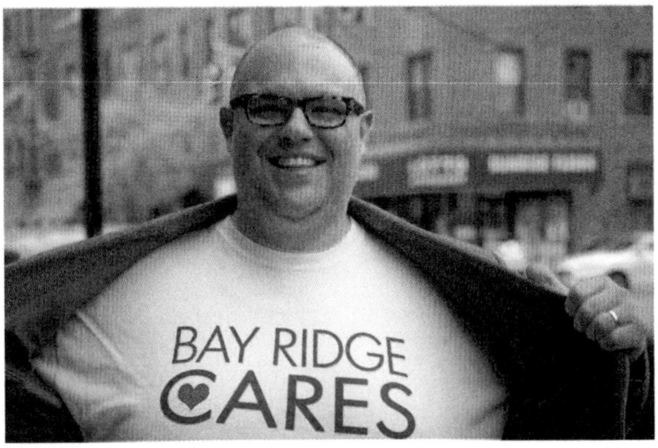
BAY RIDGE
CARES

Pizzolo: And what are the kinds of things that are determined at the local level?

Justin: In times like these, it's about getting creative and seeing just how far we can push the envelope, and how far we can go with making sure that we're protected when it comes to being a Sanctuary City or when it comes to making sure that funding and stuff is secure because we don't know what kind of cuts are coming down the pipe. So it's a very interesting time because you've got a lot of folks who are trying to figure out just how much can we do to really build a fortress to make sure that we can protect the progress that we've made and also keep the city running and keep the city strong.

I think the city has certainly been a laboratory for democracy for a very long time, and a laboratory for progressivism, and really trying to lead on so many issues, but now, it's sort of like we're trying to defend and protect those gains while also trying to just shore ourselves for what might be coming.

Pizzolo: I think that when people imagine like a City Council office or a position at a local level, there's the assumption that everything is such a bureaucracy you can't actually get anything done. Do you feel that there is the opportunity at that level to really impact people?

Justin: Absolutely. That's why I was so drawn to local government, because it was a place where I saw that I could really get things done. It's where the rubber meets the road.

I finally found a place where I could effect real change in the lives of real people in real time, whether it was helping a senior who's living alone on fixed income, helping her freeze her rent, or whether it was getting stop signs or traffic lights installed in a dangerous intersection or getting the swings replaced in a playground, and you have to fight for it -- but sometimes bureaucracy is just getting one side of the building to talk to the other side of the building, and I think sometimes it's that simple.

At the same time, I think being an outsider helps me because I don't take No for an answer when it comes to getting help for someone, and I didn't come up through the typical channels where I might be maybe more respectful of those barriers -- I just don't care, I'm here to help people and that's my job. That's why I was elected.

Representing my community, it's some of the foundational fundamental things: making sure everyone has a fair shot at opportunity no matter who they are, where they come from, but also it means making sure that our government is functioning efficiently. If you want the government to really be a tool to advance equity, it's got to first and foremost be working, and it's got to be working for all people, rich, poor, well-connected, white, black. It doesn't matter. And I think that's where I come from. I want my office to be a place where the people's voices are the most important, and that I'm always going to listen especially carefully for the marginalized and the most quiet voices. I'm always going to look to raise up those who might feel they've been shut out of the process or ignored.

I really ran a campaign that was based on creating more seats at the table and demystifying what the role of a Councilperson is, to really empower the average person to know: "Your tax dollars pay my salary and here are some of the things I can help you with."

The days of -- I mean, it's really hardly ever happened around here -- but the days of someone coming in to your office and saying, "I have a problem with X," and you telling them, "Well, I'm sorry, but you're going to have to go down the street to a congressman's office, because that's a federal problem," those days are completely over. If you've got a problem, we are here to help you with it. I'm not going to tell you "Sorry, go down the street, that's a state issue," because people are scared. There's lot of anxiety and most of it is very, very well-founded and people want to know what their rights are. It's a crazy time. So I think the role of local-elected official has really changed because now you really have to be open to all these different issues.

Pizzolo: You ran as an outsider, but you didn't go directly from being in a hardcore band straight into running for office, right? You spent 10 years learning the ropes. I think there's a lot of demand for new voices in government, but we also are struggling with a President who lacks experience at governance. How important do you think it was that you spent all that time learning the process before running for office?

Justin: I'm a big believer in certain rites of passage. I'm an unconventional guy and I sometimes have an allergy for bureaucracy and I have an allergy for rules altogether... and I don't think there's anything more inspiring you can say to me than, "I'm sorry, but this is the way it's always been done," that just makes me know that I have to find a new way to do it -- so, it's a good question, because I do think I'm a big believer in what Obama said in his farewell speech about, "If you'r disappointed by your elected officials, grab a clipboard, ge some signatures and run for office" -- I love that. But at th same time, I do believe in certain rites of passage, if onl because you've got to do the work.

The way to prove to folks that you really care is to do the work to show that you've been doing good stuff and you've bee doing the work of helping people before you decided to run fo office. Because you've got to have some sort of track recorc that's the kind of thing that matters and I think that's the kind c stuff that people are going to put their faith in. It's not where yo went to school or what you look like or how many degrees yo have or any of that nonsense. It's about what have you don in your private life or before the spotlight was on you, wha have you been doing to show that you truly care about being a servant of the people, being a public servant.

We need to be electing the people who have been doin the work and now are just so sick of the folks who've bee elected that they feel like, "Well, you know what? It's m time to step forward and lead and run," and that's really wha the government is supposed to be. It's of the people, by th people, for the people. People stepping forward and leadin and then passing the baton.

I think for activists and folks who are just really waking up t things now, they absolutely should run for office. But it pays t do the work first and to see if this is really what you want to do

Pizzolo: Out of curiosity, did you find that having been in bands and having a public presence affected your campaigning? O was it just two different worlds?

FRIDAY JAN. 15 7PM
DEJA ONE 133 WILLIS AVE
MINEOLA LI,NY
XEARTH CRISISX
INDECISION
ALL OUT WAR
MUSHMOUTH
ONE DAY CLOSER
Directions from NYC/NJ/LI (North Shore) – Take the LIE (495) east or west to exit 37, this is Willis Ave. Go south onto Willis and continue for about four miles, its on your right, it's a brick building with blue and white trim.
Directions from LI (South Shore) – Take the Southern State Parkway east or west to exit 22N, this is the Meadowbrook Parkway North. From the Meadowbrook exit at M1, this is Old Country Rd. Turn left onto Old Country Rd. and continue for about 1 ½ miles to Willis Ave. Turn right onto Willis Ave. Go across RR tracks and the venue will be on the left.

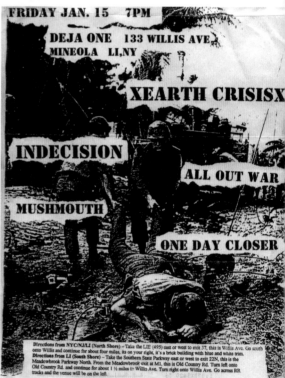

Justin: No, I mean, people in the neighborhood knew me but not because I was in the band or anything. That kind o notoriety didn't really matter. It's kind of funny, when we're doing some sort of underground thing whether it's art or music or whatever it is, 9 out 10 times your neighborhoods don't ever know that you do this stuff because it's on such a differen subcutaneous layer of life. Like your dentist has no idea tha you can go to Germany and play to a thousand kids, because why the hell would he, right?

I think if anything it just prepares you because I've been through oing interviews and that kind of stuff, so it just makes you a ttle bit more seasoned I guess. But no, that kind of notoriety idn't matter. If anything, my opponents tried to use it against ne, so, yes, they did some video about me, trying to make me ook like I was a devil worshipper and stuff and it's just like, 'es, whatever.

'izzolo: So, what was that like? Was it challenging or was it o big deal? Like, if someone's done something in the arts that ould be framed to a mainstream audience as controversial…

ustin: It's because art is in the eye of the beholder. So what's eautiful to me or you is outrage to somebody else, or feigned utrage to someone who's looking to use it as a weapon in a ampaign. There's nothing worse than feigned outrage.

knew it was coming. This goes back to what we were talking bout before, the fact that I was known for being trustworthy nd a good guy who truly cares about helping people and had elped so many people on a one-to-one level. I was able to urvive that because it just looked like someone was trying to mear me, whereas if I had just came out of the box and no ne knew who I was and suddenly someone tried to tear me own with that kind of thing, maybe it would have been a little it more effective, because no one would have known who I vas.

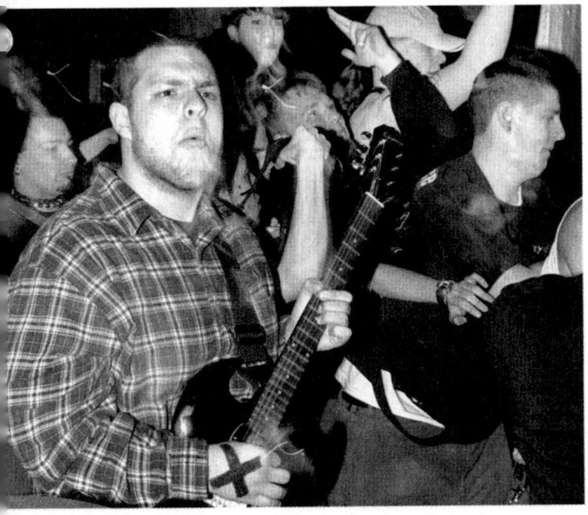

But by that point, people already knew who I was, and I never hid that I was in a band. I was never ashamed to admit that that's where I came from. A lot of people knew I was in it, that's part of my whole story. So it wasn't like I was hiding it and t wasn't like, "Oh My God, we uncovered this horrible thing about this guy." But certainly, that's another reason why you've got to do the work, because if you don't do the work, then something like that could maybe sink somebody who doesn't already have a reputation.

Pizzolo: As an outsider who also did the work, if somebody is new to all of this but is suddenly really inspired to join the political process, what kind of advice would you give them on the first steps if they don't know what it means to do the work? What are the first things that they might think about doing?

Justin: You have to at least try to get involved with your local traditional groups, your neighborhood has a Community Board -- you have to get involved in a volunteer level first and you have to see if you really like doing the work.

You can get involved politically by volunteering on a campaign, knocking on doors, stuffing envelopes -- I mean, it's all very glamorous stuff. Or there's the community service way, which is getting involved apolitically. Even though you might be a raging progressive Democrat in your heart, you don't have to do everything through that lens. It all starts by helping people and getting involved in some of your local non-profits or your civic groups, your local neighborhood civic association, that kind of thing and just to see if you've got a feel for it.

Or you just write your own path and you take an issue that's very important to you and just run with it. But in order to run for office, you have to build some sort of movement. People need to know your name and people need to see you as a leader and that means sticking your neck out on certain things and fighting. There's this famous saying like, "There go the people, I must follow them for I am their leader," right? You have to see what people are thinking about, what issues are important in your area, and make yourself a leader. Be a thought leader on stuff, and try to get folks to follow you and to believe in you.

But you can't do any of that until you start putting in the work. I think rites of passage for me… because I went to Catholic school, was raised under my dad's sort of work ethic, I believe in that -- even when we started our second band, Most Precious Blood, we could probably very easily had our first release been an album, right? Because we had just come from Indecision, but we purposely decided to put out a demo cassette, because that's what you do -- we wanted to work our way back up. And I think those rites of passage are important for a million reasons.

Pizzolo: What are some things you're excited about right now or have you feeling optimistic?

Justin: There's a lot of stuff. The opioid thing is a national issue, right? And I'm looking into doing some legislation to make sure that New York City Department of Education teaches kids in middle school and high school about opioids, the way that they used to do when we were in school, when they taught us about Mary Jane and all this nonsense just for awareness.

And I want to get civic education back into schools, so kids know the difference between their Community Board and their Congress Member. That's very important too, to understand the different levels and levers of government.

And public transportation is a huge issue. I mean, the city's public transportation system is just really deteriorated and I see public transportation a lot like how education is the great equalizer, because we're all stuck on that same subway – rich, poor, young, old. So, that's a huge issue too.

I'm certainly working on some animal welfare issues because that's really where I got my start, trying to push the envelope and I don't want San Francisco and Seattle, with all due respect to the West Coast, I don't want them to be eating New York City's lunch on any of these issues. I think that New York City really needs to lead, and I'm very focused on making our city the most humane city as far as animal protection laws and that kind of thing. So, that's something that I've really carried with me since I started. It's something where I started out with animal rights activism and now, as a lawmaker, if you want to call me that, I can focus on that. So, that's something I've carried with me from the beginning.

So, just trying to do everything I can, trying to think about all the stuff I dreamt of doing -- now I actually have a pen and I can shake some shit up.

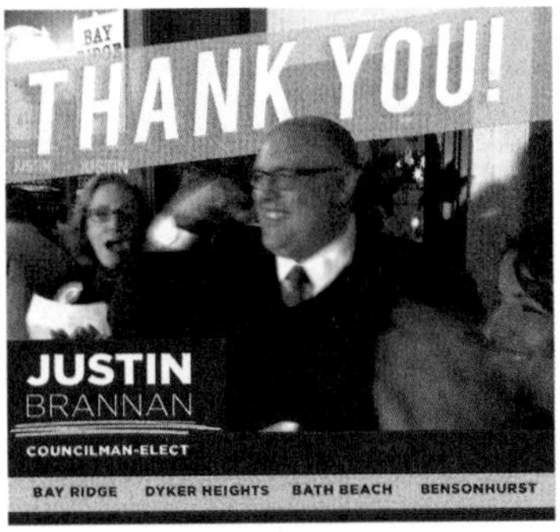
THANK YOU!
JUSTIN
BRANNAN
COUNCILMAN-ELECT
BAY RIDGE
DYKER HEIGHTS
BATH BEACH
BENSONHURST

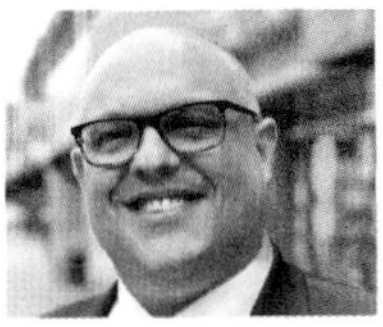

Justin Brannan was born and raised in Brooklyn, the son of a record salesman and early childhood educator. After attending PS 185, McKinley JHS and Xaverian High School, Brannan studied journalism at Fordham, before embarking on a career as a professional musician. His bands released several albums and toured the world – traveling to over fifty countries across five continents.

This interview has been lightly edited and excerpted from a much longer transcript. For the complete, unabridged interview please visit ***www.calexitcomic.com***

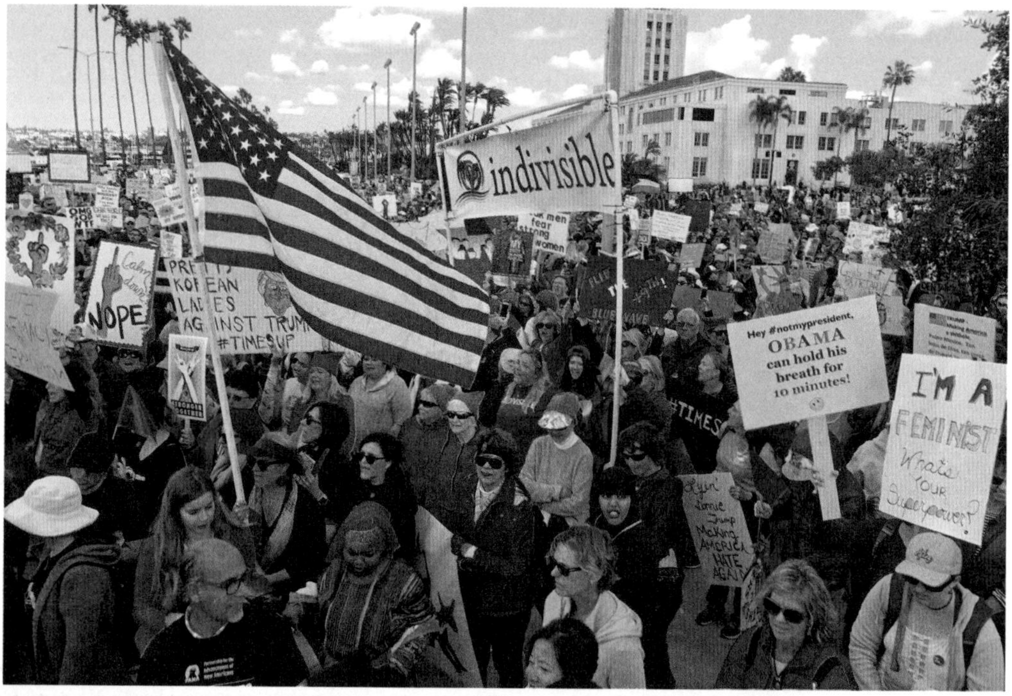
indivisible
NOPE
KOREAN
LADIES
AGAINST TRUMP
#TIMESUP
Hey #notmypresident,
OBAMA
can hold his
breath for
10 minutes!
I'M A
FEMINIST
What's
your
Superpower?

CONVERSATIONS WITH PEOPLE I FIND INTERESTING

INDIVISIBLE

***Interview by* Matteo Pizzolo**

"There are people who are very concerned we're already in a Fascist state and authoritarianism is already here, but I still have hope...we will find a way."

Pizzolo: Can you please start by explaining what Indivisible is and where it came from?

Kathy Stadler: Sure. So after the 2016 election, when we were all horrified, a group of former Hill staffers got together to talk about what they could do to make a difference and to stop what seemed to be a huge onslaught of pretty terrible things from happening policy-wise with the election of Trump. So they put together a Google Doc based on the organizing principles they had seen while they were on the Hill during the Obama Administration that the Tea Party had used successfully when Democrats controlled Congress and the White House, back when the Tea Party was interested in stopping what they thought of as the Obama Agenda. And these folks had been on the Hill at the time and saw how successful the people-powered organizing tactics were at stopping legislation -- or at least, if not stopping it, then modifying it significantly. So they wrote up a playbook for the Left to use similar tactics to stop the Trump Agenda. And the Google Doc ended up going across the country countless times.

So about 6,000 groups formed across the country, over a hundred here in San Diego. People met in living rooms, people met in restaurants, libraries, churches to start to organize -- oftentimes geographically, but not always -- about how we would use these tactics laid out in this guide to stop the agenda that was going to be coming at us.

And that's how Pam and I connected, at one of those organizing meetings with people from across San Diego County that at that point represented a number of different groups that had just started to get off the ground. And we've been working together ever since.

Pizzolo: Do you both have backgrounds in activism or political organizing or this is new?

Stadler: We both have backgrounds in organizing and activism. For me, I came from a family that was fairly active especially at a local level. The first time I remember being involved in political organizing I was carrying a sign -- I was four, my cousins were older and they made the sign -- it said "Hey, you SOB, save our beaches." Which got all kinds of laughs.

And from then on I was involved on and off throughout my life, had stepped away a little bit, but after the election -- like so many people -- I thought I need to do more and I need to get more involved. So I got involved with activist groups and particularly with Indivisible.

Pam Hughes: I also had a lot of background experience in is area, unlike most of our members who were either novices politics or hadn't been involved for decades. That is one ason Kathy and I worked a lot together, because we're a tle bit more seasoned than some of the other people in the ovement -- we were able to help provide some guidance ased on our past experience. I've been involved in politics orking in campaigns. I've been involved working in state nd federal government. I worked on the Hill in Washington, orked in advocacy groups, feminist groups, and had done a t of communication strategy over my career.

here clearly was a tremendous amount of energy that surged to the Indivisible movement after the Women's March, and ere was the need to kind of direct how it was going to go, how e we going to harness that in the best way possible to have be effective. Because there's a long history of resistance nd rebellions that pop up and fizzle out. And the threat from ump is so extreme, along with the whole Republican Agenda ankly, we felt this was something we had to get right.

o that's been the mission. Not only doing the week to week sponsive, reactive actions based on what's happening in ongress and what the President is doing, but also trying develop a longer term infrastructure that will allow this ovement to be sustainable and to grow and to thrive... ecause we can't ever find ourselves in this position again. hat was the mandate we gave ourselves: How do we keep is going? But also to be building a longterm way to channel e spirit of resistance, and to get more people plugged in who herwise might have felt that they didn't have a role, they dn't have a place.

ut the other major role we've played is targeting our ongressional delegation. Kathy, maybe you can talk about at.

tadler: Yes, here in San Diego we have a split Congressional elegation: we have three Democratic members and two epublican. With our three Democratic members, our work as mostly focused on making sure people are communicating ith them on important votes and letting them know that we're ere opening up lines of communication. We have groups that eet regularly with a couple of our members to talk about what ur priorities are, what our goals are, what they see going on, hat they see coming down the pipe and getting a dialogue oing that hasn't been happening before for a lot of people.

nd, with the two Republican members, we are looking to flip oth of those seats. So in California 49, it's currently Darrell sa's seat and you might have heard he's retiring. The folks om Indivisible in the 49th district worked in coalition with labor roups and activist groups and other progressive organizations nd they held -- well, they are still holding a pretty famous eekly rally at his office to pressure him. Sometimes there ave been upwards of 800 people. I think it averages over 00 people who attend every week at rallies that put enough ressure on Darrell Issa that it was one of the factors in his ecision to retire. And now those groups are working to make ure a Democrat will get through the June primary and get lected in November so we can flip that seat.

nd California 50, which by its registration is one of the reddest istricts in California, is currently held by Duncan Hunter Jr., ho's under FBI investigation. We are part of a coalition that got gether Indivisible groups and other groups across the district endorse a candidate that some would say is an outside of e box choice for the district: he's an Arab American candidate ho we feel could help engage parts of the electorate that may ave never had anyone to vote for. We're doing work there register new voters and get new voters engaged in the rocess, so that we can change the electorate and make it ore reflective of the district itself, and help change the seat at way.

izzolo: California 50 is the district where a number of ndivisible groups formed a coalition and endorsed one andidate all together, right?

tadler: Correct, it was the first endorsement in California and ne of the first in the country for 2018.

Pizzolo: When you put that together and organized a vote on who to endorse, there were a number of things you did that don't seem like obvious choices: you opened up the vote to 16 and 17 year olds, to immigrants who aren't eligible to vote, to people outside the district. What was the thought process behind including people who can't actually vote in the election?

Hughes: They may not be able to vote in the election, but that doesn't mean they can't impact it. 16 and 17 year olds are eligible to pre-register in California. They are also plenty eligible to walk and make phone calls and recruit and organize their neighbors to vote, and to get engaged in the process. People who are Dreamers or people who are on a path to citizenship are eligible to do the same thing, and they have a large stake in what happens in the district and what happens in the Congressional races in general. So we wanted to make engagement and inclusivity big parts of the process we set up.

Pizzolo: What was that process like? How did you organize it?

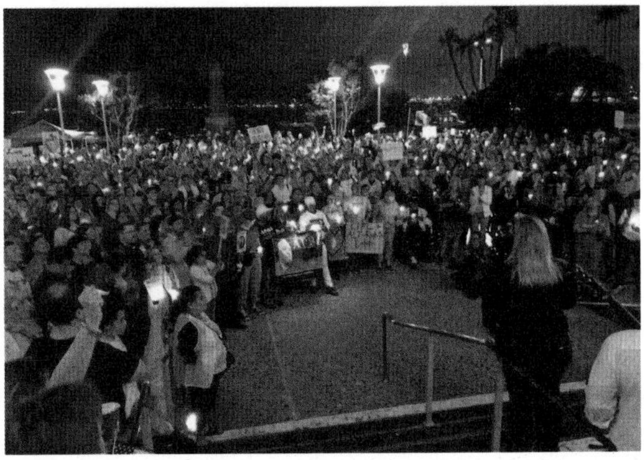

Stadler: We reached out beyond Indivisible, we reached out to Our Revolution, and we reached out to the climate groups, and we reached out to Planned Parenthood, and we said, "You don't have to be a member of Indivisible, but if you want a voice and a vote you can join us and help us endorse a Democrat to take on Duncan Hunter in this district."

And people showed up, they came. And what was surprising to us is that almost half of the voters who showed up to work in our endorsement process had not been activists in Indivisible before. So we used it as a way to open doors.

Again it's this whole theme of coalitions. How do we reach out and network so that everybody isn't in their little silo -- we're reaching across the district line, we had blue district voters come in and participate because we knew we're going to need them to help volunteer and turn out the vote. So give them a voice now and they're much more likely to show up and phone bank for you later. We brought people in from different organizations -- it's a social opportunity, face to face. It's people helping each other to do something important and getting to know people outside of our own bubble. And that worked very, very well.

Pizzolo: So all these people voted on which Democrat in the Primary to endorse for the seat?

Stadler: Correct. It's a Jungle Primary, so only the top two vote-getters get through. There's no guarantee that a Democrat would get through.

There were five or six Democrats that had expressed an interest in running, and we knew we needed to get behind one to elevate that person and help ensure that at least one Democrat would get through the Primary.

Pizzolo: So first everybody competes against one another in one big Primary that includes both Democratic and Republican candidates, and then the two winners face off head-to-head after that -- rather than having a Democratic Primary and a Republican Primary.

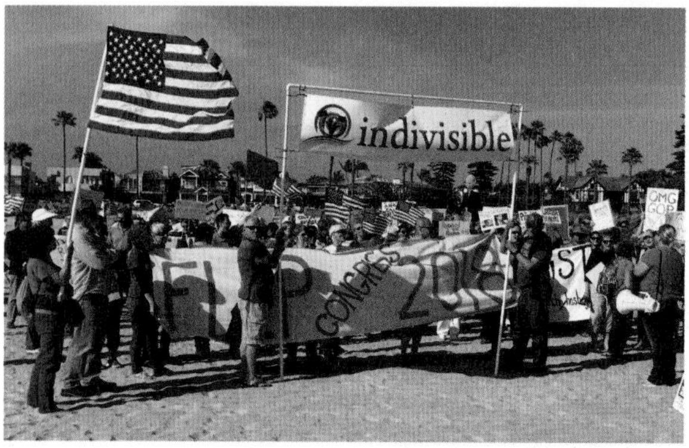
indivisible

Stadler: Right, which is a very big difference compared to states where all you're doing is competing within your base to get through the Primary and one Democrat is guaranteed to be on the ballot. We don't have that, that's why we couldn't risk splitting endorsements. We needed consensus for one Democrat that all the grassroots could get behind.

Pizzolo: And what was the process for organizing the vote for that endorsement?

Stadler: The process was going to nine different neighborhoods and getting votes from hundreds of people until there was a clear choice: and it was Ammar Campa-Najjar, a millennial Latino Arab American who really inspired people and then went on after winning our vote to secure the Democratic Party's endorsement, too -- which is interesting because if you can get somebody who has the grassroots and the establishment behind you it can put some wind at your sails. Even though it is an uphill race in a red district for a progressive minority to win. It really was a strategic advantage to have had this level of grassroots support behind him to rise with enough prominence and enough media attention and enough fundraising benefits to be able to have a chance of actually winning.

Hughes: There's an opportunity now that has never happened before that's unprecedented on the Left, where Indivisible is partnering with MoveOn and some other big groups nationally to buy their own voter list.

So there's going to be a shadow operation that does not rely on the Democratic Party, but can supplement and add to what the Democratic Party and the campaigns have been able to do. And the hope is that it can make a significant difference, so some of our Indivisible groups are going to form a coalition to work as an independent expenditure group -- so not working in coordination with the party or with the candidates, but able to work with Indivisible's national 501(c)4 and with non-corporate PACs.

There is an opportunity to bring resources to a whole different way of phone banking, of precinct walking, of getting out to vote, voter registration, and being able to activate people that haven't been able to be reached before. That's a whole untapped resource and this will be the first time it's been used.

Pizzolo: Usually the voter lists are provided by the Democratic Party? But in this case a bunch of groups are going to buy their own list?

Hughes: Yeah, they're going to be buying a voter file. Voter lists are publicly available information from the registrar of voters. Typically they provide it either through a political party or a specific candidate's campaign. 501(c)4s and PACs also typically have them, but progressive groups like Indivisible and MoveOn have never gotten together before to pool their resources and make that type of data available to grassroots organizers.

Indivisible has groups in all the Congressional districts. So to be able to make that type of data available to folks who are as on-the-ground as it gets, to be able to organize in their own neighborhoods and communities is potentially a game changer for national politics.

Pizzolo: The voter list has come up in various conversatio I've been having with organizers, and I don't fully understar the process of where that information comes from. What you' saying here is that if someone has formed an Indivisible grou on their block and they're not part of a campaign, ordinar they would not be able to get that information, right? And no they will be able to get it through Indivisible? Why is that game changer?

Hughes: It's been cost prohibitive for anybody other than th major parties or wealthy campaigns to be able to access the li and that information. For example, in each county in District 5 there are perhaps 30% Latino residents, so: What percentag of those are voters? What percentage of those are eligible be voters that we could register to vote? Which ones could w turn out if we have a young Latino millennial candidate wh might appeal to them that might make them vote when the never had anyone to vote for before? Is there an opportunity identify college students? There's a lot of young people in th district that haven't been involved.

So if we have those lists, we can target people not just ho the party wants to, but we can target people ourselves ar then develop an understanding and affinity with these votir groups, not just for 2018 but for 2020, 2022, 2024...

And we've never had the opportunity to do that before, becaus the grassroots groups would never have the resources or th people to be able to do it without the parties. Now we've g all these volunteers and all this energy and all this labor tha willing to get on its feet and walk, or get on the phone and ca or get on their phones and text, and now we're going to hav the database and the training to be able to use all that to targ the people we need to vote.

Because the only way we can win in some of these districts if we change the electorate, not just the candidate.

Yes, we need a candidate that's going to appeal, but you hav to change the electorate. You have to get people who've bee disenfranchised, who didn't vote... for example, people wh voted for Obama in 2012 and didn't vote at all in 2016 -- that the important group. Who are those people? Why didn't the vote? How can you inspire them now they really need to vo and how do we keep them voting not just in the primary but the midterm and then in the general and 2020?

And how do we keep those people feeling like their vote an important part of their life and an important habit that the will make and keep? That's part of the thinking behind thes national groups trying to do this game changing opportunity make this list available outside of working just within a party.

Pizzolo: A lot of people follow Presidential politics and they vote for President and they'll vote down ballot in Presidenti Election years, but why should people feel that midter elections and local elections are important?

Stadler: The 2016 election presented us with an opportuni at the same time it presented us with a lot of negatives. Th opportunity is to build a bench of local candidates, to build bench of people trained in working on campaigns and runnin campaigns and volunteering for them so that we will hav people to run up and down the ballot across the country.

One of the things the Republicans have been very successf at is running people in offices from Dog Catcher throug President, and that's one of the areas in which sometimes w on the Left have not been as strong as we could.

And in California on the state level, we need to elect peop who are going to lead a progressive agenda that will present the rest of the country something different than is coming o of Washington and will protect Californians and will do the be by Californians that's possible.

We have a lot of local elections here where people hav stepped up for the first time who are new to politics, who wer inspired to run by what happened in 2016. And we have peopl stepping up to work on campaigns and run campaigns that ar the same position. I think that's one of the greatest things that has come out of the election -- not just what we're seeing at the Federal level, not just that we're seeing the efforts to flip Congress, but what we're seeing at a local level as well.

Pizzolo: If someone has not participated in politics before but they feel suddenly very excited to get more involved in the process maybe because of 2016, what would you suggest are the first things they might try to do to get more involved if they don't have a background in activism or organizing?

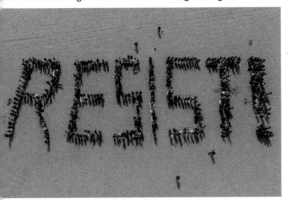

Stadler: Show up. I think the first thing is to show up. Find an issue or an office about which you are passionate, and show up. One of the things I tell a lot of people who are new to this process is a lot of this work is showing up -- and sometimes that means showing up to a city council meeting and holding a sign that indicates how you'd like to see people vote and sitting silently in solidarity with people who are most affected by that issue, or it might mean showing up and speaking at that city council meeting and offering testimony. It might mean going to your first text bank and sitting in someone's living room sending text messages into Virginia trying to remind people to get out and vote. But whatever you're passionate about, if you show up, and continue to show up regularly, you'll find a way to increase your activism, to increase your engagement, and make a difference in the things you care about.

Hughes: A lot of what we hear from people is not so much that they are "interested," the word they use is that a lot of people feel "compelled" right now. They feel compelled to do more, and yet sometimes they lack confidence in their ability to make a difference. And where Indivisible has succeeded is that we have new people all the time. We've gotten to the point where we make a habit at the beginning of every event or meeting to ask people for whom it's their first event with us, or it's their first protest, to raise their hands -- and there's always new people, and we always clap and welcome those people because it's a community. It's a community of people who believe in our own agency and who believe that the spirit of resistance can lift us out of the dark place that our country is in right now and that's contagious. People need hope.

They need to believe that they still make a difference, and that all of the things they see on the news, all the things they see happening… not just around the country -- but they're literally snatching people off the street in the community of San Diego. Very famously a few weeks ago, a mother of two was grabbed off the street by the border patrol in front of her teenage daughters who were screaming and crying, and that rattled people. That hits you with a gut punch. And it makes people want to say, "What can I do? I am compelled to do something." In Sacramento, they shot this young man Stephon Clark in his backyard 20 times for holding a cell phone. The people are desperate for something to do and some way to take action.

Every time you turn on the TV, Trump is doing something -- the EPA is going to try to gut the science that can be used to make health and environmental decisions in this country, and the scientific community in San Diego is very engaged and has never been political before but the scientists are really upset and they want a place to get involved. They want a way to have their knowledge and their expertise be relevant to try to push back against this kind of ignorance and obstruction. So

giving people a place to come and feel welcomed and to feel hope and to feel relevant to what's happening is really what we're trying to offer. I think the more people get involved, they can find a variety of different ways. Some people like to write postcards to voters in other districts or other states and they're very artistic and they design this beautiful message and they write something very heartfelt and they mail that postcard to somebody who is going to receive it and realize "Somebody reached out to me on a very personal level," and they're gonna stick it on the refrigerator and remember to vote.

Other people are going to be comfortable going out and knocking on strangers doors, which is not for everybody. Some people love it because they get to engage in conversations with voters about things they really care about. Other people are going to just want to stand up at the March For Our Lives in solidarity with these high school students and hold a sign. But there's always a way. The more we can touch people and give them hope and give them a sense of this feeling of agency back, the stronger this movement can be.

Even though, short term we do see a lot of pain: the ICE deportations, the police shootings of African Americans, the white supremacist movement being empowered, all the federal policies that are threatening people's healthcare, the foreign policy concerns we have with North Korea and the Russians' infiltration of Facebook and our voter files and Twitter… there's just so much that's disturbing and that has our alarm bells going off -- I do still feel that, for people who are active, if you really do get involved, that there is optimism for the long term.

We still have democratic institutions that -- however compromised they are, and they have been compromised -- you still have a vote, they'll try to suppress it and it might be interfered with, but we still can overwhelm with the vote. We still have the courts on our side, we still have free press, and social media to connect with each other. We still have our intelligence agencies. And we still have allies around the world who are all pulling for the United States to save our democracy and to prevent this takeover by Trump and the Republicans that is not just threatening to our people but to people all over the world.

If we do continue to work together, if we keep this spirit of resistance alive, we will be able to overcome it. There'll be a lot of pain in the meantime. There's a tremendous price that we're going to pay, but I do think that we can avoid the dystopia that many of us fear is coming. And political art like yours is a great reminder, as well as The Handmaid's Tale and other things that let you see what can happen if you don't take this seriously and if we're not all in to stop it.

Pizzolo: Hopefully it doesn't become an actual dystopia…

Hughes: There are people who are very concerned we're already in a Fascist state and authoritarianism is already here, but I still have hope that we're going to turn this around… that we're stronger than that, and we will find a way.

Pam Hughes is a communications strategist for Indivisible based in San Diego, CA. During a career in government, politics and advocacy, she worked for the National Organization for Women, Sen. Ted Kennedy, the US Department of Education and PBS.

Kathy Stadler has been a teacher, organizer, campaign manager and trailblazer in building community through innovative social media connections. She is a leading strategist for San Diego County Indivisible.

Follow them on Twitter @SDIndivisible

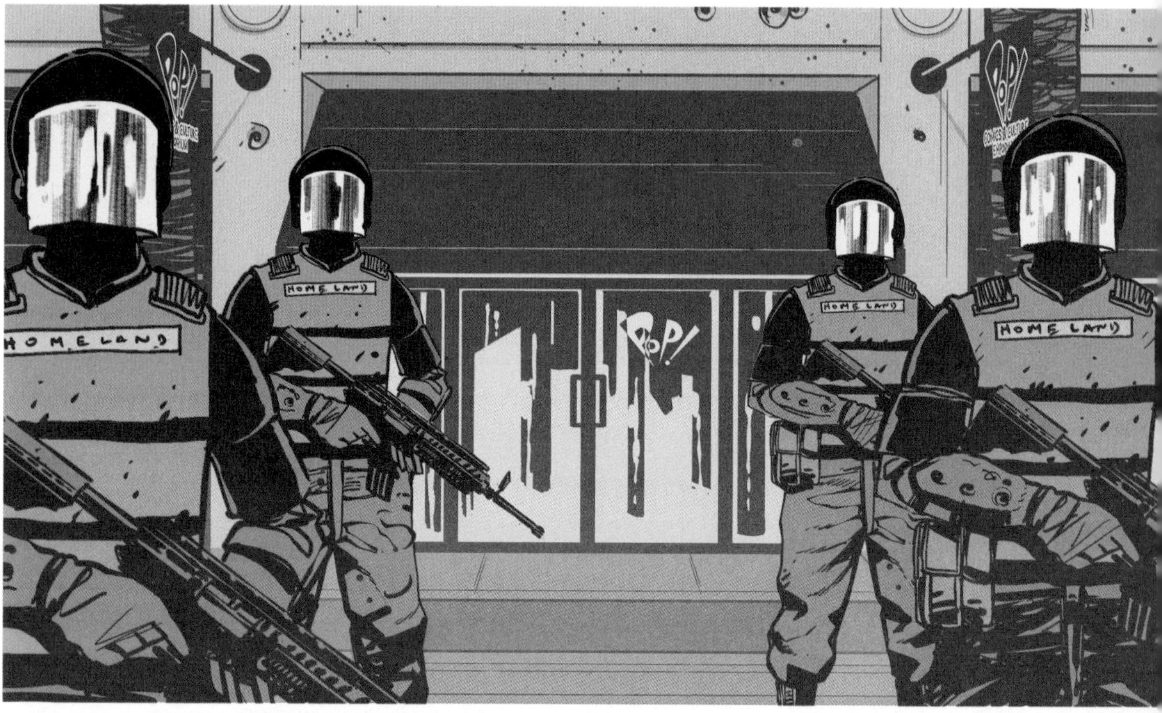
POP!
HOMELAND
HOME LAND
POP!
HOME LAND
HOME LAND
POP!

CONVERSATIONS ABOUT CALEXIT

NEW COMIC CALEXIT SEES CALIFORNIA REBELLING AGAINST PRESIDENT TRUMP

This interview was conducted by Christian Holub and first appeared in Entertainment Weekly on July 12, 2017. It is reprinted here with EW's permission. - pg 141

2017'S MOST DANGEROUS COMIC: WRITER MATTEO PIZZOLO ON GOLDEN STATE SECESSION SERIES 'CALEXIT'

This interview was conducted by Will Nevin and first appeared in The Oregonian on July 11, 2017. It is reprinted here with The Oregonian's permission. - pg 143

This interview was conducted by Christian Holub and first appeared in Entertainment Weekly on July 12, 2017. It is reprinted here with EW's permission.

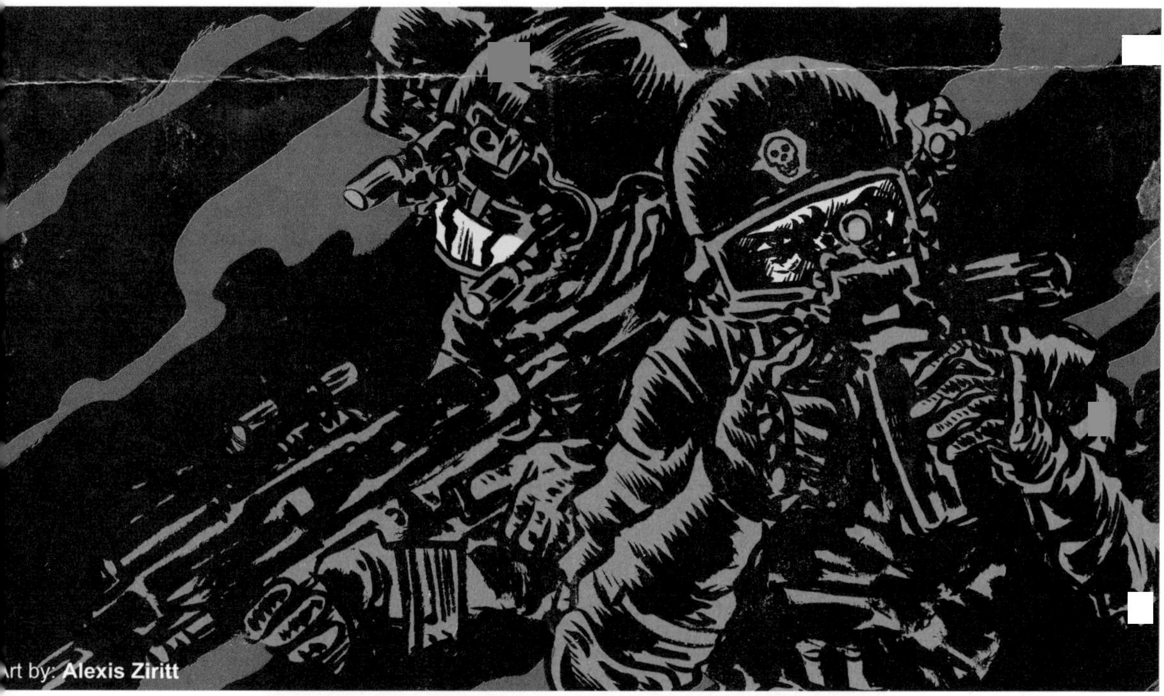

ırt by: Alexis Ziritt

CONVERSATIONS ABOUT *CALEXIT*

"NEW COMIC CALEXIT SEES CALIFORNIA REBELLING AGAINST PRESIDENT TRUMP"

***Interview by* Christian Holub**

ıe presidency of Donald Trump has certainly been eventful so far. The day after Trump was inaugurated as the 45th President the United States, millions of Americans took to the streets to make the Women's March one of the biggest protests in e country's history — and that energy has not yet subsided. Liberal opponents of Trump proudly declare themselves "The esistance," as if they were fighting the Nazi occupation of France. Constituents have been storming Republican town halls and ongressional offices to protest the Trump-led Republican Party's new health care proposal, while so-called "antifa" protestors ve more violently confronted Trump supporters on the streets. The country has rarely felt so divided.

on't worry: It can get worse! Calexit, a new comic from Black Mask Studios, portrays a near-future world in which the state California is in open rebellion against the Trump-led U.S. government. Militants clad in black bloc openly clash with federal ops to defend immigrants, painkiller addiction is widespread, and environmental decay is clear. Writer Matteo Pizzolo and ist Amancay Nahuelpan combine these elements to create a dystopia that feels far closer than many readers will probably be mfortable with.

V caught up with Pizzolo to discuss the genesis of the comic, its roots in the real world, and the spirit of resistance.

ITERTAINMENT WEEKLY: This story definitely feels like a oduct of the Trump era. The man himself shows up on the st page, and some of the action and general aesthetic looks e an extrapolation of the protests (especially antifa and black oc) which have sprung up in his term. What kind of real-world periences inspired this story? What was the moment, if there is one, where this idea really started to come together for u?

ATTEO PIZZOLO: This comes as a surprise to a lot of ople, but the project wasn't conceived under the Trump Administration. We were initially putting this all together last year. You're right though, it's become very much a product of the Trump era and we've embraced that.

The real-world experience that most inspired it is an unlikely one: the California drought. And I realize that's a bit of a local story but I think the experience rings universal. I drive my son to pre-school past a large reservoir here in Northeast L.A., and one day, at the height of the drought, I passed the reservoir and it was completely empty. Just barren. There's a park out in front of the reservoir and I remember seeing all these kids playing on the yellowed grass with this gigantic, parched wasteland behind them. It was a chilling image. If the drought were to persist or worsen, if something happened with the water pipelines coming into L.A., well… none of us [would] have very much accessible water for our children. The thought of having to rely on the federal government for something like water was scary a year ago. In 2017, it's downright terrifying. But it can also be inspiring to recognize our interdependence and get past political vitriol to work together. To my mind, the comic isn't about secession or attacking the government, it's about people learning to take care of one another at a time when it feels like we're all slipping apart.

EW: What is the role of California's culture, history, and politics (especially its Texas-like sense of being a quasi-independent state) in this story? Why did you choose California as the setting?

MP: Californians have a long history of aggressively standing up for themselves, as far back as 1846 when California seceded from Mexico up through relatively recent (and extreme) examples like the Watts Riots and L.A. Riots, and even in arguably more constructive forms like exporting entertainment and technology that celebrate rebellion, from Star Wars to Apple Computer to NWA. So California's sense of itself as semi-sovereign is deep in its DNA.

Calexit follows Zora, a Mexican immigrant who's become a leader in the resistance army, on the run with Jamil, an apolitical smuggler who salutes no flag. While I think these are universally relatable characters, they're also uniquely Californian, and the backdrop of the factionalized California they're journeying through is a perfect microcosm for the country because California is as diverse yet interdependent as America.

EW: Early on in the issue you show a map of California split up into various factions and occupied territories, not unlike real-world Syria right now. What's been happening in California in the time before this story kicks off?

MP: The setting of *Calexit* is that a fascist leader is elected U.S. President and enacts an executive order to deport all immigrants. So the governor in Sacramento responds by refusing to enforce the law, proclaiming California a Sanctuary State. What happens after that? The state itself fractures and plunges into civil war. Immigration law is as contentious within California as it is throughout the rest of the country, after all. Many of the suburban, rural, and exurb regions side with the federal government, proclaiming themselves the Sovereign Citizens Coalition, and those regions happen to control most of the major resources the cities rely on. Everything escalates from there as cities up the coast form the Pacific Coast Sister Cities Alliance to support Los Angeles and San Francisco, inciting Homeland Security to finally invade California.

It's impossible to work on a project dealing with civil war, refugees, factionalized populations, and political extremists, particularly a story like this that's partly inspired by the effects of climate change, and not look deeply at the situation in Syria. We don't pretend to be experts on the subject, but it certainly weighs on our minds heavily.

EW: How do you balance political commentary with telling a story on its own terms?

MP: The guardrail we've established for ourselves is to stay focused on the core thematic idea: to celebrate the spirit of resistance. And from there we avoid doing direct political commentary. It's peppered here and there, but we try and devote our efforts to serving the story and characters. We've sought

to do that by developing compelling characters with stro moral centers but who are conflicted and have contradicto motivations, and we plunge them into awful situations whe they have to make tough decisions under great duress. And w trust that joining them through their struggles and journeys w ultimately be inspiring, that their hearts will shine through t grim dystopia.

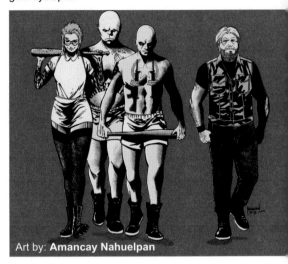

Art by: **Amancay Nahuelpan**

EW: By the end of the first issue, Zora has emerged as badass resistance leader. What can you say about her a how she came to this position?

MP: As there is a civil war raging in California, there also a war raging within Zora. She's been elevated to leadership position in the resistance because of her force will and fearlessness. People respect her and they want follow her, but what they don't realize is that she's principa driven by anger and revenge. Right now she can lead t resistance and pursue her personal revenge at the same tim but over the course of the story, she will need to decide if sh going to become a real leader or if she's only here for blood

EW: The art here is really spectacular. What would you s Amancay Nahuelpan brings to the story? How do you t work together?

MP: Amancay draws some of the most incredibly dynam action sequences I've seen anybody do, so I love givi him big set pieces he can devour — but *Calexit* also h more grounded and controlled scenes than we've ever do before. The silent moment of a father and daughter looking one another in a dark suburban yard with an unknown thre looming. Amancay is flexing totally new muscles here, an think what he's doing is just astonishing. There's a moment the tail end of the gunfight in issue 1: It ends on Zora's fac silent. She's not saying a word but Amancay manages express everything in the fierceness of her eyes and the sub clench of her jaw. He's doing work with these characters he that I just find stunning.

EW: What can you tease about what readers can expect goi forward?

MP: Readers should expect things to get pretty rough for characters, but despite the grimness of the world, we a following hopeful characters who won't give up. So expect b but complex heroes who are willing to look fascism in the fa and challenge it. If you're like me and you feel we need m heroes like that, then I hope Zora's rallying cry for resistan will stay with you after you close the book.

This interview was conducted by Will Nevin and first appeared in The Oregonian on July 11, 2017. It is reprinted here with The Oregonian's permission.

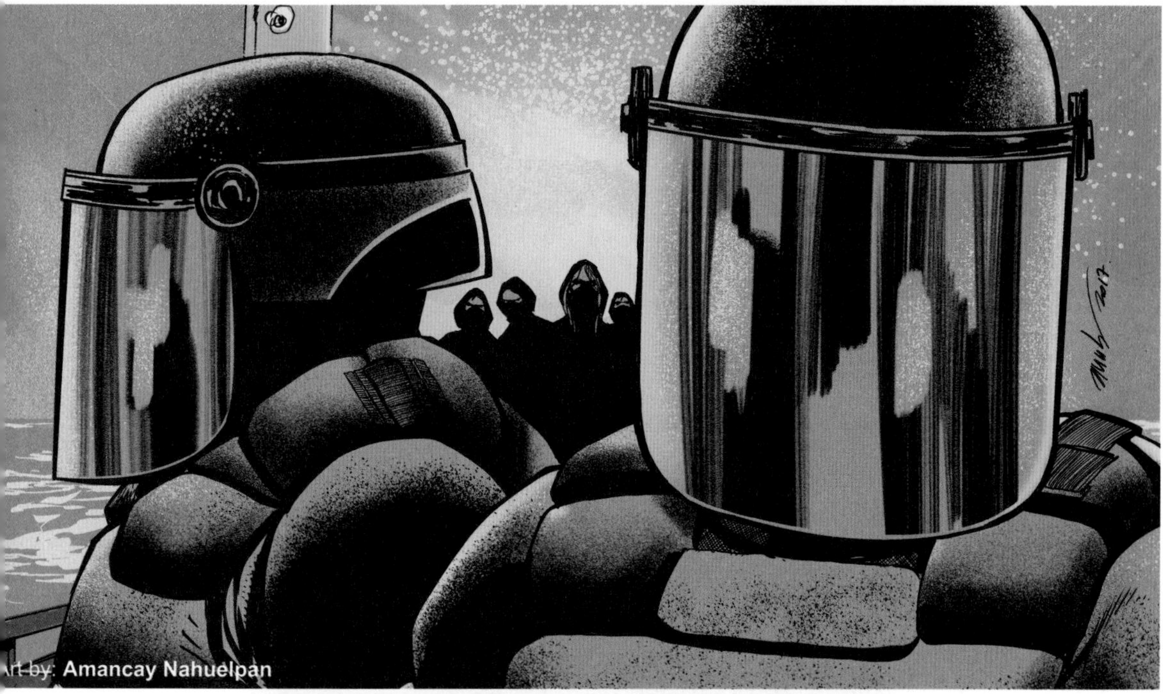

rt by: Amancay Nahuelpan

CONVERSATIONS ABOUT *CALEXIT*

"2017'S MOST DANGEROUS COMIC: WRITER MATTEO PIZZOLO ON GOLDEN STATE SECESSION SERIES 'CALEXIT'"

***Interview by* Will Nevin**

s the United States has tumbled farther from established and comfortable political norms in the last 16 months, many comic ok creators -- as much a part of the disaster as any of us -- have responded creatively, giving us some comics that have been cellent and some...not so much. This week, Black Mask Studios brings us another project that very much seems to be in that rmer group: "Calexit," by writer Matteo Pizzolo, artist Amancay Nahuelpan and colorist Tyler Boss, imagines a world in which alifornia has seceded to escape the fascist grasp of the Trump administration.

alked via email with Pizzolo on the new series, the politics of 2017 and what it was like to write the best words for the esident with the yugest hands.

LL NEVIN: How would you summarize the premise of alexit"?

ATTEO PIZZOLO: "Calexit" is the story of Zora, a resistance ovement leader, and Jamil, a smuggler, who are on the n from Homeland Security forces that are occupying Los ngeles and hunting down immigrants after California went to ar against the US Government. It's a fictitious tale of a fascist ader being elected US president and passing an executive der to deport all immigrants, which causes California to fuse enforcement of the new law and proclaim itself a nctuary state.

ings escalate from there with various cities supporting California, forming the Pacific Coast Sister City Alliance from Tijuana to Mexico, and Homeland Security invading California, all as the state itself descends into a civil war with rural regions factionalizing against the metropolitan centers.

WN: How did the book begin -- before or after the election? Would you be writing it if Clinton had won? Would there be any different emotion for you if she had? In essence, does an actual Trump presidency make this book more raw and difficult to write?

MP: We started work on the book prior to the election, developing the basic concept during the 2016 election cycle but before the actual election. So, it was conceived in the muck of the primaries and general election, but not in direct reaction to Trump winning.

Many of the political issues inspiring us to create the book have been present throughout various administrations, even if the current one is stepping things up a million notches. It was scripted and illustrated after the election, though, so obviously we knew the election results while crafting the book itself.

The Trump presidency doesn't change the core of Zora and Jamil's story journeys, but it recontextualizes everything. I think it gives us a different responsibility to make sure we don't wallow in dystopia at a time when a lot of people are feeling suddenly more at risk than they did a year ago. We don't want people to put the book down more fearful or depressed than they were when they picked it up.

So, the main change that the administration inspired was building out the back half of the book with non-fiction material featuring people who are doing inspiring, exciting, positive and constructive things. The book itself is about celebrating the spirit of resistance, but some of the issues will end on down notes, and we want to keep the whole project with a sense of positivity about it.

WN: What do artist Amancay Nahuelpan and colorist Tyler Boss bring to the book, and what do you think are their strengths?

Art by: **Amancay Nahuelpan**

MP: Well, for one thing, Amancay and Tyler bring the book itself, since nobody wants to read a comic book script. Amancay and I worked together on "Young Terrorists" before and I also work with him on "Clandestino," which he both writes and draws. He's an incredible talent who composes some of the most dynamic action panels I've seen, but he can also deliver incredibly subtle character moments which are really crucial to this book, since it's considerably less bombastic than "Young Terrorists" or "Clandestino." I think there's a lot of power in silent comic book scenes, but they're hard on a reader because they only work if the reader sees the implied word balloons even though they're not actually there. It requires

very deft visual storytelling from the artist in the crafting of th sequence as well the silent panels themselves. I can alwa trust Amancay to deliver moments like that.

Zora doesn't have a lot of dialogue scenes in issue #1 to beg with, and there are a few places where I scripted her to rea silently -- which is real dicey when the character isn't speakir too much as it is, but I trusted Amancay to convey paragrap of exposition in her eyes. And he delivered. Those are some my favorite beats in the book.

Tyler I've worked with on his book "4 Kids Walk Into A Ban which he co-created with writer Matthew Rosenberg, ar that's one of the best all-around books of the past few yea in my humble opinion. I've also worked with Tyler on desig for various other Black Mask books, and I've found him not only be a brilliant visual storyteller, but also he has a impeccable design sensibility and an intense work ethic. H is very thoughtful in each creative decision he makes, whir "Calexit" really needs.

For example, every panel has to feel authentically and unique California but still resonate as being universal. A lot of that to falls on Tyler to express; we spent a bunch of time just the color of California sunshine and basing the color pale around that. It's the kinds of thing you don't necessarily noti but impacts you during the read.

WN: At one point in issue #1, Trump is referred to as "h excellency" -- what's your take on the state of American politi and where we're going? Do you see "Calexit" as plausible implausible fiction?

MP: Well, the "His Excellency" line is delivered by the hea immigrant-hunter Father Rossie, a ruthless and fear leader of the occupation. What we're getting at there is th kind of hero-worship common to followers of fascist leade As for whether this is plausible, it's starting to feel plausib isn't it? We had no idea there would be an actual secessi ballot initiative when we put the book together. A lot of peop who'd read early drafts started emailing me when Califorr co-founded the Climate Alliance after Trump pulled out of th Paris accord and also when Trump threatened to deputize tr National Guard.

It's jarring as hell -- prescient is not an adjective I want for th book.

WN: There's no hiding that Trump is a character in the boc How did you write his dialogue? Was it strange or disturbing project those patterns and idiosyncrasies onto your imagin disasters?

MP: I actually found it really easy to write the preside character's dialogue, probably just because we've all be listening to Trump babble for the past year, so using his tonal for the president's monologue felt natural. Trump's cadeno has a fun rhythm to it, and the mix of hyperbole with zero so reflection feels refreshing when you're used to public figur speaking in such a calculated way, y'know? I mean, that's o of the reasons Trump's become so popular and why he can g away with saying things that are objectively monstrous and s come across as likeable to millions of people.

But yeah, placing that clearly Trumpian word pattern onto th dystopia strikes me as really troubling in the re-read. We're a fine line with the book where we want it to feel grounded a realistic, but it can't get too realistic or it becomes horrifying.

WN: How does California state politics play into the book w the split along the Sister Cities / Sovereign Citizen lines?

MP: One of the key premises in the book is that, in the event of secession, California would become embroiled in its own civil war before any US soldier would have the chance to be deployed. So, when Sacramento proclaims itself a Sanctuary State in the story, a lot of the rural and exurb areas revolt against that, forming the Sovereign Citizens Coalition. After all, immigration is an incredibly contentious issue in California with passionate activists on all sides. Since the Sovereign Citizen regions control a lot of the resources the metropolitan cities rely on (water pipelines, agriculture, etc), many unexpected battlegrounds emerge like the dams in Fresno and Oroville or the nuclear power plant in San Onofre or the snowpack in the Sierras.

WN: What's your take on the actual California secession movement and how it might be tied to Russia?

MP: The idea that California should secede is pretty much the first thing you hear when you get off the bus at the Greyhound station anywhere in California going back decades through every presidential administration. So, the idea isn't new. It was startling to me that it picked up so much momentum earlier this year, hard to tell how much of that is real -- I mean, it seems pretty impossible, but then again we elected Arnold Schwarzenegger governor. The setup in the comic book is that California is forced to secede when it takes a principled stance, so that is a bit different than passing a ballot initiative to secede.

Whether Russia is behind it -- I mean, again, it's not a new idea. Russia didn't suddenly convince Californians that they're aggravated by the electoral college. But, sure, why wouldn't Putin throw some money into the movement if it looked like it could become disruptive? Isn't that why France supported the American Revolution, to disrupt the British Empire? The comic will eventually widen its canvas to look at the conflict between California and the US government from a global perspective. If California has a larger economy than France, then a war between California and the US would have global implications -- for example, it would be a far larger initial conflict than the one between Austria-Hungary and Serbia that eventually escalated into World War I.

WN: How would you describe your main characters: Jamil, Zora and Father Rossie?

MP: Zora is a leader in the Mulholland Resistance who is thrust into this position of authority without very much background in revolutionary strategy or combat; she's in over her head, but so is everyone in the resistance movement. She's headstrong, hurtling forward simultaneously to build the movement and also to seek personal vengeance against Father Rossie. Right now, those two motivations are generally in accord with one another, but soon enough, she will have to decide if she is going to devote herself to what's right for the resistance or if she is going to abandon all that and seize her revenge.

Jamil, on the other hand, is a survivor who remains completely neutral and apolitical; as he likes to say, he's "got a problem with no one." Of course, as the saying goes, you can't be neutral on a moving train, and Jamil will ultimately have to choose a side -- although, knowing Jamil, he'll probably choose more than one.

Father Rossie is the most feared man in occupied Los Angeles, a cold-blooded immigrant hunter who will go to absolutely any length to capture his prey. He runs the Homeland Security forces throughout Southern California, and he's developed a personal vendetta against Zora.

WN: Is it fair to say that California -- at least the parts of it we see in #1 -- is an occupied territory? What did you draw from in crafting that world, and what was your thought process in creating an occupied state in which life for many is still normal (e.g. tourists still visit, photo op superheroes, etc.)?

MP: Not all of California is occupied, but Los Angeles and San Francisco specifically are under active military occupation. The level of control exerted by Homeland Security over the population was inspired by the early years of the Nazi occupation of France, during which time many of the French people were going through their day-to-day routines despite the constant, ubiquitous existential danger. In a certain way "Calexit" depicts everyday American life with a fascist overlay -- although a militarized police force silently watching your every move, waiting for you to step out of line really is everyday life for a lot of Americans. I think the other thing to note about the tourists seen throughout the book is that they are a far less diverse assortment of tourists than you would ordinarily see around Los Angeles. Not everyone is going through their normal daily routines.

WN: What's your goal for the book? What do you hope readers get out of it?

MP: I hope our celebration of the spirit of resistance shines through and inspires readers in a positive way. Maybe the story might do its small part to help someone feel encouraged to get out there and participate more in their community in an optimistic, constructive way.

But most of all I hope readers fall in love with Zora and Jamil and are thrilled by their journey. I feel like we need more heroes these days who aren't afraid to look fascism in the face and challenge it.

Art by: **Ben Templesmith**

CALIFORNIA REPUBLIC

All covers by **Amancay Nahuelpan** unless otherwise noted.

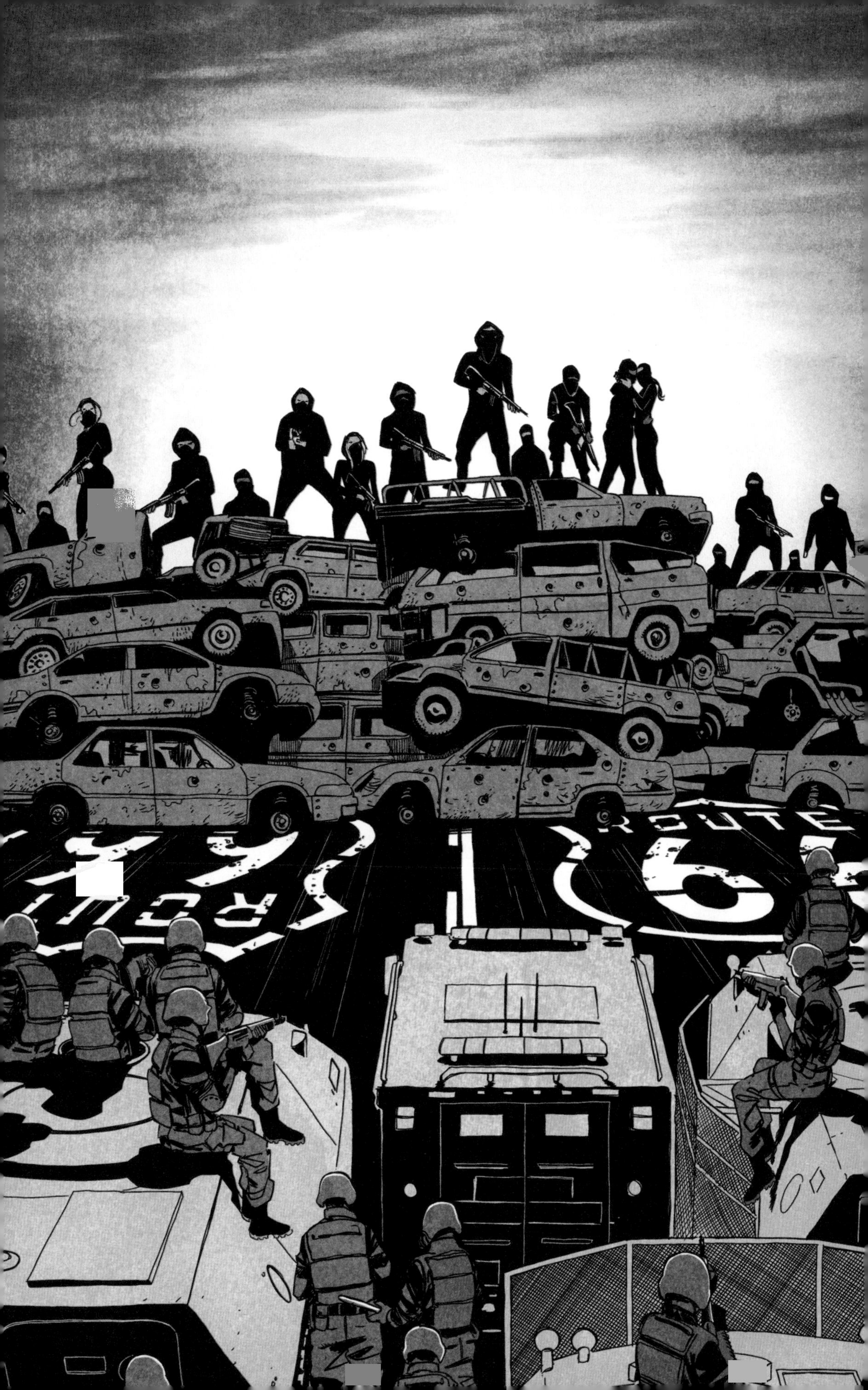
ROUTE

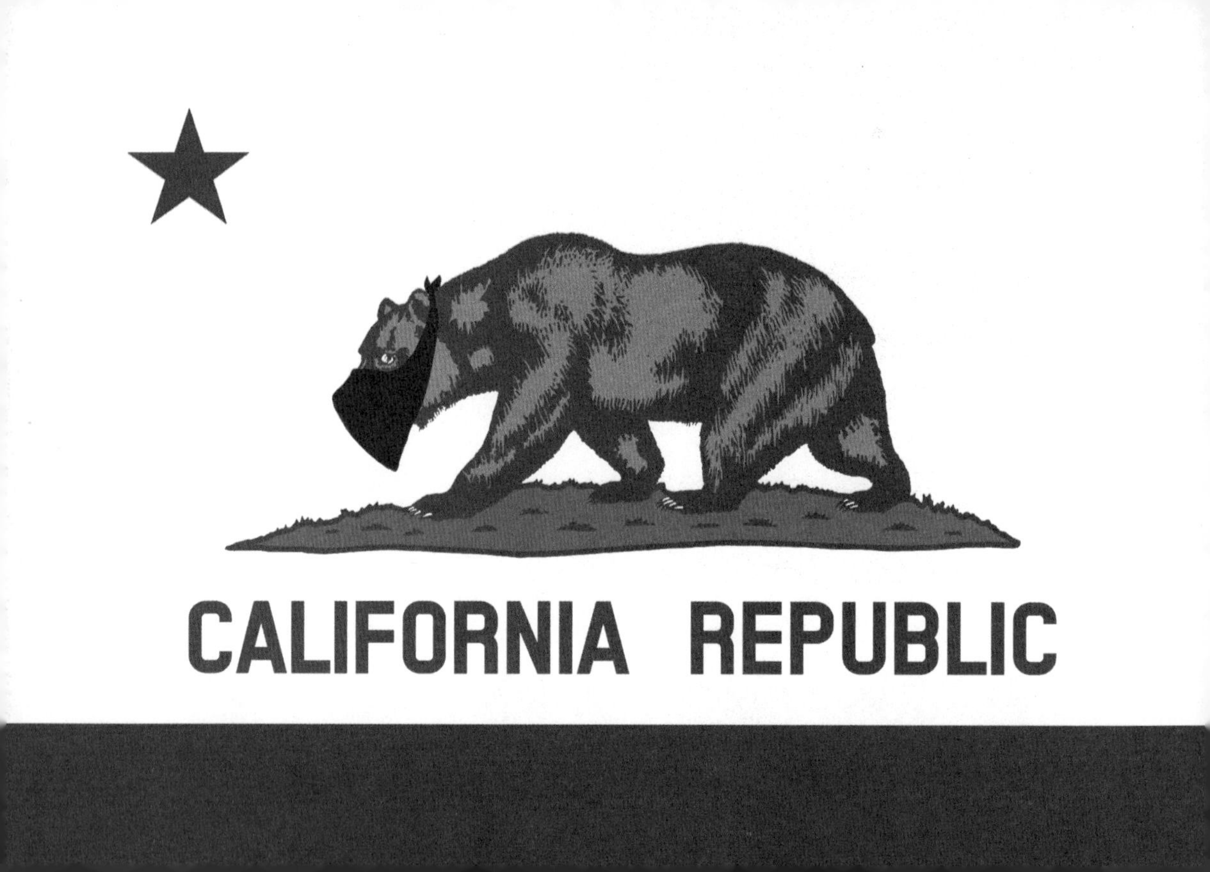
CALIFORNIA REPUBLIC

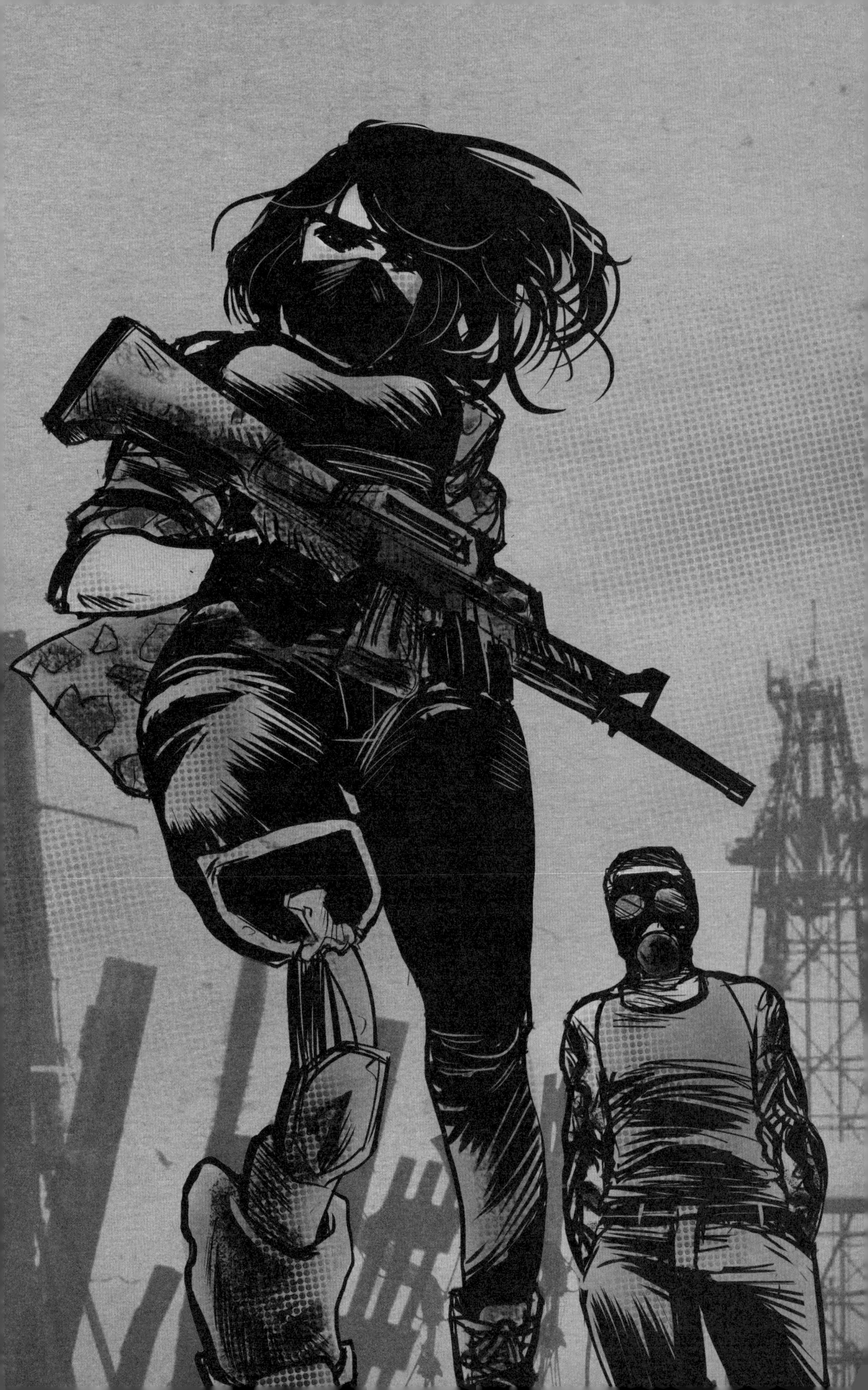

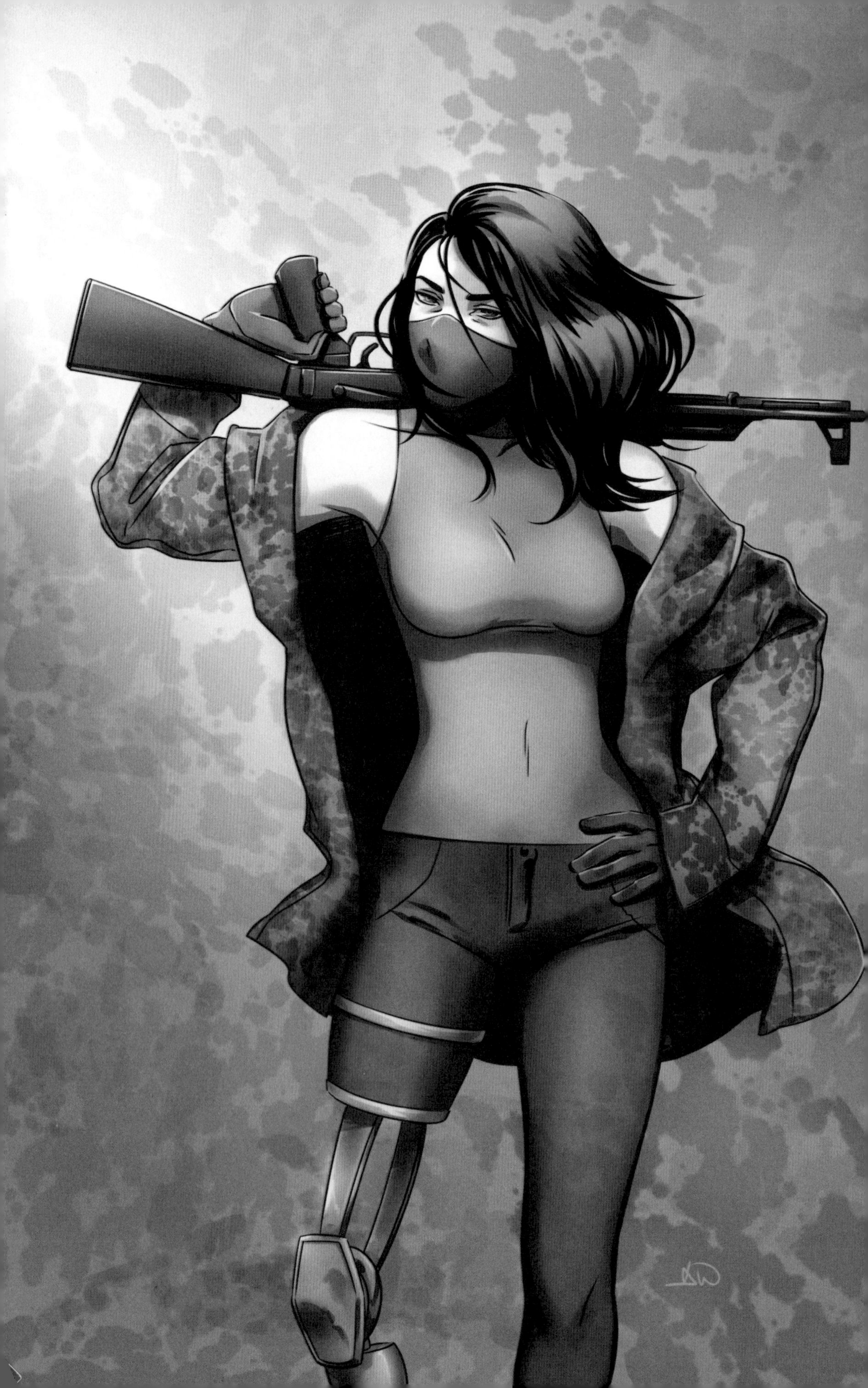

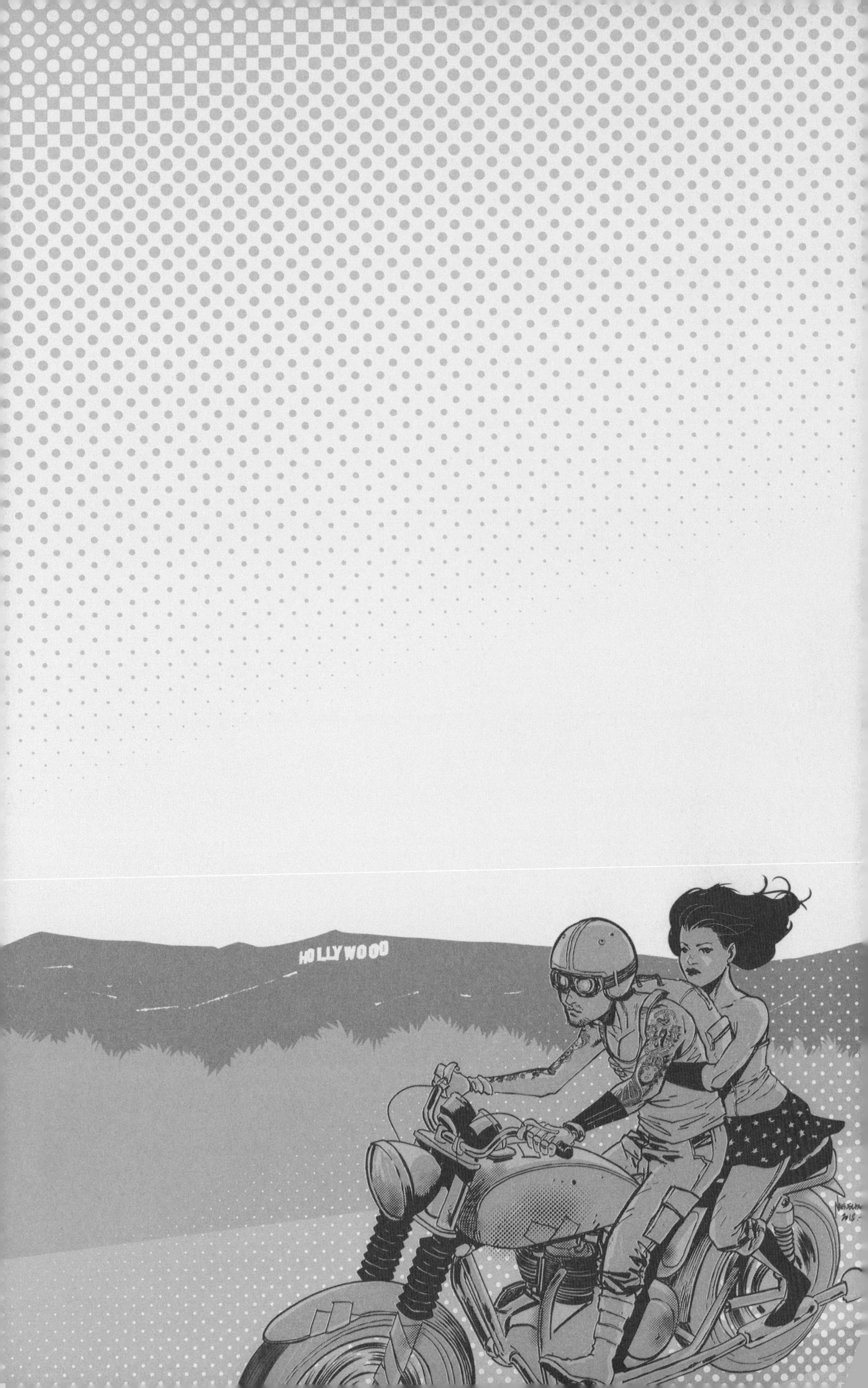
HOLLYWOOD

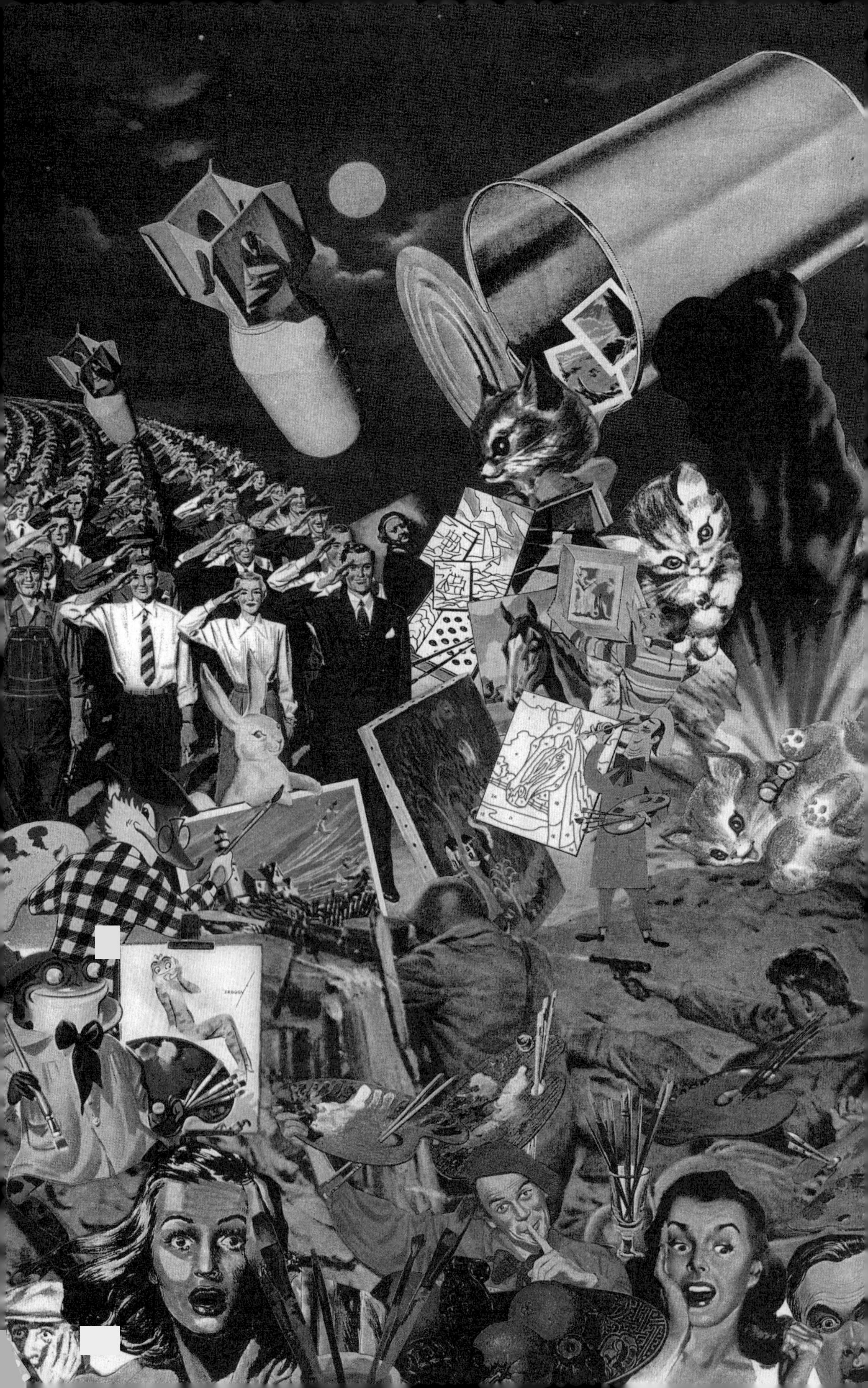

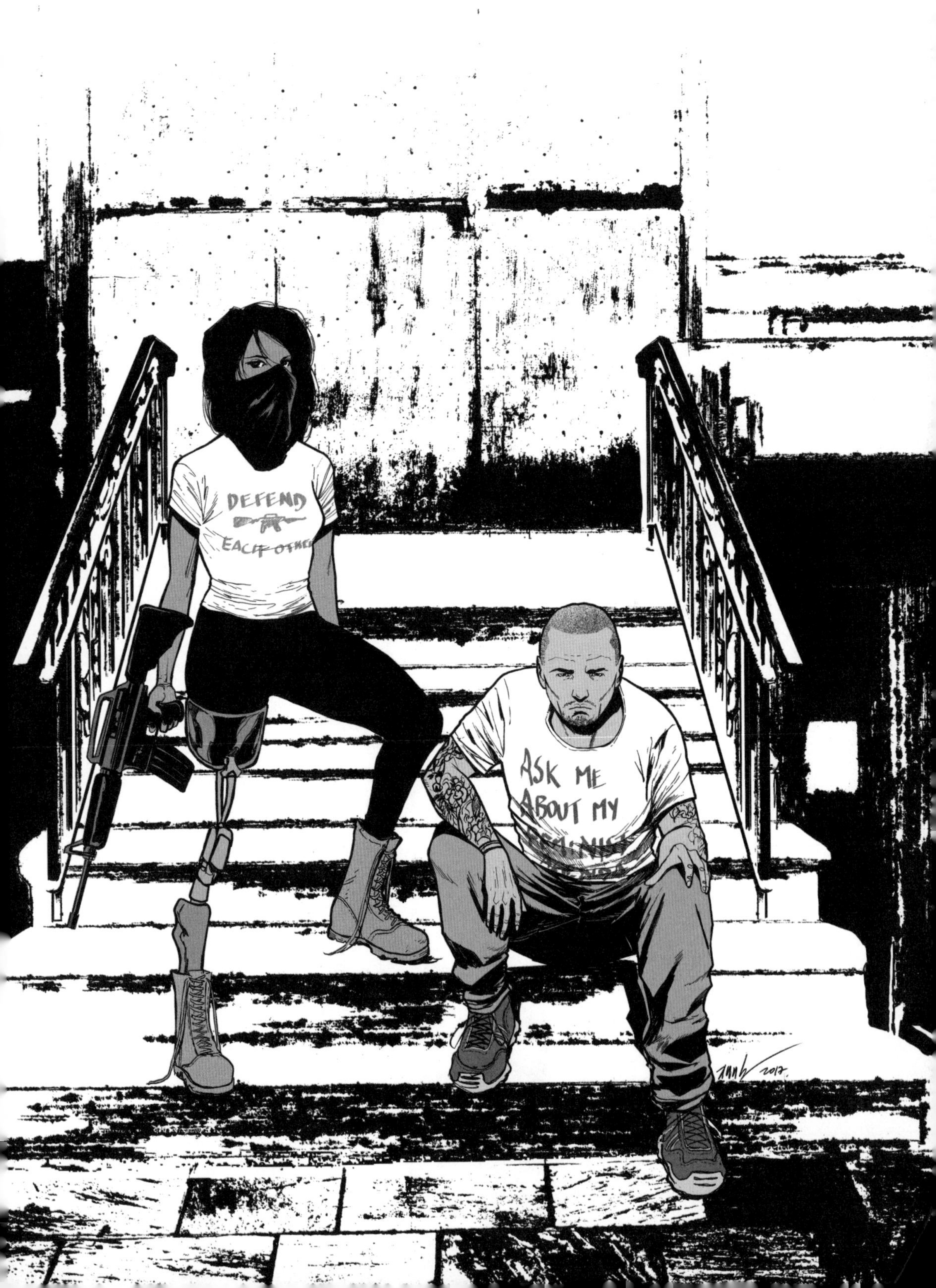
DEFEND
ASK ME
ABOUT MY

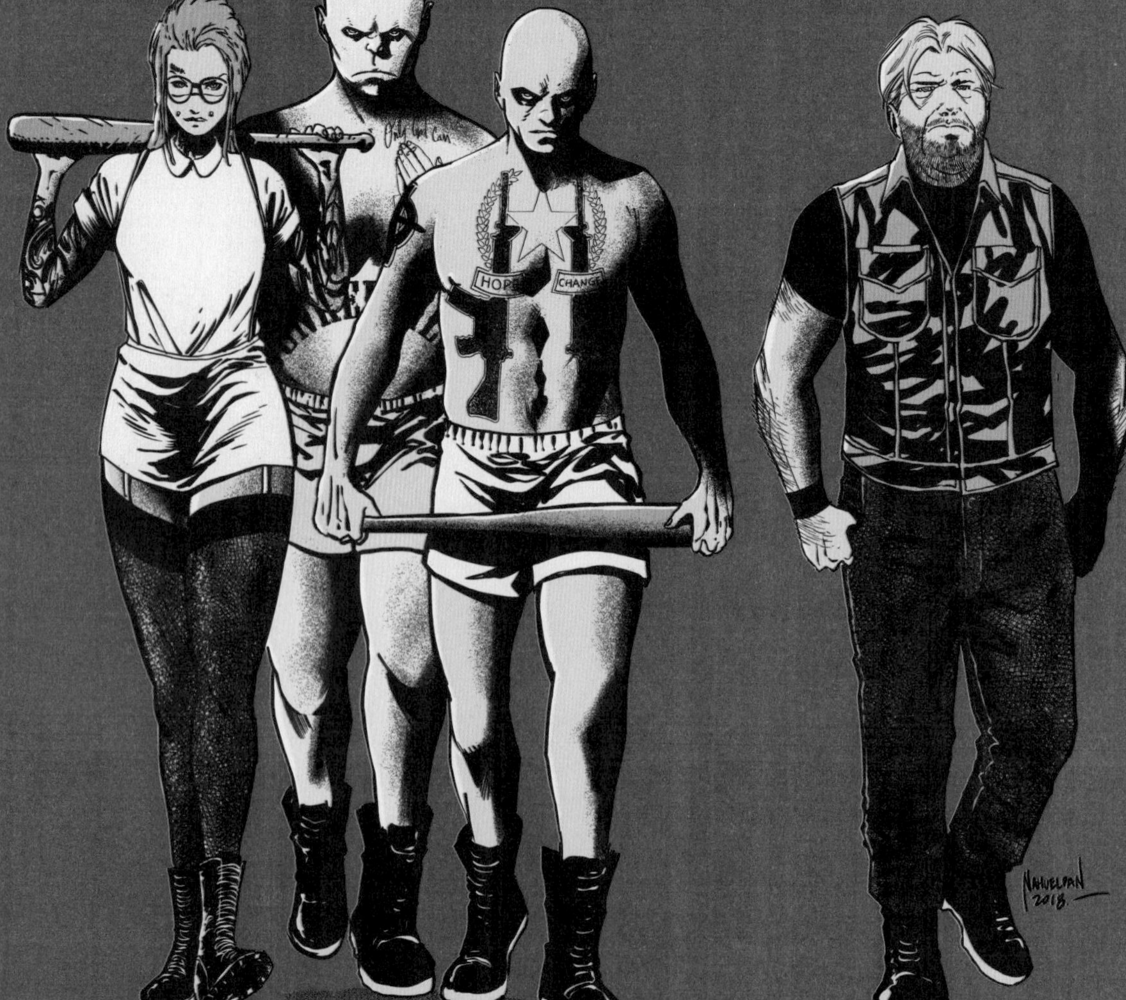
HOPE
CHANGE
NAHUELPAN 2018.

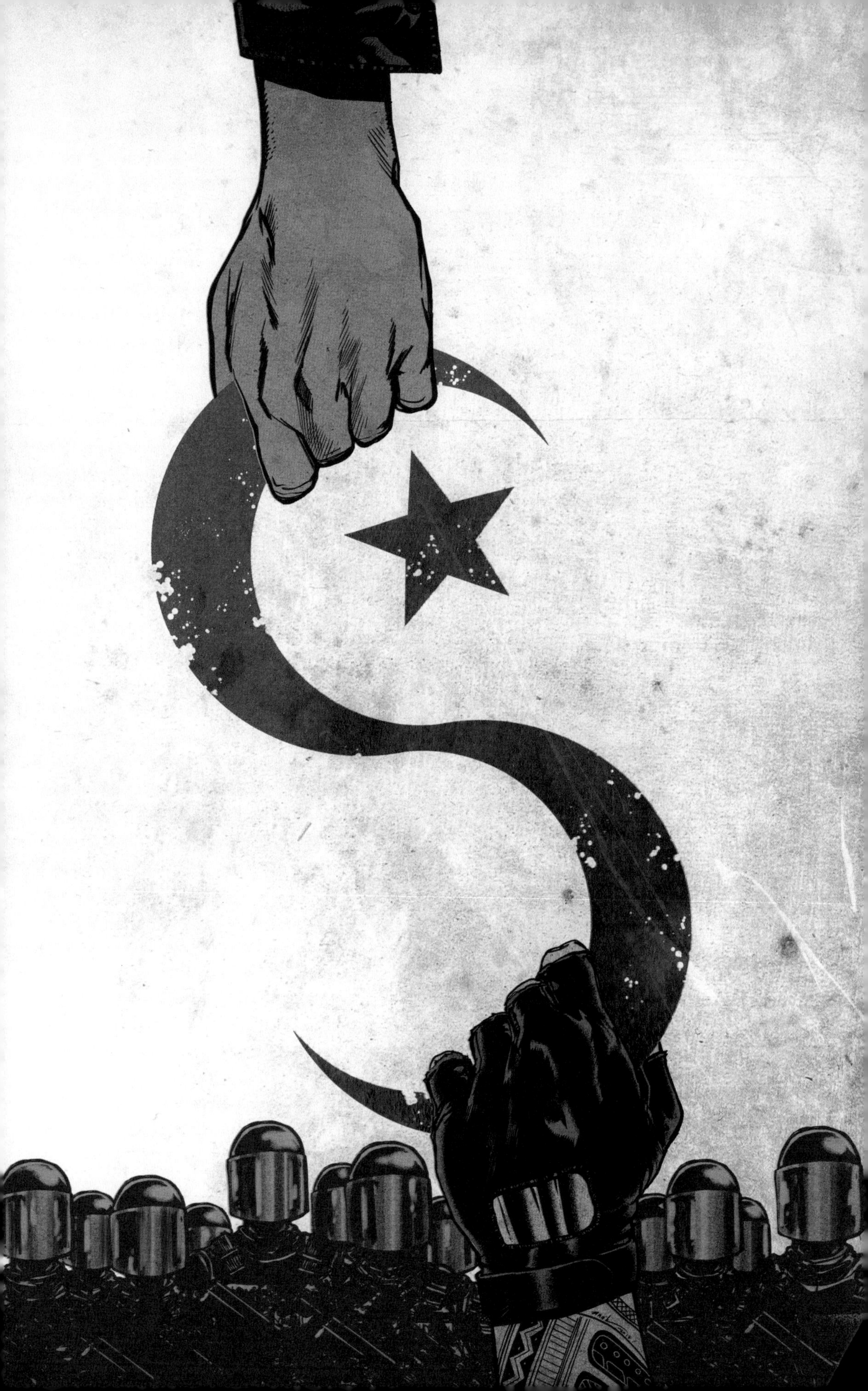

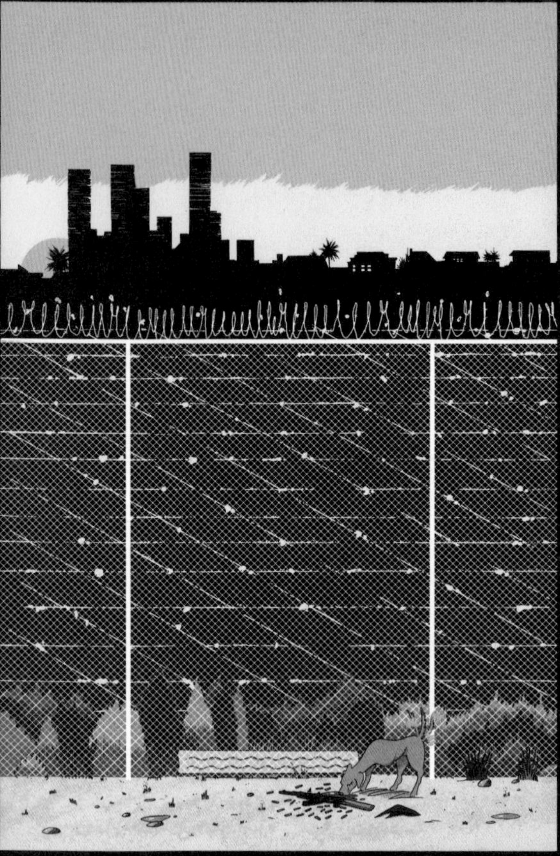

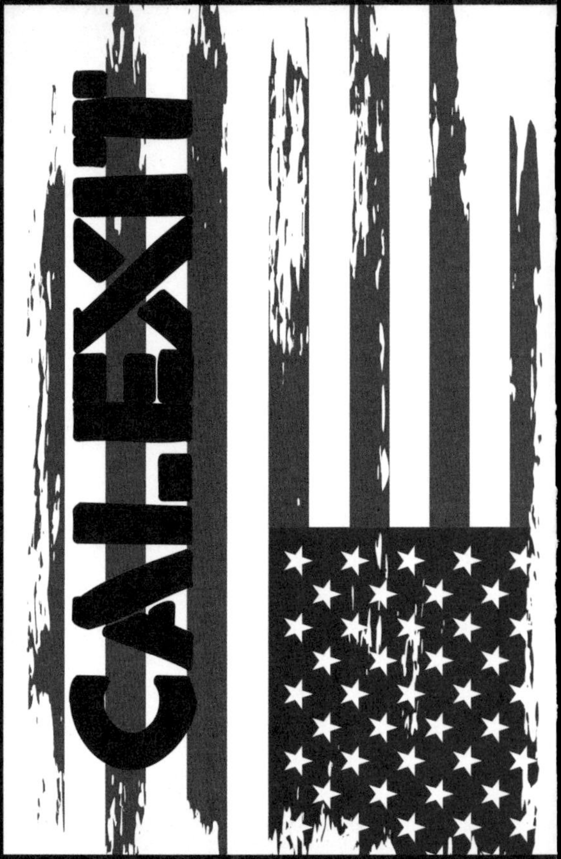
CAL-EXIT

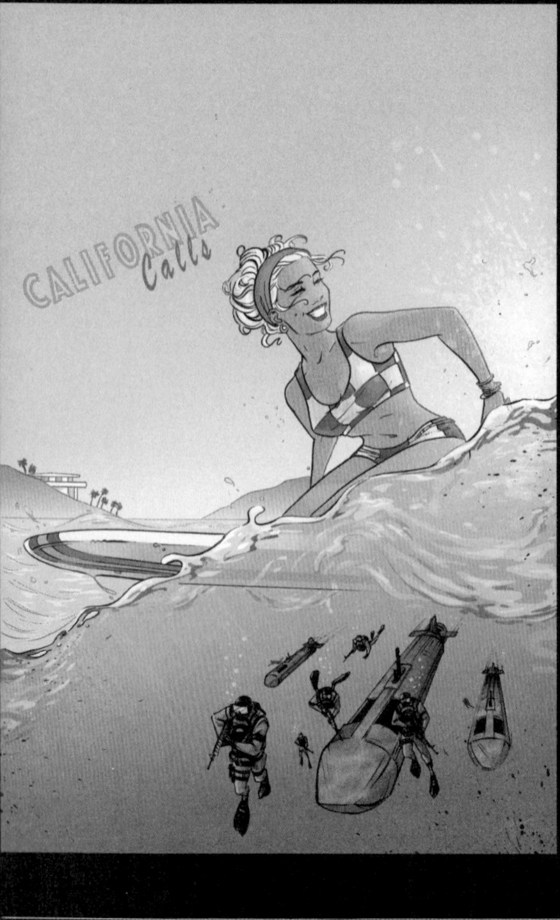
CALIFORNIA
Calls

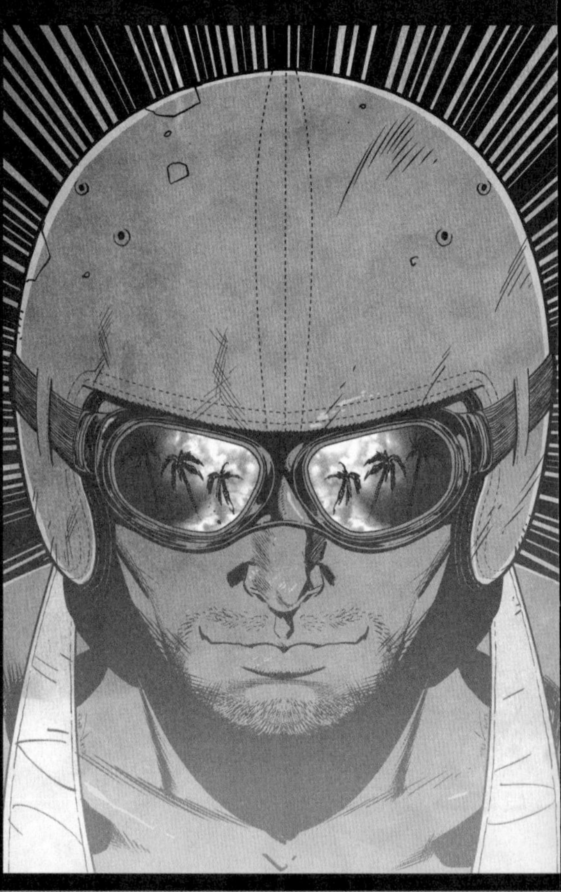

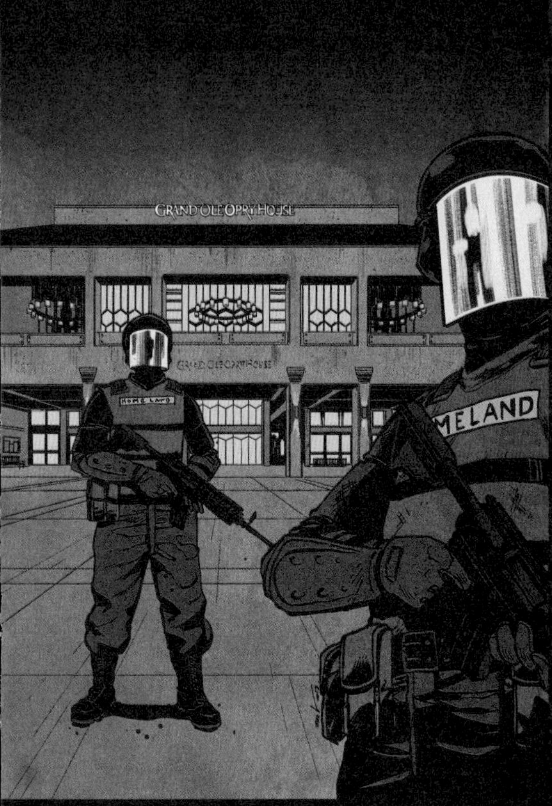
GRAND OLE OPRY HOUSE
MELAND

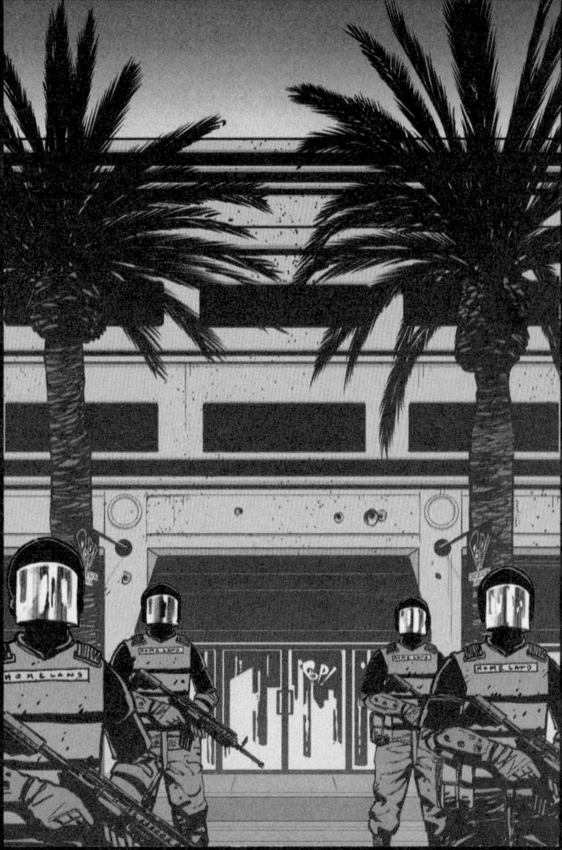

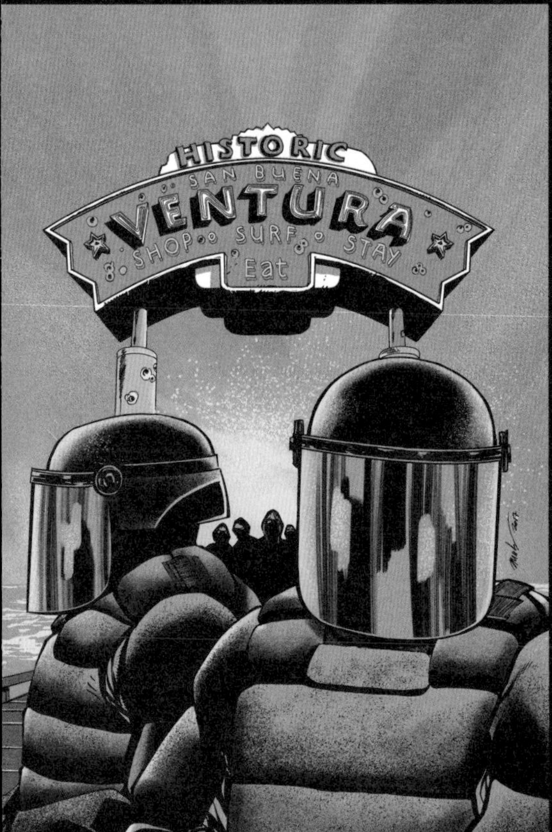
HISTORIC
SAN BUENA
VENTURA
SHOP SURF STAY
Eat

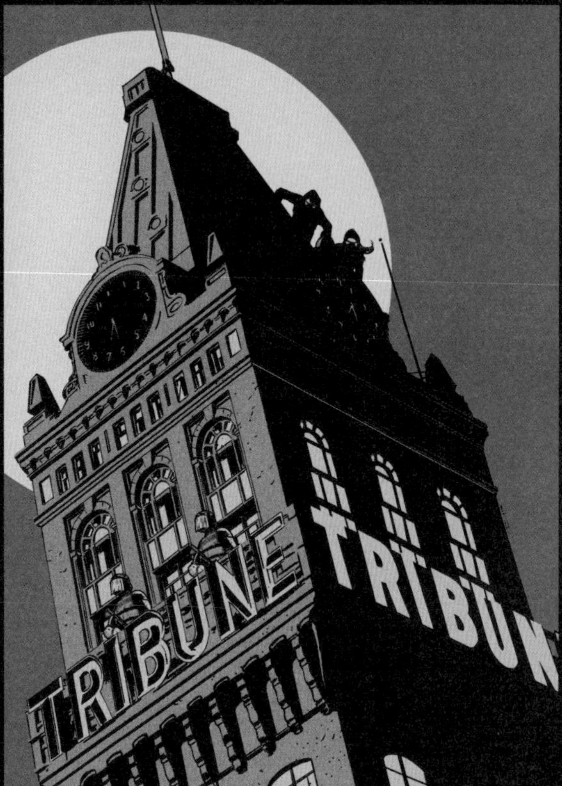
TRIBUNE
TRIBUN

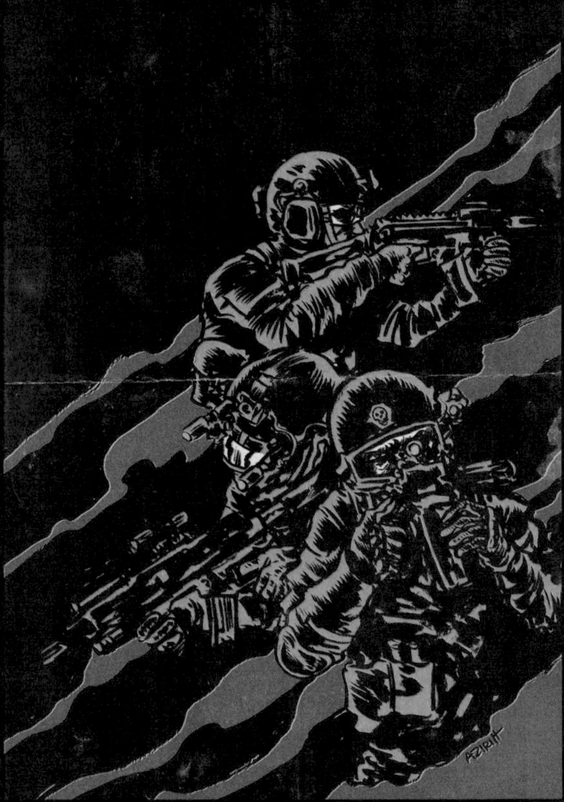

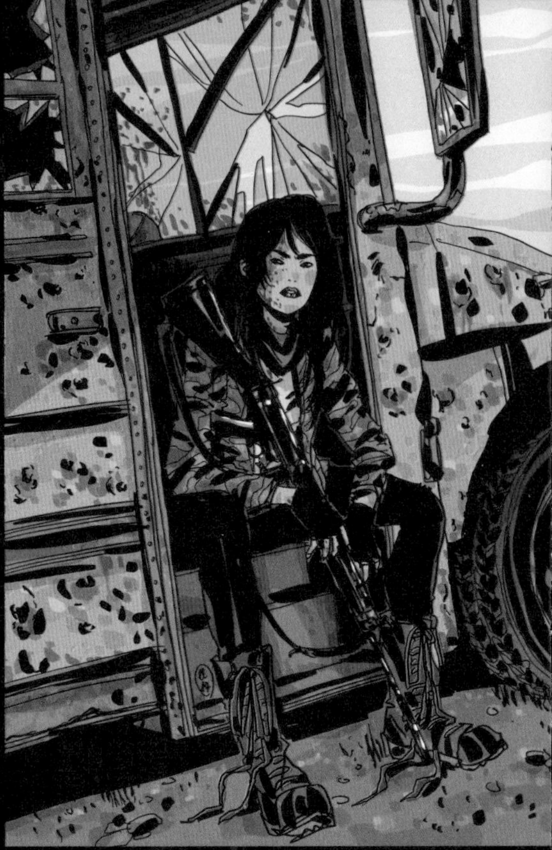

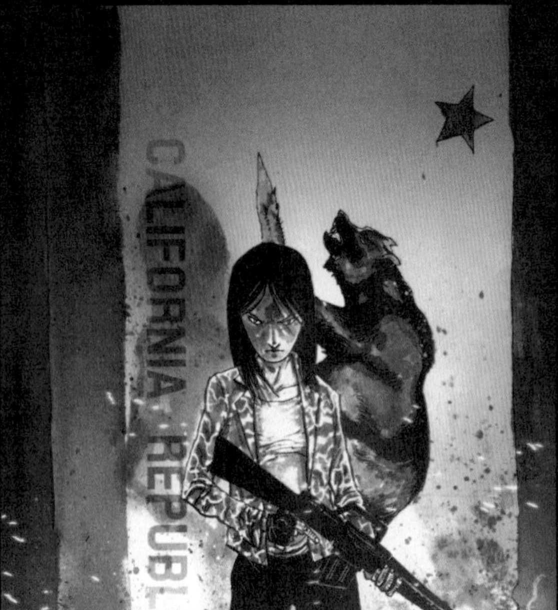
CALIFORNIA
REPUBLI

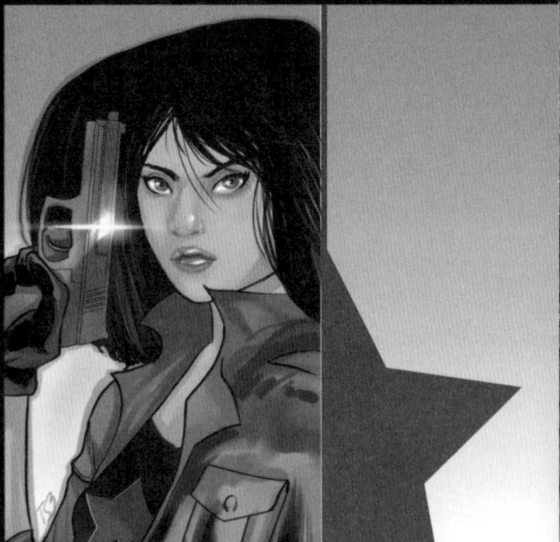

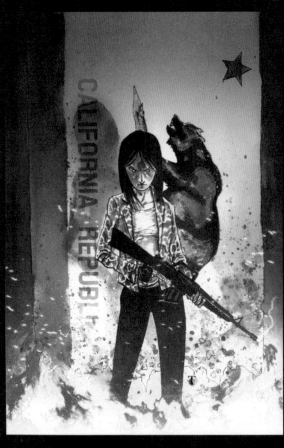

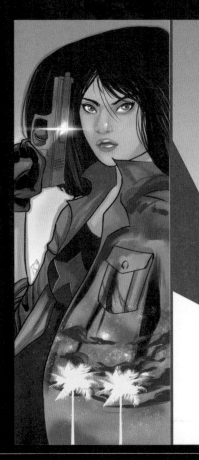